KnowThis®: *Marketing Basics*

5th Edition

Paul Christ, Ph.D.

KnowThis LLC

KnowThis®: Marketing Basics, 5ᵗʰ Edition

Paul Christ

Published By:
KnowThis LLC
Blue Bell, PA 19422

Publisher Website: KnowThis.com

ISBN: 978-0-9820722-9-5

U3-24

Contents

Preface

Why This Book?

In 1998, *KnowThis.com* was launched as one of the first internet websites to address the specific needs of those involved in marketing and related fields. The strong interest by site visitors to learn about marketing led to the first edition of ***KnowThis: Marketing Basics***, in 2009 which was well received by both the academic and business communities. The success and satisfaction received from publishing the first edition led to three more editions and now a fifth update.

Overall, the ***KnowThis: Marketing Basics, 5ᵗʰ Edition*** continues our practice of offering comprehensive coverage of marketing concepts. This new edition expands on the coverage offered in the fourth edition in several ways including:

- The 5th edition provides a <u>special focus on how evolving technologies, including artificial intelligence (AI)</u>, are impacting marketing decision making.

- The 5th edition is the <u>first edition to include marketing case studies</u> designed to enhance and apply the material presented in this book..

- The 5th edition contains <u>over 30% new material while updating or rewriting nearly 25% of other material</u> found in the previous edition

- The 5th edition presents <u>nearly 60% new or completely updated references</u> and insightful comments.

Who is the Book For?

KnowThis: Marketing Basics, 5ᵗʰ Edition was written for several audiences including:

◆ *The Marketing Novice* – This book is ideal for anyone who is new to marketing, as it covers all essential marketing areas. By reading this book, the *Marketing Novice* will gain the foundation needed to appreciate what marketers do and understand the full scope of marketing decision making. For some, reading this book may also offer insight into career options in the marketing field.

◆ *The Marketing Professional* – Experienced marketers will also find this book useful. Often, seasoned marketers tend to focus on just a few areas of marketing as part of their day-to-day activities. This book may serve as a good refresher for areas of marketing where marketers have not recently spent much time.

◆ *The Marketing Educator* – Teachers of marketing now have an alternative to high-priced marketing textbooks. This book offers nearly all of the same coverage found in expensive textbooks at a fraction of the price (educators see more information below).

Additionally, most of what is covered applies to all types of businesses including those whose objective is to make money (i.e., for-profit businesses) as well as those not driven by a profit-making motive (i.e., not-for-profit organizations). It should be noted that as part of book discussion the terms *company*, *firm*, and *organization* are used. In most cases, no matter which term is used the discussion will be applicable to both for-profit and not-for-profit businesses.

Quality at an Affordable Cost?

Yes! ***KnowThis: Marketing Basics, 5th Edition*** is written by a marketing professor and covers much of the same ground as found in much more expensive books. But it also provides insight not found in other publications and, therefore, holds its own as a unique offering and not simply a remaking of other books.

We are able to maintain affordable pricing by using printing strategies and methods that reduce overall printing and inventory carrying costs. <u>However, be assured this book does not sacrifice quality.</u> Whether this book is used in the classroom to help students learn basic concepts or used outside the classroom to assist in professional marketing activities, readers will find the material to be comprehensive and relevant. Additionally, it is written in a way that is intended to bridge the gap that often exists between business practice and academic textbooks.

For Educators

As noted, ***KnowThis: Marketing Basics, 5th Edition*** is ideal as a textbook for an entry-level marketing course or as a supplemental reference for a more advanced class. This book covers the same ground as far more expense textbooks, while also offering new information not covered in other books. Additionally:

◆ This book takes a contemporary view of marketing including covering numerous new developments and how these affect marketing. For instance, coverage includes such topics as the potential impact of artificial intelligence (AI), the effects of an unforeseen global pandemic, the implications of solar powered equipment and devices, the use of advanced payment systems, and much, much more.

◆ Slide Presentations, End-of-Chapter Discussion Questions and Activities, and Test Bank are available for qualified instructors who adopt the book.

Also, to help apply what is learned, 10 Marketing Case Studies are included. These cases, presented in a shorten format, are excellent for homework assignments, class presentations, testing, or as part of class discussion. Educators adopting our book have access to an Instructor's Teaching Guide for each case that offers insights into the issues discussed. Additionally, each case presents an Issues to Consider section that poses questions and suggests assignments for students.

For information on obtaining an educator review or desk copy, see the website for this book - *KnowThis.com*.

About the Author

Paul Christ (pronounced with soft "i") holds a Ph.D. (marketing concentration) from Drexel University. He is Professor Emeritus of Marketing at West Chester University (AACSB accredited), the largest university in the Pennsylvania State System of Higher Education and one of the largest universities in the Philadelphia region.

During 28 years of teaching Paul taught MBA-level courses titled *Marketing Management, Marketing and Technology*, and *Business Research and Data Analysis*. In addition to teaching, Paul held several administrative positions including serving as the university's MBA Program Director for 14 years. Also, in 1999 he was responsible for developing one of the first E-Commerce focused MBA programs in the world.

Paul has written and presented on marketing and technology topics in numerous academic publications, conferences and other public forums and has spoken throughout the world on the topic of marketing and internet business. In addition, Paul launched and, for over 20 years, managed one of the first websites in the world to focus on marketing and marketing-related topics.

In addition to academic experience, Paul has extensive experience in various marketing and sales positions with Fortune 500 companies and served in a management position for a successful startup in the consumer electronics industry. Additionally, he is currently a consultant to marketing and technology companies.

This edition is lovingly dedicated to my wife Carol.

P. C.

Chapter 1: What is Marketing?

Welcome to the world of marketing! The main intention of **KnowThis: Marketing Basics** is to offer a straightforward examination of an important, exciting, and challenging business discipline crucial to virtually all organizations and all industries.

In this first chapter, we lay the groundwork for our study of the field of marketing with a look at marketing's key concepts and the important tasks marketers perform. Coverage includes a close examination of the definition of marketing. A dissection of the key terms in the definition will show that marketing's primary focus is to identify and satisfy customers in a way that helps build a solid and, hopefully, sustained relationship that encourages customers to continue doing business with the marketer. We also show how the field of marketing has evolved from a process centered on simply getting as many people as possible to purchase a product to today's highly complex efforts designed to build long-term sustainable customer relationships. Additionally, we will see marketing is not only necessary for individual organizations, but it also carries both positive and negative influences at a broader societal level. Finally, we look at the key characteristics exhibited by successful marketers.

MARKETING DEFINED

Marketing is defined in many different ways. Some definitions focus on marketing in terms of what it means to an organization, such as being the main functional area for generating revenue. Other definitions lean more toward defining marketing in terms of its most visible tasks, such as advertising and creating new products. There probably is no one best way to define marketing; however, whatever definition is used should have an orientation that focuses on the key to marketing success – customers.

With this in mind, we define marketing as follows:

Marketing consists of the strategies and tactics used to identify, create, and maintain satisfying relationships with customers resulting in value for both the customer and the marketer.

Dissecting Marketing

Let's examine our definition of marketing in detail by looking at the key terms.

Strategies and Tactics

Strategies are the direction the marketing effort takes over some period of time while tactics are actionable steps or decisions made in order to follow the strategies that have been established. For instance, if a company's strategy is to begin selling its products in a new country, the tactics may involve the marketing decisions made to carry this out. Performing strategic and tactical planning activities in advance of taking action is considered critical for long-term marketing success.

Identify

Arguably, the most important marketing function involves efforts needed to gain knowledge of customers, competitors, and markets (i.e., where organizations do business). To gain the necessary knowledge, marketers continually strive to better understand their customers by undertaking marketing research.

Create

Competition forces marketers to be creative. When marketers begin a new venture, such as starting a company, it is often based around something that is new (e.g., a new product, a new way of reaching customers, a new advertising approach, etc.). However, once something new is launched innovation does not end. Competitive pressure is continually felt by the marketer, who must respond by again devising new strategies and tactics that help the organization remain successful. For marketers, no matter how successful, the cycle of continuous innovation never stops.

Maintain

Today's marketers work hard to ensure their customers return to do business with them again and again. Long gone are the days when success for a marketer was measured simply by how many sales are made each day. Now, in most marketing situations, marketing success is evaluated not only in terms of sales but also by how long a marketer retains their customers. Consequently, marketers' efforts to attract customers do not end when a customer completes their first purchase. It continues in various ways for, hopefully, a long time after the initial purchase.

Satisfying Relationships

A key objective of marketing is to provide goods and services that customers really want AND to make customers feel their contact with the marketer is helping build a strong relationship between the two. In this way, the customer becomes a partner in the transaction, not just a source of revenue for the marketer. While this concept may seem intuitive and a natural part of what all businesses should do, as Box 1-1 points out, this has not always been the case.

Value for Customer and Marketer

Value refers to the perception of benefits received for what someone must give up. For customers, value is most often measured by how much benefit they feel they are getting for their money, though the value one customer feels may differ from what another customer feels even though they purchase the same product. On the other

---

Box 1-1

EVOLUTION OF THE MARKETING CONCEPT

In the early days of marketing (before the 1950s), sellers of products were keen on identifying strategies and tactics that focused solely on selling more goods and services with little regard for what customers really wanted. Often this meant companies embraced a "sell-as-much-as-we-can" philosophy with little concern for building long-term customer relationships.

But starting in the mid-1900s, companies began to see that their old ways of selling products were wearing thin with customers. As competition grew stiffer across most industries, organizations looked to the buyers' side of the transaction for ways to improve. What they found was an emerging philosophy suggesting that the key factor in successful marketing is understandings the needs of customers. Now known as the *Marketing Concept*, this approach suggests decisions made by marketers should flow from FIRST knowing their customers and what they want. Only then should an organization initiate the process of developing and marketing goods and services.

Today, the *Marketing Concept* continues as the root of most marketing efforts. Marketers know they can no longer limit their marketing efforts to just getting customers to purchase more, but rather must have an in-depth understanding of who their customers are and what their customers really want to satisfy their needs.

---

side of the transaction, the marketer for a for-profit organization may measure value in terms of how much profit they make for the marketing efforts and resources expended. For a successful marketing effort to take place, both the customer and the marketer must feel they are receiving something worthwhile in return. Without a strong perception of value, it is unlikely a strong relationship can be built.

THE MARKETER'S TOOLKIT

To reach the goal of creating a relationship that holds value for customers and the organization, marketers use a diverse Toolkit (Figure 1-1). The Toolkit represents the key tasks performed by the marketer. These tasks include:

1. Selecting Target Markets

This task involves the selection of customers identified as possessing needs the marketer believes can be addressed by its marketing efforts. In most cases, marketers identify target markets prior to making other decisions since satisfying the needs of the target market drives all other marketing decisions. This task is discussed in detail in Chapter 5.

2. Creating Products

Marketers use tangible (e.g., goods) and intangible (e.g., services) solutions to address the needs of their target market. For many customers, the product is the main reason why the customer will or will not do business with the marketer. Product decisions have several dimensions and are discussed in detail in Chapters 6 and 7.

3. Establishing Distribution

Products are only of value to the target market if they can be obtained. Selecting distribution methods that enable customers to acquire products requires extremely careful consideration of different options. As we will discuss in Chapters 8 through 10, for most marketers gaining distribution almost always requires they seek assistance from other organizations.

4. Developing Promotions

Most organizations must communicate information about their products to their target market. While advertising is the most notable form of promotion, there are others, including sales promotion, personal selling, and public relations. In-depth coverage of promotion is discussed in Chapters 11 through 16.

5. Setting Price

Marketing often results in a transaction taking place between customers and the marketing organization. While product decisions determine what the marketer will exchange with the customer, it is pricing decisions that determine what the customer will give up in order to obtain the product. Pricing decisions can be quite complex and are addressed in detail in Chapters 17 and 18.

Figure 1-1: The Marketer's Toolkit

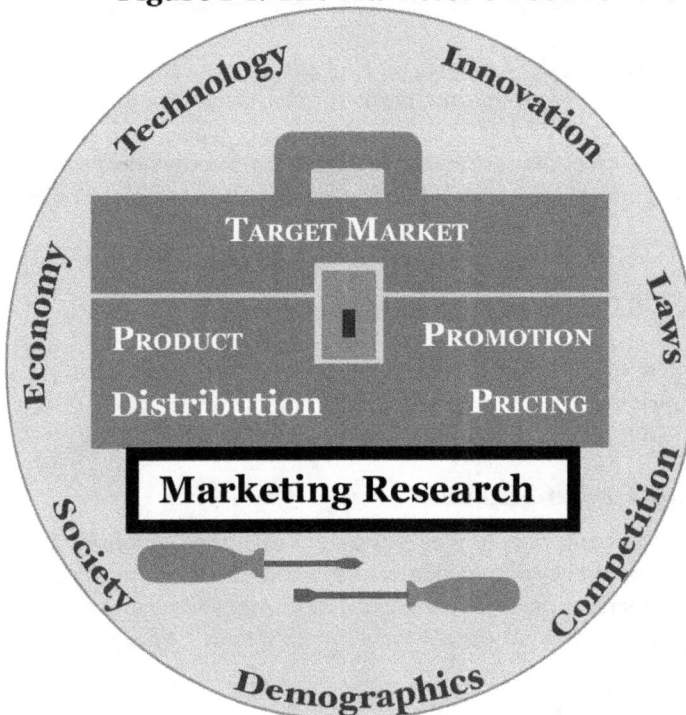

Characteristics of the Marketer's Toolkit

In addition to containing the five key marketing decisions, other important characteristics of the Toolkit include:

INTEGRATION OF TASKS

Each task within the Marketer's Toolkit is tightly integrated with all other tasks so that a decision on one task could, and often does, impact decisions on others. For instance, a change in pricing, such as lowering the price of a product sold at retail stores, could affect the distribution area by requiring increased product shipments to retail stores to cover an anticipated increase in customer demand.

SEQUENCE OF TASKS

While the five key marketing tasks are shown with a number, the order of decision making does not necessarily follow this sequence. However, as we will discuss, marketers will generally first identify target markets (#1) prior to making decisions #2 through #5 (also called the **marketing mix**) since these decisions are going to be directed toward satisfying the desired target markets.

ADDITIONAL SKILLS

To use the Toolkit properly, marketers must possess additional skills including the ability to:

- Conduct Marketing Research – As we will see in Chapter 2, marketing decisions should not be made without first committing time and resources for gathering and analyzing information through marketing research. For this reason, marketing research can be viewed as the foundation of marketing and, as shown in Figure 1-1, is used to support nearly all marketing decisions.

- Understand Customers – While the Marketer's Toolkit centers on making decisions that satisfy customers, marketers must take extra steps to know as much as they can about their customers. In Chapters 3 and 4, we will see what marketers do to understand and manage their customers.

- Monitor the External Environment – As shown in Figure 1-1, options within the Marketer's Toolkit are affected by factors that are not controlled by the marketer. These factors, discussed in Chapter 19, include economic conditions, legal issues, technological developments, innovation, demographics, social/cultural changes, and many more. While not managed in the way marketers control their Toolkit, these external factors must be monitored and dealt with since these have the potential to cause considerable harm to the organization. Also, ignoring outside elements can lead to missed opportunities in the market, especially if competitors are the first to take advantage of the opportunities. (1)

- Create a Marketing Plan – While some marketers may find success making decisions on the spur of the moment, most marketers must put much more deliberate thought and effort into their decision making. As we will discuss in Chapter 20, this often means it is critical for marketers to spend time developing a formal marketing plan

MARKETING'S ROLE

The primary objective of an organization's marketing efforts is to develop satisfying relationships that benefit both the customer and the organization. These efforts lead marketing to serve a pivotal role within most organizations and within society.

At the organizational level, marketing is a vital business function that is necessary in nearly all industries whether the organization operates as a for-profit or not-for-profit. For the for-profit organization, marketing is responsible for most tasks that generate revenue and profits. For the not-for-profit organization, marketing is responsible for attracting customers needed to support the not-for-profit's mission, such as raising donations or supporting a cause.

Marketing is also the organizational business area that interacts most frequently with the public; consequently, what the public knows about an organization is determined by their interactions with marketers. For example, customers may believe a company is dynamic and creative based on its advertising message.

At a broader level, marketing offers significant benefits to society. These include:

◆ Developing products that satisfy needs, including products that enhance society's quality of life.

◆ Creating a competitive environment that helps lower product prices.

◆ Developing product distribution systems that offer access to products to a large number of customers and many geographic regions.

◆ Building demand for products that require organizations to expand their labor force.

◆ Offering techniques that possess the ability to convey messages that influence societal behavior in positive ways (e.g., using promotional methods to help improve public health [2]).

CRITICISMS OF MARKETING

While marketing is viewed as offering significant benefits to organizations and to society, the fact that marketing is a business function operating in close contact with the public opens this functional area to extensive criticism.

Among the issues cited by those who criticize marketing are:

Marketing Makes People Purchase What They Do Not Need

Possibly the criticism most frequently made about marketing is that marketers are only concerned with getting customers to buy whether they need the product or not. The root of this argument stems from the belief that marketers are only out to satisfy their own needs and really do not care about the needs of their customers.

While many marketers are guilty of manipulating customers into making unwanted purchases, the vast majority understand such tactics will not lead to loyal customers, and therefore is unlikely to lead to long-term success.

Marketers Embellish Product Claims

Marketers are often criticized for exaggerating the benefits offered by their products. This is especially the case with methods used for customer communication, such as advertising. The most serious issues arise when product claims mislead customers into believing a product can offer a certain level of value that, in fact, it cannot.

But sometimes there is a fine line between what a rational person should accept as a "reasonable exaggeration" and what is considered downright misleading. Fortunately, many countries offer customers some level of protection from misleading claims since such business practices may subject the marketer to legal action. Of course, using such tactics is also likely to lead to marketing failure as customers will not be satisfied with their experience and will not return. (3)

Marketing Discriminates in Customer Selection

A key to marketing success is to engage in a deliberate process that is intended to identify customers who offer marketers the best chance for satisfying organizational objectives. This method, called **target marketing** (see Chapter 4), often drives most marketing decisions, including product development and price setting. But some argue target marketing leads marketers to focus their efforts primarily on customers who have the financial means to make more expensive purchases. They contend this intentionally discriminates against others especially lower income customers, who cannot afford to purchase higher priced products. Additionally, critics say lower income customers are targeted with lower quality products.

While this criticism is often valid, it is worth noting that while many "lower quality" products are inferior to current high-end products, comparison of these "lower quality" products to similar products from just a few years ago often shows there has been significant improvement. For instance, low-cost consumer electronics equipment, such as big screen "smart" televisions, offer more features compared to low-cost televisions of just a few years ago. Thus, while certain customer groups may not be the primary target market for some new product offerings, within a short period of time they may benefit from the development of high-end products.

Marketing Contributes to Environmental Waste

One of the loudest complaints voiced against marketing concerns its impact on the environment through:

- the use of excessive, non-biodegradable packaging (e.g., use of plastics, placing small products in large packages, etc.)

- the continual development of resource consuming products (e.g., construction of new buildings on previously undeveloped land, growth of landfills for unrecyclable products, etc.)

- the proliferation of unsightly and wasteful methods of promotions (e.g., outdoor billboards, direct mail, etc.)

Marketers have responded to these concerns by introducing **green marketing** campaigns that are not only intended to appease critics but also take advantage of potential business opportunities. For example, today's automakers are aggressively moving into the production and marketing of fuel-efficient electric vehicles (EV), the demand for which has accelerated due to the heightened awareness of the environmental impact of gasoline-powered vehicles. Also, awareness of environmental issues can be seen in other marketing and business decisions, such as those that focus on reducing an organization's carbon footprint. It is expected that, as environmental awareness continues to gains political clout and more consumer support, marketers will see even more opportunity to develop and market environmentally friendly products.

Marketing Encroaches on Customers' Right to Privacy

For marketers, a vital step in making smart marketing decisions is to gather and analyze information about the market in which they conduct business. Often the most valuable information deals with customers' buying behavior and especially determining which factors influence how customers make purchase decisions.

But to some, digging deep into customer behavior crosses the line of what they consider to be private information. Of most concern to privacy advocates is marketers' use of methods that track user activity. In particular, they are critical of the growing utilization of advanced technologies allowing marketers to gain access to customers' shopping and information gathering habits (see Box 1-2).

Privacy issues are not restricted to marketing research. Other areas of marketing have also experienced problems. For instance, there have been many incidents affecting consumer purchasing, most notably those involving mishandled credit card payment information, where a breach in privacy has placed customers at risk. Customer privacy is likely to become one of the most contentious issues marketers face in the coming years and could lead to greater legal limits on how marketers gather customer information and perform other activities.

ETHICAL AND SOCIAL CONCERNS

In addition to problems cited above, some critics also argue that the money-making motive of some marketers has encouraged many to cross the line in terms of ethical and social business behavior.

Ethical Issues

Ethics is concerned with what is right and wrong. Many people assume that only actions that violate laws are considered unethical. While it is true that illegal activity is also unethical, a business activity can be unethical even though no laws are violated. For instance, some consider it unethical for companies to aggressively promote unhealthy foods to children, though such promotional practices are generally not viewed as illegal.

Box 1-2

TRACKING CUSTOMERS ONLINE AND OFFLINE

Marketers have at their disposal numerous highly advanced techniques for tracking user activity both online and offline.

Online Tracking

At the most rudimentary level, marketers operating websites and digital applications or "apps" (e.g., apps for smartphones, smart televisions, TV streaming services) can track user activity that may include determining: how many are using a service (e.g., visit a website), what areas of the service are used (e.g., pages viewed within an app), how they arrived at the service (e.g., via a search engine), where in the world users are located (e.g., geographic location), and many other types of information. This information is left by visitors each time they access a website or app and does not require the marketer to do much extra work to obtain the data. Additionally, through **cross-channel** or **cross-platform** marketing, companies can track and then market to users as they move from one device to another (e.g., from tablet to smartphone).

While online tracking is widely used and generally considered an acceptable marketing tool, some marketers do engage in questionable practices, such as loading tracking software onto digital devices (e.g., computers, smartphones, TV streaming) without the knowledge or permission of the user. For instance, one type of tracking software, called **adware**, allows marketers to monitor the actions of unsuspecting users, such as tracking the websites a user visits. They then use this information to deliver advertisements based on the users' activity. There are also rising concerns with potential tracking that may occur with other connected digital devices. For instance, customer information may be gathered through television apps and set-top boxes, voice-activated speakers, digital thermostats, and other so-called "smart devices." (For more see *Trends in Marketing Research* in Chapter 2.)

Offline Tracking

Privacy issues are not limited to concerns with online tracking; marketers also use techniques to track customers' offline purchase activities. One example of offline tracking occurs when retail stores match sales transactions to individual shoppers. This is easy to do when customers use **purchase cards** (a.k.a. loyalty cards, discount cards, club cards, etc.) or related smartphone apps as part of the buying process. This information can then be used to create individualized promotions, such as printing coupons, that are based on the customer's previous buying activity.

In the U.S., several consumer advocacy groups and politicians have raised the prospect of legislation to limit the extent to which tracking techniques are used. While a comprehensive federal law dealing with tracking does not yet exist, individual U.S. states have addressed this. In Europe, a more aggressive approach to control tracking exists with implementation of the General Data Protection Regulation. (4)

Sometimes the line between what is ethical and unethical is difficult to distinguish since what is right and wrong differs depending on such factors as nationality, culture, and even industry. For example, many websites offer users free access to their online content (e.g., articles, videos, audio clips, etc.), but do so only if users register and provide contact information, including an email address. Some of these sites then automatically add registrants to promotional email mailing lists. Some view the practice of automatic "**opt-in**" to a mailing list as being unethical since customers do not request it and are forced to take additional action to be removed from the list ("**opt-out**"). However, many marketers see no ethical issue with this practice and simply view adding registered users to an email list as part of the "cost" to customers for accessing content.

MARKETING CODE OF ETHICS

The call for marketers to become more responsible for their actions has led to the development of a code of ethics by many companies and professional organizations.

Company Code

A company code of ethics includes extensive coverage of how business is conducted by members of an organization. For instance, Google's code of ethics, titled *Code of Conduct* and posted on their parent company's website, lays out an extensive list of what is expected of their employees. (5) Among the issues covered are:

- Offering Gifts – "We want to avoid the possibility that the gift, entertainment, or other business courtesy could be perceived as a bribe, so it's always best to provide such business courtesies infrequently and, when we do, to keep their value moderate."

- Receiving Gifts – "Google's Non-Government Related Gifts & Client Entertainment Policy provides specific guidance on when it is appropriate for Googlers to accept gifts, entertainment, or any other business courtesy (including discounts or benefits that are not made available to all Googlers) from any of our competitors or business partners."

- Competitor Information – "If an opportunity arises to take advantage of a competitor's or former employer's confidential information, don't do it."

- Friends and Relatives – "Don't tell your significant other or family members anything confidential, and don't solicit confidential information from them about their company."

Organization Code

Marketers often join professional organizations for the purpose of associating with others who share similar interests. These organizations include industry associations, whose membership is mostly limited to those working within a particular industry, and professional services associations, whose membership consists of those sharing similar job responsibilities. Marketers joining these organizations often find that a code of ethics has been developed that is intended to be followed by all organization members. For example, the Canadian Marketing Association lays out rules for its members, which includes marketers from many for-profit and not-for-profit organizations, in its *Code of Ethics & Standards and Practice*. (6) The Code discusses such issues as:

- Accuracy of Representation – "Marketers must not materially misrepresent a product, service, marketing program or make any other representation that is misleading in a material respect, even if not directly related to the product or service, and must not materially mislead by statement or manner of demonstration."

- Support of Claims – "Marketers must be able to prove the basis for any performance, efficacy or length of life claim or comparison and must not imply a scientific, factual or statistical basis where none exists."

- Use the Word "Free" – "Products or services offered without cost or obligation on the part of the consumer or business may be described as "free", or similar."

- Comparative Advertising – "Comparisons included in marketing communications must be factual, verifiable and not misleading. They must compare similar aspects of the products or services being assessed."

The concern over ethical behavior in marketing continues to draw attention from customers, the news media, and other external groups. The issue is so important many for-profit and not-for-profit organizations now mandate their employees engage in ethics training and commit to performing their work with an understanding of what falls inside and outside of ethical boundaries. As more questionable marketing practices are publicized for potential ethical violations, marketers may expect to hear an increasing call for more emphasis in this area.

Social Responsibility in Marketing

Most marketing organizations do not intentionally work in isolation from the rest of society. Instead, they find greater opportunity exists if the organization is visibly accessible and involved with the public. As we've seen, because marketing often operates as the "public face" of an organization, when issues arise between the public and the organization marketing is often at the center. In recent years, the number and variety of issues raised by the public has increased. One reason for the increase is the growing perception that marketing organizations are not just sellers of products but also have an inherent responsibility to be more socially responsible, including being more responsible for its actions and more responsive to addressing social concerns.

Being socially responsible means an organization shows concern for the people and environment in which it transacts business. It also means these values are communicated and enforced by everyone in the organization and, in some cases, with outside business partners, such as those that sell products to the organization (e.g., supplier of raw material for product production) and those that help the organization distribute and sell to other customers (e.g., retail stores).

In addition to ensuring these values exist within the organization and its business partners, an organization can often pursue social responsibility through methods that fall under the heading of **cause marketing**. As the name suggests, these techniques involve activities intended to align an organization or a product with a specific cause. For instance, marketers may sponsor charity events, produce cause-related advertising, or create new products that are specifically intended to serve as fundraisers.

Marketers who are pursue a socially responsible agenda should bear in mind such efforts do not automatically translate into increased revenue or even in an improved public image. Additionally, if not handled correctly, a poorly implemented socially responsible activity could negatively affect an organization. However, organizations that consistently exhibit socially responsible tendencies may eventually gain a strong reputation that could pay dividends in the form of increased customer loyalty.

CHARACTERISTICS OF THE MODERN MARKETER

As we've seen, marketing is a critical business function operating in an environment that is highly scrutinized and continually changing. Today's marketers undertake a variety of tasks as they attempt to build customer relationships while also meeting organizational objectives. The "know-how" needed to perform these tasks successfully is also varied. Possessing basic marketing knowledge is just the beginning. Successful marketers must also be comfortable with a wide range of knowledge and skill sets including:

Basic Business Skills

Marketers are first and foremost businesspeople who must perform necessary tasks required of all successful businesspeople. Many of these tasks depend on marketers possessing an assortment of basic skills, including problem analysis and decision making, oral and written communication, quantitative skills, and the ability to work well with others.

Understanding Marketing's Impact

Marketers must know how their decisions will impact other areas of their organization and their business partners. They must realize that marketing decisions are not made in isolation and that decisions made by the marketing team could lead to problems for others both inside and outside the organization. For example, a decision to run a special sale that significantly lowers the price of a product could present supply problems if the production area is not informed well in advance of the sale.

Technology Savvy

Today's marketers must have a strong understanding of technology on two fronts. First, marketers must be skilled in using technology as part of their everyday activities. Not only must they understand how basic computer software is used to build spreadsheets or create slide presentations, but marketers must also investigate additional technologies that can improve their effectiveness and efficiency, including tools offered in the rapidly evolving field of **artificial intelligence (AI)**. (7).

Second, as we will see throughout this book, the evolution of digital networks, including internet and mobile technologies, is transforming many marketing functions . While this is evident through the tremendous growth of customer purchasing that is now transacted on websites and through digital apps, nearly all areas of marketing have also been dramatically affected (e.g., the impact of **social media** on promotion decisions). Consequently, marketers must pay close attention to emerging technologies and associated applications in order to spot potential business opportunities as well as potential threats.

The Need for a Global Perspective

Thanks in large part to the internet, nearly any company can conduct business on a global scale. Yet just having a website or social media account that is accessible to hundreds of millions of people worldwide does not guarantee success. Marketers selling internationally must possess a thorough understanding of the nuances of international trade and cultural differences that exist between markets. One key issue facing marketers selling globally is choosing the appropriate strategy for reaching international customers. As discussed in Box 1-3, two distinctly different methods are often pursued.

Box 1-3

APPROACHES TO GLOBAL MARKETING

Marketers seeking to expand beyond their home market face many decisions. For most organizations the most important decision is deciding whether they should follow a marketing approach that is the same worldwide (i.e., standardization) or one that is customized for the markets served (i.e., adaptation). This topic is a broad one encompassing not only issues regarding decisions to produce the same or different products but all marketing mix decisions.

Standardization

Under a standardization strategy, an organization follows a "one-for-all" approach, where all global markets are targeted with the same combination of marketing mix elements. The main advantage to standardization is the cost savings realized from common production, research and development, and similar marketing decisions deployed across multiple countries. On the downside, standardization may only be effective if there are enough customers in each market who share similar needs.

Adaptation

Under an adaptation strategy, firms operating globally allow both conception and execution of the marketing plan to originate in the foreign market. This provides local managers the opportunity to custom design the marketing mix for local conditions. The main advantage of this approach is that it fits the Marketing Concept by allowing local management to satisfy the target market's needs while taking into consideration issues that may exist within the local environment. However, the cost of implementation of this approach can be higher compared to standardization as costs cannot be spread over all markets the way these can with standardization.

Information Seeker

The field of marketing is dynamic. Changes occur continually and often quickly. Marketers must maintain close contact with these changes through a steady diet of information. As we will see, information can be obtained through formal marketing research methods involving extensive planning that includes the use of a variety of information gathering techniques. However, marketers also must be in tune with day-to-day developments by paying close attention to news that occurs in their industry, in the markets they serve, and among their potential customers.

Flexible to Changing Market Conditions

Through continual information seeking, marketers often will find that unanticipated market changes will require they quickly adjust their marketing strategy. This may occur for many reasons, such as competitors launching an unexpected new product, unanticipated changes in market demand (e.g., COVID-19 pandemic)), or the marketer's product suddenly being in great demand due to influential comments and reviews (e.g., mentions by social media influencers).

Successful marketers respond to market changes by quickly gathering information and ideas from both inside (e.g., members of other departments) and from outside (e.g., customers, business partners) the organization. For some situations, there may be benefit in preparing a "what-if" plan in case a situation affects the organization. For instance, a plan could be developed that spells out what the organization may do in the event of a sudden product shortage (e.g., product loss due to fire) or in situations where customers claim to be negatively affected using the organization's product (e.g., physical injury). No matter how a potential problem or opportunity is addressed, marketers must be accepting of change and be ready to respond.

REFERENCES

1. There is no better example of the need to monitor uncontrollable marketing conditions than what organizations experienced in wake of the COVID-19 outbreak when most marketers were forced to quickly make adjustments to their regular marketing plan.

2. For more on marketing and public health issues in the U.S. see: "Public Health Campaigns." *NIH.* https://prevention.nih.gov/research-priorities/dissemination-implementation/nih-public-health-campaigns.

3. For more on misleading advertising see: "Truth in Advertising." *Federal Trade Commission.* https://www.ftc.gov/news-events/topics/truth-advertising.

4. For more on tracking laws see: "Do Not Track Legislation." *Wikipedia.* https://en.wikipedia.org/wiki/Do_Not_Track_legislation.

5. "Google Code of Conduct." *Alphabet.* https://abc.xyz/investor/google-code-of-conduct.

6. "Code of Ethics and Standards of Practice." *Canadian Marketing Association.* https://thecma.ca/resources/code-of-ethics-standards.

7. Artificial intelligence (AI) tools, such as ChatGPT and Google Gemini, are already being deployed across many marketing areas. Throughout this book we will reference AI tools and see how these are expected to impact marketing decisions.

Chapter 2: Marketing Research

Many organizations find the markets they serve are dynamic with customers, competitors, and market conditions continually changing. They also recognize that marketing efforts that work today cannot be relied upon to be successful in the future. Meeting changing conditions requires marketers have sufficient market knowledge in order to make the proper adjustments to their marketing strategy. For marketers, gaining knowledge is accomplished through marketing research.

In this chapter, we look at the importance of research in marketing. We explore what marketing research is and see why it is considered the foundation of marketing. Our examination includes a detailed look at the methods marketers utilize to gather relevant information. Finally, we look at the important trends shaping marketing research.

THE FOUNDATION OF MARKETING

Research, in general, is the process of gathering information to learn about something that is not fully known. Nearly everyone engages in some form of research. From the highly skilled microbiologist investigating the underlying structure of a potentially lethal virus to the author of best-selling spy novels seeking insight into new surveillance techniques to the model train hobbyist spending hours hunting down the manufacturer of an old electric engine, each is driven by the quest for information.

For marketers, research is not only used for the purpose of learning, it is also a critical component needed to make good business decisions. Marketing research does this by giving marketers a picture of what is occurring (or likely to occur) and, when done well, offers alternative choices that can be made. For instance, research may suggest multiple options for introducing new products or entering new markets. In most cases, marketing decisions prove less risky (though these are never risk free) when the marketer can select from more than one option.

Using an analogy of a house foundation, marketing research can be viewed as the foundation of marketing. Just as a well-built house requires a strong foundation to remain sturdy, marketing decisions need the support of marketing research in order to be viewed favorably by customers and to stand up to competition and other external forces. Consequently, all areas of marketing and all marketing decisions should be supported with some level of research.

While research is important for marketing decision making, it does not always need to be elaborate to be effective. Sometimes small efforts, such as doing a quick search on the internet, will provide the needed information. However, for most marketers there are times when more elaborate research work is needed and understanding the right way to conduct research, whether performing the work themselves or hiring someone else to handle it, can increase the effectiveness of these projects.

Research in Marketing

As noted, marketing research is undertaken to support a wide variety of marketing decisions. Table 2-1 presents a small sampling of the research undertaken within marketing decision areas. Many of the issues listed under Types of Research are discussed in greater detail in other parts of this book.

Table 2-1: Examples of Research in Marketing

Marketing Decision	Types of Research
Target Markets	sales, market size, demand for product, customer characteristics, purchase behavior, customer satisfaction, website and app usage, and search engine traffic
Product	product development, package protection, packaging awareness, brand name selection, brand recognition, brand preference, product positioning
Distribution	distributor interest, assessing shipping options, online shopping trends, retail store site selection
Promotion	advertising recall, advertising copy testing, sales promotion response rates, sales force compensation, public relations media placement, social media engagement, search engine optimization
Pricing	price elasticity analysis, optimal price setting, discount options
External Factors	competitive analysis, legal environment, social and cultural trends, technological developments, economic conditions
Other	company image, test marketing

Options for Gathering Research Information

Marketers engage in a wide range of research from simple methods done spur of the moment to extensive, highly developed research projects taking months or even years to complete. To gather research, marketers have three choices:

◆ The marketer can acquire pre-existing research conducted by others.

◆ The marketer can undertake their own new research.

◆ The marketer can outsource the task of new research to a third-party, such as a marketing research company.

The first option is associated with **secondary research**, which involves accessing information that was previously collected. The last two options are associated with **primary research**, which involves the collection of original data generally for one's own use. In many instances, the researcher uses both secondary and primary data collection as part of the same research project. While both secondary and primary research have advantages and disadvantages, as discussed in Box 2-1, the value in using these is generally dependent on how the information is collected.

Box 2-1

RISK AND DOING RESEARCH RIGHT

Marketing research is a process that investigates both organizations and people. Of course, organizations are made up of people so when it comes down to it, marketing research is a branch of the social sciences. Social science studies people and their relationships, and includes such areas as economics, sociology, and psychology. To gain understanding into their fields, social science researchers use scientific methods that have been tested and refined over hundreds of years. Many of these methods require the institution of tight controls on research projects. For instance, many companies conduct surveys (i.e., by asking questions) of a small percentage of their customers (called a **sample**) to see how satisfied they are with the company's efforts. (1)

For this information to be useful when evaluating how the organization's larger customer base feels, controls may define sample selection (e.g., how are those in the sample chosen) and methods used to acquire customer information (e.g., types of questions). Additionally, for results to be truly relevant, research must stand up to scrutiny using **statistical analysis**. If these and other controls are not properly utilized, relying on results of research conducted incorrectly to make decisions could prove problematic if not disastrous.

But marketers must also be aware that following the right procedures to produce a relevant study does not ensure the results of research will be 100 percent correct as there is always the potential that results are wrong. Because of the risks associated with research, marketers are cautioned not to use the results of marketing research as the only input when making marketing decisions. Rather, smart marketing decisions require considering many factors, including management's own judgment. But being cautious with how research is used should not diminish the need to conduct research. While making decisions without research input may work sometimes, long-term success is not likely to happen without regular efforts to collect information.

SECONDARY RESEARCH

By far the most widely used method for collecting data is through secondary data collection, commonly called secondary research. This process involves collecting data from either the originator or a distributor of primary research (see *Primary Research* discussion below). In other words, accessing information that is already gathered.

In most cases, this means finding information from third-party sources, such as industry research reports, company websites, news outlets, and numerous other sources. But in actuality any information previously gathered, whether from sources external to the marketer's organization or from internal sources, such as previously undertaken marketing research, old sales reports, accounting records and many others, falls under the heading of secondary research.

ADVANTAGES

Secondary research offers several advantages for information gathering including:

- Ease of Access – Before the internet era, accessing reliable secondary data required marketers visit libraries or wait until a report was shipped by mail. When online access initially became an option through early computer dial-up services, marketers needed training to learn different rules and procedures for accessing each data source. However, the internet has changed how secondary research is accessed by offering convenience (e.g., easy, nearly anywhere access) and generally standardized usage methods for accessing data sources.

- Low Cost to Acquire – Researchers are often attracted to secondary data because getting this information is much less expensive than if the researchers had to carry out the research themselves.

- May Help Clarify Research Question – Secondary research is often used prior to larger scale primary research to help clarify what is to be learned. For instance, a researcher doing competitor analysis, but who is not familiar with competitors in a market, could access secondary sources to locate a list of potential competitors and use this information as part of her/his own primary research study.

- May Answer Research Question – As noted, secondary data collection is often used to help set the stage for primary research. In the course of doing so, researchers may find the exact information they are looking for is available via secondary sources, which eliminates the need and expense of carrying out primary research.

- May Show Difficulties in Conducting Primary Research – The originators of secondary research often provide details on how the information was collected. This may include discussion of any difficulties that were encountered. For instance, a consumer research report written by a large marketing research company may reveal that a high percentage of people declined to take part in the research. After obtaining this study, a marketer contemplating doing similar research may decide it is not worth the effort given the potential difficulties in conducting the study.

DISADVANTAGES

While secondary research is often valuable, it also has drawbacks that include:

- Quality of Researcher – As we will discuss, research conducted using primary research methods is largely controlled by the marketer. However, this is not the case when it comes to data collected by others. The quality of secondary research should be scrutinized closely since the origins of the information may be questionable. Organizations relying on secondary data as an important component in their decision making must take care to evaluate how the information was gathered, analyzed, and presented to ensure the research was done correctly and is relevant (see Box 2-1).

- Not Specific to Researcher's Needs – Secondary data is often not presented in a form that exactly meets the marketer's needs. For example, a marketer decides to obtain an expensive research report examining how different age groups feel about certain products within the marketer's industry. Unfortunately, the marketer may be disappointed to discover the way the research divides age groups (e.g., under 13, 14-18, 19-25, etc.) does not match how the marketer's company designates its age groups (e.g., under 16, 17-21, 22-30, etc.). Because of this difference the results may not be useful.

- Not Available in All Markets – In some cases, marketers will find that the secondary research available in one market is not available in all markets. This is especially the case for marketers seeking to expand into foreign markets. They may discover that secondary research that is readily available in their home market is either not available or the quality of research that is available is poor. Also, there may be differences in how the data was collected and presented making it difficult to compare the different markets.

- Inefficient Spending for Information – If the research received is not specific to the marketer's needs, an argument can be made that research spending is inefficient. That is, the marketer may not receive a satisfactory amount of information for what is spent.

- Incomplete Information – Many times a researcher finds research that appears to be promising is, in fact, a "teaser" released by the research supplier. This may occur when a small portion of a research study is disclosed, often for free, but to gain access to the entire report may require payment of a sizable fee..

- Not Timely – Caution must be exercised in relying on secondary data that was collected well in the past. Out-of-date information generally offers little value especially for companies competing in fast changing markets.

- Not Proprietary Information – In most cases, secondary research is not undertaken specifically for one organization. Instead, it is made available to many either for free or for a fee. Consequently, there is rarely an information advantage gained by those who obtain the research.

Types of Low-Cost Secondary Research

Many marketers mistakenly believe marketing research is something that is far too expensive to do on their own. While this is true for some marketing decisions, not all marketing research must be expensive to be useful. There are secondary research sources that are easily obtainable at relatively low cost and, in many cases, offer free access to information. These include:

TRADE ASSOCIATIONS

Trade associations are generally membership-supported organizations whose mission is to offer assistance and represent the interests of those operating in a specific industry. One of the many tasks performed by trade associations is to provide research information and industry metrics through efforts, such as conducting member surveys. Accessing this information may be as simple as visiting a trade association's website, although some associations limit access to the best research to members only, in which case joining the association (if they permit) may include paying dues.

GOVERNMENT SOURCES

Many national, regional, and local governments offer a full range of helpful materials, including information on consumers, domestic businesses, and international markets. For those operating in the United States, information available through the U.S. Federal Government is staggering. The U.S. Federal Government is a behemoth with agencies and offices found in more nooks and crannies than one could ever imagine, and the uninitiated can spend hours on end trying to find relevant information. But once found and digested, the reports are often very useful for many marketing purposes.

COMMUNITY GROUPS AND ORGANIZATIONS

When searching for information related to regional business areas, marketers can often tap into groups and organizations connected to these areas. Some examples of groups offering access to low-cost secondary data include regional chambers of commerce, economic development agencies, local colleges and universities, and not-for-profit organizations.

COMPANY-PROVIDED INFORMATION

If the need is for information on a specific company and if research seekers are willing to believe what a company reports in its own literature, then value may be found in company-provided information. While many materials published by companies are promotional pieces (see *Research as Promotional Tool* discussion below), there may be beneficial information found amongst the hype. Options for finding information include company websites, annual reports, press releases, white papers, social media postings, and presentations.

NEWS AND MEDIA SOURCES

Possibly the most widely used method for acquiring secondary research is through articles and other reports found through commercial news sources. Options include magazines, newspapers, television news, podcasts, and other video/audio programming. Nearly all of these sources are available online.

ACADEMIC RESEARCH

College professors often cite industry research as part of their scholarly efforts when they conduct their own research studies. Many of these academic works can be found in academic journals. A search of Google Scholar may be a good place to start for locating this information. (2) Research may also be found within academic research centers established by many universities. The websites of these centers frequently post articles and working papers containing market data, most of which are freely accessible. An internet search using the keywords "research center" along with industry or product keywords may yield a list.

CAUSE-RELATED GROUPS

Many not-for-profit groups have an organizational mission directed at supporting causes they feel are not well supported in society. Examples include groups focusing on the environment, education, and health care. As would be expected, a considerable portion of their focus looks at how business issues impact these causes. Research seekers will find the best funded of these cause-related groups carry out an active marketing research agenda with many of their studies freely available on their websites.

Types of High-Cost Secondary Research

While research seekers can get lucky finding information through inexpensive means, the reality is that, in many situations, locating in-depth market information is difficult and expensive. Companies in the business of producing market studies are mostly doing so to make money and do not give the information away for free. Consequently, in many research situations, especially those in which reliable market numbers and estimates are critical, acquiring the most comprehensive information will require the marketer pay a substantial fee.

Expensive sources of information generally include accessing reports from the originators of the research, such as marketing research companies. However, since gaining access to quality research can be costly, on the surface it may not seem practical for small organizations or individuals to take advantage of these sources. Yet research seekers also know that the level of detail available in a single report may be enough to provide answers to most of their questions, in which case these reports can be real time savers (though marketers are cautioned against relying on a single source of information when making marketing decisions).

Also, while the cost of certain secondary research reports can appear prohibitive, today's reports are much more accessible than in the past when research suppliers often required clients to sign up for high-priced subscription services. Purchasing a subscription would then give the client access to a large number of reports. Today, many information sources permit the purchase of a single research report without the requirement to commit to a subscription. It should be noted that some of these sources may make a limited amount of material available for free, so for those seeking marketing research information it is worth a look no matter how much money the research seeker has to spend.

High-cost marketing research sources include:

MARKETING RESEARCH COMPANIES

Many companies engaged in marketing research services offer both customized research activities (i.e., produce work only for a specific client) and commercial research (i.e., produce work that nearly anyone can buy). Commercial reports produced by reputable firms are often well researched and contain extensive product/industry metrics and statistics, including forecasts and trend analysis. Often these reports are generated by a specific researcher, who has been following the market/industry for many years. An industry-focused researcher will produce regular updates, which include offering comments and insights that go beyond the numbers. But these reports often come with a high price tag. It is not uncommon to pay a large sum for a report that is less than 100 pages long. However, many research reports are updates of existing reports and the older reports may be available for lower cost.

FINANCIAL SERVICES COMPANIES

Financial institutions, such as brokerage firms and other financial consulting firms, are also in the business of producing original research. Financial firms assist investors by offering research reports presenting the financial firm's analysis of an industry or company, including providing market metrics. While such reports may be free to a broker's clients, many reports can also be purchased by non-clients through financial portal websites, such as Bloomberg and BizMiner.

CONSULTING FIRMS

Consulting firms consist of individuals specializing in particular business areas, such as by job function (e.g., sales training), business need (e.g., strategy development), or industry (e.g., transportation). In addition to working for individual clients, consulting firms also produce reports covering their specialties that are made available to the general public. By and large, the bigger the consulting firm the more valid and reliable are the reports they produce. One group of companies to consider as a starting point is large accounting firms. Nearly all major accounting firms have divisions focused on management consulting. These divisions regularly make available industry reports.

MARKET INFORMATION DEALERS

The marketing research business consists of a large number of suppliers who provide many products (i.e., research studies and other documents) targeted to a wide range of buyers. To get research into the hands of buyers, the creators of the research can attempt to sell the reports themselves or they can enlist the services of companies serving an intermediary role (i.e., those bringing buyers and sellers together). For their services, these marketing research dealers receive a percentage of the sale price.

For research seekers, these dealers offer several advantages. First, they carry reports from many different suppliers increasing the likelihood of finding a report that meets the researcher's needs. Second, they allow for the purchase of individual reports and, in some cases, pieces of reports offered at lower cost. By comparison, marketing research creators often require clients purchase a complete report at full price. Third, they offer excellent search functionality making it easy to locate reports.

COMPREHENSIVE INFORMATION SOURCES

Marketers, who frequently need to locate market information, may consider establishing an account with one of the major comprehensive information sources. These are the heavyweight providers of business research used by university libraries and leading corporations.

Comprehensive sources offer one-stop shopping for research reports, industry news, and even government information. In fact, much of the information available from sources already mentioned is also available through comprehensive information sources. However, gaining access to these services can be prohibitively expensive. Fortunately, several comprehensive information sources are now offering pay-per-item access.

PRIMARY RESEARCH

When marketers conduct research to collect original data for their own needs it is called primary research. This process has the marketer or someone working for the marketer designing and then carrying out a research plan. Primary research is often undertaken after the researcher has gained some insight into the issue by collecting secondary data.

While not as frequently used as secondary research, primary research still represents a significant part of overall marketing research. For many organizations, especially large firms, spending on primary research far exceeds spending on secondary research.

The primary research market consists of marketers carrying out their own research as well as an extensive group of research companies offering their services to marketers. These companies include:

◆ <u>Full-Service Marketing Research Firms</u> – These companies develop and carry out the full research plan for their clients.

◆ <u>Partial-Service Research Firms</u> – These companies offer expertise addressing a specific part of the research plan. Their services include developing methods for data collection (e.g., designing surveys), locating research participants, or performing data analysis.

◆ <u>Research Tools Suppliers</u> – These firms provide tools used by marketing researchers that assist with data collection (e.g., survey software and apps), data analysis (e.g., data visualization software), and report presentation products (e.g., online presentation software).

ADVANTAGES

Marketers often turn to primary data collection because of the benefits it offers including:

● <u>Addresses Specific Research Issues</u> – Carrying out its own research allows the marketing organization to address issues specific to its particular situation. Primary research is designed to collect the information the marketer wants to know and report it in ways benefiting the marketer. For example, while information reported with secondary research may not fit the marketer's needs, rarely do such problems exist with primary research since the marketer is the one who determines the research design.

● <u>Greater Control</u> – Primary research enables the marketer to focus on specific issues and have a higher level of control over how the information is collected. In this way, the marketer can decide such issues as the size of project (e.g., how many responses are needed), the location of research (e.g., geographic area), and the time frame for completing the project.

● <u>Efficient Spending for Information</u> – As noted, unlike secondary research where the marketer may spend for information that is not needed, primary data collection focuses on issues specific to the researcher. This helps improve the chances research funds will be spent efficiently.

● <u>Proprietary Information</u> – Information collected by the marketer using primary research is its own and is generally not shared with others. Thus, information can be hidden from competitors and potentially offer an **information advantage** to the company that undertook the primary research.

DISADVANTAGES

While primary data collection is a powerful method for acquiring information, it does pose several significant problems including:

● <u>Cost</u> – Compared to secondary research, primary data collection may be very expensive since it often requires both a high degree of marketer involvement and high cost for the tools and methods used to carry out the research.

- Time Consuming – To be done correctly, primary data collection requires the development and execution of a research plan. Going from the starting point of deciding to undertake a research project to the end point of having results is often much longer than the time it takes to acquire secondary data.

- Not Always Feasible – Some research projects, while potentially offering information that could prove quite valuable, are not within the reach of a marketer. Many are just too large to be carried out by all but the largest companies while some research projects are not feasible at all. For instance, it would not be practical for Starbucks to attempt to interview every customer visiting its stores on a certain day since doing so would require hiring an enormous number of researchers, which would be an unrealistic expense. Fortunately, there are ways for Starbucks to use other methods (e.g., sampling) to meet its needs without talking to all customers.

Types of Primary Research

In general, there are two basic types of primary research – quantitative data collection and qualitative data collection.

Quantitative Data Collection

Quantitative data collection involves the use of numbers to assess information. This information can then be evaluated using statistical analysis, which offers researchers the opportunity to dig deeper into the data to look for greater meaning (see Box 2-2). Quantitative data collection comes in many forms with the most popular being:

- Surveys – This method captures information through the input of responses to a research instrument, such as a questionnaire. Information can be input either by respondents themselves (e.g., complete an online survey) or the researcher can input the data (e.g., phone survey, shopping mall intercept). The main methods for distributing surveys are via websites, mobile apps, postal and electronic mail, phone calls, and in person.

- Tracking – With tracking research marketers monitor the behavior of customers as they engage in a variety of activities. This can be seen with digital media, where tracking is used for monitoring website visits, mobile app usage, podcasts listenership, television viewing, and more. Yet tracking research also has offline applications (see Box 1-2 in Chapter 1), including using point-of-purchase scanners to track product purchases at retail stores. This method of research is expected to grow significantly as more devices are introduced with tracking capability.

- Experiments – Marketers often undertake experiments to gauge how the manipulation of one marketing variable affects another (i.e., **causal research**). The use of experiments has applications for many marketing decision areas, including product testing, advertising design, setting price points, and creating packaging. Unfortunately, performing highly controlled experiments can be quite costly. Some researchers have found the use of computer simulations can work nearly as well as experiments and may be less expensive, though the number of simulation applications for marketing decisions is still fairly limited.

Box 2-2

RESEARCH BY THE NUMBERS

Primary research is collected using a **research instrument** designed to record information for later analysis. Marketing researchers use many types of instruments from basic methods that record participant responses to a survey on a piece of paper to highly advanced electronic measurement that use body sensors to measure participants' response. Depending on the type of research instrument used, the researcher may be able to evaluate the results by turning responses into numbers, which then allows for analysis using statistical methods (see Box 2-1).

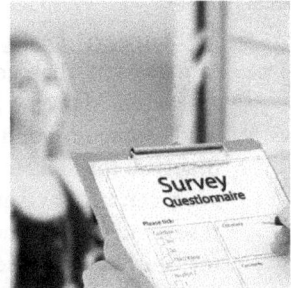

Of course, certain information is by nature numerical. For example, asking a person their actual age or weight will result in a number. But under the right circumstances, numbers can also be used to represent certain characteristics, which are not on the surface considered numerical. This most often occurs with data collected within a structured and well-controlled scientific **research design**. For instance, a company researching its customers' attitudes toward products they purchased may ask a large number of customers to complete a survey. Contained in the survey is the following:

Place an "X" on the line that best indicates your impression of the overall quality of our company's products:

Poor _ _ _ _ _ _ _ **Excellent**

In this example each line, which represents a potential customer response, could be assigned a number. For example, checking the left-most line could result in the researcher entering a "1", the next line a "2", the next line a "3", and so on.

Once research is gathered for all customers completing the survey, information for this item can then undergo statistical analysis and interesting comparisons can be made. For example, different types of customers (e.g., female vs. male) can be compared on their mean or average score for this item. Statistical analysis can then be used to determine if a difference exists in how they responded.

Qualitative Data Collection

Often called "touchy-feely" research, qualitative data collection requires researchers to interpret the information gathered, most often without the benefit of statistical support. If the researcher is well trained in interpreting respondents' comments and activities, this form of research can offer valuable insight. However, this method of data collection may not hold the same level of relevancy as quantitative research due to the lack of scientific controls. An additional drawback of qualitative research is that the process can be time consuming, expensive, and only a very small portion of the marketer's desired market can participate. Due to the lack of strong controls in the qualitative research design, using results to estimate characteristics of a larger group is more difficult.

Qualitative data collection options include:

● <u>Individual Interviews</u> – Talking to someone one-on-one allows a researcher to cover more ground than may be covered if a respondent was completing a survey. The researcher can dig deeper into a respondent's comments to find out additional details that might not emerge from initial responses. Unfortunately, individual interviews can be quite expensive and may be intimidating to some participants, who are not comfortable sharing details with a researcher.

● <u>Focus Groups</u> – To overcome the drawbacks associated with individual interviews, marketers can turn to focus groups. Under this research format, a group of respondents (generally numbering 8-12) is guided through a discussion by a moderator. The power of focus groups as a research tool rests with the environment created by the interaction of the participants. In well-run sessions, members of the group are stimulated to respond by the comments and the support of others in the group. In this way, the depth of information offered by a respondent may be much greater than that obtained through individual interviews. However, focus groups can be costly to conduct especially if participants must be paid. To help reduce costs, researcher often utilize video conferencing. While the fact that respondents are not physically present may somewhat diminish the benefits gained from in-person group dynamics, continual technology improvements have made video focus groups a cost-effective research option.

● <u>Observational Research</u> – Marketers can gain valuable insight by watching customers as they perform activities, especially when they are observed in a natural setting (e.g., using products at home). In fact, an emerging research technique called **ethnographic research** has researchers following customers as they shop, work, and relax at home in order to see how they make decisions, use products, and more.

TRENDS IN MARKETING RESEARCH

In its role as the foundation of marketing, marketing research is arguably the crucial ingredient in making marketing decisions and a critical factor in gaining advantage over competitors. Because organizations recognize the power information has in helping create and maintain customer relationships, there is an insatiable appetite to gain even more insight into customers and markets. Marketers in nearly all industries are expected to direct more resources to gathering and analyzing data, especially in highly competitive markets. Many of the trends discussed below are directly related to marketers' quest to acquire large amounts of customer, competitor, and market information

ARTIFICIAL INTELLIGENCE

There is little doubt that generative artificial intelligence (AI) (3) is the most impactful technological development to affect marketing (and nearly all other areas of business) since the evolution of the internet and, more recently, mobile technologies. While still in its infancy, the field of AI is rapidly evolving with developments potentially enhancing or, in some cases, supplanting many existing marketing methods, including those involving marketing research. Not only are new AI-supported research techniques being envisioned and, in many cases, already being deployed, but AI is also becoming an integral component in many of the research methods discussed throughout this book. For instance, AI is being used to help assess the "emotional tone" of customers by evaluating customers' email, social media postings, online chats and other areas where customers share their thoughts and feelings. This so-called **sentiment analysis** can help marketers gain a better understanding of how their customers respond to marketing decisions, such as their feelings about new products or promotional messages. (4)

DIGITAL DEVICE TECHNOLOGIES

In addition to enhancing data collection with AI, marketing companies utilize many other digital technologies to assist in the information gathering process. One area where these technologies are widely deployed is associated with measuring the activities of website visitors, mobile apps users, and smart TVs viewers. These technologies include::

- Enhanced Tracking – Digital technologies offer an unparalleled ability to track and monitor customers. For instance, each time a visitor accesses a website or uses a mobile application they provide marketers with extensive information (see Box 1-2 in Chapter 1). The information provided by various tracking options has spawned the concept of **customer engagement research**, which offers insight into how customers interact with a digital outlet (e.g., amount of time spent, movement around the outlet). With tracking software becoming more sophisticated, many marketers now view it as an indispensable research tool.

- Improved Communication – Internet and mobile technologies offer a significant improvement in customer-to-organization communication, which is vital for marketing research. For instance, the ability to encourage customer feedback on an organization's goods and services (e.g., product ratings) is easy with website popup messages, social media posts, text messages, and email reminders.

- Research Tools – Many internet websites and app developers offer services to assist with the collection of market information. These include advanced data analytics, survey tools, virtual focus groups, and access to large databases containing previous research studies (i.e., secondary research).

OTHER TECHNOLOGIES

In addition to technologies discussed above, marketing research has benefited from other technological improvements including:

- Global Positioning Systems (GPS) – GPS enables marketers to track product shipments and even to track sales and service personnel. GPS is also a common feature contained within customers' communication devices, such as smartphones, offering marketers the potential to locate and track customers.

- Virtual Reality and Simulations – Marketers now have the capability of using computer-developed virtual worlds or **metaverse** to simulate real-world customer activity, such as in-store shopping. The emergence of research applications involving virtual reality enables marketers to test new product concepts and gain more insight into customer buying behavior. (5)

- Eye Tracking - Technologies that track eye movement have been around for some time, and most notably have been used in evaluating customer response to advertising and website layout. Typically, eye tracking research is conducted in a testing laboratory. However, recent advancements have led to the development of special glasses that offer the advantage of conducting research in real-world environments, such as in real stores, rather than in a controlled laboratory setting.

- Data Analysis Software – The research process not only includes gathering information, it also involves a full analysis of what is collected. A number of software and statistical programs have been refined to give marketers greater insight into what the data really means. In fact, everyday spreadsheet programs, such as Microsoft Excel, now offer advanced statistical tools that previously were only available with more expensive computer programs.

- Neuro-Research – Companies have begun to explore the use of brain-imaging technology for marketing research. Using such technologies as Magnetic Resonance Imaging (MRI) and Electroencephalogram (EEG) sensors, researchers scan the brains of research subjects as they are exposed to neuro-stimuli, such as imagery and sound (e.g., advertisements), in order to detect any effect potentially attributable to the stimuli.

AFFORDABLE RESEARCH

For many years, formal research projects were considered something only the largest marketers could afford due to the expense in carrying out such projects. However, many of the technologies discussed above make it affordable for organizations of all sizes to engage in research. For instance, surveying customers is quick and easy using one of the many online survey services, which charge low fees to create, distribute, and analyze results.

MERGING OF DATA SOURCES

Marketers' constant quest for information has resulted in data being gathered across many areas within an organization. For instance, as we will discuss in Chapter 3, there may be multiple contact points where customers can interact with a marketer (e.g., in person, on the web, via phone call). In the past, the information gathered at these points was often stored separately and not easily accessible to those in other areas. However, with advances in data storage technologies including cloud-based services, organizations now see the value in knowing what customers do across all contact points, and consequently they now integrate customer information from many sources. Alos, some marketers go outside their own data collection and seek customer information from other sources, such as credit card companies. This information is then merged with the company-owned information to get a fuller picture of customer activity.

PRIVACY CONCERNS AND CUSTOMER COOPERATION

As we discussed in Chapter 1, the continual demand for customer information, along with advances in technology, has led marketing organizations to gather information in ways that are raising privacy concerns. While such concerns have been expressed for some time by privacy advocates and government regulators, particularly in Europe (6), marketers are now finding that awareness of these issues is increasing among their customers. The growing concern with privacy is leading many customers to limit their participation in research activities, including choosing not to respond to company requests to take part in research studies and by using techniques to restrict marketers tracking efforts. For instance, marketers can place small data files called **cookies** on customers' digital devices and then use these to track user activity. Many customers are learning to change the privacy setting on their digital devices to reject tracking and, in doing so are limiting marketer's ability to monitor customer activity. As customers' awareness of tracking and other research methods increases, marketers may find customer research will become even more challenging.

RESEARCH AS A PROMOTIONAL TOOL

While most people do not equate marketing research with promotion, many companies are discovering research can also function as an influential promotional tool. The practice of distributing company-produced research reports to potential customers and the news media has been used for several years in scientific and technology industries. Recently the practice has expanded into many other fields, particularly among firms involved in consulting, healthcare, and financial services. Such reports, which often provide information related to company products, comparisons with competitor's offerings and target market perceptions, are produced using high quality graphics and charts backed up by carefully created narratives that proudly emphasize the company's strengths.

Unfortunately, many reports produced for promotional reasons are not scientific; therefore, these may not carry much value. While companies may claim the research supports their products, many of these claims may, in fact, be more fluff than substance since they are not grounded in sound research methodology.

REFERENCES

1. For more on the different methods of sampling see: "Survey Sampling Methods." *Stat Trek*. https://stattrek.com/survey-research/sampling-methods.

2. "Google Scholar." *Google*. https://scholar.google.com.

3. For more on why it is called generative artificial intelligence see: "Generative Artificial Intelligence". *Wikipedia*. https://en.wikipedia.org/wiki/Generative_artificial_intelligence.

4. For more on sentiment analysis see: "What is Sentiment Analysis." *Amazon Web Services*. https://aws.amazon.com/what-is/sentiment-analysis.

5. For more on how virtual reality may impact research see: "Virtual Reality Market Research." *Explorer Research*. https://explorerresearch.com/virtual-reality-market-research.

6. In 2018, the European Union instituted the General Data Protection Regulation (GDPR) that impacts how marketers and others can gather customer information. For a summary of GDPR and its requirements see: "Complete Guide to GDPR Compliance" *GDPR.EU*. https://gdpr.eu.

Chapter 3: Managing Customers

In Chapter 1, we noted marketers make decisions which result in value to both the marketing organization and its customers. Throughout *KnowThis: Marketing Basics*, we emphasize the importance customers play in helping marketers meet their business objectives. To drive home this point, in Chapter 3 we concentrate our discussion on understanding customers and examining customers' role in the marketing process. We show that for most marketers understanding customers is necessary not only because of their effect on marketing decisions but because customers' activities have the potential to influence the entire organization.

In this chapter, we explore the techniques marketers use to manage customers. We begin by defining what a customer is and why they are important to an organization. We then look at what tools and strategies must be in place to manage customers skillfully, including the crucial requirement that marketers work hard to build relationships with their customers. Finally, we conclude with a discussion of how servicing customers after a relationship is established (e.g., after a purchase) is often just as critical as the marketing efforts that were needed to begin the relationship.

WHAT IS A CUSTOMER?

In general terms, a customer is a person or organization that a marketer believes will benefit from the goods and services offered by the marketer's organization. As this definition suggests, a customer is not necessarily someone who is currently purchasing from the marketer. In fact, customers may fall into one of three groups:

EXISTING CUSTOMERS

The first group consists of customers who have purchased or otherwise used an organization's goods or services, typically within a designated period of time. For some organizations, the time frame may be short. For instance, a coffee shop may only consider someone to be an existing customer if they have purchased within the last three months. Other organizations may view someone as an existing customer even though they have not purchased in the last few years (e.g., automobile manufacturer).

Existing customers are by far the most important of the three customer groups since they have a current relationship with an organization, and consequently they give an organization a reason to remain in contact with them. Additionally, existing customers also represent the best market for future sales, especially if they are satisfied with the relationship they presently have with the marketer. Getting existing customers to purchase more products is significantly less expensive and less time consuming than finding new customers. This is because existing customers know and hopefully trust the marketer and, if managed correctly, are easy to reach with promotional appeals (e.g., texting a special discount offer for a new product). Yet, as discussed in Box 3-1, not all existing customers should be treated the same as some customers offer more value to the marketer than others.

FORMER CUSTOMERS

This group consists of those who have formerly had a relationship with the marketing organization, typically through a previous purchase. However, the marketer no longer feels the customer is an existing customer because they have not purchased from the marketer within a certain time frame or due to other indications (e.g., a former customer just purchased a similar product from the marketer's competitor).

The value of this group to a marketer will depend on whether the customer's previous relationship was considered satisfactory to the customer or to the marketer. For instance, a former customer who felt she was not treated well by the marketer will be more difficult to persuade to buy again compared to a former customer who liked the marketer but decided to buy from another company offering a similar product but at a lower price.

POTENTIAL CUSTOMERS

The third category of customers includes those who have yet to purchase but possess what the marketer believes are the requirements to become customers. As we will see in Chapter 5, the requirements to become a potential customer include such issues as having a need for a product, possessing the financial means to buy, and having the authority to make a buying decision.

Locating potential customers is an ongoing process for two reasons. First, existing customers may become former customers (e.g., decide to buy from a competitor) and must be replaced by new customers. Second, while we noted above that existing customers are the best source for future sales, often it is new customers that are needed for a business to expand. For example, a company selling only in its own country may see less room for sales growth if a high percentage of people in the country are already existing customers. To realize stronger growth, the company may seek to sell their products in other countries where the percentage of potential customers may be quite high.

Box 3-1

THE "GOOD" CUSTOMER

For marketers, simply finding customers who are willing to purchase their goods or services is not enough to build a successful marketing strategy. Instead, as we note in our definition of marketing in Chapter 1, marketers should look to manage customers in a way that will "identify, create, and maintain satisfying relationships." By using marketing efforts that are designed to "maintain satisfying relationships" rather than simply pursuing a quick sale, the likelihood increases that customers will be more trusting of the marketer and exhibit a higher level of satisfaction with the organization. In turn, satisfied customers are more likely to become "good" customers.

For our purposes, we define a "good" customer as one who holds the potential to undertake activities offering long-term value to an organization. The activities performed by "good" customers not only include purchasing products, but these also include such things as:

♦ offering a higher level of profitability since they buy more while costing proportionally less to satisfy

♦ making prompt payment for their purchases

♦ offering feedback that helps create new products and improve services

♦ voluntarily promoting the organization's products to others

These activities, along with many others, represent the value (i.e., benefits obtained for costs spent) an organization receives from its customers. In the case of "good" customers, their potential for providing value should be a signal for marketers to direct additional efforts in building, strengthening, and sustaining customer relationships.

The fact that we place the descriptive term "good" in front of customers should not be taken lightly. Not all existing customers, who currently have relationships with an organization, should be treated on an equal level. Some consistently spend large sums to purchase products from an organization; others do not spend large sums but hold the potential to do so; and still others use a large amount of an organization's resources (e.g., constantly call customer service) but contribute little revenue. Clearly there are lines of demarcation between those in the existing customer category. For marketers, identifying the line that separates "good" customers from others is critical. For larger marketers, this may be done with so-called **customer lifetime value (CLV)** computer models that calculate a customer's potential to contribute profitably to an organization. For smaller organizations, CLV assessment may be done using "gut instincts" gained from experience rather than by analytical means. No matter what method is used to assess the value of customers, limited resources force nearly all marketers to establish a line of separation between customers that offer value and those customers that do not. (1)

CUSTOMERS AND THE ORGANIZATION

For most organizations, understanding customers is the key to success, while not understanding them is likely to result in failure. It is so important that the constant drive to satisfy customers is not only a concern for those responsible for carrying out marketing tasks, but also a concern of everyone in the entire organization.

Whether someone's job involves direct contact with customers (e.g., salespeople, delivery drivers, service representatives) or indirect contact (e.g., production workers, accounting department), all members of an organization must appreciate the role customers play in helping the organization meet its goals. To ensure everyone understands the customer's role, many organizations continually preach a "customer is most important" message in department meetings, organizational communication (e.g., internal emails), and corporate training programs. To drive home the importance of customers, the message often contains examples of how customers impact the organization. These examples may include:

SOURCE OF INFORMATION AND IDEAS

Satisfying the needs of customers requires organizations maintain close contact with them. Marketers can get close to customers by conducting research, such as surveys and other feedback methods (e.g., rate-our-service messages), that encourages customers to share their thoughts and feelings. With this information, marketers can learn what people think of their present marketing efforts and receive suggestions for making improvements. For instance, research and feedback methods can offer marketers insight into new goods and services sought by their customers.

AFFECTS ACTIVITIES THROUGHOUT THE ORGANIZATION

For most organizations, customers not only affect decisions made by the marketing team they are also the key driver for decisions made throughout the organization. For example, consider how customers may affect a manufacturer. Customers' reaction to the design of a product may influence the type of raw materials used in the product manufacturing process. With customers impacting such a significant portion of a company, creating an environment geared to locating, understanding, and satisfying customers is imperative.

NEEDED TO SUSTAIN THE ORGANIZATION

Finally, customers are the reason an organization is in business. Without customers or the potential to attract customers, an organization is not viable. Consequently, customers are not only key to revenue and profits they are also crucial to creating and maintaining jobs within the organization.

CHALLENGE OF MANAGING CUSTOMERS

While on the surface, the process for managing customers may seem to be intuitive and straightforward, in reality, organizations struggle to accomplish this. The challenges marketers face when it comes to managing customers include:

CUSTOMERS ARE DIFFERENT

One reason managing customers can be difficult is because no two customers are the same. What is appealing to one may not work for another. For instance, a marketer may change its coupon promotion (see *Coupons* in Chapter 14) by reducing the frequency of issuing coupons by regular mail and instead direct customers to digital coupons on their website, in emails, or displayed on a shopping app. The marketer makes this move with the hope it will lead to cost savings (e.g., coupons sent by mail require postage expense), allow the marketer to acquire more customer information (e.g., monitor activities when customers visit the website or app), and give the marketer the opportunity to sell more products to the customer (e.g., special promotional messages after coupon is used). However, while many customers will prefer using digital coupons, some long-time customers may feel they will now need to do more work to acquire coupons compared to having these delivered by regular mail. In this example, the change in coupon delivery may satisfy some customers while irritating others.

CUSTOMERS INTERACT AT DIFFERENT CONTACT POINTS

Managing customers can also be an issue due to the many contact points that can be used to connect with an organization. A contact point is the method customers utilize to communicate with an organization. These include:

- <u>In-Person Assistance</u> – Customers seek in-person assistance by visiting retail stores and other outlets, or through discussion with company salespeople who visit customers at business locations or in homes. While some in-person support is intended to help with a customer's purchase decision, other support is designed to offer help once a purchase is made. Often these services are handled by specialist such as product trainers, delivery people, and service technicians.

- <u>Telephone</u> – Customers seeking to make purchases or looking to have problems resolved may find it more convenient to do so through phone contact. In many organizations, a dedicated department (e.g., **call center**) handles incoming phone inquiries.

- <u>Digital Networks</u> – The fastest growing contact points are communications made over the internet and mobile networks. Not only are these networks widely used to make purchases, but customers are also becoming comfortable using digital technologies when seeking assistance. While email is a digital technology that has been part of customer-company communication for many years, organizations now rely on several newer methods for addressing customer issues, including social media, video conferencing, and mobile apps. Additionally, monitoring and responding to questions and comments posted to online forums and product review websites has also become a key method for connecting with customers.

- Kiosks – A kiosk is a standalone, interactive computer, often equipped with a touchscreen, offering customers such service options as product information, real-time purchasing, and review of a customer's account. Kiosks are now widely used for airline check-in, in-store purchases, paying for parking, and much more.

- Assistance Through Other Departments – As noted in the next section, customer contact may also occur through departments that are not part of the marketing area. For instance, employees in a company's credit department may help customers arrange the funds necessary to make a purchase while personnel in accounts receivable may work with customers who experience payment problems.

The challenge of ensuring customers are handled properly no matter the contact point they use is daunting for many organizations. For some, the customer contact points cited above operate independently of others. For instance, retail stores may not be directly connected to telephone **customer service**. The result is that, for different contact points, many organizations have developed different procedures and techniques for handling customers. And, for some organizations, there exists little integration between contact points so customers communicating through one point one day and another point the next day may receive conflicting information. In such cases, customers are more likely to become frustrated and question the organization's ability to provide adequate service. As discussed in Box 3-2, one way organizations can maintain a consistent relationship with customers across different contact points is through the implementation of methods for managing customer relationships.

CUSTOMER SERVICE AND MARKETING

As we have noted, to manage customers effectively, marketers must be concerned with the entire experience a customer has with an organization. While much of the value sought by customers is obtained directly from the consumption or use of goods or services they purchase (i.e., benefits from using the product), customers' satisfaction is not limited only to benefits from the actual product. Instead, customers are affected by the entire purchasing experience, which is a mix of product and **non-product benefits**.

When it comes to managing customers, a pivotal non-product benefit that can have an important effect on customers' feelings about an organization is customer service. We define customer service as activities used by the marketer to support purchasers' experience with a product. Customer service includes several activities such as: (2)

- Training – services needed to assist customers in learning how to use a product
- Repair – services needed to handle damaged or malfunctioning products
- Financial Assistance – services needed to help customers with the financial commitment required to purchase or use the product
- Complaint Resolution – services needed to address other problems that have arisen with customers' use of a product

Box 3-2

CUSTOMER RELATIONSHIP MANAGEMENT

In order to overcome the challenges faced as they attempt to cultivate and manage customers, many marketers must continually conduct marketing research to evaluate customers to determine what they want. And uncovering what customers want is made significantly easier if a company establishes methods designed to manage its customers. The most widely adopted method for managing customers is a business concept known as Customer Relationship Management (CRM).

CRM and "Good" Customers

CRM is a strategic approach whose goal is to get everyone in an organization, not just the marketing department, to recognize the importance of customers. Under CRM, the key driver for marketing success is to treat "good" customers in a way that will increase the probability they will stay "good" customers. This is accomplished, in part, by ensuring a customer receives accurate information and has a consistent and satisfying experience every time they interact with the organization.

CRM and Other Customers

While CRM is primarily used to manage existing customers, it also has application for other customer groups. For instance, CRM is used to help identify former customers that may hold potential to buy again. This is often possible due to the amount of information obtained and subsequently retained within a CRM system when former customers were considered existing customers. Additionally, CRM can serve an integral role in helping locate potential customers. As we will explore in Chapter 5, one method for locating potential customers is to use information contained in CRM to determine key characteristics exhibited by existing customers. This information can then be used to pursue new customers in untapped markets who possess similar characteristics.

CRM and Technology

Digital technology plays a critical part in carrying out CRM. A proper technology-based system is needed so that nearly anyone in an organization that comes into contact with a customer (e.g., sales force, service force, customer service representatives, accounts receivable, etc.) has access to information and is well prepared to deal with the customer. For large firms with many employees, this requires the purchase of expensive CRM software along with the necessary hardware to implement CRM throughout the company. For smaller firms with only a few employees, a more cost-effective and potentially less complicated way is to use internet-based services that charge monthly fees to utilize CRM technology. (3)

In many industries, customers' experience with an organization's customer service can significantly affect their overall opinion of the product. Companies producing superior products may negatively impact their products if they back these up with shoddy service. On the other hand, many companies compete not because their products are superior to their competitors' products but because they offer a higher level of customer service. In fact, many believe customer service will eventually become the most significant benefit offered by an organization as global competition increases the number of similar products found in a market. The increased competition may make it more difficult for an organization's products or services to offer unique advantages.

Customer service manifests itself in several ways with the most common being a dedicated department to handle customer issues. Whether a company establishes a separate department or spreads the function among many departments, being responsive and offering reliable service is critical and likely to be demanded by customers.

Trends in Customer Service

Marketers have seen the customer service process evolve from an area receiving only marginal attention into a primary functional area. In response to customers' demands for responsive and reliable service, organizations are investing heavily in innovative methods and processes to strengthen their service level. These innovations include:

INCREASED CUSTOMER SELF-SERVICE

A major trend in customer service is to encourage customers to be involved in helping solve their own service issues. For instance, complaints of slow checkout lines have led many retailers to offers customers the ability to improve service speed. This ranges from customers placing their own products in shopping bags all the way to having customers do their own checkout, including scanning products and making payment. Also, as we will soon discuss, customers seeking helpful information are being encouraged by companies to undertake the effort themselves, often by visiting special company-provided information areas (see *Knowledge Base* discussion below). Only after they have explored these options are customers advised to contact a customer service representative. (4)

REVENUE GENERATORS

Organizations maintaining a customer service staff have found these employees not only help solve customer problems, but they also may be in a position to convince customers to purchase more. Many companies now require sales training for their customer service personnel. At a basic level, customer service representatives may be trained to ask if customers are interested in hearing about other goods or services. If a customer shows interest, then the representative will transfer the customer to a sales associate. At a more advanced level, the representative will shift to a selling role and attempt to get the customer to commit to additional product purchases.

OUTSOURCING

One of the most controversial developments impacting customer service is the move by many organizations around the world to establish customer service functions outside of either their home country or the country in which their customers reside. Called outsourcing, companies pursue this strategy to both reduce cost and to increase service coverage. For instance, having multiple customer service facilities around the world allows customers to talk via phone with a service person no matter what time of day.

Yet moving customer service to another country has raised concerns on two fronts. First, many see this trend as leading to a reduction of customer service jobs within a home country. Second, customer service personnel located offshore may not be sufficiently trained and often lack an understanding of the conditions within the customer's local market, both of which can affect service levels. At the extreme, a poorly managed move to outsource customer service can lead to a decrease in customer satisfaction, which in the long run could affect sales.

CUSTOMER SERVICE TECHNOLOGIES

As we will see throughout this book, technological innovation has significantly impacted all areas of marketing. Within the customer service function, improvements in hardware and software, as well as expansion of internet and mobile networks, has led to numerous innovative methods for addressing customer needs. These include:

- AI-Powered Chatbots – As noted in Chapter 1, the evolution of artificial intelligence has made a strong impact across marketing. Rapidly evolving tools powered by AI have been particularly embraced for handling customer service issues. One tool, commonly referred to as **chatbots**, have been programmed to respond in ways that mimic a conversation with a real customer service representative,. While early chatbots were primarily text-based, advances in AI can now engage customers with voice responses. Additionally, while early customer service chatbots were pre-programmed with responses to customers' messages, these have now evolved to being able to learn more about the customer as a **virtual attendant** engages and guides customers to an answer. This provides more detailed and individualized responses to a customer's service issue. Additionally, chatbots enable an organization to offer support at any time even after an organization's normal business hours. (5)

- Social Media – The use of social media offers marketers an easy method for engaging customers who have service issues. For instance, many organizations use an account on X (formerly known as Twitter) to respond to customer service questions. However, using social media for customer service is not limited to only responding when a customer poses a question on an organization's social media account. Instead, organizations can proactively use social media to inform and alert customers to important issues that may arise.

- Knowledge Base – For years organizations have addressed customers' desire to be more involved in solving their own problems with technological solutions geared toward customer self-service. The predominant method for doing this has been to maintain a collection of text-based answers to **frequently asked questions (FAQ)**. However, this service tools has also seen the impact of AI as customers seeking answers are guided to a potential answer rather than requiring customers to hunt for answers in a knowledge base.

- <u>Collaborative Browsing</u> – This technology, also called co-browsing, allows customer service representatives to manipulate a customer's web browser during a servicing session by sending webpages containing relevant information to the customers digital device.

- <u>Text Messaging and Specialized Apps</u> – In recent years, text messaging and mobile apps have found a useful place as customer service tools. Many companies and organizations, including colleges and universities, now use these as a means to communicate with their customers. For instance, colleges and universities have set up instant alert security systems, where students can receive a text message or an app alert in the case of an on-campus emergency or weather-related problem.

- <u>Intelligent Call Routing</u> – Another innovation associated with telephone support deals with technologies for identifying and filtering incoming calls. One method is the use of software that attempts to identify the caller (usually based on the incoming phone number) and then automatically directs the call for proper servicing. For instance, an appliance manufacturer may be able to distinguish between those who purchased refrigerators and those who purchased ovens. But some marketers go a step further and program their call routing system to distinguish "good" customers from others. This may result in these customers receiving preferential placement in the calling order so they will be serviced before lower rated customers who sequentially called before the "good" customer.

REFERENCES

1. For more on customer lifetime value see: "Customer Lifetime Value." *Wikipedia*. https://en.wikipedia.org/wiki/Customer_lifetime_value.

2. In addition to the activities listed, customer service may perform other tasks, such as helping customers place orders, gathering customer feedback, and assisting customers with switching services from another provider.

3. For a review of CRM products for small businesses see: Gadjo Sevilla and Neil McAllister. "The Best CRM Software of 2023." *PC Magazine*. June 8, 2023. https://www.pcmag.com/picks/the-best-crm-software.

4. Many experts predict that technological advances will make it easy for customers to simply walk out of stores with their purchases without having to stop at make payment. However, such developments have been slow to take hold as evidenced by Amazon's closing of several Amazon Go stores. "Amazon to Close Eight Go Convenience Stores in Cost-Cutting Move." *CNBC*. March 3, 2023. https://www.cnbc.com/2023/03/03/amazon-to-close-eight-go-convenience-stores-in-cost-cutting-move.html.

5. For more on AI-powered chatbots see: "What is a Chatbot?" *IBM*. https://www.ibm.com/topics/chatbots.

6. For insight on how to effectively use social media for customer service see: Molly Murphy. "9 Tips for Providing Great Social Media Customer Service." *Zendesk*. September 8, 2023. https://www.zendesk.com/blog/customer-service-through-social-media.

Chapter 4: Understanding Customers

Possibly the most challenging concept in marketing deals with understanding why buyers do what they do. Such knowledge is critical for marketers since having a strong understanding of buyer behavior helps shed light on what is important to the customer, including what influences their purchasing.

However, factors affecting how customers make decisions are extremely complex. Buyer behavior is deeply rooted in psychology with dashes of sociology thrown in just to make things more interesting. Since every person in the world is different, it is impossible to have simple rules explaining how buying decisions are made. But those who have spent many years analyzing customer activity have presented us with useful "guidelines" for how someone decides whether or not to make a purchase.

In this chapter, we look at how customers make purchase decisions. We begin with a discussion of customer needs and why understanding this is fundamental to understanding why customers make purchases. The perspective we take in this chapter is to touch on just the basic concepts that appear to be commonly accepted as influencing customer behavior. We look at the buying behavior of consumers (i.e., when people buy for personal reasons) and we also examine factors that influence buyers' decisions in the business market.

WHY CUSTOMERS BUY

Customers make purchases in order to satisfy **needs**. Some of these needs are basic and must be filled by everyone on the planet (e.g., food, shelter), while others are not required for basic survival and vary depending on the person or organization making a purchase. It probably makes more sense to classify needs that are not a necessity as **wants** or **desires**. In fact, in many countries where the standard of living is high, a significant portion of the population's income is spent on wants and desires rather than on basic needs.

Whether the buyer is buying for personal use (i.e., consumer purchase) or the purchase is for use by a business, it is critical for marketers to understand how their customers make decisions, including the dynamics that influence the decision-making process.

We use the term customer to refer to the actual buyer, the person spending the money. But it should be pointed out the one who does the buying is not necessarily the user and others may be involved in the buying decision. For example, in planning for a family trip the mother may make the hotel reservations but others in the family may have input into the hotel choice. Similarly, a father may purchase snacks at the grocery store, but his young child may be the one who selects these from the store shelf. Consequently, analysis of factors affecting why customers buy should not be limited to only the person doing the buying transaction; others who are not performing the purchasing activity may also be involved.

Influences on Customer Purchasing

The decision-making process used by customers to make purchases is anything but straightforward. There are many factors affecting this process. In fact, the number of potential influences on customer buying behavior is nearly limitless. However, marketers are well served to understand the key influences. By doing so, they may be in a position to tailor their marketing efforts to take advantage of these influences in a way that will satisfy the customer.

The influences on purchasing break down into two main categories: Internal and External (see Fig 4-1). For the most part, the influences are not mutually exclusive. Instead, they are all interconnected and work together to form who we are and how we behave. Additionally, not all influences affect all buying decisions. For example, a business buyer mulling over a purchase decision for high-priced telecommunications equipment that his company has never purchased before may be influenced by different factors compared to a consumer seeking to make a low-priced purchase she makes several times a week. Finally, while purchase situations facing consumers may be different from those facing business buyers, in many ways the influences on both types of decisions are similar. For this reason, we present the influences as covering both consumer and business purchasing.

INTERNAL INFLUENCES

We start our examination of the influences on customer purchase decisions by first looking inside ourselves to see which are the most important internal factors affecting how we make choices.

Perceptual Filter

Perception is how we see ourselves and the world we live in. However, what ends up being stored inside us does not always get there in a direct manner. Often our mental makeup results from information consciously or subconsciously filtered as we experience it, a process we refer to as a perceptual filter. To us this is our reality, though it does not

Figure 4-1: Influences on Customer Purchasing

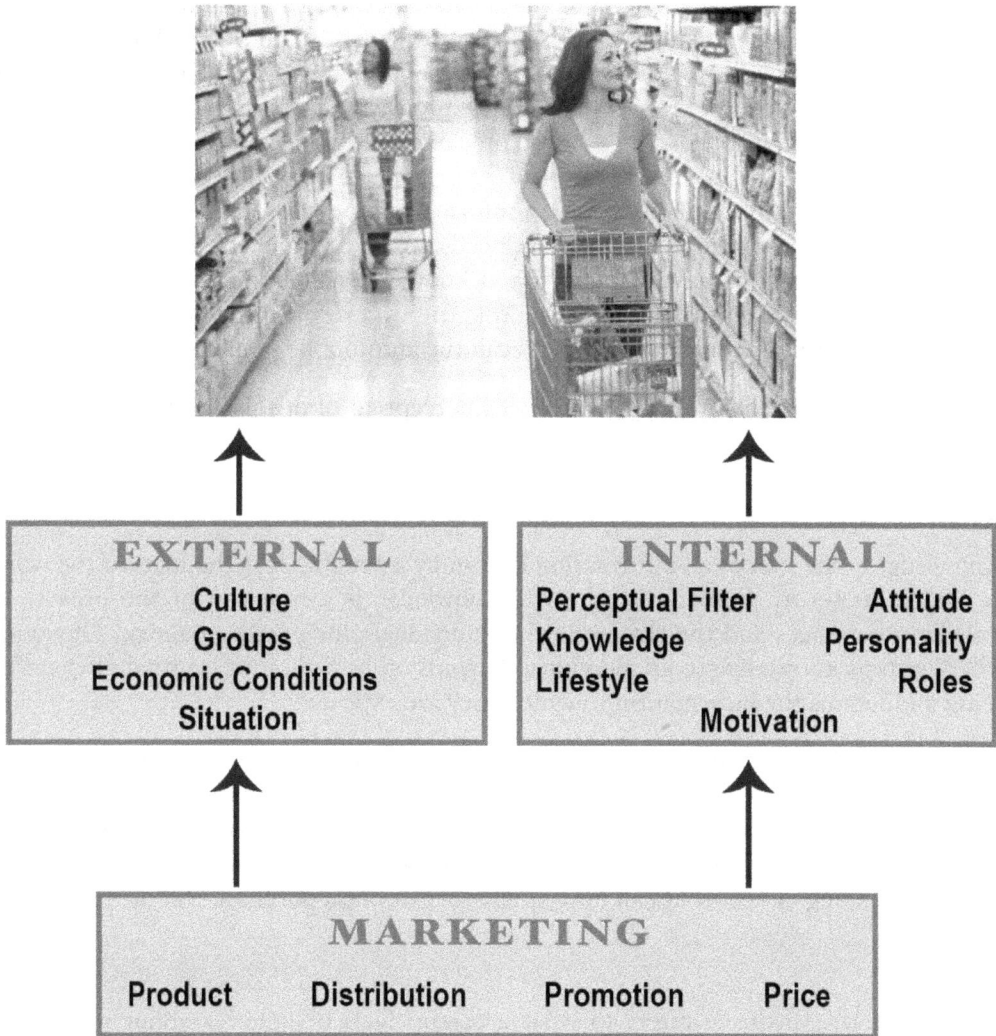

mean it is an accurate reflection of what is real. Thus, perception is the way we filter stimuli (e.g., someone talking to us, listening to a podcast) and then attempt to make sense of it.

Perception has several steps:

- Exposure – sensing a stimulus (e.g., seeing an advertisement)
- Attention – an effort to recognize the nature of a stimulus (e.g., recognizing it is an advertisement)
- Awareness – assigning meaning to a stimulus (e.g., it is a humorous advertisement for a particular product)
- Retention – adding the meaning to one's internal makeup (i.e., this product has fun advertisements)

How these steps are eventually carried out depends on a person's approach to **learning**. By learning we mean how a person changes what they know, which in turn may affect how they act. There are many theories of learning, a discussion of which is beyond the scope of this book; however, suffice to say people are likely to learn in different ways. For instance, one person may be able to focus intensely on a certain advertisement and retain the information after being exposed only one time while another person may need frequent exposure to the same advertisement before she/he even recognizes what it is. Customers are also more likely to retain information if a person has a strong interest in the stimulus. For example, if a person needs a new car, they are more likely to pay attention to automobile advertisements and know the name of the automobile being advertised, while someone who is not looking to buy a new car may be exposed to the advertisement many times but is unable recall the automobile name.

For marketers, getting through a customer's perceptual filter takes careful planning as outlined in Box 4-1.

Knowledge

Knowledge is the sum of all information known by a person. It is the facts of the world as she/he knows it. Someone's depth of knowledge is a function of the breadth of worldly experiences and the strength of an individual's long-term memory. Obviously, what exists as knowledge to an individual depends on how their perceptual filter makes sense and retains the information to which they are exposed.

As we will see in this chapter, many factors can influence how customers make purchase decisions. In most cases, these factors are shaped by the knowledge a customer possesses. Thus, for marketers, developing methods that encourage customers to add to what they know, such as offering incentives for watching a product video, may affect other influencing factors that can impact whether or not a purchase will be made.

Attitude

In simple terms, attitude refers to what a person feels or believes about something. Additionally, attitude may be reflected in how an individual acts based on his or her beliefs (i.e., knowledge). Once formed, attitudes can be difficult to change. If a customer has a negative attitude toward a particular product or organization, it may take considerable effort to change what the customer believes to be true.

Marketers facing customers with negative attitudes toward their product must work to identify the key issues shaping a customer's attitude then adjust marketing decisions (e.g., advertising) in an effort to change the attitude. Also, when competing against a competitor, whose customers possess a strong positive attitude toward the competitive company, a key strategy for a marketer is to work to see why customers feel positive toward the competitor and then try to meet or beat the competitor on these issues. Alternatively, an organization can try to locate customers who have negative feelings toward the competitor and then target its efforts to this group.

Box 4-1

GETTING THROUGH THE PERCEPTUAL FILTER

A key goal of most marketers is to get customers to form positive impressions of the organization and its products. But clearly the existence of a perceptual filter can make this a difficult goal to achieve. As discussed below, each stage in the perceptual filter presents challenges and opportunities:

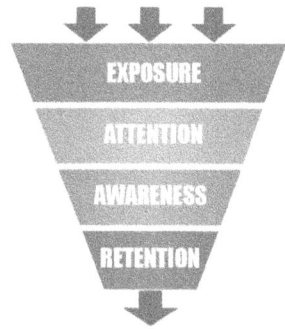

Stage 1: Exposure

Exposing customers to a product can be extremely difficult especially when competing products are attempting to accomplish the same objective. To stand out from others requires marketers be creative and use a variety of different methods (e.g., different types of promotion) to deliver their message. Additionally, marketers often find that many attempts to expose customers to their message (e.g., frequently running advertisements) must be made before customers are aware to their product.

Stage 2: Attention

Once the message reaches the customer, it must be viewed as interesting in order to capture his/her attention. This often means the marketer's message must not only be engaging but must also highlight a product's benefits and how these can satisfy customers' needs. It is important to understand that being exposed to a product does not mean a customer will pay attention to it. Of course, most people experience this every day as they are bombarded with products in stores or ads on the internet, but they attend to only a very small percentage.

Stage 3: Awareness

Simply attending to the marketer's message is not enough for a customer to retain the message. For marketers, the most critical step in getting through the perceptual filter is the one that occurs with awareness or the point where customers give meaning to what they experience. To ensure the message is getting through as intended (i.e., a customer accurately interprets the message), marketers must continually monitor and respond if their message becomes distorted in ways that negatively shape its meaning. This can happen due, in part, to competitive activity, such as a competitor creating advertisements that position their product in a stronger light than the marketer's product, or through published comments, such as online customer ratings containing negative and possibly inaccurate statements related to the marketer's product.

Stage 4: Retention

Finally, making sure customers are retaining positive product information requires continual customer research. If the marketer discovers customers are retaining the wrong information (e.g., wrong idea of how product works) then new strategies must be employed to address this (e.g., change the product's message). Marketers can reinforce the retention process by establishing ongoing communication with customers. This can be achieved through such techniques as social media updates, email newsletters, and follow-up service calls.

Personality

An individual's personality relates to perceived personal characteristics they consistently exhibit, especially when interacting with others. In most, but not all, cases the behaviors projected in one situation are similar to the behaviors exhibited in another situation. In this way, personality is the sum of sensory experiences others get from experiencing a person (i.e., how one talks, responds in certain situations, etc.).

While one's personality is often interpreted by those we interact with, a person has her/his own vision of their personality, called **self-concept**, which may or may not be the same as how others view them. For marketers, it is necessary to know how customers, and especially consumers, make purchase decisions to support their self-concept. Using research techniques to identify how customers view themselves may give marketers insight into products and promotion options that are not readily apparent. For example, when targeting consumers, a marketer may initially build its marketing strategy around more obvious clues to consumption behavior, including consumers' demographic indicators, such as age, occupation, and income (see Chapter 5 for more on demographic targeting). However, in-depth research may yield information showing consumers are purchasing products to fulfill self-concept objectives that have little to do with the demographic category they fall into. For instance, research by a clothing manufacturer may show senior citizens, who are not currently targets for a company's product, are making purchases because it makes them feel younger. In this example, appealing to consumers' self-concept needs could expand a product's customer base by including customers not initially envisioned to be in the target market.

Roles

Roles represent the position we feel we hold, or others feel we should hold in a group environment, whether in a personal or business situation (see Box 4-2). These positions carry certain responsibilities, yet it is essential to understand that some of these responsibilities may be perceived and not spelled out or even accepted by others. In support of their roles, customers make product choices that vary depending on which role they are assuming. As an illustration, an employee responsible for selecting snack food for an office party, which the company's CEO will be attending, may choose higher quality snack products than that person would normally purchase for their family.

Advertisers often show how the benefits of their products aid customers as they perform certain roles. Typically, the underlying message of this promotional approach is to suggest that using the advertiser's product will raise one's status in the eyes of others while using a competitor's product may have a negative effect on their status.

Lifestyle

This internal influencing factor relates to the way we live through the activities we engage in and interests we express. In simple terms, it is what we value out of life. Lifestyle is often determined by how we spend our time and money. Additionally, customers often associate with others who share similar lifestyles.

Box 4-2

ROLES IN THE BUYING CENTER

In the business market, those associated with the purchase decision are known to be part of a Buying Center, which consists of individuals within an organization performing one or more of the following roles:

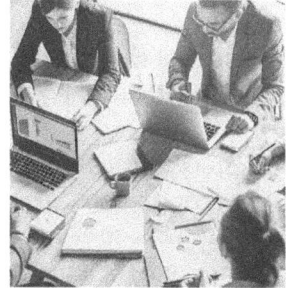

♦ <u>Buyer</u> – responsible for dealing with suppliers and placing orders (e.g., purchasing agent)

♦ <u>Decider</u> – has the power to make the final purchase decision (e.g., CEO)

♦ <u>Influencer</u> – has the ability to affect what is ordered, such as setting order specifications (e.g., engineers, researchers, product managers)

♦ <u>User</u> – those who will actually use the ordered product (e.g., office staff)

♦ <u>Initiator</u> – any Buying Center member who first determines that a need exists

♦ <u>Gatekeeper</u> – anyone who is in a position to control access to other Buying Center members (e.g., administrative assistant)

For marketers confronting a Buying Center, it is crucial that first they identify who plays what role. Once identified, the marketer must address the needs of each member, which may differ significantly. For instance, the Decider, who may be the company president, wants to make sure the purchase will not negatively affect the company financially while the Buyer wants to be assured the product is delivered on time. The way each Buying Center member is approached and marketed to requires careful planning in order to address their unique needs.

In the consumer market, products are purchased to support consumers' lifestyles. Marketers work hard researching how consumers live their lives since this information can impact many marketing decisions, such as offering insight on possible new products (e.g., observe how consumers use products in unexpected ways), suggesting more effective promotional methods (e.g., shift digital advertising to growing podcast market), and determining how best to distribute products (e.g., growth of home delivery services). (1)

Motivation

Motivation relates to our desire to achieve a certain outcome. Many internal factors we've already discussed can affect a customer's desire to achieve a certain outcome, but there are others. For instance, when it comes to making purchase decisions, customers' motivation could be affected by such issues as financial position (e.g., Can I afford the purchase?), time constraints (e.g., Do I need to make the purchase quickly?), overall value (e.g., Am I getting my money's worth?), emotional attachment (e.g., Will this product remind me of something that is special to me?), and perceived risk (e.g., What happens if I make a bad decision?).

Motivation is closely tied to the concept of **involvement**, which relates to how much effort a customer exerts in making a decision. Not all products have a high percentage of highly involved customers. For example, purchasing milk is generally a low involvement decision as most customers choose whatever is easy to select on the store shelf. But other product decisions find customers being highly motivated during the purchasing process. For these products, customers will want to get mentally and physically involved in learning about the product.

Marketers who sell goods and services with a high level of customer involvement should prepare options to attract this group. For instance, marketers should make it easy for customers to learn about their product (e.g., information on website, free video preview) and, for some products, allow customers to experience the product (e.g., free trial) before committing to the purchase. In fact, some companies offer **experiential marketing** opportunities, where prior to purchase, customers can immerse themselves in the product at a location or in a situation in which they are most likely to use it. (2)

EXTERNAL INFLUENCES

As customers around the world experienced during the COVID-19 pandemic, purchase decisions can be affected by factors beyond their control. While the pandemic represented a once-in-a-century example of the impact of uncontrollable external factors, many more common ones have direct or indirect effect on how customers live and what they consume.

Culture

Culture represents the behavior, beliefs, and, in many cases, the way we act which is learned by interacting with and observing other members of society. In this way, much of what we do is shared behavior passed along from one member of society to another. Culture is learned from those with whom we directly interact (e.g., family, co-workers) and from those that we observe from a distance (e.g., movie stars).

Culture can be analyzed from many levels. At a broad level, cultural attributes are shared by a large portion of society, such as citizens of a country sharing patriotic beliefs. However, marketers are much more concerned with culture as it pertains to smaller groups or **subcultures**. Customers simultaneously belong to multiple subcultures whose cultural attributes may be different. For instance, people may simultaneously belong to different groups based on ethnicity, religious beliefs, geographic location, musical tastes, sports team allegiance, environmental concerns, and countless others. In a business situation, there may exist several subcultures within an organization. For example, the organization's formal policies and procedures may be pivotal in developing an overall corporate culture, while other subcultures are developed in less formal ways (e.g., members of the company bowling team).

As part of their efforts to convince customers to purchase their products, marketers often use cultural representations, especially in promotional appeals. The objective is to connect with customers using cultural references that are easily understood and often embraced by customers. By doing so, marketers hope customers feel comfortable with or can relate better to their products since these correspond with their cultural values.

Additionally, smart marketers use strong research efforts to identify differences in how subcultures behave. These efforts help pave the way for spotting trends within a subculture, which the marketer can capitalize on through new marketing tactics, such as developing new products.

Finally, when selling globally marketers must understand cultural differences are pervasive. Many marketers make the mistake of assuming that what works in their home market will also work in foreign markets. Unfortunately, when success does not come the marketer may discover that cultural differences are at the root of the problem and until these differences are addressed marketing efforts will continue to struggle.

Other Group Membership

In addition to cultural influences, customers belong to many other groups with which they share certain characteristics, and which may influence purchase decisions. Some of the basic groups include:

- Social Class – This group represents the social standing one has within a society based on such factors as income level, education, and occupation.

- Family – Someone's family situation (e.g., family size, religious influences, etc.) can have a strong effect on how purchase decisions are made.

- Associated Reference Groups – Most customers simultaneously belong to many other groups with which they associate (e.g., community sports league, book club, etc.) and which may influence what they purchase.

- Dissociated Reference Groups – Customers may also feel the need to dissociate with certain groups, which they do not want to belong to (e.g., an opposing political party). This may influence them to make certain purchase decisions that they believe will not place them in these groups.

- Industry Groups – An organization and many of its employees may belong to a large number of trade and community groups.

Identifying and understanding groups, which customers belong to, is a key strategy for marketers. And, as discussed in Box 4-3, marketers can gain further insight through those who are perceived to be group leaders.

Box 4-3

MARKETING TO OPINION LEADERS

When appealing to groups, a key marketing strategy is to seek out group leaders and others to whom group members look to for advice, direction, or other important information. Termed opinion leaders, these individuals may have influence over what others purchase if they are perceived as well respected by the group.

Marketers may find value in researching opinion leaders to learn more about how they behave and the means by which they influence a group. For instance, marketing research may show that someone with a strong following on social media (i.e., **social media influencer**) is viewed as an opinion leader by a group within the marketer's industry and regularly following this person could yield insight into what may be occurring with the group. (3)

Additionally, marketers may find promotional opportunities with opinion leaders. For instance, marketers may target influential podcasters with free products and other material hoping this effort will encourage podcasters to discuss the product. Also, opinion leaders can be approached to represent the company in a promotional way, such as serving as a spokesperson for the marketer's products.

Economic Conditions

The current state of economic conditions has a direct impact on buyers. While in certain cases a customer's financial status is controllable (i.e., able to control wasteful spending), in other instances what the customer has available for spending is affected by economic factors that are beyond their control. Clearly, if someone has suddenly lost their job, the impact on purchasing may be immediate and force major adjustments in what is purchased.

Additionally, expectation of future economic conditions could impact purchasing. For instance, if the sentiment exists that the economy is posed to grow then buyers may feel that engaging in purchasing of expensive items holds less risk than if the same decision were made during times when the forecast is for an economic slowdown. (4)

Situation

A purchase decision can be strongly affected by the situation in which people find themselves. This external factor can be influenced by many elements including the circumstances which a buyer currently faces or will be facing in the future (e.g., hosting a party that is unexpectedly running out of food), existing market conditions when a buyer makes a purchase (e.g., the normally purchased product is now in short supply), time constraints (e.g., has a limited amount of time to make a purchase), and features found within a buyer's current physical environment (e.g., presence of an in-store display). (5)

On many occasions, a situation facing a customer is not controllable, in which case they may not follow their normal purchase decision process. For instance, if a person needs a product quickly and a retailer does not carry her/his normal brand, the customer may have little choice then to buy a competitor's product.

Marketers can sometimes take advantage of decisions made in uncontrollable situations in at least two ways. First, marketers can use promotional methods to reinforce a specific selection of products when the customer is confronted with a particular situation. For example, some automotive manufacturers provide services promising to offer assistance if the user runs into problems anywhere and at any time. Second, marketers can use marketing methods to convince customers a situation is less likely to occur if the marketer's product is used. This can be seen with financial services firms targeting business customers, where marketers explain that their clients' assets are protected in the case of unexpected economic problems.

HOW CUSTOMERS BUY

So now that we have discussed the factors influencing a customer's decision to purchase, our next task is to examine the process customers follow when making purchase decisions. Our focus is on the types of decisions two different customer groups – consumers and businesses – face and the steps they may take in getting to their final decision. We define consumers as those making purchases for their own or others personal consumption while businesses make purchases for organizational use.

However, before we describe how each group makes buying decisions, we first examine how the purchasing characteristics of consumers differs from those associated with business purchasing.

How Consumer and Business Purchasing Differs

It is necessary for marketers to understand that while the influences on purchasing are similar, the circumstances surrounding purchase decisions are quite different for consumers and businesses. The differences between these customers require marketers take a different approach when selling to business customers than they do when selling to consumers. Among the differences between consumer and business customers are:

- How Decisions Are Made – In the consumer market, a large percentage of purchase decisions are made by a single person. In the business market, while single person purchasing is not unusual, a large percentage of buying, especially within larger organizations, requires the input of many (see Box 4-2).

- Purchasing Experience – Businesses often employ purchasing agents or professional buyers whose job is to negotiate the best deals for their organization. Unlike consumers, who often lack information when making purchase decisions, professional buyers are generally as knowledgeable about the product and the industry as the marketer who is selling to them.

- Decision-Making Time – Depending on the product, business purchase decisions can drag on for an extended period. Unlike consumer markets, where **impulse purchasing** (i.e., purchase decisions that are not planned) is rampant, the number of people involved in business purchase decisions can result in decisions taking weeks, months, or even years!

- Size of Purchases – For products regularly used and frequently bought, businesses will often purchase a larger volume at one time compared to consumer purchases. Because of this, business purchasers often demand price breaks (e.g., discounts) for higher order levels.

- Importance of Price – In certain business markets, purchase decisions hinge on the outcome of a bidding process between competitors offering similar products. In these cases, the decision to buy is often simply who has the lowest price. Unlike consumer markets, where customers will often purchase a brand with little consideration for its price, in business purchasing this is generally not the case.

- Number of Buyers – While there are several million organizations worldwide operating in the overall business market, within a particular market the number may be relatively small. For instance, within some industries, buyers are highly concentrated in a few geographic areas (e.g., pharmaceutical and biotech clusters) and may number less than a few hundred. Consequently, compared to consumer products, where millions of customers may make up a market, marketing efforts for the business market may be confined to a smaller targeted group.

- Promotional Focus – Companies that primarily target consumers likely use methods of mass promotion (e.g., advertising) to reach an often widely dispersed market. For business-to-business marketers, the size of individual orders along with a smaller number of buyers makes person-to-person contact using sales representatives a more effective means of reaching their customers.

Types of Consumer Purchase Decisions

Consumers are faced with purchase decisions nearly every day. But not all decisions are treated the same. Some decisions are more complex than others requiring more effort by the consumer. Other decisions are fairly routine and require little effort. In general, consumers face four types of purchase decisions:

- ◆ Minor New Purchase – These purchases represent something new to a consumer. However, in the consumer's mind, it is not a critical purchase in terms of need, money, or other reason (e.g., what is purchased does not affect the consumer's status within a group).

- ◆ Minor Repurchase – These are the most routine of all purchases and often the consumer returns to purchase the same product without giving much thought to other product options (i.e., consumer is loyal to a particular product).

- ◆ Major New Purchase – These purchases are the most difficult of all purchases because the product is considered important to the consumer. However, the consumer often lacks experience making these decisions. The lack of confidence in making this type of decision often (but not always) requires the consumer to engage in an extensive decision-making process.

◆ <u>Major Repurchase</u> – These purchase decisions are also important to the consumer, though the consumer feels more confident in making the decision since they have previous experience purchasing the product.

For marketers, it is essential to understand how consumers treat the purchase decisions they face. If a company is targeting customers who feel a purchase decision is difficult (i.e., Major New Purchase), its marketing strategy may vary considerably compared to a company targeting customers who view the purchase decision as routine. In fact, the same company may face both situations at the same time; for some consumers the product is new, while others see the purchase as routine. The implication for marketers is that different purchase situations require different marketing efforts.

Steps in Consumer Purchasing Process

The consumer purchasing process can be viewed as a sequence of five steps (Figure 4-2). However, whether a consumer will actually carry out each step depends on the type of purchase decision that is faced. For instance, for Minor Repurchases the consumer may be quite loyal to a certain brand and the decision is a routine one (i.e., buy that same product) with little effort needed to make a purchase decision.

In cases of routine **brand loyal** purchases, consumers may skip several steps in the purchasing process since they know exactly what they want (See *Advantages of Brands* in Chapter 6). This allows the consumer to move quickly to the actual purchase. But for more complex decisions, such as Major New Purchases, the purchasing process can extend for days, weeks, or months. While evaluating these steps, marketers should realize that, depending on the circumstances surrounding the purchase, the importance of each step may vary.

STEP 1: NEED RECOGNIZED

In the first step, a consumer determines that he/she is not happy with a perceived level of satisfaction for a particular need. Consequently, the consumer seeks to improve to a desired level of satisfaction. For instance, internal triggers, such as hunger or thirst, may tell the consumer that food or drink is needed. External factors can also trigger consumers' needs. Marketers have long used methods, such as advertising, in-store displays, and the intentional use of scent (e.g., perfume counters in retail stores), as triggers. More recently, online marketers have deployed sophisticated computer-based **product recommendation systems** (a.k.a. **recommender systems**), which offer product suggestions it believes the customer may find of interest. Additionally, these systems may utilize a technique called **collaborative filtering** that suggests products to online shoppers and app users based, in part, on purchases made or activities performed by others (e.g., movies watched on Netflix) who show similar behavioral patterns. (6)

At this stage, the decision-making process may stall if a consumer is not motivated to continue (see *Motivation* discussion above). However, if a consumer does have the internal drive to satisfy the need, they will continue to the next step.

Figure 4-2: Decision Making Process

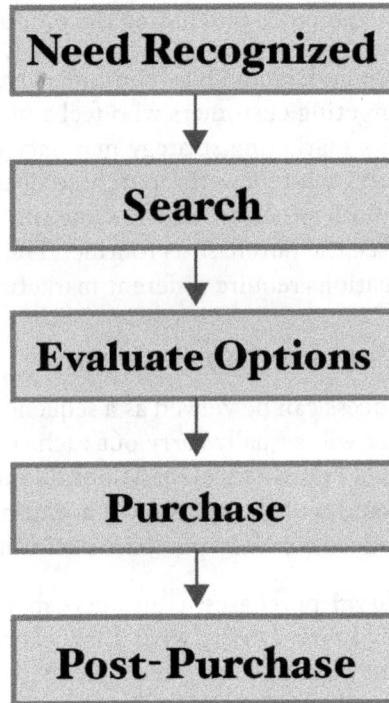

```
┌─────────────────────────┐
│    Need Recognized      │
└─────────────────────────┘
             │
             ▼
┌─────────────────────────┐
│        Search           │
└─────────────────────────┘
             │
             ▼
┌─────────────────────────┐
│    Evaluate Options     │
└─────────────────────────┘
             │
             ▼
┌─────────────────────────┐
│       Purchase          │
└─────────────────────────┘
             │
             ▼
┌─────────────────────────┐
│     Post-Purchase       │
└─────────────────────────┘
```

STEP 2: SEARCH FOR INFORMATION

Assuming a consumer is motivated to satisfy a need, they will next undertake a search for information on possible solutions. The sources used to acquire this information may be as simple as remembering information from past experience (i.e., memory) or the consumer may expend considerable effort to locate information from outside sources (e.g., internet searching, talking with others, etc.). How much effort the consumer directs toward searching depends on such factors as the importance of satisfying the need, familiarity with available solutions, and the amount of time available to search. To appeal to consumers who are at the search stage, marketers should make efforts to ensure consumers can locate information related to their product. For example, for marketers, whose customers rely on the internet for information gathering, it may be critical to utilize certain strategies (see *Search Engine Optimization* in Chapter 15) so that a link to product information appears as one of the first listings on the search results page for likely keyword searches.

STEP 3: EVALUATE OPTIONS

Consumers' search efforts may result in a set of options from which a choice can be made. It should be noted there may be two levels to this stage. At level one, a consumer may create a set of possible solutions to their needs (i.e., different product types), while at level two a consumer may be evaluating particular products (i.e., different individual brands) within each solution. For example, when someone moves to a new apartment and wants a television service, he/she will likely have a few solutions to choose from, including subscribing to cable or using a TV streaming service. While the apartment complex may only offer a single cable option, live streaming via an internet connection may offer multiple options from which to choose. Marketers need to understand how consumers evaluate product options and why some products are included in a consumer's evaluation while others are not. Most importantly, marketers must determine which criteria consumers are using in their selection of possible options and how each criterion is evaluated. Returning to the television service example, marketing tactics will be most effective when the marketer can tailor their efforts by knowing: 1) what benefits are most relevant to consumers (e.g., channel options, brand name, reliability, price, etc.); and 2) determining the order of importance of each benefit.

STEP 4: PURCHASE

In many cases, the solution chosen by the consumer is the same as the product whose evaluation is the highest. However, this may change when it is actually time to make the purchase. The "intended" purchase may be altered for many reasons, such as the product is out-of-stock, a competitor offers an incentive at the point-of-purchase (e.g., store salesperson mentions a competitor's online coupon), the customer lacks the necessary funds (e.g., credit card not working), or members of the consumer's reference group take a negative view of the purchase (e.g., a friend is critical of the potential purchase). Marketers, whose product is most desirable to the consumer, must make sure the transaction goes smoothly. For example, internet retailers have worked hard to prevent consumers from abandoning an online purchase (i.e., **online shopping carts**) by streamlining the checkout process. (7) For marketers whose product is not the consumer's selected product, last chance marketing efforts may be worth exploring, such as offering incentives to store personnel to "talk up" the marketer's product at the checkout counter (e.g., *"That's a nice iPhone cover but did you know XYZ company also sells nice phone covers for a lower price?"*).

STEP 5: POST-PURCHASE EVALUATION

Once the consumer has made the purchase they are faced with an evaluation of the decision. If the product performs below the consumer's expectation, then they will question their decision. At the extreme, this may result in the consumer returning the product and seeking a replacement or a refund, while in less extreme situations the consumer will retain the purchased item but may take a negative view of the product. Such evaluations are more likely to occur in cases of expensive or highly important purchases. To help ease the concerns consumers have with their purchase evaluation, marketers need to be receptive and even encourage consumer contact. Customer service centers and follow-up marketing research are useful tools in helping to address purchasers' concerns.

Types of Business Purchase Decisions

While it would appear business customers face the same four purchase situations that are faced by consumers (Minor New Purchase, Minor Repurchase, Major New Purchase, Major Repurchase), marketers targeting business buyers often see little value in pursuing business customers who undertake minor purchases (e.g., small orders) compared to consumer marketers who may actively pursue such customers. Consequently, while minor purchases certainly do occur in the business market, especially within small businesses, few suppliers choose to direct significant selling efforts to this type of purchase due to the low potential for generating enough revenue to offset marketing expense. Instead, suppliers focus on purchase situations that offer greater opportunity.

For this reason, the types of purchase situations of interest to marketers in the business market are:

◆ Straight Repurchase – These purchase situations involve routine ordering. In most cases, buyers simply reorder the same products previously purchased. Many larger companies have programmed repurchases into an automated ordering system that initiates an **electronic order** when inventory falls below a certain predetermined level. For the supplier benefiting from a Straight Repurchase, this situation is ideal since purchasers are not looking to evaluate other product options (i.e., may be loyal to one supplier). For competitors, whose products are not being repurchased, it may require extensive marketing efforts to persuade the buyer to consider other product options.

◆ Modified Repurchase – These purchases occur when products previously considered a Straight Repurchase are now under a re-evaluation process. There are many reasons why a product is moved to the status of a Modified Repurchase including a purchasing contract in which a buyer agrees to purchase from a seller has expired, there is a change in who is involved in making the purchase, a supplier is removed from an approved suppliers list, a mandate has come from the top level of the organization to re-evaluate all purchasing, or a strong marketing effort by competitors has made the company re-evaluate purchasing. In this circumstance, the incumbent supplier faces the same challenges they faced when they initially convinced the buyer to make the purchase. For competitors, the door is now open, and they must work hard to make sure their message is heard by the buyer's key decision makers.

◆ New Task Purchase – These purchases are ones the buyer has never or rarely made before. While not all New Task Purchases are considered to have equal importance, in general, the buyer will spend considerably more time evaluating alternatives than would be considered for repurchase situations. For marketers, the goal when selling to a buyer facing a New Task Purchase is to make sure to be included in the set of evaluated products as discussed in Step 2 of the business purchasing process (discussed below).

Steps in Business Purchasing Process

Business purchasing follows the same five-step buying process (Figure 4-2) faced by consumers – Need Recognition, Search, Evaluate Options, Purchase, and After-Purchase Evaluation. While the steps are the same, the activities occurring within each step are quite different.

As we examine the business purchasing process, it is necessary to keep in mind the Buying Center concept discussed in Box 4-2. In particular, marketers must be aware that members of the Buying Center can affect the process at different stages.

STEP 1: NEED RECOGNIZED

In a business environment, needs arise from just about anywhere within the organization. The Buying Center concept shows Initiators are the first organizational members to recognize a need. In most situations, the Initiator is also the User or Buyer. Users are inclined to identify the need for new solutions (i.e., new products), while Buyers are more likely to identify the need to repurchase products. But marketers should also understand more companies are replacing human involvement in repurchase decisions with automated methods, which makes it more challenging for competitors to convince buyers to replace currently purchased products. In Straight Repurchase situations, the purchasing process often jumps from Step 1 to Step 4 since little search activity will be performed.

As part of this step, a specifications document may be generated laying out the requirements of the good or service to be purchased. Several members of the Buying Center may be involved in the creation of the specifications. For the marketer, establishing close contact with those who draw up the specifications may help position the marketer's product for inclusion in the search phase.

STEP 2: SEARCH FOR INFORMATION

The search for alternatives to consider for satisfying recognized needs is one of the most significant differences between consumer and business purchasing. Much of this has to do with an organization's motive to reduce costs. While a consumer will not search hard to save a few cents on gas, a company with a large fleet of cars will. In fact, this step in the purchasing process is where professional buyers make their mark. The primary intention of their search efforts is to identify multiple suppliers who meet product specifications and then, through a screening process, offer a selected group of suppliers the opportunity to present their products to members of the Buying Center. Although, in some industries, online marketplaces and auction websites offer buyers access to supplier information without the need for suppliers to present to the Buying Center.

For suppliers, the key for success at this step is to make sure they are included within the search activities of the Buyer or others in the Buying Center. In some instances, this may require a supplier work to be included within an approved suppliers list. In the case of online marketplaces and auction websites, suppliers should work to be included within these relevant sites.

STEP 3: EVALUATE OPTIONS

Once the search has produced options, members of the Buying Center then choose among the alternatives. In more advanced purchase situations, members of the Buying Center evaluate each option using a checklist of **features and benefits** sought by the buying organization. Each feature/benefit is assigned a weight that corresponds to its importance to the purchase decision. In many cases, especially when dealing with government and not-for-profit markets, suppliers must submit bids with the lowest bidder often being awarded the order, assuming goods or services meet specifications.

STEP 4: PURCHASE

To actually place the order may require the completion of certain documents, such as a **purchase order**. Acquiring the necessary approvals can delay the order for an extended period. And for extremely large purchases, such as buildings or large equipment, financing options may need to be explored.

STEP 5: POST-PURCHASE EVALUATION

After the order is received, the purchasing company may spend time reviewing the results of the purchase. This may involve the Buyer discussing product performance issues with Users. If the product is well received, it may end up moving to a Straight Repurchase status, which eliminates much of the evaluation process on future purchases.

REFERENCES

1. For insight into the worldwide growth of home food delivery services see: "Online Food Delivery – Worldwide." *Statista Market Insights*. https://www.statista.com/outlook/dmo/online-food-delivery/worldwide.

2. Amazon highlights experiential marketing as an option for marketers who are part of their advertising program. To learn more see: "Experiential Marketing." *Amazon*. https://advertising.amazon.com/blog/experiential-marketing.

3. For one listing of top social media influencers in different industries see: Nicole Fallon. "The Top 5 Social Media Influencers by Industry." *U.S. Chamber of Commerce*. https://www.uschamber.com/co/grow/marketing/top-social-media-influencers.

4. For more on the impact of *Economic Conditions* see Chapter 19.

5. In-store displays are a common type of Sales Promotion found within many retail stores. For more see Chapter 14.

6. For more on the Netflix recommendation system see: David Chong. "Deep Dive into Netflix's Recommender System." *Towards Data Science*, April 30, 2020. https://towardsdatascience.com/deep-dive-into-netflixs-recommender-system-341806ae3b48.

7. One estimate suggests the abandonment rate for online shopping carts exceeds 75%. For details see: Stephen Serrano. "Complete List of Cart Abandonment Statistics." *Barilliance*. https://www.barilliance.com/cart-abandonment-rate-statistics.

Chapter 5: Targeting Markets

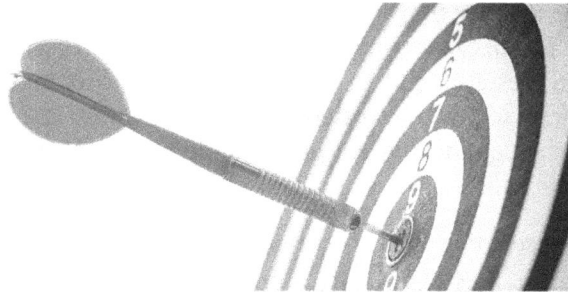

In Chapters 1 - 4, we saw that the essential building blocks for creating a strong marketing program rests with marketing research and a deep understanding of customers. With this groundwork in place, it is now time to turn our attention to strategic decisions undertaken by the marketer to address customers' needs and help the organization meet its objectives.

In this chapter, we examine decisions affecting the selection of target markets. This is a critical point in marketing planning since all additional marketing decisions are going to be directed toward satisfying customers in the markets selected. We explore what constitutes a market and look at basic characteristics of consumer and business markets. We will see not all markets are worth pursuing, and marketers are often better served developing a plan identifying specific markets to target. In particular, we look at the process of market segmentation where larger markets are carved into smaller segments offering more potential. Our discussion includes methods used to identify markets holding the best potential. Finally, we discuss the concept of product positioning and see how this is used as part of a target marketing strategy.

WHAT IS A MARKET?

The simple definition of a market is that it consists of all the people or organizations that may have an interest in purchasing an organization's goods or services. In other words, a market comprises all customers who have needs that may be fulfilled by an organization's offerings. Yet just having a need is not enough to define a market. Several other factors also come into play.

The first factor is that markets consist of customers who are qualified to make a purchase. As discussed below, customers must meet several criteria to be qualified. A second factor for defining a market is that a market can only exist if the solutions sought by customers can be satisfied with the marketer's offerings. Thus, if a company identifies a group of customers qualified to make purchases, the company can only consider these customers to be a market if the company is in a position to execute marketing activities designed to satisfy these customers (e.g., the company markets products these customers seek).

Therefore, a market is defined as all people or organizations that are <u>qualified</u> to obtain (e.g., purchase) goods or services that a marketer is able to offer.

Criteria for Qualifying Customers

Many people may say they have a need for a California mansion overlooking the Pacific Ocean. Yet just because someone says they have a need for this type of property does not mean a real estate agent will automatically consider them to be a potential customer. Instead, marketers are interested in customers who are qualified; they meet certain criteria which suggest they are good candidates to be the target of an organization's marketing efforts.

In general, there are five basic criteria customers must meet to be considered qualified:

Must Seek a Solution to a Need

The customer must either consider the marketer's product to be a potential solution to a need or the marketer must believe the customer is likely to do so. In some cases, the customer may not realize or accept they have a need (e.g., *I don't need insurance*). These so-called **latent needs** may be unknown until something triggers them. For instance, latent needs may be triggered by exposure to certain marketing actions, such as product demonstrations, testimonials and other promotional methods, leading the customer to decide a previously unknown need does actually exist.

Must be Eligible to Make a Purchase

Some marketers limit who is eligible to purchase their products. The best example is legal restrictions on who can purchase alcohol, firearms, and tobacco products. Other examples of limitations include manufacturers only selling to certain retailers (see Chapter 9) and legal firms only handling certain types of clients.

Must Possess the Financial Ability to Make a Purchase

In our example of the California mansion, financial ability is most likely the criterion that will disqualify most people. Marketers are not inclined to consider someone to be a customer if they do not have the funds to make a purchase. This is a major evaluative measure in the business market, where purchasing companies lacking a strong financial position may be viewed as a risk to a supplying firm.

Must Have the Authority to Make the Purchase Decision

In some buying situations, the person responsible for the decision may not be the one with the need for a product. For example, in our Buying Center discussion in Chapter 4 (see Box 4-2), the Decider may be the one with the power to make the decision, but Users are the ones with the need for the product. In these situations, while Users may fit the criteria of need, eligibility and financial ability, they ultimately may not have the authority to make the purchase.

Must be Reachable

What good are potential customers if the marketer is not able to communicate with them? When the marketer is unable to reach a customer, it is not reasonable to consider them as a qualified customer even though they meet all other criteria. For example, a newly created small business selling custom high-end dress shoes may feel presidents of leading companies are potential customers yet establishing personal communication with these executives may prove all but impossible. Thus, it would be a stretch for these executives to be reasonably considered qualified customers.

It is crucial to note a customer must meet ALL criteria listed above to be considered qualified. However, in some markets the customer may have a **surrogate** who handles some of these qualifications. For instance, a market may consist of pre-teen customers who have a need for certain clothing items, but the actual purchase may rest with the pre-teen's parents. So, the parents could possibly assume one or more surrogate roles (e.g., financial ability, authority) that will result in the pre-teen being a qualified customer.

CONSUMER AND BUSINESS MARKETS

As we discussed in Chapter 4, a marketer's customers may be consumers, businesses, or both. A brief profile of each of these broad markets is presented below.

Consumer Market

The consumer market is comprised of anyone who buys goods and services for their own personal consumption or for the personal consumption of others (e.g., household members, gift for friend, etc.). Most consumer purchasing takes place at retail outlets of which there are many types (see *Retail Formats* in Chapter 9), though consumers also spend in other ways, such as through online auctions, flea markets, and yard sales.

For 2021, it was estimated that worldwide consumer spending (measured as household final consumption expenditure) was over (US) $53 trillion. (1) Yet this number is most likely much higher as it does not account for many unreported purchases, such as those that occur with private exchanges (e.g., neighbor selling to another neighbor). In the United States, according to the U.S. Bureau of Labor, the average annual consumer expenditure for a household (measured as Average Annual Expenditures per Consumer Unit) was over (US) $73,000 in 2022. (2)

When marketers look at the overall consumer market for a specific geographic area, they will see total spending tends to change at slow rates from one year to the next. For instance, barring extraordinary and unforeseen events (e.g., coronavirus pandemic), in developed countries total consumer spending, adjusted for inflation (i.e., price increases), may rise or fall by less than a few percentage points from one year to the next.

WHO MAKES UP THE CONSUMER MARKET

The consumer market is made up of nearly everyone in the world! This means nearly 7.9 billion people exist in the consumer market. Within this population, companies create markets by locating customers that share similar needs. For instance, the consumer market can be subdivided into a large number of categories based on needs, such as food, clothing, digital devices, entertainment, leisure, etc. Furthermore, each of these can be subdivided. For example, clothing has hundreds of **submarkets**, such as women, men, children, athletic, formal, and many, many more.

Business Market

The business market is comprised of organizations involved in the manufacture, distribution, or support of products sold or otherwise provided to other organizations. Many believe the business market dwarfs total spending in the consumer market even though there are far fewer buyers than are found in the consumer market. This is because the business market not only includes businesses making purchases for their own needs (e.g., equipment, office supplies, services), it also includes purchases of items that are contained in the products businesses produce (e.g., raw materials) and purchases of items that one business resells to another business (see *Resellers* discussion below). (3) Additionally, as we noted in Chapter 4, the size of orders placed by businesses tends to much higher compared to orders placed by consumers.

The demand by businesses for goods and services is affected by consumer purchases (called **derived demand**) and because so many organizations play a part in creating consumer items, a small swing in consumer demand can create significant changes in overall business purchasing. Automobile purchases offer a good example. If consumer demand for cars increases, companies connected with the automobile industry also see demand for their goods and services increase (we will later refer to these companies as supply chain members). Under these conditions, companies ratchet up their operations to ensure demand is met, which leads to new purchases by a large number of companies. An increase of just one or two percent for consumer demand can increase business demand for products and services by five or more percent. Unfortunately, the opposite is true if consumer demand declines. Trying to predict these swings requires those selling in the business market to undertake marketing research to better assess the conditions facing their direct customers (e.g., retail stores, other businesses) as well as customers to whom they do not sell directly (e.g., final consumer).

WHO MAKES UP THE BUSINESS MARKET

There are millions of organizations worldwide selling their goods and services to other businesses. They operate in many industries and range in size from huge multinational companies with thousands of employees to one-person small businesses. For our purposes, we will categorize the business market based on the general business function an organization performs rather than by industry (of which there are thousands). We break the business market down into two broad categories – Supply Chain Members and Business User Markets.

Supply Chain Members

The supply chain consists of companies engaged in activities involving product creation and delivery. Essentially the chain represents major steps needed to manufacture a product that is eventually sold as a final product.

The supply chain includes:

- <u>Raw Materials Suppliers</u> – These organizations are generally considered the first stage in the supply chain and provide basic products (e.g., mining, harvesting, fishing, etc.) that are key ingredients in the production of higher-order products. *Example: a copper mine that extracts and refines copper from copper ore.*

● Processed Materials or Basic Components Manufacturers – Firms at this level use raw materials to produce more advanced materials or products contained in more advanced components. *Example: an electrical wire manufacturer purchases copper.*

● Advanced Components Manufacturers – These companies use basic components to produce products offering a significant function needed within a larger product. *Example: a manufacturer of electrical power products purchases electrical wire.*

● Product Manufacturers – This market consists of companies purchasing both basic and advanced components and then assembling these components into a final product designated for a user. These products may or may not be sold as stand-alone products and instead some may be included as parts within larger products. *Example: a smartphone manufacturer purchases electrical power supplies.*

● Supporting Firms – These companies offer services at almost any point in the supply chain and to buyers in the business user market (see *Business User Markets* discussion below). Some services are directly related to the product while others focus on areas of the business not directly related to product production. *Example: a trucking company moves products from one supply chain member to another.*

Business User Markets

Several additional business markets also make purchases for their own consumption or with the intention of redistributing to others. We refer to members of this market as business users. In most of their purchase situations, the buyer does not radically change the product from its original purchased form. While technically these markets are also part of the supply chain, members of the business user market do not, in most cases, engage or directly assist in production activities.

The business user market consists of:

● Governments – They use purchases to assist with the functioning of the government, which may include redistributing to others, such as medical supplies. *Examples: federal, state, local, and international governments.*

● Not-For-Profits – This category includes organizations whose tax structure precludes earning profits from operations and whose mission tends to be oriented to assisting others. *Examples: educational institutions, charities, and hospitals.*

● Resellers – Also called distributors, these companies operate in both consumer and business markets. Their function involves purchasing large volumes of products from manufacturers (and sometimes from other resellers) and selling these products in smaller quantities. *Examples: wholesalers, retailers, and industrial distributors.* (Resellers are discussed in detail in Chapters 9 and 10.)

THE NEED FOR TARGET MARKETS

Earlier we defined a market as consisting of customers who are qualified to purchase goods or services offered by an organization. Yet as we saw in our discussion of consumer and business markets, depending on how a market is categorized, qualified customers can exist in multiple markets. With potential customers in many markets, marketers face the challenge of deciding on the best approach for reaching these customers.

For many inexperienced marketers, the strategy for reaching these customers is simple: "*We will just sell to whoever wants to buy.*" However, for most marketing organizations, the notion of marketing to ALL qualified customers is unrealistic because:

REACHING CUSTOMERS REQUIRES RESOURCES

The fact customers are qualified by no means ensures they will do business with the marketer. No matter where customers are located, marketers must invariably spend money reaching them. In situations where qualified customers are spread throughout many markets, (e.g., across many geographical regions), the idea of reaching all potential customers is both ineffective and inefficient as the marketer is likely to drain resources in its quest to locate those willing to buy.

SATISFYING BASIC CUSTOMER NEEDS MAY NOT BE ENOUGH

How customers' needs are defined (see *Criteria for Qualifying Customers* discussion above) is critical to determining a market. One approach to defining needs is to identify markets as consisting of qualified customers who have a basic need that must be satisfied. For example, one could consider the beverage market as consisting of all customers that want to purchase liquid refreshment products to solve a thirst need. While this may be the largest possible market a company could hope for (it would seem to contain just about everyone in the world!), in reality, there are no manufactured products that would appeal to everyone in the world since individual nutritional needs, tastes, purchase situations, economic conditions, and many other issues lead to differences in what people seek to satisfy their thirst needs.

Instead of directing resources to every conceivable customer, marketers are better off being selective in the markets they will target with their marketing efforts. **Target markets** are the markets that offer the best fit for an organization's goals and objectives. In using a target market approach, an organization attempts to get the most from its resources by following a planned procedure to identify customers that appear to be the best candidates to respond to the marketer's message.

With this in mind, we now turn our attention to examining the process marketers follow to choose which markets are best to target with their marketing effort.

TARGETING MARKETS THROUGH SEGMENTATION

The market(s) selected by an organization as the target for its marketing efforts is critical since all subsequent marketing decisions will be directed toward satisfying the needs of these customers. But what approach should be taken to select markets that an organization will target?

As we saw in Chapter 4, marketers strive to understand as much as possible about their customers, including identifying the main benefits they seek. However, with the exception of basic commodity items, such as home heating oil, a single marketing strategy often does not address the unique needs of all members of a market. Because people are different and seek different ways to satisfy their needs, nearly all organizations, whether for-profit or not-for-profit, must select their target markets using a **market segmentation** approach.

Market segmentation divides broad markets, consisting of customers possessing different characteristics including different needs, into smaller market segments in which customers are grouped by characteristics shared by others in the segment.

To successfully target markets using a segmentation approach, organizations should engage in the following three-step process:

1. Identify segments within the overall market.
2. Choose the segment(s) that fits best with the organization's objectives and goals.
3. Develop a marketing strategy that appeals to the selected target market(s).

Below we examine these steps in detail.

Step 1: Identify Market Segments

The first step in targeting markets through market segmentation is to separate customers, who make up large general markets, into smaller groupings based on selected characteristics (called **bases of segmentation**) shared by those in the group. General markets are most often associated with basic product groups, such as automobile, beverage, footwear, home entertainment, etc. The purpose of segmentation is to look deeper within a general market to locate customers who: 1) possess specific needs (e.g., seek electric-powered automobiles); and 2) who share similar characteristics (e.g., college educated, support environmental issues, etc.). When grouped together, these customers may form a smaller segment of the general market (e.g., segment of the automobile market). By focusing marketing research on these smaller segments, the marketer can learn a great deal about these customers and, with this information, craft highly targeted marketing campaigns.

The variables used to segment markets can be classified into a three-stage hierarchy (Figure 5-1) with higher stages building on information obtained from lower stages in order to reach greater precision in identifying shared characteristics. More precise segmentation efforts require sufficient funding, strong research skills, and other capabilities. For instance, a marketer entering a new market may not have the ability to segment beyond the first two stages since the precision needed in Stage 3 segmentation may demand an established relationship with customers in the market.

The three-stage segmentation process presented below works for both consumer and business markets, though the variables used to segment each market may differ. In our discussion, each segmentation stage includes an explanation along with suggestions for segmentation variables the marketer should consider. This is not meant to be an exhaustive list, as other variables are potentially available. However, for marketers new to segmentation, these offer a good starting point for segmenting markets.

Figure 5-1: Stages of Segmentation

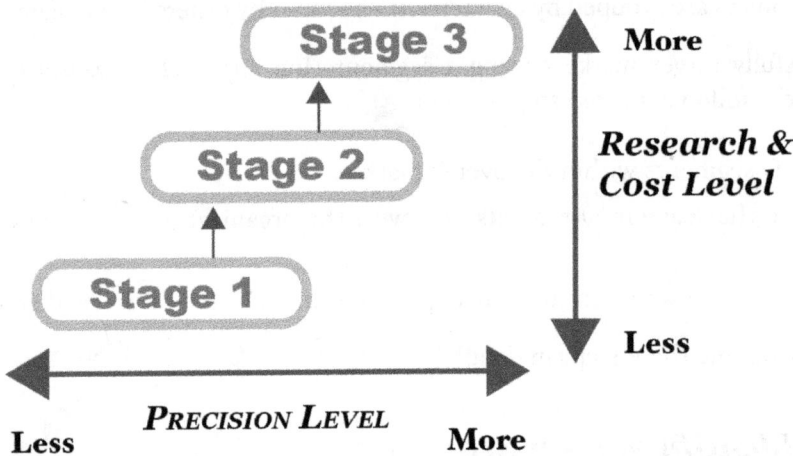

STAGE 1 SEGMENTATION VARIABLES

Stage 1 segmentation consists of variables (see Table 5-1) that can be easily identified through **demographics** (i.e., statistics describing a population), geographical characteristics (i.e., location), and financial information. For both consumer and business segmentation (see Box 5-1), this information focuses mostly on easy to obtain data from such sources as government data (e.g., census information), examining secondary data sources (e.g., news media), industry trade associations, and financial reporting services. While Stage 1 segmentation does not offer the segmentation benefits available with higher-level stages, the marketer generally benefits from accomplishing the segmentation task in a short time frame and at relatively lower cost.

Table 5-1: Stage 1 Segmentation Variables

Segmentation Variables Consumer Markets	Segmentation Variables Business Markets
Demographics age group (e.g., teens, retirees, young adults), gender, education level, ethnicity, income, occupation, social class, marital status **Geographical Characteristics** location (e.g., national, regional, urban/ suburban/rural, international), climate	**Demographics** type (e.g., manufacturer, retailer, wholesaler), industry, size (e.g., sales volume, number of retail outlets), age (e.g., new, young growth, established growth, mature) **Geographical Characteristics** facility locations (e.g., main headquarters, external offices/plants), markets served (e.g., local, regional, national, international) **Business Arrangement** ownership (e.g., private versus public, independent versus chain), financial condition (e.g., credit rating, income growth, stock price, cash flow)

Box 5-1

FINDING BUSINESS TARGET MARKETS

On the surface, segmentation of business markets may not always seem to be as clear as segmenting consumer markets. This can especially be a problem for marketers who are not familiar with a particular business market. For these marketers, a convenient starting point for segmentation efforts is to utilize one or more business classification systems, such as the North American Industry Classification System - NAICS (4) and, for European countries, the International Standard Industrial Classification - ISIC (5). These systems provide descriptions of hundreds of industry classifications. For instance, the table below shows how U.S. operators of retail "Golf Pro Shops" are listed in the NAICS coding system. Note the numeric sequence that occurs as one "drills down" in order to locate individual industry groups.

Level	NAICS Code	Description
Sector	44-45	Retail Trade
Subsector	459	Sporting Goods, Hobby, Musical Instruments, Book & Misc.
Industry Group	4591	Sporting Goods, Hobby & Musical Instruments
Industry	459111	Sporting Goods (general)
US Industry	4591110	Golf Pro Shops (and other types of sporting goods retailers)

Once industry codes are known, these can be used within various government and industry research reports to locate industry information, such as the number of firms operating in the industry, total industry sales, number of employees, and more. Additionally, these codes can be used to locate individual businesses. This can be done through business directory services specializing in listing company information.

STAGE 2 SEGMENTATION VARIABLES

Some firms, especially organizations with limited funds or those that feel they need to move quickly to get their product to market, stop the search for segmentation variables at the Stage 1 level. However, moving beyond Stage 1 segmentation offers a rich amount of customer information allowing marketers to target customers' needs more effectively..

To segment using Stage 2 variables (see Table 5-2), marketers must use research techniques to gain insight into customers' current purchase situations and the environment in which customers operate. Information at this stage includes learning what options customers have chosen to satisfy their needs, what circumstances within customers' environment affect how purchases are made, and understanding local conditions impacting purchase decisions.

Marketers might locate some of this information through the same sources used in Stage 1 segmentation, but most variables in Stage 2 require the marketer to engage in at least casual contact with customers in the market. This can be done through primary research methods, such as surveying the market, having sales personnel contact customers, purchasing research reports from commercial marketing research firms, or hiring consultants to undertake research projects. The cost and time needed to acquire this information may be significantly greater than the efforts needed for Stage 1 segmentation.

Table 5-2: Stage 2 Segmentation Variables

Segmentation Variables Consumer Markets	Segmentation Variables Business Markets
Current Purchasing Situation brands used, purchase frequency, current suppliers **Purchase Ready** possess necessary equipment, property, knowledge, skill sets **Local Environment** cultural, political, legal	**Current Purchasing Situation** brands used, purchase frequency, current suppliers **Purchase Ready** possess necessary equipment, property, knowledge, skill sets **Local Environment** cultural, political, legal **Customers Served by the Business** identify the business' market **Business' Perceived Image** identify how targeted businesses are perceived by their customers

STAGE 3 SEGMENTATION VARIABLES

Marketers choosing to segment at the Stage 3 level face an enormous challenge in gathering useful segmentation information but, for those committed to segmenting at this level, the rewards may include gaining competitive advantage over rivals whose segmentation efforts have not dug this deep. However, the marketer must invest significant time and money to amass the detailed market intelligence needed to achieve Stage 3 segmentation.

Additionally, much of what is needed at Stage 3 is information that is often well protected and not easily shared by customers. In fact, many customers are unwilling to share certain personal information (e.g., feelings, attitudes) with marketers with whom they are not familiar.

Consequently, segmenting on Stage 3 variables (see Table 5-3) is often not an option for marketers new to a market unless they acquire this highly detailed information via other means (e.g., hire a consultant who knows the market). To get access to this information, marketers, who already serve the market with other products, may be able to use primary research, such as focus groups, in-depth interviews, observational research, and other high-level marketing research techniques. Additionally, companies with advanced customer relationship management (CRM) technologies may be in position to tap into their customer information in order to identify customer characteristics that may potentially lead to new segments.

Table 5-3: Stage 3 Segmentation Variables

Segmentation Variables Consumer Markets	Segmentation Variables Business Markets
Benefits Sought price, overall value, specific feature, ease-of-use, convenience, support services, etc.	**Benefits Sought** price, overall value, specific feature, services, profit margins, promotional assistance, etc.
Product Usage how used, why used, situation when used, used in combination with other goods or services, etc.	**Product Usage** how used (e.g., raw material, component product, major selling item at retail level), situation when used, etc.
Purchase Conditions time of day/month/year when purchased, require product usage assistance, credit terms, trade-in option, etc.	**Purchase Conditions** length of sales cycle, specific product specifications, bid pricing, credit terms, trade-in option, product handling, etc.
Characteristics of Individual Buyer purchase experience, how purchase is made, influencers on purchase decision, importance of purchase	**Characteristics of Buying Center** purchase experience, number of members, make-up of key influencers, willingness to assume risk
Psychographics personality, attitudes, and lifestyle combined with demographics	

Step 2: Choosing Market Segments

The second step in selecting target markets requires the marketer to critically evaluate the segments identified in Step 1 in order to select those which are most attractive. For small firms, this step may not be very involved since they may lack the resources to do it effectively. Consequently, these firms are often left with using their own intuition or judgment to determine which segments are the most promising. For organizations with the time and money to commit to this step, the results may offer greater insight as to which segments are primary candidates for current marketing efforts. Additionally, it may identify segments that could serve as future targets for the marketer's offerings.

In determining whether a segment is a worthwhile target market, the marketer needs to address the following:

◆ *Is the segment large enough to support the marketer's objectives?* This is an especially critical question if the marketer is entering a market served by many competitors.

◆ *Is the segment showing signs of growth?* One of the worst situations for a marketer is to enter a market whose growth is flat or declining, especially if competitors have begun to exit the market.

◆ *Does the segment meet the mission of the organization?* The segment should not extend too far beyond the direction the organization has chosen to take in order to meet its marketing objectives.

◆ *Does the organization have the necessary skills, knowledge, and expertise to service the segment?* The marketer should understand and be able to communicate with customers in the segment, otherwise they may face a significant learning curve in understanding how to market effectively to these customers.

Once one or more segments have been identified the marketer must choose the most attractive option(s) for its marketing efforts. At this point, the choice becomes the firm's target market(s).

Step 3: Develop Strategy to Appeal to Target Market(s)

In the final step of the segmentation process, the marketer must decide a strategy for reaching the segments identified in Step 2. The options include the following target marketing strategies:

◆ <u>Undifferentiated or Mass Marketing</u> – Under this strategy, the marketer attempts to appeal to one large market with a single marketing strategy. While this approach offers advantages in terms of lowering development and production costs since only one product is marketed, there are few markets in which all customers seek the same benefits. This approach was extremely popular in the early days of marketing (e.g., Ford Model-T), but today few companies view this as a feasible strategy. (6)

◆ <u>Differentiated or Segmentation Marketing</u> – Marketers choosing this strategy try to appeal to multiple smaller markets with a unique marketing strategy for each market. The underlying concept is that bigger markets can be divided into many submarkets and an organization then chooses different marketing strategies to reach each submarket it targets. Most large consumer products firms follow this strategy as they offer multiple products (e.g., running shoes, basketball shoes) within a larger product category (e.g., footwear). (7)

◆ <u>Concentrated or Niche Marketing</u> – This strategy combines mass and segmentation marketing by using a single marketing strategy to appeal to markets that are only a fraction of the size of larger markets. It is primarily used by smaller marketers, who have identified small **subsegments** of a larger segment that are not served well by bigger firms. In these situations, a smaller company can do quite well marketing a single product to a narrowly defined target market. (8)

◆ <u>Customized or Micro Marketing</u> – This target marketing strategy attempts to appeal to targeted customers with individualized marketing programs. For micro marketing segmentation to be effective, the marketer must, to some degree, allow customers to "build-their-own" products. This approach requires extensive technical capability for marketers to reach individual customers and allow customers to interact with the marketer. Digital networks, in particular internet and mobile technologies, have been catalysts for micro marketing strategy. As more companies become comfortable utilizing these technologies, micro marketing is expected to flourish.

POSITIONING PRODUCTS

No matter which target marketing strategy is selected, the overall marketing strategy should involve the process of positioning the firm's offerings in ways that will appeal to targeted customers. Positioning is concerned with the perception customers hold regarding a product or company. In particular, it relates to marketing decisions an organization undertakes to get customers to think about a product or company in a certain way when compared to its competitors.

The goal of positioning is for marketers to convince customers their product offers key benefits not found with competitors' offerings. For instance, if a customer has discovered she has a need for an affordable high-definition television (HDTV), a company, such as Vizio, may come to mind since its marketing efforts position its products as offering good value at a reasonable cost.

To position successfully, the marketer must have thorough knowledge of the key benefits sought by the market. Obviously, the more effort the marketer expends on segmentation (i.e., reached Stage 3 segmentation) the more likely it will know the benefits sought by the market. Once known, the marketer must: 1) tailor marketing efforts to ensure its offerings satisfy the most sought-after benefits, and 2) communicate to the market in a way that differentiates the marketer's offerings from competitors.

For firms seeking to appeal to multiple target markets (i.e., segmentation marketing), positioning strategies may differ for each market. For example, a marketer may sell the same product to two different target markets but in one market the emphasis is on styling while in another market the emphasis is on ease-of-use benefits. The key point is that the overall marketing strategy must be evaluated separately for each target market since what works well in one market may not work as well in another market. (9)

REFERENCES

1. "Households and NPISHs Final Consumption Expenditure." *The World Bank*. https://data.worldbank.org/indicator/NE.CON.PRVT.CD.

2. It should be noted that consumer spending was impacted by the highest inflation rate in over 40 years. For more see: "Consumer Expenditures in 2022." *Bureau of Labor Statistics – United States Department of Labor*. December, 2023. https://www.bls.gov/opub/reports/consumer-expenditures/2022/home.htm.

3. It should be noted that a significant portion of business spending is on the labor required to produce and support an organization's products and services.

4. For details on the North American Industry Classification System see: "2022 NAICS Manual." *United States Census Bureau*. https://www.census.gov/naics.

5. For details on the International Standard Industrial Classification see: "Introduction to ISIC." *United Nations Statistics Division*. https://unstats.un.org/unsd/classifications/Econ/ISIC.cshtml.

6. While the Ford example is categorized as a good (i.e., car), mass marketing can also apply to services as well. For example, leading internet and mobile technologies, including Google, TikTok and Facebook, can be classified as offering mass market products as each of these are freely available to anyone with online or mobile access.

7. For an example of a highly segmented product lines including athletic shoes and clothing see: *Nike*. https://www.nike.com.

8. For more on niche markets especially as these pertain to small businesses see: Kelly Quinn. "What Is a Niche Market? 15 Examples and How to Find One." *Indeed*. June 1, 2023. https://www.indeed.com/career-advice/career-development/market-niches.

9. For examples of companies that repositioned their business model see: Chuck Nelson. "12 Companies That Reinvented Themselves to Stay Relevant." *Cheapism*. April 20, 2022. https://blog.cheapism.com/companies-that-reinvented-themselves.

Chapter 6: Product Decisions

As we stress throughout this book, organizations attempt to provide value to a target market by offering solutions to customers' needs. These solutions include tangible or intangible (or both) product offerings marketed by an organization. In addition to satisfying the target market's needs, the product is crucial because it is how organizations generate revenue. It is what a for-profit company sells in order to realize profits and satisfy their financial stakeholders (e.g., stockholders). Products are also important for many not-for-profit organizations where they are used to generate revenue needed to support operations (e.g., fundraising). Without a well-developed product strategy that includes input from the target market, a marketing organization will not have long-term success.

In this chapter, we define what a product is and look at how products are categorized. We also take a close look at the key decisions marketers face as they formulate their product offerings. These decisions may involve what features to include in a product, how a product's identity is established through branding, important issues in packaging design, and what to consider when labeling products. We discuss each in detail and see how these impact product strategy.

WHAT IS A PRODUCT?

In marketing, the term product is used as a catch-all word to identify solutions a marketer provides to its target market. We will use the term "product" to cover offerings that fall into one of the following categories:

GOODS

Something is considered a good if it is a tangible item. That is, it is something that is felt, tasted, heard, smelled, or seen. For example, bicycles and donuts are all examples of tangible goods. In some cases, there is a fine line between items that affect the senses and whether these are considered tangible or intangible. We often see this with digital goods (e.g., music, games, 3D imaging) accessed using technology devices, such as laptops, smartphones, virtual reality headsets, and other devices. For these products, there does not appear to be anything that is tangible or real since it is essentially computer code providing the solution. However, for our purposes, we distinguish these as goods rather than services, since these products are built (albeit using computer code), are stored (e.g., on cloud servers), and generally offer similar benefits each time (e.g., quality of a digital song is always the same).

SERVICES

Something is considered a service if a customer obtains value through the work or labor of someone else. Services can result in the creation of tangible goods (e.g., a magazine publisher hires a researcher to locate information for an article), but the main solution purchased is the service. Unlike goods, services are not stored and are only available at the time of use (e.g., hair salon), and the consistency of the benefit offered can vary from one purchaser to another (e.g., not exactly the same hair styling each time).

IDEAS

Something falls into the category of an idea if the marketer attempts to convince the customer to alter his/her behavior or perception in some way. Marketing an idea is often an approach used by not-for-profit organizations and governments in order to get targeted groups to avoid or change certain behavior. This is seen with public service announcements produced by the not-for-profit Ad Council directed toward such activity as ending hunger, child car safety, texting while driving, and shelter pet adoption. (1)

While some marketers offer solutions providing both tangible and intangible attributes, for most organizations their primary offering is concentrated in one area. So, while a manufacturer may offer intangible services or a service firm provides certain tangible equipment, these are often add-ons that support the organization's main product.

Categories of Consumer Products

Most products intended for consumer use can be further categorized as:

◆ Convenience Products – These products appeal to an extremely large market segment. Products in this category tend to be consumed regularly and purchased frequently. Examples include most household items, such as food, cleaning products, and personal care products. Because of the high purchase volume, pricing per item is often relatively low and consumers often see little value in shopping around since additional effort to find a better deal often yields minimal savings. From the marketer's perspective, the low price of convenience products means that profit per unit sold is generally low. In order to make high profits, marketers must sell in large volume. Consequently, marketers attempt to distribute these products in mass through as many retail outlets as they can possibly support (see *Mass Coverage* in Chapter 8).

◆ Shopping Products – These are products consumers purchase and consume on a less frequent schedule compared to convenience products. Consumers spend more time locating shopping products since these are relatively more expensive than convenience products and because these may possess additional **psychological benefits** (see Box 6-1) for purchasers, such as raising their perceived status level within their social group. Examples include many clothing products, personal services, digital products, and household furnishings. Because consumers are purchasing less frequently and are willing to spend time locating these products, the target market for shopping products is much smaller than for convenience goods. Therefore, marketers often are more selective when choosing distribution outlets in which to sell these products (see *Selective Coverage* in Chapter 8).

◆ Specialty Products – These are products that carry a high price tag relative to convenience and shopping products. Consumption may occur at the same rate as shopping products, but consumers are much more selective. In fact, in many cases consumers know in advance which product they prefer and will not shop to compare products. But they may shop at retailers that provide the best value. Examples include high-end luxury automobiles, expensive champagne, and celebrity hairstylists. The target markets are generally very small and outlets selling the products are highly limited to the point of being exclusive (see *Exclusive Coverage* in Chapter 8). (2)

In addition to the three main categories above, consumer products are also classified in at least two additional ways:

◆ Emergency Products – These are products sought due to sudden events and for which pre-purchase planning is not considered. Often the decision is one of convenience (e.g., whatever works to fix a problem) or personal fulfillment (e.g., perceived to improve purchaser's image in an unplanned situation). (3)

◆ Unsought Products – These are products whose purchase is unplanned but occur as a result of marketers' actions. For instance, such purchase decisions may be made when a customer is exposed to certain promotional activity, such as a salesperson's persuasive presentation, or to a an unexpected purchase incentive, such as a special discounted price. These marketing activities often lead customers to engage in impulse purchasing.

Categories of Business Products

Products sold within the business market fall into the following categories:

◆ Raw Materials – These are products obtained through such methods as mining, harvesting, and fishing that become key ingredients in the production of higher-order products.

◆ Processed Materials – These are products created through the processing of basic raw materials. In some cases, original raw materials are refined while in other cases the process combines different raw materials to create something new. For instance, certain crops, including corn and sugar cane, can be processed to create ethanol used as fuel to power motor engines.

◆ Equipment – These are products used to help with production or with important business operations activities. Examples include material mixers, conveyor belts, and buildings housing a company's operations.

◆ Basic Components – These are products used within more advanced components and are often built with raw or processed materials. Electrical wire is an example.

◆ Advanced Components – These are products that use basic components to produce products offering a significant function needed within a larger product. By itself, an advanced component is not a final product. In computers, the motherboard is an example since it contains many basic components but without the inclusion of other products (e.g., memory chips, microprocessor, power connector, etc.) it would have little value.

◆ Product Components – These are products used in the assembly of a final product, though these could also function as stand-alone products. Dice included as part of a children's board game is an example.

◆ MRO (Maintenance, Repair and Operating) Products – These are products used to assist with the operation of an organization but are not directly used in producing goods or services. Office supplies, parts for a truck fleet, and natural gas to heat a factory would fall into this category.

Components of a Product

On the surface, it seems a product is simply a marketing offering, whether tangible or intangible, that someone wants to purchase and consume. One might believe product decisions are focused exclusively on designing and building the consumable elements of goods, services, or ideas. In actuality, while decisions related to the consumable parts of the product are extremely important, the **total product** consists of more than what is consumed. The total product offering, and the decisions facing the marketer for the product, can be broken down into three main parts:

Core Benefits

As we discussed in Chapter 1, customers seek to obtain something of value from marketers in exchange for their willingness to give up something they value, generally money. What customers obtain are solutions to their needs or, stated another way, they receive benefits. For customers, benefits drive their purchase decisions (see Box 6-1). Consequently, at the very heart of all product decisions is being able to determine the core benefits a product should provide. These benefits, hopefully, address those sought by the marketer's target market. In most cases, the core benefits are offered by features of the actual product (see *Actual Product* discussion below), though, for some customers, benefits offered by other aspects or augmented features (see *Augmented Product* discussion below) of the product may also be important (e.g., access to customer service).

Actual Product

For most customers, the core benefits are offered through the components that make up the actual product. When a consumer returns home from shopping and takes an item out of her shopping bag, the actual product is the item she holds in her hand. Within the actual product is the **consumable product**, which is the main good, service, or idea the customer is buying. For example, while toothpaste comes in a package that makes dispensing it easy, the consumable product is the

Box 6-1

MARKETERS SELL BENEFITS

The benefits a customer obtains from a product are contained within the actual and augmented product through product features. Features are the separate attributes of a product. For example, features of so-called "smart televisions" may include screen size, screen resolution, internet-enabled, HDMI ports, remote control, and overall weight.

The benefits a customer receives from the purchase and use of the product fall into two main categories:

Functional Benefits

These are benefits derived from features that are part of the consumable product. For instance, in our television example, features and benefits may include:

Feature	Functional Benefit
◆ screen size	offers greater detail and allows for more distant viewing
◆ screen resolution	provides clear, more realistic picture quality
◆ internet-enabled	access a wide range of streaming services
◆ HDMI ports	offers connections for multiple add-on components
◆ remote control	allows for greater comfort and control while viewing
◆ lightweight	can be easily hung on a wall

The benefits offered by these features are called functional because these lead to benefits the user directly associates with the product. Functional benefits are often the result of materials, design, and production decisions. How the product is built can lead to benefits, such as increased speed, ease-of-use, durability, and cost savings.

Psychological Benefits

These are benefits the customer perceives he/she receives when using the product. These benefits address psychological needs, such as status within a group, risk reduction, sense of independence, and happiness. Such benefits are developed through promotional efforts that are aimed at customers' internal influences on purchase behavior (see Chapter 4).

In communicating with customers, marketers should always associate a benefit with a product feature. Benefits are what customers seek; the feature is simply how the benefit is delivered. In our smart television example, an online advertisement promoting a TV is more effective if it speaks directly to the benefits it offers such as:

Our new 75-inch smart television offers a screen resolution **(feature)** *that provides the clearest, most realistic picture* **(functional benefit)** *that will make your house the place to be* **(psychological benefit)** *for the big game!*

paste that is placed on a toothbrush. But marketers must understand that while the consumable product is the most critical of all product decisions, as we will soon see, creation of the actual product involves many separate product decisions, including product features, branding, packaging, labeling, and more.

Augmented Product

Marketers often surround their actual product with goods and services that provide additional value to the customer's purchase. While these factors may not be key reasons leading customers to purchase (i.e., these factors do not offer core benefits), for some customers the inclusion of these items strengthens the purchase decision while for others failure to include these may cause the customer not to buy. Items considered part of the augmented product include:

- Guarantee – This provides a level of assurance that the product will perform up to expectations and, if not, the company marketing the product will support the customer's decision to replace, repair, or return the product for a refund.

- Warranty – This offers customers a level of protection often extending past the guarantee period to cover repair or replacement of certain product components.

- Customer Service – As discussed in detail in Chapter 3, these services support customers through such methods as training, repair, and other types of assistance.

- Complementary Products – The value of some product purchases is enhanced with add-ons or complementary products. Such items make the main product easier to use or use in more situations (e.g., laptop carry bag), provides more protection (e.g., smartphone case), or extends functionality (e.g., portable keyboard for tablet computers). Complementary products can also include services. For instance, the retail warehouse chain Sam's Club offers customers purchasing tires free tire rotation for the life of the tires. (4)

- Availability – How customers obtain the product can affect its perceived value depending on such considerations as how easy it is to obtain (e.g., stocked at nearby store, delivered directly to office), the speed at which it can be obtained, and the likelihood it will be available when needed.

KEY PRODUCT DECISIONS

The actual product is designed to provide the core benefits sought by the target market. The marketer offers these benefits through a combination of factors making up the actual product. Below we discuss four key factors – features, branding, packaging, and labeling – that together help shape the actual product.

Consumable Product Features

As noted in Box 6-1, features are characteristics of a product that offer benefits to the customer. When it comes to developing a consumable product, marketers face several decisions related to product features including:

◆ <u>Set of Features vs. Cost</u> – For marketers, an important decision focuses on the quantity and quality of features to include in a product. In most cases, the more features that are included or the higher the features quality level, the more expensive the product is to produce and market.

◆ <u>Is More Better?</u> – Even if added cost is not a major concern, the marketer must determine if more features help or hurt the target market's perception of the product. A product containing too many features could be viewed by customers as being complicated and too difficult to use.

◆ <u>Who Should Choose the Features?</u> – Historically marketers determined what features to include in a product. However, the Customized or Micro Marketing targeting strategy we discussed in the Chapter 4 offers customers the opportunity to choose their own features to custom build a product. For instance, for the vast majority of websites, the actual computer files that produce the site reside on computer servers managed by a website hosting service. Such services charge a fee that varies depending on the service features the website owner chooses (e.g., data storage options, processing speed). Also, for traditional products, such as clothing, companies may allow customers to stylize their purchases with logos and other personalized options.

Branding

Branding involves decisions establishing an identity for a product with the goal of distinguishing it from competitors' offerings. In markets where competition is fierce and where customers may select from among many competitive products, creating an identity through branding is essential. It is particularly important in helping position the product (see *Positioning Products* in Chapter 5) in the minds of targeted customers.

While consumer products companies have long recognized the value of branding, it has only been within the last 30 years or so that organizations selling in the business market have begun to focus on brand building strategies. Intel, maker of computer component products such as computer chips, was one of the first business market companies to brand its products with its now famous 1990s "Intel Inside" slogan. Intel's success has led many other business-to-business marketers to incorporate branding within their overall marketing strategy. (5)

BRAND NAMES AND BRAND MARKS

At a basic level, branding is achieved through the use of unique brand names and brand marks. Developing a brand name, which may be the individual product name or a name applied to a group or family of products, offers several advantages. First, brand names may suggest to customers what the product is or does (e.g., Mop & Glo). This can catch the attention of customers needing a product for a certain usage or who are seeking a specific benefit but do not know what product to choose. Second, the brand name is often what customers say when they are discussing a product with others. This is helpful in creating and spreading product awareness.

The brand mark is a design element that provides visual or auditory recognition for the product. This can be represented by a symbol (e.g., Nike swoosh), a logo (e.g., Google color graphic), a character (e.g., Keebler elves), or even a sound (e.g., Intel Inside sound).

The creation of brand names and brand marks must be done carefully if a marketer seeks to expand outside its home country. This can especially be a problem if an organization looks to follow a standardization approach to global marketing (see Box 1-3 in Chapter 1), where a single brand name and mark is used throughout the world. Whether using a single name and mark or developing a new name and mark for each market that is entered, marketers must fully understand the local language to ensure there are no issues in the translation of these branding elements.

BRANDING STRATEGY

With competition growing more intense in almost all industries, establishing a strong brand allows an organization's products to stand out and avoid potential pitfalls, such as price wars. A clear understanding of branding is essential in order to build a solid product strategy. Marketers should be aware of various branding approaches that can be pursued and deployed to establish a product within the market. The purpose of these approaches is to build a brand that will exist for the long term. Making smart branding decisions in the early stages of a new product is crucial since the organization may have to live with the decision for a long period of time.

Branding approaches include:

- Individual Product Branding – With this branding approach, new products are assigned new names with no obvious connection to a company's existing brands. Under individual product branding, the marketing organization must work hard to establish the brand in the market since it cannot ride the coattails of previously introduced brands (see *Family Branding* discussion below). The chief advantage is it allows brands to stand on their own. which may lessens threats that may occur to other brands marketed by the company. For instance, if a company receives negative publicity for one brand this news is less likely to influence the company's other brands since these carry their own unique names. Under individual branding, each brand builds its own separate equity (see *Brand Equity* discussion below), which allows the company to potentially sell off individual brands without impacting other brands the company owns. The most famous company to follow this strategy is Procter & Gamble, which has historically introduced new brands without any link to other brands or even to the company name. (6)

- Family Branding – Under this branding approach, new products are placed under the umbrella of an existing brand. The principle advantage of family branding is it enables rapid building of market awareness and acceptance of a new product, since the brand is already established and known to the market. The potential disadvantage is that the market already has established perceptions of the brand. For instance, a company selling low-end, lower priced products may have a brand viewed as an economy brand. If the company attempts to introduce higher-end, higher priced products using the same brand name, customers may be confused with their perception of the brand, which could negatively impact sales for all products. Additionally, any negative publicity for one product within a brand family could spread to all other products that share the same brand name.

- Co-Branding – This approach takes the idea of individual and family branding a step further. With co-branding, a marketer seeks to partner with another firm, which has an established brand, in hopes the synergy of two brands on a product is more powerful than a single brand. The partnership often has both firms sharing costs but also sharing the gains. For instance, major credit card companies, such as Visa and MasterCard, offer co-branding options to organizations. The cards carry the name of a co-branded organization (e.g., university name) along with the name of the issuing bank (e.g., Citibank) and the name of the credit card company. Besides tapping into awareness for multiple brands, the co-branding strategy is designed to appeal to a larger target market, especially if each brand, when viewed separately, does not have extensive overlapping target markets with their co-brand partner. Therefore, co-branding allows all partners to tap into market segments where they previously did not have a strong position.

- Private Label or Store Branding – Some suppliers are in the business of producing products for other companies, including placing another company's brand name on the product. This is most often seen in the retail industry where stores or online sellers contract with suppliers to manufacture the retailer's own branded products. In some cases, the supplier not only produces products for the retailer's brand but also markets its own brand so that a store's shelves and website will contain both brands. For retailers, store brands often offer higher profit margins than brand name products. Consequently, in recent years, the rapid growth of private label products has resulted in more shelf space being dedicated to these products and less to branded products.

- No-Name or Generic Branding – Certain suppliers provide products that are intentionally "**brandless**." These products are mostly basic commodity-type products consumer or business customers purchase as low-price alternatives to branded products. Basic household products, such as paper goods, over-the-counter medicines and even dog food, are available in a generic form.

- Brand Licensing – Under brand licensing, a contractual arrangement is created in which an organization owning a brand name allows others to produce and supply products carrying that brand name. This is often seen when a brand is not directly associated with a particular product category. For instance, several famous children's characters, such as Sesame Street's Elmo, have been licensed to toy and food manufacturers, who market products using the branded character's name and image.

ADVANTAGES OF BRANDS

A strong brand offers many advantages for marketers including:

- Enhances Product Recognition – Brands provide multiple sensory stimuli to enhance customer recognition. A brand can be visually recognizable from its packaging, logo, shape, etc. It can be recognizable via sound, such as hearing the name on a radio advertisement or verbally when someone mentions the product.

- Helps Build Brand Equity – Strong brands can lead to financial advantages through the concept of brand equity (see *Brand Equity* discussion below) in which the brand itself becomes valuable. Such gains can be realized through the outright sale of a brand or through licensing arrangements.

- Helps Build Brand Loyalty – Brand loyal customers are frequent and enthusiastic purchasers of a particular brand. Cultivating brand loyalty among customers is the ultimate reward for successful marketers since these customers are far less likely to switch to other brands compared to non-loyal customers.

- Helps with Product Positioning – Well-developed and promoted brands make product positioning efforts more effective. The result is that upon exposure to a brand (e.g., hearing it, seeing it) customers conjure up mental images or feelings of the benefits of that brand. The reverse is even better. When customers associate benefits with a particular brand, the brand may have attained a significant competitive advantage. In these situations, a customer, who recognizes she/he needs a solution to a problem (e.g., needs to bleach clothes), may automatically think of one brand that offers the solution to the problem (e.g., Clorox). This association of "benefit = brand" can provide a significant advantage for the brand.

- Aids in Introduction of New Products – A successful brand can be extended by adding new products under the earlier discussed Family Branding strategy. Such branding may allow companies to introduce new products more easily since the brand is already recognized within the market.

BRAND EQUITY

For marketers, intellectual property (see Box 6-2), particularly trademarks, is important in building a brand's identity. As we discussed, a uniquely identified brand, that is well known to a target market, may occupy a position in the minds of customers that sets it apart from other brands (e.g., Apple iPhone vs. Samsung Galaxy) or associates it with a specific feature or benefit (e.g., music streaming service = Spotify). By doing this, the marketer is creating a company asset from a recognizable name, symbol, or other unique feature. Called brand equity, the marketer's work can lead to an asset that can grow in value and eventually offer the organization a financial reward.

For example, Company A may have a well-recognized brand (Brand X) within a market, yet they have decided to concentrate efforts on selling other brands they own. Company B is looking to enter the same market as Brand X. If circumstances are right, Company A could sell to Company B the rights to use the Brand X name without selling any other part of the company. That is, Company A simply sells the legal rights to the Brand X name while retaining all other parts of Brand X, such as the production facilities and employees. These other parts can then be redirected to the production of other Company A brands. In cases of well-developed brands, this kind of transaction may carry a large price tag. Thus, through strong branding efforts Company A achieves a large financial gain by simply signing over the rights to the brand name.

But why would Company B seek to purchase a brand for such a high price tag? Because, by buying the brand Company B has already achieved a significant marketing goal – building awareness within the target market. The fact the market is already familiar with the brand allows Company B to concentrate on other marketing decisions.

Box 6-2

BRANDS AND INTELLECTUAL PROPERTY

When most people think of a business asset they generally think of machinery, digital technology, buildings, and other physical items purchased and used by a business. But companies can also create and grow their own assets that are, in essence, intangible. These assets principally exist as legally protected "rights" that often prevent others from doing the same thing. If managed well, such rights can become enormously valuable.

In marketing, the most likely source for acquiring protected rights is through government-controlled registration systems collectively referred to as intellectual property. Intellectual property provides protection in four ways (7):

Patent

Offers legal protection for inventions, such as new products, preventing others from offering the same product for a specified period of time. For example, a company may develop certain features in a product that others cannot include in their product for the period of the patent, which may be as long as 20 years.

Trademark

Offers legal protection on unique words, names, symbols, and other identifiable features that distinguish one item from another. For example, a product's name, the design of a logo, special symbols, and even special characters associated with a brand (e.g., sports team mascot) can be trademarked.

Copyright

Offers legal protection for original authored work, such as writings and recordings. For example, in addition to protecting authors of books and music, copyright can also be used to protect website materials, music tied to product advertising, and print advertising copy.

Trade Secret

Offers legal protection for information, tightly protected by a company, which is used within the regular course of doing business and is intended to give a company an advantage over competitors. For example, the formula used to produce Coca-Cola is protected as a trade secret.

Packaging

Nearly all tangible products (i.e., goods) are sold to customers in a container or package that can serve many purposes, including protecting the product during shipment. In a few instances, such as with certain produce items or with tool items such as a hammer, the final customer may purchase the product without a package, but the marketer of these products still faces packaging decisions when it comes to shipping to others, such as shipping to resellers. As a result, for many products there are two packaging decisions – final customer package and distribution package.

Final Customer Package

This relates to the package the final customer receives in exchange for payment. When the final customer makes a purchase, she or he is initially exposed to the outermost container holding the product. This exterior package generally contains product information (see *Labeling* discussion below), graphic design (e.g., logo, color scheme), special handling features (e.g., a carrying handle), and other characteristics.

Depending on the type of product being purchased, there may be several components to the package holding the product. These components can be divided into the following:

- First-Level Package – This represents the packaging that holds the consumable product (e.g., Tylenol bottle holding tablets). In some cases, this packaging is minimal since it only serves to protect the product. For instance, certain frozen food products are sold to consumers in a cardboard box with the product itself contained in a plastic bag found inside the box. This plastic bag represents the first-level package. In other cases, frozen food products are sold to final customers only in plastic bags. In these cases, the plastic bag is the only packaging obtained by the customer.

- Second-Level Package – For some products, the first-level package is surrounded by one or more outer packages (e.g., box holding the Tylenol bottle). This second-level package would then serve as the exterior package for the product.

- Package Inserts – Marketers use a variety of other methods to communicate with customers after they open the product package. These methods are often inserted within, or sometimes on, the product's package. Package insertions include product information, including instruction manuals and warranty cards; promotional incentives, including coupons; and items that provide additional value, including recipes.

Distribution Package

This packaging is used to transport the final customer package through the supply chain. It generally holds multiple final customer packages and offers a higher level of damage protection than what is available with customer packaging. The most obvious examples are cardboard boxes and wooden crates. A single box or crate may contain a large number of customer packages.

FACTORS TO CONSIDER WHEN MAKING PACKAGING DECISIONS

Packaging decisions are crucial for several reasons including:

- Protection – Packaging is used to protect the product from damage during shipping and handling, and to lessen spoilage to certain products (e.g., fruits and vegetables) if these are exposed to air or other elements. Products being shipped long distances, such as overseas, are likely to require more durable packaging in order to protect the product from damage that can occur due to potential temperature fluctuations and repeated handling.

- Visibility – Packaging design is used to capture customers' attention as they are shopping or glancing through a catalog, website, or app. This is particularly useful for customers who are not familiar with the product or in situations where a product must stand out among thousands of other products, such as those found in grocery stores. Packaging designs that stand out are more likely to be remembered on future shopping trips.

- Added Value – Packaging design and structure can add value to a product. For instance, benefits can be obtained from package structures that make the product easier to use while stylistic designs can make the product more attractive to display in the customer's home (e.g., design of plug-in air fresheners).

- Distributor Acceptance – A packaging decision must not only be accepted by the final customer, but it may also have to be accepted by distributors who sell the product for the marketer. For instance, a retailer may not accept a product unless the packaging conforms to requirements the retailers has for storing products on its shelves (e.g., fits maximum height or weight requirements).

- Total Cost – Packaging can represent a significant portion of a product's selling price. For example, in the cosmetics industry, it is estimated packaging cost for some products may be as high as 40 percent of a product's retail selling price. Consequently, smart packaging decisions can help reduce costs and possibly lead to higher profits.

- Expensive to Create – Developing new packaging can be extremely expensive. The costs involved in creating new packaging include graphic and structural design, production, customer testing, possible destruction of leftover old packaging, and possible advertising to inform customers of the new packaging.

- Long-Term Decision – When companies create a new package it is most often with the intention of having the design on the market for an extended period of time. In fact, changing a product's packaging too frequently can have negative effects since some customers become conditioned to locating the product based on its package and may be confused if the design is altered.

- Environmental or Legal Issues – Packaging decisions must also include an assessment of its environmental impact especially for products with packages that are frequently discarded. Packages that are not easily biodegradable could draw customer and governmental reaction. Also, caution must be exercised in order to create packages that do not infringe on another firm's intellectual property, such as copyrights, trademarks, or patents.

Labeling

Most packages, whether final customer packaging or distribution packaging, are imprinted with information intended to assist customers and distributors. For consumer products, careful focus on labeling decisions is often needed for the following reasons:

- <u>Captures Attention</u> – Labels serve to capture the attention of shoppers. The use of catchy words and eye-catching graphics may cause strolling retail customers to stop and evaluate the product.

- <u>Offers First Impression</u> – The label is often the first thing a customer sees when first exposed to a product leading to his/her initial impression of the product.

- <u>Provides Information</u> – The label provides customers with product information to aid their purchase decision or help improve customers' experience when using the product (e.g., recipes).

- <u>Aids Purchasing and Inventory</u> – Packaging generally includes scannable universal product code (UPC) labels making it easy for resellers, such as retailers, to process customers' purchases (e.g., scan at checkout) and manage inventory.

- <u>Addresses Needs in Global Markets</u> – For companies serving international markets or diverse cultures within a single country, it may be necessary to include bilingual or multilingual labels. (8)

- <u>Meets Legal Requirements</u> – In some countries, certain products, including food and pharmaceuticals, are required by law to contain certain labels, such as a listing of product ingredients, providing nutritional information, or including usage warning information.

REFERENCES

1. For examples of these and many other Ad Council campaigns see: "All Campaigns." *Ad Council*. https://www.adcouncil.org/all-campaigns.

2. For additional insight on luxury goods and why consumers purchase these see: "The Psychology Behind Why People Buy Luxury Goods." Vanessa Page. *Investopedia*. June 29, 2023. https://www.investopedia.com/articles/personal-finance/091115/psychology-behind-why-people-buy-luxury-goods.asp.

3. Sudden demand for emergency products may also lead to inventory shortages as was seen . For instance, during the Covid-19 pandemic extensive product shortages occurred for such items as toilet paper, hand sanitizers, bicycles, and even swimming pools.

4. "Tire Buying Guide." *Sam's Club*. https://www.samsclub.com/content/tire-buying-guide.

5. For more on the history behind the Intel Inside branding see: "End User Marketing and Intel Inside." *Intel*. https://www.intel.com/content/www/us/en/history/virtual-vault/articles/end-user-marketing-intel-inside.html.

6. For a listing of all P&G products see: "Brands." *Procter & Gamble*. https://us.pg.com/brands.

7. For more on intellectual property see: "Intellectual Property (IP) Policy." *United States Patent and Trademark Office*. https://www.uspto.gov/ip-policy.

8. For examples of excellence in packaging and labeling around the world see: *Dieline*. https://thedieline.com.

Chapter 7: Managing Products

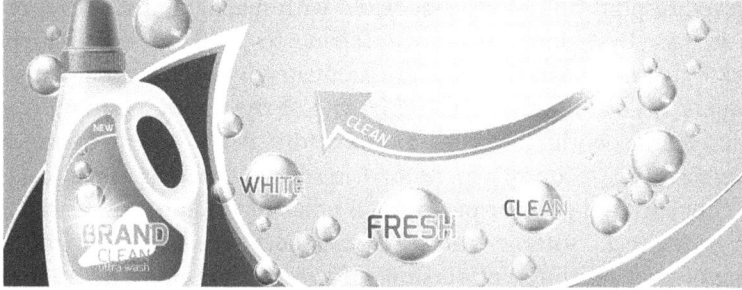

In Chapter 6, we saw how marketers are confronted with many issues when building the product component of their marketing strategy. While product decisions represent just one aspect of marketers' overall activities, these decisions are often the most critical because these lead directly to the reasons (i.e., benefits offered, solutions to problems) why the customer decides to choose the organization's goods, services, or ideas. Consequently, it is often the marketing decision that consumes the most time for marketers and for their organizations.

In this chapter, we extend the coverage of product decisions by exploring additional product issues facing the marketer. First, we look at how companies structure their product offerings and identify the scope of a marketing manager's responsibilities within this structure. Second, we spend a large part of this chapter covering the importance of new product development, including an analysis of the steps organizations may follow to bring new products to market. Finally, we show that once new products have been established in the market numerous factors may force the marketer to adjust its product decisions. As part of this, we examine the concept of the Product Life Cycle and see how it offers valuable insight and guidance for product decisions.

STRUCTURE OF PRODUCT MANAGEMENT

Marketers are often responsible for a wide array of decisions required to manage an organization's product offerings. As we will discuss shortly, these decisions include both creation of new products and management of existing products. But the tasks a marketer performs on a day-to-day basis will depend on the structure an organization has established for its product decisions. Possible structures include:

PRODUCT ITEM MANAGEMENT

At this managerial level, responsibilities are associated with marketing a single product or brand. By "single" we are limiting the marketer's responsibility to one item. For instance, an AI software development company may initially market just one product. In some organizations, the person in charge has the title Product Manager, though in smaller companies this person may simply be the Marketing Manager.

BRAND PRODUCT LINE MANAGEMENT

At this level, responsibilities are associated with managing two or more similar product items. By "similar" we are referring to products carrying the same brand name that fit within the same product category and offer similar solutions to customers' needs. Procter & Gamble, one of the largest consumer products companies in the world, markets Tide laundry detergent in many different packaging sizes (e.g., 46oz., 92oz., 146oz.), in several different forms (e.g., regular powder, concentrated powder packs, high efficiency liquid), and with different added features (e.g., softener, bleach, freshener) resulting in a product line consisting of over 60 different versions of the product. (1) Differences in the product offerings indicate these are targeted to different segments within the larger market (e.g., those preferring liquid vs. those preferring powder packs); however, it may also represent a choice for the same target market who may seek variety. A product line is measured by its depth, relative to competitors, with deep product lines offering extensive product options. Brand product lines are often managed by a Brand or Product Line Manager.

CATEGORY PRODUCT LINE MANAGEMENT

At this level, responsibilities are associated with managing two or more brand product lines, generally within the same product category. In this situation, the marketer may manage products offering similar basic benefits (e.g., detergent to clean clothes) but target its offerings to slightly different needs (e.g., products for tough to clean clothing vs. products to clean delicate clothing). Multiple brand product lines allow the marketer to cover the needs of more segments, and consequently increases its chances of generating sales. Often in larger companies, category product lines are the responsibility of the Product Category or Divisional Marketing Manager, who may have several Brand or Product Line Managers reporting to her/him.

PRODUCT MIX MANAGEMENT

At this level, responsibilities include two or more category product lines directed to different product categories. In some cases, the category product lines may yield similar general solutions (e.g., cleaning) but are aimed at entirely different target markets (e.g., cleaning dishes vs. cleaning automobiles). In large companies, the product lines are often diverse and offer different solutions. For example, BIC sells writing instruments, shaving products, and gas lighters. (2) This diversification strategy cushions against an "all-eggs-in-one-basket" risk that may exist for a company that directs all resources to a single product category. A product mix can be classified based on its **width** (how many different category product lines) and its **depth** (how many different brand product lines within a category product line). In most situations, responsibility for this level belongs to a company's Vice President or Director of Marketing.

MANAGING NEW PRODUCTS

By its nature, successful marketing requires marketers frequently develop new ideas that adjust or even dramatically reshape an organization's marketing plan. New ideas are essential for responding to changing market demand and competitive pressure. The reasons for developing new products will vary by organization and industry. Yet, for most organizations, the motivation to develop new products is a direct result of the need to respond to one or more of the following situations:

◆ Customers Change – Over time customers' needs may evolve. What attracted customer interest in the past is not guaranteed to do the same in the future. This is especially the case for products targeted to narrow age groups, where not only are customers' needs changing but customers themselves change. For example, Nickelodeon, a cable television network targeted to young children and teenagers, faces a situation where customers are only in their target market for 10 to 12 years (from young child to early teen). The constant influx of new customers, along with continually losing existing customers, requires frequent evaluation of programming to ensure the network is meeting the needs of an ever-changing target market. (3)

◆ Attract Different Customers – Almost all companies face a point at which appealing to the current target market is not enough to grow the business. Instead, the company must attract different customers, who are not yet major purchasers of the company's products. To appeal to new customers often requires a different set of products than what the organization presently offers.

◆ Profit in Newer Products – Many new products earn higher profits than older products. This is often the case for products considered innovative or unique, which may enjoy success and initially face little or no competition.

◆ Keep Ahead of Competition – Fierce global competition and technological developments make it much easier for competitors to learn about products and replicate them. In other instances, marketers may find their own brands are being duplicated by unapproved manufacturers, especially in foreign markets. These "**knockoff**" products are then sold to unwitting customers. To stay ahead of true competitors and product duplicators, requires marketers to innovate with new offerings.

◆ Helps with Repositioning – New products can help reposition the company in customers' minds. For instance, a company with a reputation for selling low-priced products with few features may shift customers' perceptions by introducing products with more features and slightly higher pricing.

◆ Fill Out Product Line – Companies with limited product line depth may miss out on more sales unless they add new products to fill out the line. For example, companies may have a strong high-end, high priced product but lack a good quality, mid-price offering.

◆ Expand Product Mix – Some firms market seasonal products that garner their highest sales during a certain time of the year or sell cyclical products whose sales fluctuate depending on economic factors (e.g., slow sales during an economic recession). Expanding the firm's product mix into new areas may help offset these fluctuations. For manufacturing firms, an additional benefit is realized as new products utilize existing production capacity that is under-used when seasonal or cyclical products are not being produced.

◆ Respond to Significant Market Changes – While not a common occurrence in most markets, sometimes marketers are confronted with a situation that requires they develop new products to either survive a changing market or to take advantage of unplanned opportunities. Certainly, the best example of this can be seen with how the coronavirus pandemic resulted in many new products in order to address not only the medical issues associated with the pandemic but also unexpected conditions faced by customers. (4)

Categories of New Products

New products fall into several categories defined by: 1) the type of market the product is entering, which includes newly created, existing but not previously targeted, or existing and previously targeted; and 2) the level of product innovation, which includes radically new, new, or improved.

Create New Market with Radically New Products

This category is represented by new breakthrough products that are so revolutionary they create an entirely new market. A relatively recent example can be seen with evolution of ridesharing services, such as Uber and Lyft. Highly innovative products are rare so very few new products fall into this category.

Enter Existing but Not Previously Targeted Market with New Products

In this category, a marketer introduces a new product or product line to an existing market which they did not previously target. Often these products are similar to competitors' products already available in the market but with some level of difference (e.g., different features, lower price, etc.). Apple's introduction of the HomePod into the existing voice-controlled smart speaker market is an example.

Stay in Existing and Previously Targeted Market with New or Improved Products

Under this category, the marketer attempts to improve its current market position by improving or upgrading existing products or by extending a product line by adding new products. This type of new product is seen in our earlier example of Procter & Gamble's Tide product line, which contains many product variations.

How New Products Are Obtained

Marketers have several options for obtaining new products. First, products can be developed within an organization's own research operations. For some companies, such as service firms, this may simply mean the marketer designs new service options to sell to its target markets. For instance, a marketer for a mortgage company may design new mortgage packages offering borrowers different rates or payment options. At the other extreme, companies may support an extensive research and development effort, where engineers, scientists, or others are engaged in new product discovery.

A second way to obtain products is to acquire them from external sources. This can occur in several ways including:

◆ <u>Purchase the Product</u> – With this option, a marketer buys the product outright from another firm. The advantage is the product is already developed, which reduces the purchasing organization's time and potential costs related to developing it themselves. The disadvantage is the purchase cost may be quite high and, under some conditions, the purchase may not include valuable assets (e.g., equipment, facilities, people) associated with the product.

◆ <u>License the Product</u> – Under this option, the marketer negotiates with the owner of the product for the rights to market the product. This may be a particularly attractive option for companies that have to fill a new product need quickly (e.g., give a product line more depth) or it may be used as a temporary source of products while the marketer's company is developing its own product. On the negative side, the arrangement may have a limited time frame at which point the licensor may decide to end the relationship leaving the marketer without a source for the product.

◆ <u>Purchase Another Firm</u> – Instead of purchasing another company's products marketers may find it easier just to purchase the whole company owning the products. One key advantage to this is that the acquisition often includes the people and resources that developed the products, which may be a key consideration if the acquiring company wants to continue to develop and market their own products.

New Product Development Process

Because introducing new products is necessary to the future success of many organizations, marketers in charge of product decisions often follow set procedures for bringing products to market. In the scientific area, this may mean the establishment of ongoing laboratory research programs for discovering new products (e.g., medicines), while other industries may pull together resources for product development on a less structured basis.

In this section, we present a 7-Step process comprising the key elements of new product development. While some organizations may not follow a deliberate step-by-step approach, the steps are useful in showing the information input and the decisions required to develop new products successfully. The process also shows the importance marketing research plays in developing products.

However, while the new product development process offers insight into how products come to market, marketers should also understand potential limitations with this approach that include:

◆ Developing Radically New Products – While the 7-Step process works for most industries, it is less effective in developing radically new products (see *Categories of New Products* discussion above). This is due to the target market's inability to provide sufficient feedback on advanced product concepts, as they often find it difficult to understand radically different ideas. So, while many of these steps are used to research breakthrough ideas, the marketers of radically new products should exercise caution when interpreting the marketing research information gathered in this 7-Step process.

◆ New Product Development in Less-Developed Markets – Marketers should recognize that it may be more difficult to obtain significant marketing research information in less-developed markets (e.g., underdeveloped countries) compared to what can be obtained in more-developed markets. Often this is due to the lack of a reliable communication infrastructure. Though it may not be possible to gain the same level of market analysis in less developed markets, some level of marketing research should still be considered as even a small amount of research may prove to be useful.

STEP 1: IDEA GENERATION

The first step of new product development requires gathering ideas to be evaluated as potential product options. For many marketers, idea generation is an ongoing process with contributions from inside and outside the organization. Many marketing research techniques are used to encourage ideas including:

● Conducting focus groups with customers, channel members, and the company's sales force

● Encouraging customer comments and suggestions via toll-free telephone numbers, social media postings, website comment forms, email, or online discussion forums

● Gaining insight on competitive product developments through secondary research sources

One effective research technique used to generate ideas is **brainstorming**, where open-minded, creative thinkers from inside and outside the organization gather and share ideas. The dynamic nature of group members floating ideas, where one idea often sparks another idea, can yield a wide range of possible product options that can be further explored. (5)

STEP 2: SCREENING

In Step 2, the ideas generated in Step 1 are critically evaluated to isolate the most attractive options. Depending on the number of ideas, screening may be done in rounds with the first round involving the organization's executives judging the feasibility of ideas while successive rounds may utilize more advanced research techniques. As the ideas are whittled down to a few attractive options, rough estimates are made of an idea's potential in terms of revenue, production costs, profit potential, and competitors' response if the product is introduced. Acceptable ideas move on to the next step.

STEP 3: CONCEPT DEVELOPMENT AND TESTING

With a few ideas in hand, the marketer now seeks initial feedback from customers, business partners (e.g., distributors), and its own employees. Generally, focus groups are convened where the ideas are presented to a group, often in the form of **concept board** or **storyboard** presentations. For instance, customers may be shown a concept board displaying drawings of a product idea or even an advertisement featuring the product. In some cases, focus groups are exposed to a **mock-up** of the idea, which is a physical but, in most cases, a nonfunctional version of the product concept. During focus groups with customers the marketer seeks information including likes and dislikes of the concept, level of interest in purchasing the product, frequency of purchase (used to help forecast demand), and price points to determine how much customers would be willing to spend to acquire the product.

STEP 4: BUSINESS ANALYSIS

At this point in the new product development process, the marketer has reduced a large number of ideas down to one or two options. Now in Step 4, the process becomes highly dependent on marketing research as efforts are made to analyze the viability of the product ideas. At this step, the key objectives for the marketer are to obtain useful forecasts of market size (e.g., overall demand), operational costs (e.g., production costs), and financial projections (e.g., sales, profits). Additionally, the organization must determine if the product fits within the organization's overall mission and strategy. Much effort is directed at both internal research, such as discussions with production and purchasing personnel, and external marketing research, such as customer and distributor surveys, secondary research, and competitor analysis.

STEP 5: PRODUCT AND MARKETING MIX DEVELOPMENT

Ideas passing through business analysis are given serious consideration for development. Companies direct their research and development teams to construct an initial design or **prototype** of the idea. Marketers begin to construct a Marketing Plan for the product (see *The Marketing Plan* in Chapter 20). Once the prototype is ready, the marketer seeks customer input. However, unlike the concept testing stage, where customers were only exposed to the idea, in this step the customer gets to experience the real product as well as other aspects of the marketing effort, such as advertising, pricing, and distribution options (e.g., retail store, direct from company, etc.). Favorable customer reaction helps solidify the marketer's decision to introduce the product and provides other valuable information, such as estimated purchase rates and understanding how the customer will use the product. Less favorable reaction may suggest the need for adjustments to elements of the Marketing Plan. Once these are made the marketer may have the customer test the product again. In addition to gaining customer feedback, this step is used to gauge the feasibility of large-scale, cost-effective production for manufactured products.

STEP 6: MARKET TESTING

Products surviving to Step 6 are ready to be tested. While, in some cases, the marketer accepts what was learned from concept testing (Step 3) and skips over market testing to launch the idea as a fully marketed product, many companies will seek more input from a larger group before moving to commercialization (Step 7). The most common type of market testing, used especially for consumer products sold at retail outlets, uses methods that make the product available to a selective, small segment of the target market, such as selling in just one city. Customers in this market are then exposed to a full marketing effort, just as they would be with most other products they can purchase. In **conventional test markets**, the marketer must work hard to get the product into the market by convincing distributors to purchase and place the product on their store shelves or website. In more **controlled test markets**, distributors may be paid a fee for agreeing to make the product available for customers to purchase. Another form of market testing for consumer products, which is even more controlled, uses methods to recruit customers to a "laboratory" store where they are given shopping instructions. Product interest is then measured based on customers' shopping responses. Finally, there are several high-tech approaches to market testing, including virtual reality and computer simulations. With **virtual reality testing**, customers are exposed to a computer-simulated environment and asked to locate and select products. With **computer simulation testing**, customers may not be directly involved at all. Instead, key research variables are entered into sophisticated computer programs, including those built on newly developed artificial intelligence (AI) platforms, and estimates of a target market's response are calculated.

STEP 7: COMMERCIALIZATION

If market testing displays promising results, the product is ready for market introduction. Some firms introduce or roll-out the product in waves with different parts of their target market receiving the product on different schedules. This allows the company to ramp up production in a more controlled way and to fine-tune marketing decisions as the product is distributed to new areas.

MANAGING EXISTING PRODUCTS

Marketing strategies developed for initial product introduction almost certainly need to be revised as the product settles into the market. While commercialization may be the last step in the new product development process, it is just the beginning of managing the product. Adjusting the product's marketing strategy is required for many reasons, such as changes in customers' tastes and preferences, threats from domestic and foreign competitors, changes in economic conditions, and innovative technological advances.

To stay on top of possible threats, the marketer must monitor all aspects of their marketing strategy and make changes as needed. Such efforts may lead to continual refinement of the product's Marketing Plan. In fact, marketing strategies change as a product moves through time leading to the concept called the Product Life Cycle.

The Product Life Cycle

The basic premise of the Product Life Cycle (PLC) is that products go through several stages of "life" with each stage presenting new challenges that must be met with different marketing approaches. For example, marketers may find what works when appealing to customers early in the life of a product may not be as effective when targeting new customers after the product has been on the market for a while.

There have been several attempts over the years to define the stages that make up the PLC. Unfortunately, the PLC may be different for different products, different markets, and different market conditions (e.g., economic forces). Consequently, there is not a one-model-fits-all PLC. Yet there is enough evidence to suggest most products and product groups (see Box 7-1) experience patterns of activity that divide the evolution of the product into five distinct stages. As shown in Figure 7-1, these stages are:

◆ Development – Occurs before the product is released to the market and is principally a time for honing the product offering, finding funding to launch the product, and preparing the market for product introduction.

◆ Introduction – The product is released to the market and sales begin though often gradually as the market becomes aware of the product.

◆ Growth – If the product is accepted it may reach a stage of rapid growth in sales and profits.

◆ Maturity – At some point, sales of a product may stabilize. For some products, the maturity phase can be the longest stage as loyal customers continue to purchase. However, while overall sales may grow year-over-year, sales in terms of percentage increase may be smaller compared to previous years.

◆ Decline – All products eventually see demand decline as customers no longer see value in purchasing the product. Similar to the Maturity stage, the Decline stage may last for a long time.

Figure 7-1: Stages of the Product Life Cycle

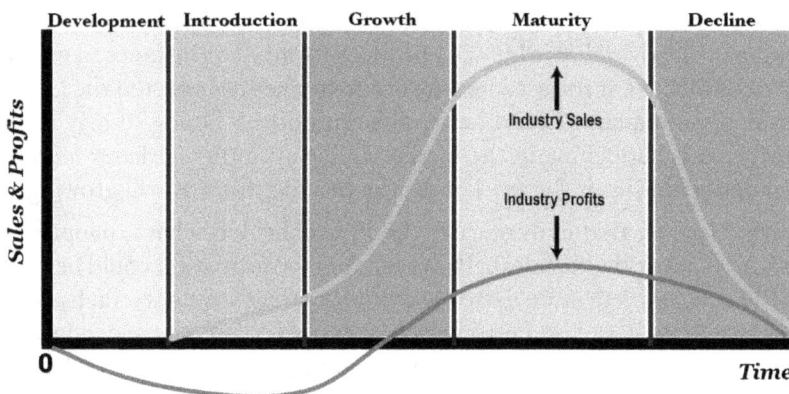

Box 7-1

LEVELS OF ANALYSIS OF THE *PLC*

The Product Life Cycle is often referenced in business media outlets as a way of describing conditions facing a market or product. The fact it is used to describe either markets or individual products points out the need to understand the three different levels of analysis for which the PLC can be used:

Product Category

This level considers the macro market view for the general category of products that meet a general need. For instance, automobiles would be a general category that meets the need for personal motorized transportation (obviously there are others, such as motorcycles, scooters and trucks, but we will focus only on automobiles) and includes many products. Since the PLC for a product category includes sales for all products, the time frame for the automotive PLC is quite long with the Introduction stage beginning around 1900.

Product Form

This level looks at product groupings that fall within a product category. The product form contains many different groupings that, taken together, make up the product category. These groupings include products that not only satisfy the general need of the product category but do so by also offering additional benefits. In our example, electric cars would be a product form, since it satisfies the general need for personal motorized transportation and offers additional benefits, including fuel efficiency and environmental friendliness. Other product forms in the product category include sports cars, SUVs, luxury sedans, etc. Clearly there can be a unique PLC for each form of a product. Marketers are very concerned with analysis at this level since it provides evidence for what is occurring in specific markets and, for this reason, is considered the most important level of analysis.

Individual Brand

This level concerns the life cycle of a specific brand within a product form. In our example, this would include the Tesla Model 3. While it may seem marketers would be most concerned with this level, they actually gain more value from analyzing what is happening in the overall market (i.e., product form). For instance, a marketer may make a serious mistake if she assumes the entire market has entered the Decline stage just because her company's brand has seen a sales drop. Doing so may mean a total misread of what is happening in the market and lead to the marketer missing out on additional opportunities if the market for the product form is still growing.

It's important to note that in most cases the PLC considers what is happening for the total market (i.e., worldwide sales). However, more information could be obtained by applying PLC concepts to more narrowly defined market segments, such as geographic regions or segments based on customer characteristics (e.g., by age, education level, etc.). For more on the PLC, see *Planning and Strategy with the PLC* in Chapter 20.

Adoption of New Products

The PLC is tied closely to the concept of the **Diffusion of Innovations**, which explains how information and acceptance of new products spreads through a market. Innovation can be viewed as anything new that solves needs by offering a significant advantage over existing methods (e.g., other products) customers use (see *Innovation* in Chapter 19). Innovation can encompass both highly advanced technology products, such as new computer chips, and non-technological products, such as a new soft drink. In fact, the seminal work of the Diffusion of Innovations concept occurred in the 1950s when researchers in the agricultural industry observed how new corn seeds were adopted by farmers in the U.S. Midwest. (6)

For marketers, a key concept to emerge from research on new product diffusion is the identification of adopter categories into which members of a market are likely to fall. These categories include:

Innovators

These adopters represent a small percentage of the market that is at the forefront of trying new products. These people are often viewed as enthusiasts and are eager to try new things, often without regard for the price. While a useful test ground for new products, marketers find Innovators often do not remain loyal as they continually seek new products.

Early Adopters

This group contains more members than the Innovators category. They share Innovators' enthusiasm for new products, though they tend to be more practical about their decisions. They also are eager to communicate their experiences with the Early Majority (next group) and, because of their influence, they are vital to the future success of new products (i.e., act as opinion leaders).

Early Majority

This represents the beginning of entry into the mass market (i.e., large number of potential customers). The Early Majority accounts for up to one-third of the overall market. The Early Majority like new things but tend to wait until they have received positive opinions from others (i.e., Early Adopters) before purchasing. Adoption by the Early Majority is key if a new product is to be profitable. On the other hand, many new products die quickly because they are not accepted beyond early trials by Innovators and Early Adopters and never reach mass market status.

Late Majority

Possibly as large as the Early Majority, this group takes a wait-and-see approach before trying something new. Marketers are likely to see their highest profits once this group starts to purchase.

Laggards

This is the last group to adopt something new and, in fact, may only do so if they have no other choice. Depending on the market this group can be large, though, because of their reluctance to accept new products, marketers are not inclined to direct much attention to them.

ADOPTER CATEGORIES AND THE PLC

The adopter categories help explain the shape of the life cycle for many products. For instance, consider how a new household cleaning product may become successful. At first Innovators may experience the product during the Development stage and then become the key targeted customers at the beginning of the Introduction stage. Early Adopters will also be targeted during the Introduction stage and their adoption will determine whether the product makes it to the Growth stage. If the product survives the Innovator and Early Adopter stages, it moves to the Growth stage where acceptance by the Early Majority means the product is entering the mass market. The product can continue to be successful as it is adopted by the Late Majority and, to a much lesser extent, by Laggards. Eventually product sales decline as Innovators and Early Adopters move on to something new and the cycle starts over.

It should be noted, an assumption of a person's placement in a certain adopter category for one product does not imply that person will also occupy the same category for other products. For example, someone who is an Innovator for one product may be a Laggard for another. However, with research marketers may find an individual's adopter classification for one product applies across a similar set of products. For instance, those classified as Innovators for new fitness routines may have a high probability of being categorized the same for high-performance energy drinks. This assumption may be necessary as an energy drink company develops its target marketing strategies in advance of launching a new product.

Additionally, marketers should not view an adopter category as being a single market segment. Instead, each adopter classification consists of multiple market segments that together make up the category. For example, the Early Majority may be made up of many markets that can be segmented on different variables, such as geographic location, age, income, etc. Therefore, aiming to satisfy all customers in an adopter category using a single marketing plan is likely not an effective strategy.

Criticisms of the PLC

The PLC has the ability to offer marketers guidance on strategies and tactics as they manage products through changing market conditions. Unfortunately, the PLC does not offer a perfect model of markets as it contains drawbacks preventing it from being applicable to all products. Among the problems cited are:

◆ Shape of Curve – Some product forms do not follow the traditional PLC curve. For instance, clothing may go through regular up and down cycles as styles are in fashion then out then in again. **Fad products**, such as a certain toy, may be popular for a period of time only to see sales drop dramatically until a future generation renews interest in the toy.

◆ Length of Stages – The PLC offers little help in determining how long each stage will last. For example, some products can exist in the Maturity stage for decades while others may be there for only a few months. As a result, it may be difficult to determine when adjustments to the Marketing Plan are required to meet the needs of different PLC stages.

◆ Competitor Reaction is Not Predictable – As we discuss in greater detail in Chapter 20, the PLC suggests competitor response occurs in a somewhat consistent pattern. For example, for a new product form, the PLC says competitors will not engage in strong brand-to-brand competition until the product form has gained a foothold in the market. The logic is that, until the market is established, it is in the best interest of all competitors to focus on building interest in the general product form and refrain from claiming one brand is better than another. However, competitors do not always conform to theoretical models. Some will always compete on brand first and leave it to others to build market interest for the product form. Arguments can also be made that competitors will respond differently than what the PLC suggests on such issues as pricing, number of product options and spending on declining products, to name a few.

◆ Patterns May Not Apply to All Global Markets – Marketers who base their strategies on how the PLC plays out in their home market may be surprised to see the PLC does not follow the same patterns when they enter other global markets. The reason is that customer behavior may be quite different within each market. For instance, a company may find that while customers in their home market easily understand how the company's new product could save them time in performing a certain task, customers in a foreign market may not easily see the connection.

◆ Impact of External Forces – The PLC assumes customers' decisions are primarily impacted by the marketing activities of the companies selling in the market. In fact, as we will discuss in more detail in Chapter 19, there are many other forces affecting a market which are not controlled by marketers. Such forces (e.g., social changes, technological innovation) can lead to changes in market demand at rates that are much more rapid than would occur if only an organization's marketing decisions were being changed (i.e., if everything was held constant except for the marketer's decisions). (7)

◆ Use for Forecasting – The impact of external forces may create challenges in using the PLC as a forecasting tool. For instance, factors not directly associated with the marketing activities of market competitors, such as economic conditions, may have a greater impact on a reduction in product demand. Consequently, what may be forecasted as a decline in the market, signaling a move to the Maturity stage, may be the result of declining economic conditions and not a decline in customers' interest in the product. In fact, it is likely demand for the product will recover to growth levels once economic conditions improve. Yet if a marketer does not recognize this and instead follows the strict guidance of the PLC, he/she may conclude that strategies should now change to those for a product in the Maturity stage (see *Planning and Strategy with the PLC* in Chapter 20). However, doing so may be an overreaction that could hurt market position and profitability.

◆ Stages Not Seamlessly Connected – Some high-tech marketers question whether one stage of the PLC naturally follows into another stage. In particular, technology consultant Geoffrey Moore suggests that for high-tech products targeted to business customers, a noticeable space or **chasm** occurs between the Introduction and Growth stages that can only be overcome by altering marketing strategy beyond what is suggested by the PLC. (8)

While not perfect, the PLC is a marketing tool that should be well understood by marketers since its underlying message, that markets are dynamic, supports the need for frequent marketing planning. Also, for many marketers the principles presented by the PLC will, in fact, prove to be very much representative of the conditions they will face in the market. We will return to the concepts associated with the PLC in much greater detail in *Planning and Strategy with the PLC* discussion in Chapter 20.

REFERENCES

1. "Laundry Detergent and Fabric Care Products – Tide." *Procter & Gamble*. https://tide.com.

2. "The Whole BIC Universe." *BIC*. https://us.bic.com.

3. For more on the Nickelodeon business model see: "Nickelodeon." *Wikipedia*. https://en.wikipedia.org/wiki/Nickelodeon.

4. For examples of products that experienced growth during the pandemic and continue to remain viable see: "17 Pandemic Innovations That Are Here to Stay." *Politico*. December 10, 2021. https://www.politico.com/news/2021/12/10/17-ways-covid-hit-fast-forward-on-the-future-523845.

5. Marketers should also pay close attention to the development of artificial intelligence tools as a source of new product ideas. While AI is still in its infancy in terms of assisting with product development, this will likely change in the coming years. For example see: Christian Terwiesch and Karl Ulrich. "M.B.A. Students vs. ChatGPT: Who Comes Up With More Innovative Ideas?" *The Wall Street Journal*. 9/9/2023. https://www.wsj.com/tech/ai/mba-students-vs-chatgpt-innovation-679edf3b.

6. Everett. M. Rogers. *Diffusion of Innovations, 5th ed.* The Free Press, 2003.

7. Of course, a once-in-a-century pandemic experienced with Covid-19 is an external force. However, unlike other forces, the rarity of this event is generally not something marketers consider when developing a new product strategy. Though for a few years after the end of this pandemic, it would not be a surprise to see marketers adding a special "unusual events" section to their plan just in case another pandemic or other unique event occurs.

8. Geoffrey Moore. *Crossing the Chasm, 3rd ed.* HarperBusiness, 2014.

Chapter 8: Distribution Decisions

Our coverage in Chapters 6 and 7 indicates product decisions may be the most important of all marketing decisions since these can lead directly to the reasons why customers decide to make a purchase (i.e., offer benefits that satisfy needs). But having a strong product does little good if customers are not able to easily and conveniently obtain it. With this in mind, we turn to the second major marketing decision area – distribution.

In this chapter, we cover the basics of distribution, including defining what channels of distribution are, examining the key functions and parties within a distribution system, and evaluating the role distribution serves within the overall marketing strategy. Also, we look at the major types of channel arrangements and the factors affecting the creation of effective distribution channels. We conclude with a discussion of different distribution design options and look at the issues global marketers face when distributing beyond their home country.

IMPORTANCE OF DISTRIBUTION

Distribution decisions focus on establishing the path, termed **channel of distribution**, which moves the product from the marketer to the customer. For most marketers, this means making decisions on the activities that will ultimately give customers access to and permit purchase of a marketer's product.

Distribution decisions are relevant for nearly all types of products. While it is easy to see how distribution decisions impact physical goods, such as laundry detergent or truck parts, distribution is also necessary for digital goods (e.g., television streaming, podcasts, online music) and services (e.g., income tax services). Whether a marketer is distributing products that are physical, digital or service, the bottom line is a marketer's distribution system must be both effective (i.e., delivers a good or service to the right place, in the right amount, and in the right condition) and efficient (i.e., delivers at the right time and for the right cost).

As discussed in Box 8-1, creating an effective and efficient distribution system requires the marketer carefully consider the benefits offered versus the costs for establishing and maintaining the system.

Box 8-1

DISTRIBUTION TRADE-OFF ANALYSIS: SERVICE LEVEL VS. COST

As part of developing a successful distribution strategy, marketers strive to provide an optimal level of service to their customers. However, "optimal" does not always translate into using the "best" options for distributing their product. Instead, the service level marketers choose for their distribution activities is often determined using trade-off analysis.

With service level trade-off analysis, the marketer compares the number and quality of distribution features (e.g., speed of delivery, ease of placing orders, order tracking, etc.) it would like to offer versus the cost of providing the features. While customers may want quick delivery, a marketer may find fast delivery is an expensive proposition leading the organization to lose money on a customer purchase.

Since most distribution activities represent a cost to the marketer, the distribution system choice may not always be the "best" available in terms of getting the product into customer's hands as fast as possible. Consequently, the marketer's choice for what is optimal will be determined by first analyzing distribution features and costs, and then evaluating how these will best fit within the marketer's overall objectives.

Distribution Activities

The primary activities involved in establishing the channel of distribution are presented in Table 8-1. While some marketers may choose to handle all distribution activities on their own, most marketers find many of these tasks are best left to others. Whether handled by the marketer or contracted to others, these activities are crucial when structuring a cost-effective and efficient distribution system.

TYPE OF CHANNEL MEMBERS

Channel activities may be carried out by the marketer or by specialist organizations that assist with certain functions. We can classify specialist organizations into two broad categories: resellers and specialty service firms.

Resellers

These organizations, also known within some industries as **intermediaries**, **distributors**, or **dealers**, generally purchase or take ownership of products from a marketer with the intention of selling to others. If a marketer utilizes multiple resellers within its distribution channel strategy this is called a **reseller network**, which is classified into several subcategories including:

◆ <u>Retailers</u> – Organizations selling products directly to final consumers.

◆ <u>Wholesalers</u> – Organizations purchasing products from suppliers and selling these to other resellers, such as retailers or other wholesalers.

◆ <u>Industrial Distributors</u> – Firms working in the business-to-business market selling products obtained from industrial suppliers. (1)

Specialty Service Firms

These are organizations providing additional services to help with the exchange of products, though they generally do not purchase the product:

◆ <u>Agents and Brokers</u> – Organizations working to bring suppliers and buyers together in exchange for a fee. (2)

◆ <u>Distribution Service Firms</u> – Offer services aiding in the movement of products, such as assistance with transportation, storage, and order processing.

◆ <u>Others</u> – This category includes firms providing additional services, such as insurance and transportation routing assistance.

Table 8-1: Channel of Distribution Activities

Distribution Activity	Explanation
Order Processing	Includes methods for handling customer purchase requests.
Inventory Management	Includes methods to ensure the right products in the right amount are available to fill customer orders.
Physical Handling	Includes methods to prepare products for movement that reduces damage.
Storage	Includes facilities for holding inventory.
Shipping	Includes providing means for getting the products to customers in a timely manner.
Display	Includes having resellers place products in locations that can be seen by customers.
Promotion	Includes the need for resellers to assist in communicating products to the target market.
Selling	Includes the need for resellers to provide personal promotion to help sell products.
Information Feedback	Includes the need for methods to encourage resellers and customers to provide marketing research information to the marketer.

WHY DISTRIBUTION HELP IS NEEDED

As noted, distribution channels often require the assistance of others in order for the marketer to reach its target market. But why exactly does a company need others to help with the distribution of its product? Wouldn't an organization that handles its own distribution functions be in a better position to exercise control over product sales and potentially earn higher profits? Also, doesn't the internet make it much easier to distribute products, which then lessens the need for others to be involved in selling a marketer's product?

While, on the surface, it may seem to make sense for an organization to operate its own distribution channel (i.e., handling all aspects of distribution), there are many factors preventing them from doing so. While companies can do without the assistance of certain channel members, for many marketers some level of channel partnership is needed. For example, L.L. Bean, which sells a large percentage of its products over the internet and through catalogs, is successful without utilizing other resellers to sell their products. However, L.L. Bean still needs assistance with certain parts of the distribution process, primarily with delivery of customer orders (e.g., FedEx, UPS and USPS). In L.L. Bean's case, creating its own transportation system makes little sense given how large such a system would need to be in order to service their customer base. Therefore, by using shipping companies, L.L. Bean is taking advantage of the benefits these services offer to the company and to its customers.

When choosing a distribution strategy, a marketer must determine what value a channel member adds to its products. Remember, as we discussed in Chapter 6, customers assess a product's value by looking at many factors, including those surrounding the product (i.e., augmented product). Several surrounding features can be directly influenced by channel members, such as customer service, delivery, and availability. Consequently, selecting a channel partner involves a value analysis in the same way customers make purchase decisions. That is, the marketer must assess the benefits received from utilizing a channel partner versus the cost incurred for using their services.

It should be noted, that while we talk about marketers "selecting a channel partner," it is necessary to recognize that the channel member is the one who ultimately decides which products they will distribute. In most industries, it is not possible for a channel member to handle all products sold by all suppliers(e.g., a retailer cannot carry all products). As a result, competition between suppliers to gain distribution through a specific channel member can be intense. To gain access to a channel member often requires a supplying company have strong knowledge of the market. Additionally, it requires the marketer have a well-developed marketing strategy that will help in persuading a channel member to offer their services to the marketer.

Benefits Offered by Channel Members

Marketers seeking distribution assistance will find that channel members can offer a number of advantages including:

◆ Offer Cost Savings Through Specialization – Members of the distribution channel are specialists in what they do and can often perform tasks better and at lower cost than companies that do not have distribution experience. Marketers attempting to handle too many aspects of distribution may end up exhausting company resources as they learn how to distribute, resulting in the company being "a jack of all trades but master of none."

◆ Reduce Exchange Time – Not only are channel members able to reduce costs by being experienced at what they do, they often perform their job more rapidly resulting in faster product delivery. This can be seen in Box 8-2.

◆ Allow Customers to Conveniently Shop for Variety – Marketers have to understand what customers want in their shopping experience. Referring back to our grocery store example, consider a world without grocery stores and instead each marketer of grocery products sells through its own stores. As it is now, many customers find shopping to be a time-consuming activity, but consider what would happen if customers had to visit many different retailers each week to satisfy their grocery needs. Hence, resellers within the channel of distribution serve two fundamental needs: 1) they give customers the products they want by purchasing from many suppliers (termed **accumulation** and **assortment** services); and 2) they make it convenient to purchase by offering products in a single location.

Box 8-2

EFFICIENCY IN DELIVERY

The evolution of channels of distribution can be tied directly to the need for efficiency in the distribution system. For instance, consider what would happen if a grocery store received direct shipment from EVERY manufacturer that sells products in the store. This delivery system would be chaotic as hundreds of trucks line up each day to make deliveries, many of which would consist of only a few boxes. On a busy day, a truck may sit for hours waiting for space so it can unload its products.

Instead, a better distribution scheme may have the grocery store purchasing its supplies from a grocery wholesaler (discussed in Chapter 10) that has its own warehouse for handling simultaneous shipments from a large number of suppliers. The wholesaler distributes to the store in the quantities the store needs, on a schedule that works for the store, and often in a single truck, all of which speeds up the time it takes to get the product on the store's shelves.

◆ Resellers Sell Smaller Quantities – Channel members, and particularly resellers, allow purchases in quantities that work for their customers. This is an especially valuable channel function because handling orders for small quantities is not what works best for most suppliers. Suppliers prefer to ship their products in large quantities since this is more cost effective than shipping smaller amounts (see Box 10-1 in Chapter 10). The ability of intermediaries to purchase large quantities but to resell them in smaller quantities (termed **bulk breaking**), provides customers with two key advantages. First, it makes products available to those who do not want large quantities, such as a small retail store. Second, the reseller is able to pass along to its customers a significant portion of the cost savings gained by purchasing in large volume, thus allowing its customers to purchase smaller quantities at competitive prices.

◆ Create Sales – Channel partners are at the front line when it comes to creating demand for the marketer's product. In some cases, resellers perform an active selling role using persuasive techniques to encourage customers to purchase a marketer's product. In other cases, they encourage sales of the product through their own advertising efforts and using other promotional means, such as special product displays and product sampling. (3)

◆ Offer Access to More Customers – For marketers, channel partners may offer access to more customers in a much shorter time frame than the marketer can accomplish on its own. This can be particularly beneficial to organizations that are new to a market and do not have an established distribution network, or existing organizations that have had difficulty gaining distribution using their own methods.

◆ Offer Financial Support – Channel partners often provide programs enabling their customers to more easily purchase products by offering financial options that ease payment requirements. These programs may include allowing customers to purchase on credit, purchase using an extended payment plan, delay the start of payments, and allow trade-in or exchange options.

◆ Provide Information – Companies utilizing channel members for selling their products depend on these distributors to provide information that can help improve the product. High-level intermediaries, such as major retailers, may offer their suppliers real-time access to sales data, including information showing how products are selling by such characteristics as geographic location, type of customer, and product location (e.g., where located within a store, where found on a website). Even if such high-level information is not available, marketers can often count on resellers to provide feedback as to how customers are responding to products. This feedback can occur either through surveys or interviews with a reseller's employees, or by requesting a reseller to allow the marketer to survey the reseller's customers. (4)

Costs of Utilizing Channel Members

While distribution assistance can be beneficial to a marketer, there are several potential drawbacks that must be considered prior to establishing these relationships:

◆ Loss of Revenue – Channel members are not likely to offer services to a marketer unless they see financial advantages in doing so. Firms obtain payment for their services as either direct payment (e.g., marketer pays specialty service firm for shipping costs) or, in the case of resellers, by charging their customers more than what they paid the marketer for acquiring the product (see *Markup Pricing* in Chapter 18). For the latter, marketers have a good idea of what the final customer will pay for their product, which means the marketer must charge less when selling the product to resellers. In these situations, marketers are not reaping the full sale price by using resellers, which they may be able to do if they sold directly to the customer.

◆ Loss of Communication Control – Marketers not only give up revenue when using channel partners, they may also give up control of the message being conveyed to customers. If the reseller engages in communication activities, such as when a retailer uses salespeople to sell to customers, the marketer is no longer controlling what is being said about the product. This can lead to miscommunication problems with customers, especially if the reseller embellishes or makes misstatements about the benefits the product provides. While marketers can influence what is being said by offering sales training to resellers' salespeople, they lack ultimate control of the message.

◆ Loss of Product Importance – Once a product is out of the marketer's hands, the importance of that product is left up to channel members. If there are pressing issues in the channel, such as transportation problems, or if a competitor is using promotional incentives in an effort to push its product through resellers, the marketer's product may not receive as much of the resellers' attention as the marketer feels it should.

CHANNEL ARRANGEMENTS

The distribution channel consists of many parties each seeking to meet their own business objectives. Clearly for the channel to work well, relationships between channel members must be strong. For product distribution to flow smoothly, each member must understand and trust others on whom they depend. For instance, a small sporting goods retailer trusts a wholesaler to deliver required items on time in order to meet customer demand, while the wholesaler counts on the retailer to place regular orders and to make prompt payments.

Relationships in a channel are in large part a function of the arrangement that occurs between the members. These arrangements can be divided in two main categories: independent and dependent.

Independent Channel Arrangement

Under this arrangement, a channel member negotiates deals with others that do not result in binding relationships. In other words, a channel member is free to make whatever arrangements they feel is in its best interest. This so-called **conventional distribution arrangement** often leads to significant conflict as individual members decide what is best for them and not necessarily for the entire channel (see *Channel Conflict* discussion below). On the other hand, an independent channel arrangement is less restrictive than dependent arrangements by making it easier for a channel member to move away from relationships they feel are not working to its benefit.

Dependent Channel Arrangement

With a dependent channel arrangement, a channel member feels tied to one or more members of the distribution channel. Sometimes referred to as **vertical marketing systems**, this approach makes it more difficult for an individual member to make changes to how products are distributed. However, the dependent approach provides much more stability and consistency since members are united in their goals.

The dependent channel arrangement can be further broken down into three types:

Corporate

Under this arrangement, a supplier operates its own distribution system in a manner that produces an integrated channel. This occurs most frequently in the retail industry where a supplier operates a chain of retail stores. Starbucks is a company that does this. They import and process coffee, and then sell it under its own brand name in thousands of its own stores. It should be mentioned that Starbucks also distributes its products in other ways, such as through grocery stores and online sales (see *Multichannel or Hybrid System* discussion below).

Contractual

With this approach, a legal document obligates members to agree on how a product is distributed. Often times, the agreement specifically spells out which activities each member is permitted to perform or not perform. This type of arrangement can occur in several formats including:

- Wholesaler-sponsored – where a wholesaler brings together and manages many independent retailers, including having the retailers operate under the same name

- Retailer-sponsored – this format also brings together retailers, but the retailers are responsible for managing the relationship

- Franchised Arrangement – where a central organization controls nearly all activities of its members (5)

- Licensing Agreement – where a central organization controls some activities of its channel members, but it does not control all activities of the members

Administrative

In certain dependent channel arrangements, a single member may dominate the decisions within the channel. These situations occur when one channel member has achieved a significant power position (see *Channel Power* discussion below). This most likely occurs if a manufacturer has brands that are in strong demand by its target markets (e.g., Apple) or if a retailer has significant size and market coverage (e.g., Walmart). In most cases, the arrangement is understood to occur and is not bound by legal or financial arrangements.

FACTORS IN CREATING DISTRIBUTION CHANNELS

Like most marketing decisions, a great deal of research and thought must go into determining how to carry out distribution activities in a way that meets a marketer's objectives. In particular, the marketer must consider three key issues when establishing a distribution system: marketing decision issues; infrastructure issues; and channel relationship issues.

Marketing Decision Issues

Distribution strategy can be shaped by how decisions are made in other marketing areas. These include:

PRODUCT ISSUES

The nature of the product often dictates the distribution options available, especially if the product requires special handling. For instance, companies selling delicate or fragile products, such as flowers, look for shipping arrangements that are different from those sought by companies selling extremely tough or durable products, such as steel beams.

PROMOTION ISSUES

Besides issues related to physical handling of products, distribution decisions are affected by the type of promotional activities needed to sell products to customers. For products needing extensive salesperson-to-customer contact (e.g., automobile purchases), the distribution options are different compared to products where customers typically require little or no assistance when making a purchase (e.g., bread purchases).

PRICING ISSUES

The desired price at which a marketer seeks to sell its product can impact how they choose to distribute. As previously mentioned, the inclusion of resellers in a marketer's distribution strategy may affect a product's pricing since each member of the channel seeks to make a profit for their contribution to the sale of the product. If too many channel members are involved, the eventual selling price may be too high to meet sales targets, in which case the marketer may explore other distribution options.

TARGET MARKET ISSUES

A distribution system is only effective if customers can obtain the product. Consequently, a key decision in setting up a channel arrangement is for the marketer to choose the approach that reaches customers in the most effective way possible. The most important decision with regard to reaching the target market is to determine the level of distribution coverage needed to meet customers' needs.

Distribution Coverage

Distribution coverage is measured in terms of the **intensity** of product availability. For the most part, distribution coverage decisions are of most concern to consumer products companies, though there are many industrial products that also must decide how much coverage to give its products.

There are three main levels of distribution coverage – mass, selective, and exclusive.

- Mass Coverage – The mass coverage strategy (also known as **intensive distribution**) attempts to distribute products widely in nearly all locations in which that type of product is sold. This level of distribution is only feasible for relatively low-priced products that appeal to extremely large target markets (e.g., consumer convenience products). A product such as Coca-Cola is a classic example since it is available in a wide variety of locations, including grocery stores, convenience stores, vending machines, hotels, and many, many more. With such a large number of locations selling the product, the cost of distribution is extremely high and must be offset with very high sales volume.

- Selective Coverage – Under selective coverage, the marketer deliberately seeks to limit the locations in which its product is sold. To the non-marketer, it may seem strange for an organization not to want its product distributed in every possible location. However, the logic of this strategy is tied to the size and nature of the product's target market. Products with selective coverage appeal to smaller, more focused target markets (e.g., consumer shopping products) compared to the size of target markets for mass marketed products. Consequently, because the market size is smaller, the number of locations needed to support the distribution of the product is fewer.

- Exclusive Coverage – Some high-end products target narrow markets having a relatively small number of customers. These customers are often characterized as "discriminating" in their taste for products and seek to satisfy some of their needs with high-quality, though expensive products. Additionally, many buyers of high-end products require a high level of customer service from the channel member from whom they purchase. These characteristics of the target market may lead the marketer to sell its products through a very select or exclusive group of resellers. Another type of exclusive distribution may not involve high-end products, but rather products only available in selected locations, such as company-owned stores. While these products may or may not be higher priced compared to competitive products, the fact these are only available in company outlets gives exclusivity to the distribution.

We conclude this section by noting that while the three distribution coverage options just discussed serve as a useful guide for envisioning how distribution intensity works, the advent of the digital technology has brought into question the effectiveness of these schemes. For all intents and purposes, all products available for purchase over the internet or through mobile devices are distributed in the same way – mass coverage. So, a better way to look at the three levels is to consider these as options for distribution coverage of products that are purchased by customers at a physical location (i.e., walk-in to purchase)..

Infrastructure Issues

The marketer's desire to establish a distribution channel is often complicated by what options are available to them within a market. While in the planning stages the marketer has an idea of how the distribution plan should be executed, the organization may find that certain parts of the distribution channel may not be what they expected. For example, a supplier of high-end, specialty snack foods may find a promising target market for their products is located in a mountain ski area in Colorado. However, the company may also discover that no suitable distributor in that area possesses the required refrigerated storage space that is necessary to store the product in the proper way specified by the marketer.

This concern is even greater when a marketer looks to expand into international markets. Marketers often find the type of distribution system they are used to employing is lacking or even nonexistent (e.g., poor transportation, few acceptable retail outlets). In fact, depending on the type of product, a marketer could be prevented from entering a foreign market because there are no suitable options for distributing the product. More likely, marketers will find options for distributing their product but these options (see *Distribution in Global Markets* discussion below) may be different, and possibly inferior, from what has made them successful in their home country. While viewed as risky, organizations entering foreign markets often have little choice but to accept the distribution structure that is in place if they want to enter these markets.

Relationship Issues

An appropriate distribution strategy takes into account not only marketing decisions, but also considers how relationships within the channel of distribution can impact the marketer's product. In this section, we examine three such issues:

CHANNEL POWER

A channel can be made up of many parties each adding value to the products purchased by customers. However, some parties (see Box 8-3) within the channel may carry greater weight than others. In marketing terms, this is called channel power, which refers to the influence one party within a channel has over other channel members. When power is exerted by a channel member, they are often in the position to make demands of others. For instance, they may demand better financial terms (e.g., will buy only if prices are lowered, will sell only if suggested price is higher) or demand their channel members perform certain tasks (e.g., do more marketing to customers, perform more product services).

Box 8-3

WHO HAS THE POWER

Channels of distribution can be dominated by certain channel members who hold something of value that is needed by other members. Examples of those holding power include:

Backend or Product Power

This occurs when a product manufacturer or service provider markets a brand that has a high level of customer demand. The marketer of the brand is often in a power position since other channel members have little choice but to carry the brand or risk losing customers. Organizations considered having this power include Apple and Procter & Gamble.

Middle or Wholesale Power

This occurs when a channel intermediary, such as a wholesaler, services smaller retailers with products obtained from a large number of manufacturers or product suppliers. In this situation, the wholesaler can exert power since small retailers, who purchase only a few items at a time, are often not in the position to directly purchase products cost-effectively from manufacturers or in as much variety as what is offered by the wholesaler. Organizations consider having this power include Ace Hardware (hardware stores) and Independent Grocers Alliance (grocery stores).

Front or Retailer Power

As the name suggests, the power in this situation rests with the retailer who can command considerable concessions from its suppliers. This type of power is most prevalent when the retailer generates a significant percentage of sales in the market it serves and others in the channel are dependent on sales generated by the retailer. For example, small suppliers looking to sell to Walmart may be surprised to see how much information the world's largest retailer demands from its suppliers. The requirements include having financial information listed on Dun & Bradstreet, showing evidence of product liability insurance, and allowing for an onsite factory audit. (6)

CHANNEL CONFLICT

In an effort to increase product sales, marketers are often attracted by the notion that sales can grow if the marketer expands distribution by adding additional resellers. However, such decisions must be handled carefully so that existing dealers do not feel the new distributors are encroaching on their customers and siphoning potential business. For marketers, channel strategy designed to expand product distribution may, in fact, do the opposite if existing channel members feel conflict will arise if the marketer increases the number of resellers. If existing members sense a conflict and feel the marketer is not sensitive to their needs, they may choose to stop handling the marketer's products. (7)

NEED FOR LONG-TERM COMMITMENTS

Channel decisions have long-term consequences for marketers since efforts to establish new relationships can take an extensive period of time, while ending existing relationships can prove difficult. For instance, Company A, a marketer of kitchen cabinets that wants to change distribution strategy, may decide to stop selling its product line through industrial supply companies, who distribute cabinets to building contractors, and instead sell through large retail home centers. If, in the future, Company A decides to once again enter the industrial supply market they may run into resistance since supply companies may have replaced Company A's product line with other products and, given what happened to the previous relationship, may be reluctant to deal with Company A again. Considering these potential problems, Company A may need to give serious thought to whether breaking its long-term relationship with industrial suppliers is in the company's best interest.

OVERALL DISTRIBUTION DESIGN

When settling on a design for its distribution network, the marketer may have several potential options from which to choose. We stress that distribution options "may" be available but are not guaranteed. This is because important marketing decision factors (e.g., product, promotion, pricing, target markets), infrastructure limitations, or the nature of distribution channel relationships may not permit the marketer to pursue a particular option. For example, selling through a desired retailer may not be feasible if the retailer refuses to handle a product.

For marketers, the choice of distribution design comes down to selecting between direct or indirect methods, or in some cases choosing both.

Direct Distribution System

With a direct distribution system, the marketer reaches the intended final user of its product by distributing the product directly to the customer. That is, there are no other parties involved in the distribution process that take ownership of the product. The direct system can be further divided by the method of communication taking place when a sale occurs. These methods are:

◆ Direct Marketing Systems – With this system, the customer places the order either through information gained from non-personal contact with the marketer, such as by visiting the marketer's website, or through personal communication with a customer representative, who is not a salesperson, such as through toll-free telephone ordering.

◆ Direct Retail Systems – This type of system exists when a product marketer also operates its own physical retail outlets under an independent channel arrangement. As previously discussed, Starbucks' own stores would fall into this category.

◆ Personal Selling Systems – The key to this direct distribution system is that a person, whose primary job responsibilities include creating and managing sales (e.g., salesperson), is involved in the distribution process, generally by persuading the buyer to place an order. While the order itself may not be handled by the salesperson (e.g., buyer physically places the order online or by phone), the salesperson plays a role in generating the sale.

◆ Assisted Marketing Systems – Under this distribution system, a seller relies on others to provide information about their products but handles distribution directly to the customer. The classic example of assisted marketing systems is eBay, which helps bring sellers and buyers together for a fee. Others including agents and brokers (discussed in Chapter 16) would also fall into this category.

Indirect Distribution System

With an indirect distribution system, the marketer reaches the intended final user with the help of others. These resellers usually take ownership of the product though, in some cases, they may sell products on a consignment basis (i.e., only pay the supplying company if the product is sold). Under this system, intermediaries may be expected to assume many responsibilities to help sell the product. Indirect methods include:

◆ Single-Party Selling System – Under this system, the marketer engages another party who sells and distributes directly to the final customer. This is most likely to occur when the marketer sells products directly to large store-based retail chains or through online retailers.

◆ Multiple-Party Selling System – This indirect distribution system has the product passing through two or more distributors before reaching the final customer. The most likely scenario is when a wholesaler purchases from the manufacturer and sells the product to retailers.

Multichannel or Hybrid System

In cases where a marketer utilizes more than one distribution design, the marketer is following a multichannel or hybrid distribution system. Starbucks follows this approach as its distribution design not only includes using a direct retail system by selling their products in company-owned stores, but they also utilize several other distribution systems, including a single-party selling system by selling through grocery stores and a direct marketing system as they sell product via an online store.

By using a multichannel approach, a marketer can expand distribution and reach a wider market. However, as we discussed, the marketer must be careful with this approach due to the potential for channel conflict.

DISTRIBUTION IN GLOBAL MARKETS

Organizations looking to distribute outside their home market may experience challenges that are significantly greater than what they face in their home market. Marketers, who are new to selling internationally, often discover the learning-curve for doing this effectively can be quite steep. In addition to potentially significant cultural differences that exist between customers in their home market and targeted customers in a new foreign market, marketers may find many other barriers to effective distribution, including legal, political, and infrastructure limitations (see *Infrastructure Issues* discussion above). They may also face financial burdens in terms of differences in exchange rates, heightened shipping expense, and additional packaging costs. Consequently, upon entering a new foreign market, many companies discover that strategies they utilized successfully in their home market do not work in the new market.

Because organizations often find it difficult to replicate their success when entering new markets, they may need to consider different strategies for establishing a marketing presence beyond their home country. In general, marketers have available the following options for gaining distribution in global markets:

◆ Exporting – With this distribution method, a marketer does not set up a physical presence in a foreign market. Instead, product is shipped by the company to buyers in the foreign market. In the simplest arrangement, a marketer will accept customer orders on their website then arrange for international shipment to reach the customer (e.g., FedEx shipment). In some exporting arrangements, the marketer negotiates with a marketing firm located in the foreign country to assist in generating orders, managing customers, and possibly handling some distribution activities. The main benefit of the export option is that risks and costs are relatively low. On the downside, exporting may not enable a company to realize full demand for the product since the marketer does not have a local presence. Therefore, the marketer cannot dedicate full attention to developing the market. (8)

◆ Joint Operation – In general, this is a relationship where two or more organizations team to market products. For instance, a company may agree on a licensing arrangement where the marketer allows another company in a foreign country to handle its products. This arrangement may even extend to allowing the foreign company to manufacture the product. Other forms of joint operation occur when a marketer develops a partnership with a company in the host country, often resulting in the creation of a new company. Ownership in such an arrangement may be equally split or one partner may have a greater percentage of the final company. Under this arrangement, the risk is split between the partnering organizations.

◆ <u>Direct Investment</u> – This represents the most involved business situation where the marketer owns nearly all key aspects of conducting business in another country. The main advantage with direct investment is the control it offers as the company can make all decisions and retain all profits. However, the risks are quite high as the marketer must often invest heavily to establish and maintain operations.

Finally, when it comes to global distribution, marketers must be aware of unauthorized distributors selling the marketer's product. Often such distributors operate in a "**gray or grey market**," where they obtain products from legitimate distributors, who may be approved to handle a product but are not approved to sell to certain distribution outlets. These unauthorized distributors can be difficult to control and, depending on the country in which they are selling the product, their activities may prove challenging for the marketer to stop. (9)

REFERENCES

1. To learn more about industrial distributors and to see a listing of the top companies see: "MDM Top Distributors List." *Modern Distribution Management*. https://www.mdm.com/top_distributors.

2. For more information on agents and brokers see *Wholesale Formats* in Chapter 10.

3. For detailed discussion of the various marketing promotions available to marketers see Chapters 11 - 16.

4. For an example of services and support offered by a wholesaler to independent retail customers see: "Our Services." *C&S Wholesale Grocers*. https://www.cswg.com/services.

5. For more on franchising see Box 9-1 Franchising Basics in Chapter 9.

6. For more details on Walmart's requirements for potential suppliers see: "Suppliers." *Walmart*. https://corporate.walmart.com/suppliers.

7. An example of channel conflict can be seen in the retail industry. Following the Covid-19 pandemic many suppliers raised prices above existing inflation rates which caused tension with their customers including big names retailers, such as Walmart and Whole Foods. For more see: Jaewon Kang. "Whole Foods Asks Suppliers to Lower Prices." *The Wall Street Journal*. January 31, 2023. https://www.wsj.com/articles/whole-foods-asks-suppliers-to-lower-prices-as-costs-ebb-11675115155.

8. To gain more understanding of what is involved in exporting see: "Exporting Mechanics Training Video Series." *United States International Trade Administration*. https://www.export.gov/training.

9. For more on gray (grey) market goods including examples see: "Grey Market." *Wikipedia*. https://en.wikipedia.org/wiki/Grey_market.

Chapter 9: Retailing

In an ideal business world, most marketers would prefer to handle all their distribution activities by way of the corporate channel arrangement we discussed in Chapter 8. Such an arrangement gives the marketer total control in dealing with their customers, which can make it easier to build strong, long-term relationships. Unfortunately, for many marketing organizations a corporate channel arrangement is not feasible. Whether due to high cost or lack of experience needed to run a channel efficiently, most marketing organizations must seek help from third-party channel members in order for their products to reach customers. For most organizations that sell goods and services this means enlisting the assistance of resellers.

In this chapter, we begin our discussion of resellers by examining the role retailers serve in reselling a marketer's products. We begin by setting out reasons why selecting resellers is an important decision that should not be taken lightly. We then turn our attention to a detailed look at retailing, which in terms of sales volume and number of employees is one of the largest sectors of most economies. We show that retailing is quite diverse and marketers, who want to distribute through retailers, must be familiar with the differences that exist among different retail options. The chapter concludes with a look at the key concerns facing today's retailers.

IMPORTANCE OF RESELLERS

As we discussed in Chapter 8, many marketers must enlist the assistance of others to get their products into the hands of customers. This is especially the case for marketers selling to the final consumer, though business-to-business marketers also face such decisions. One main type of channel member linking marketers to their customers is the reseller, who purchases products from supplying firms and then resells these to its customers. Examples of resellers include retailers, wholesalers, and industrial distributors.

Choosing a reseller for product distribution is crucial since the characteristics of a reseller, including how they handle customers, can affect how customers view the marketer's organization and the products it offers. For instance, a reseller's reputation (e.g., high-quality vs. low-quality) and customers' experience when they interact with the reseller to make a purchase (e.g., how long it takes to be serviced), may impact how customers feel about the products they purchase through the reseller. Consequently, marketers must take into consideration many issues when selecting a reseller including:

◆ Is the target market served by the reseller the same as the target market sought by the marketer?

◆ Does the reseller offer the expertise needed to address customers' questions regarding the marketer's product?

◆ Will the reseller help the marketer in promotional activities?

◆ Will the reseller share customer information with the marketer?

◆ Does the reseller carry competitor's products?

Once resellers have been identified a much bigger task still lies ahead for the marketer: convincing the reseller to enter a relationship.

How to Establish Reseller Relationships

Convincing resellers to handle a product requires marketers use the same marketing skills they use to sell to their final customers. And, just as they do when selling to the final customer, marketers' first step when selling to resellers is to identify their needs, which are much different than those of the final customer. For instance, when it comes to selling to resellers, marketers should consider the following reseller needs:

◆ Products – Primarily resellers seek products of interest to their customers. For instance, a buyer for a large retailer may personally not like a particular product but, nonetheless, will purchase it as long as customers are willing to buy. Thus, selling to resellers means the marketer must show convincing evidence the customers serviced by the reseller will purchase the products.

◆ Delivery – Resellers want the product delivered on time and in good condition to meet customer demand and avoid inventory out-of-stocks. A product supplier must present a clearly articulated distribution plans when convincing resellers to sell their product.

◆ Profit Margin – Resellers are in business to make money so a key factor in their decision to handle a product is how much money they will make on each product sold. They expect the difference (i.e., margin) between their cost for acquiring the product from a supplier and the price they charge to sell the product to their customers will be sufficient to meet their profit objectives.

◆ Other Incentives – Besides profit margin, resellers may want other incentives to entice them, especially if they are required to give extra effort selling the product. These incentives may be in the form of additional free products or even bonuses (e.g., money, free trips) for achieving sales goals (see *Trade Sales Promotions* in Chapter 14).

◆ Packaging – Resellers want to handle products as easily as possible and want their suppliers to ship and sell products in packages that fit within their system. For example, retailers may require products be a certain size or design so these fit on their shelves, or the shipping package must fit within the wholesaler's warehouse or receiving dock space.

♦ <u>Training</u> – Some marketers require their resellers have strong knowledge of the products they are distributing. This is particularly pertinent in selling situations where product demonstrations are needed. To address the need for reseller knowledge, marketers must consider offering training to ensure resellers present the product accurately.

♦ <u>Promotional Help</u> – Resellers often seek additional help from the product supplier to promote the product to customers. Such help may come in the form of funding for advertisements, online how-to videos, point-of-purchase product materials, or in-store demonstrations.

With an understanding of what resellers are, we now turn our attention to one of the most important types of resellers – retailers.

WHAT IS RETAILING?

Retailing is defined as selling products to consumers for their personal use. A retailer is a reseller from which consumers purchase products. This includes businesses selling physical goods and also those selling services (e.g., restaurants). Retailing is one of the largest sectors of most economies. In the U.S. alone, there are over 1 million retail outlets employing nearly 16 million (1) and generating over $7 trillion (2) in annual sales.

In the vast majority of retail situations, the organization from which a consumer makes purchases is a reseller of products obtained from others and is not the product manufacturer. (Though as we discussed in Chapter 8, some manufacturers do operate their own retail outlets in a corporate channel arrangement.) While consumers are the retailer's buyers, a consumer does not always buy from retailers. For instance, when a consumer purchases from another consumer (e.g., eBay), the purchase would not be classified as a retail purchase. This distinction can get confusing but, in the United States and other countries, the dividing line is whether the party selling to consumers is classified as a business (e.g., legal and tax purposes) or the party is selling as a hobby without legal business standing.

Benefits of Retailers

As a reseller, retailers offer many benefits to suppliers and customers as we discussed in Chapter 8. The major benefits for each include:

♦ <u>Access to Customers</u> – For suppliers, the most valuable benefits provided by retailers are the opportunities they offer for reaching the supplier's target market, building product demand through retail promotions, and providing consumer feedback. The knowledge and skills offered by retailers are key for generating sales, profits, and customer loyalty for suppliers (see *Concerns of Retailers* discussion below).

♦ <u>Access to Product</u> – For consumers, the most significant benefits offered by retailers relate to the ability to purchase products that may not otherwise be easily available if the consumers had to deal directly with product suppliers.

In particular, retailers provide consumers with the ability to purchase small quantities of a wide assortment of products at prices that are considered reasonably affordable. Additionally, when it comes to retailers with physical locations (e.g., retail stores), these are likely to be located near the retailer's target market. For consumers, having retail stores in close proximity to where they live or work enables them to acquire products faster than if they had to visit a supplier's facility or wait for an internet purchase to be delivered.

WAYS TO CLASSIFY RETAILERS

There are many ways retailers can be classified depending on the characteristics being evaluated. We separate retailers based on six factors directly related to key marketing decisions:

◆ Target Markets Served

◆ Product Offerings

◆ Distribution Method

◆ Pricing Structure

◆ Promotional Emphasis

◆ Service Level

and on one operational factor:

◆ Ownership Structure

However, these groupings are not meant to be mutually exclusive. In fact, in some way all retailers can be placed into each classification.

Target Markets Served

The first classification looks at the type of markets a retailer intends to target. These categories are identical to the levels of distribution classification scheme discussed in Chapter 8 and include:

◆ Mass Market – Mass market retailers appeal to the largest market possible by selling products of interest to nearly all consumers. With such a large market from which to draw potential customers, competition among these retailers is often quite fierce.

◆ Specialty Market – Retailers categorized as servicing the specialty market are likely to target buyers looking for products having certain features that go beyond mass marketed products, such as customers who require more advanced product options or a higher level of customer service. While not as large as the mass market, the target market serviced by specialty retailers can be sizable.

◆ <u>Exclusive Market</u> – Appealing to this market means appealing to discriminating customers who are often willing to pay a premium for products containing special or unique features, and offering highly personalized services. Since this target market is generally small, the number of retailers addressing this market within a given geographic area may also be small.

Products Carried

Under this classification, retailers are divided based on the width (i.e., number of different product lines) and depth (i.e., number of different products within a product line) of the products they carry. Within this classification are:

◆ <u>General Merchandisers</u> – These retailers carry a wide range of product categories (i.e., broad width), though the number of different items within a particular product line is generally limited (i.e., shallow depth). A retailer such as Target would be considered a general merchandiser.

◆ <u>Multiple Lines Specialty Merchandisers</u> – Retailers classified in this category stock a limited number of product lines (i.e., narrow width). However, within the product groups they handle, these retailers often offer a greater selection (i.e., extended depth) than is offered by general merchandisers. For example, a home improvement retailer, such as Home Depot, would fall into this category.

◆ <u>Single Line Specialty Merchandisers</u> – Some retailers limit their offerings to just one product line (i.e., very narrow width), and sometimes only one product (i.e., very shallow depth). This can be seen online where a small website may sell a single product, such as computer gaming software. Another example may be a small jewelry store that only handles watches and other timepieces.

Distribution Method

Retailers sell in many formats with some requiring consumers visit a physical location while others sell to customers within a virtual space. It should be noted that many retailers are not tied to a single distribution method but operate using multiple store-based and non-store methods.

Store-Based Sellers

By far the predominant method consumers use to obtain products is to acquire these by physically visiting retail outlets (also called **brick-and-mortar retailers**). Store outlets can be described based on characteristics of the building in which it operates. One distinguishing building characteristic is whether a retailer is physically connected to other businesses, such as other retail stores. These include:

● <u>Stand-Alone</u> – These are retail outlets that are not connected to other businesses.

● <u>Strip-Shopping Center</u> – A retail arrangement where two or more businesses are physically connected or share physical resources (e.g., share parking lot).

● <u>Shopping Area</u> – A local center of retail operations containing many retail outlets that may or may not be physically connected but are in close proximity to each other, such as a city shopping district.

● <u>Regional Shopping Mall</u> – Consists of a large, self-contained shopping area with many connected outlets.

Non-Store Sellers

Under this approach, retailers sell products to customers who do not physically visit a retail outlet. In fact, in many cases customers make their purchase from within their own homes or on mobile devices when outside the home.

- Online Sellers – The fastest growing retail distribution method allows consumers to purchase products via the internet and mobile apps. In most cases, delivery is then handled by a third-party shipping service, though several retailers now offer pickup of online orders at physical locations, such as a store or a **lockbox**.

- Direct Marketers – This category includes retailers principally selling via direct methods other than online (e.g., television, catalog). While these retailers may have a central location that handles customer orders, these orders are primarily received via phone or mail rather than in-person customer shopping.

- Vending – While purchasing through vending machines does require the consumer to physically visit a location, it is considered non-store retailing as the vending operations are not located at the vending company's place of business.

Pricing Strategy

Retailers can be classified based on their general pricing strategy. Retailers must decide whether their approach is to use price as a competitive advantage or to seek competitive advantage in non-price ways. The key pricing strategy options are:

- Discount Pricing – Discount retailers are best known for selling low-priced products having a low profit margin (i.e., price minus cost). To make profits these retailers look to sell in high volume. Typically discount retailers operate with low overhead costs by vigorously controlling operational spending on such things as real estate (e.g., locate in less expensive areas), store design issues (e.g., less elaborate store layout), and by offering fewer services to their customers (e.g., do not offer help in fitting clothing).

- Competitive Pricing – The objective of some retailers, particularly those selling specialty products, is not to compete on price, though they do not want to be perceived as charging the highest price. These retailers aggressively monitor the market to ensure their pricing is competitive, but they do not desire to get into price wars with discount retailers. Thus, other elements of their marketing strategy (e.g., higher quality products, more attractive store setting) are used to create higher value for which the customer will pay more.

- Full-Price Pricing – Retailers targeting exclusive markets find such markets are far less price sensitive than mass or specialty markets. In these cases, the additional value added through increased operational spending (e.g., expensive locations, more attractive design, more services) justify higher retail prices. While these retailers are likely to sell in lower volume than discount or competitive pricing retailers, their profit margins are often much higher.

Promotional Emphasis

Retailers generate customer interest using a variety of promotional techniques, yet some retailers rely on certain methods more than others as their principle promotional approach. Promotional options include:

◆ Advertising – Many store-based retailers continue to spend on traditional mass promotional methods of advertising, such as television and newspapers, though their use of digital advertising, including ads on websites, social media, within apps and through email, is growing. As would be expected, internet and app advertising methods are used extensively by online sellers.

◆ Direct Mail – A form of advertising that many retailers use for the bulk of their promotion is direct mail – advertising through postal mail. Using direct mail for promotion is the primary way catalog retailers distribute their materials. It also is utilized by smaller companies, who promote using postcards and other types of low-cost mailing methods.

◆ Sales Promotion – Retailers use short-term promotions, called sales promotion, to encourage customers to undertake certain activity, such as making a purchase or visiting a store (see *Sales Promotion* in Chapter 14). One common type of sales promotion is the customer **rewards program** offering special discounts or cash back for reaching predefined purchase levels.

◆ Personal Selling – Retailers selling expensive (e.g., automobiles) or high-end products (e.g., custom clothing) find a considerable amount of their promotional effort is spent while engaging in person-to-person contact with customers. While many of these retailers use other promotional methods as well, especially advertising, the consumer-salesperson relationship is key to persuading consumers to make purchase decisions.

Service Level

Retailers attract customers not only with desirable products but also by offering services that enhance the purchase experience. There are at least three levels of retail service:

◆ Self-Service – This service level allows consumers to perform most or all of the services associated with retail purchasing. For some consumers, self-service is considered a benefit while others may view it as an inconvenience. Self-service can be seen with: 1) **self-selection** services, where customers choose their own products, such as online purchasing and vending machine purchases; and 2) **self-checkout** services, where customers may or may not get help selecting products, but they use self-checkout options (e.g., scanning products, making payments) to process the purchase. (3)

◆ Assorted-Service – The majority of retailers offer some level of service to consumers. Services include handling the point-of-purchase transaction, assisting with product selection, arranging payment plans, offering delivery, and many more.

◆ <u>Full-Service</u> – The full-service retailer attempts to handle nearly all aspects of the purchase to the point where all consumers do is select the item they wish to buy. Retailers following a full-price pricing strategy often use the full-service approach as a way of adding value to a customer's purchase.

Ownership Structure

Finally, retailers can be classified based on their ownership structure which include:

◆ <u>Individually Owned and Operated</u> – Under this ownership structure, an individual or corporate entity owns and operates one or a very limited number of relatively small outlets or a single online store.

◆ <u>Corporate Chain</u> – A retail corporate chain consists of multiple outlets owned and operated by a single entity all performing similar retail activities. While the number of retail outlets required to be classified as a chain has never been specified, we will assume that any business owning more than five retail locations would be considered a chain.

◆ <u>Corporate Structure</u> – This classification covers large retailers operating less than five locations, such as automotive dealers and furniture stores. It also includes those operating in the non-store arena, such as online sellers, catalog retailers, and vending companies.

◆ <u>Contractually Licensed and Individually Operated</u> – The contractual channel arrangement discussed in Chapter 8 has led to a retail ownership structure in which operators of the retail outlet are not the outright owners of the business. Instead, the arrangement often involves a legal agreement in which the owner of the retail concept allows the operator to run the owner's business concept in exchange for financial considerations, such as a percentage of revenue. This structure is most often seen in the retail franchising business model (see *Franchise* discussion below).

RETAIL FORMATS

Now that we have presented ways in which retailers can be classified, we can use these categories to distinguish general formats or business models that best describe retail operations. These categories are designed to identify the primary format a retailer follows. In some cases, particularly with the advent of the internet and mobile technologies, a retailer will be involved in multiple formats.

Mom-and-Pop

These represent small retail outlets that are individually owned and operated. In many cases, these are family-run businesses catering to a local community often with a high level of service but relatively small product selection.

Mass Discounter

These retailers can be either general or specialty merchandisers, but either way their main focus is on offering discount pricing (e.g., Walmart). Compared to other store types, mass discounters offer fewer services and often lower quality products.

Boutique

This retail format is best represented by a small store carrying highly specialized and often high-end merchandise. In many cases, a boutique is a full-service retailer following a full-price pricing strategy.

Specialty Store

A step above the boutique store is the specialty store, which is generally represented by mid-sized stores carrying more depth than boutique stores. The service level of specialty stores is not as focused as it is with boutiques, though customer service is a key element to their success. Michaels is an example in the arts and crafts industry.

Category Killer

Many major retail chains have taken what previously were narrowly focused, small specialty store concepts and have expanded these to create large specialty stores. These so-called "category killers" can be found in such specialty areas as electronics (e.g., Best Buy), office supplies (e.g., Staples), and sporting goods (e.g., Dick's Sporting Goods).

Department Store

These retailers are general merchandisers offering mid-to-high quality products and a strong level of services, though in most cases these retailers would not fall into the full-service category. While department stores are classified as general merchandisers, and at one time carried a wide range of products (e.g., Sears), today most carry a more selective product line. For instance, Nordstrom focus is mainly on clothing and personal care products. (4)

Warehouse Store

This is a form of mass discounter that often provides even lower prices than traditional mass discounters. In addition, they may require buyers make minimum purchases in packaged quantities that are greater than what can be purchased at mass discount stores. These retail outlets provide few services and product selection can be limited. Furthermore, the retail design and layout are, as the name suggests, warehouse style with consumers often selecting products off the ground from the shipping package. Some forms of warehouse stores, often called warehouse clubs (e.g., Costco, Sam's Club), require customers purchase annual memberships in order to gain access to the outlet.

Catalog Retailer

Many retailers, including Lands' End and L.L. Bean, have built their businesses by having customers place orders after seeing products that appear in a mailed catalog or online. Orders are then delivered by a third-party shipper.

Franchise

As noted in Chapter 8, a franchise is a form of contractual channel in which one party, the **franchisor**, controls the business activities of another party, the **franchisee**. Under these arrangements, an eligible franchisee agrees to pay for the right to use the franchisor's business methods and other key business aspects, such as the franchise name. Franchises offer several advantages as discussed in Box 9-1.

Box 9-1

FRANCHISING BASICS

Starting a new retail operation is a dream for many aspiring entrepreneurs. But the risks involved can be substantial. Whether starting a store-based or online retail outlet, the costs for creating a presence, such as opening a store, building a website and acquiring inventory, can be steep. Yet even for retailers having the financial resources to establish a retail location, they still face the difficult hurdle of gaining customer recognition. In fact, opening a store may be easy compared to the efforts needed to build store traffic.

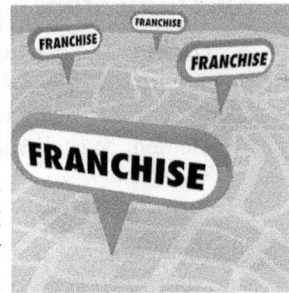

Because of the risk involved in building a retail outlet, acquiring a franchise may be an attractive option for entrepreneurs looking to move quickly from initial investment to producing revenue. In fact, the success rates for franchises tends to be higher compared with starting a business in more traditional ways. This is particularly the case when joining a well-established franchise operation. Franchise business opportunities are available in a wide variety of categories and offered by such companies as Subway, Dunkin' Donuts, and Holiday Inn. (5)

Under a franchise arrangement, a franchisor (i.e., franchise owner) allows someone, known as franchisee, to employ its business model in exchange for a fee. For instance, McDonald's is a well-known franchisor that allows individuals to use the McDonald's name and methods to deliver food to consumers. Payment to acquire a franchise is usually in the form of both a one-time, upfront franchise fee and an on-going percentage of revenue.

For a franchisee, the cost for obtaining a franchise may be quite high and there are often many restrictions on what the franchisee can do as they operate their business. And, of course, there are no guarantees a franchise will be successful, and some may eventually face bankruptcy. Yet, despite these issues, this form of retailing offers several advantages. First, it allows a franchisee to open a business that may already be known to local customers, thus reducing the promotional effort required to establish awareness. Second, training provided by a franchisor may enable a franchisee to be successful much faster than if the franchisee attempted to start their own business.

For the franchisor, the key benefit of the franchise model is that it allows for faster expansion with less capital requirements since funds needed to expand the business (e.g., acquiring retail space, local advertising) are often supported by the franchisee's upfront fee. Additionally, overall revenue may grow faster in a shorter time if demand for the franchise is strong.

Convenience Store

As the name implies, these general merchandise retailers cater to offering customers a relatively easy purchase experience. Convenience is offered in many ways, including through easily accessible store locations, small store size that allows for quick shopping, and fast checkout. The product selection found at these retailers (e.g., 7-Eleven) is extremely limited and pricing can be high.

e-tailer

Possibly the most publicized retail model to evolve in the last 100 years is the retailer that principally sells via the internet. There are thousands of online-only retail sellers of which Amazon is the most famous. These retailers offer shopping convenience including being open for business all day, every day and accepting orders via mobile apps. Electronic retailers or e-tailers also have the ability to offer a wide product selection since all they really need to attract orders is a picture and description of the product. That is, they may not need to have the product readily available the way physical stores do. Instead, an e-tailer can wait until a customer order is received before placing its own order with its suppliers. This cuts down significantly on the cost of maintaining an inventory of products.

Vending

Within this category are self-service mechanisms allowing consumers to make purchases and quickly acquire products. Vending started in the 1800s and until the last 20 years has principally been done by mechanical machines. However, today vending machines are highly automated and many are supported by either internet or telecommunications access, which permits consumers to purchase using credit and debit cards, or other electronic payment methods. While most consumers are well aware of vending machines for the purchase of basic items, such as beverages and snack foods, newer devices are entering the market that have greatly expanded product options, including vending machines that sell fresh food, electronic equipment, and clothing. (6)

Retailing Format Summary

In Table 9-1, we summarize each retail format by using the seven classification characteristics. The characteristics identified for each format should be viewed as the "most likely" case for that format and are not necessarily representative of all retailers that fall into that format.

CONCERNS OF RETAILERS

While much of the discussion in this chapter deals with retailers' role in the marketing strategy for consumer products companies, it is necessary to understand that retailers face their own marketing challenges. (7) Among the marketing issues facing retailers are:

◆ <u>Acquiring the Right Products</u> – Customers will only be satisfied if they can purchase the right products to satisfy their needs. Since a large percentage of retailers do not manufacture their own products, they must seek suppliers who

Table 9-1: Retailing Format Summary

Format	Target Market	Products Carried	Pricing Strategy	Promotion Emphasis	Distribution	Service Level	Ownership Structure
Mom-and-Pop	mass specialty	general specialty	competitive	advertising direct mail	stand-alone strip center shopping area	assorted	individually owned/oper.
Mass Discounter	mass	general	discount	advertising sales promotion	stand-alone strip-center	self	corp. chain
Boutique	specialty exclusive	specialty	full	selling	stand-alone strip center shopping area	full	individually owned/oper. corp. chain
Specialty	specialty	specialty	full competitive	selling advertising	shopping area shopping mall	full	corp. chain
Category Killer	mass	specialty	discount competitive	advertising sales promotion	stand-alone strip center	assorted	corp. chain
Department Store	specialty	general	competitive	advertising sales promotion	shopping area shopping mall	assorted	corp. chain
Warehouse Store	mass	general	discount	advertising	stand-alone	self	corp. chain
Catalog	mass specialty	general specialty	discount competitive	direct mail	direct marketer	assorted	corp. structure
Convenience	mass	general	full	advertising	stand-alone strip center	self	individually owned/oper. corp. chain
Franchise	mass specialty	specialty	competitive	advertising sales promotion	stand-alone strip center	assorted	contractual
e-tailer	mass specialty	general specialty	discount competitive full	advertising sales promotion	online seller	self	individually owned/oper. corp. structure
Vending	mass	specialty	full	none	vending	self	corp. structure

will supply products demanded by customers. Thus, an important objective for retailers is to identify the products customers will demand and negotiate with suppliers to obtain these products.

◆ Presenting Products to Generate Interest – Once obtained, products must be presented or merchandised to customers in a way that generates interest. **Retail merchandising** requires hiring talented people who understand their target market and can present products in a way that attracts customers' attention. This is often accomplished with creative in-store displays, website videos, useful apps, and attractive catalog images.

◆ Building Customer Traffic – Like any marketer, retailers must use promotional methods to build customer interest. For retailers, an important measure of interest is the number of people shopping at a retail location, visiting a website, or using the retailer's app. Building "traffic" is accomplished with a variety of promotional techniques, including advertising, and specialized promotional activities, such as coupons and other incentives.

◆ Creating an Attractive Retail Layout – For store-based retailers, a store's physical layout is an essential component in creating a retail experience that will attract customers. The physical layout is more than just deciding in what part of the store to locate products. For many retailers, designing the right shopping atmosphere (e.g., color, objects, light, sound) can add to the appeal of a store. Layout is also crucial in the online world where **website navigation** or **mobile app functionality** may be deciding factors in whether an online retailer will be successful.

◆ Keeping Pace with Technology – Technology has become an essential component for many retail activities including for managing customer information (e.g., CRM software), tracking product movement (e.g., use of **radio frequency identification (RFID)** tags for tracking [8]), streamlining the point-of-purchase (e.g., scanners, kiosks, **contactless payments** [9], self-serve checkouts), utilizing web and mobile technologies (e.g., product recommendation systems, social media), and many more. Because adopting technology can potentially lead to having a competitive advantage, it is important retailers pay close attention to technologies impacting their market.

◆ Finding Good Locations – For brick-and-mortar stores, where to physically locate may help or hinder store traffic. Well-placed stores with high visibility and easy access, while possibly commanding higher land usage fees, may hold significantly more value than lower cost sites that yield less traffic. Consequently, evaluating the trade-off between store location costs and potential benefits is a necessary task when looking to expand retail operations. (10)

◆ Improving Customer Satisfaction – Retailers know that satisfied customers are loyal customers. Consequently, they must develop strategies and methods that will allow them to fully understand and appeal to their customers. By gaining a deep understanding of their customers, retailers are in a better position to build stronger customer-retailer relationships. (11)

REFERENCES

1. "2017 Economic Census for Retail Trade." *United States Census Bureau.* https://www.census.gov/data/datasets/2017/econ/economic-census/naics-sector-44.html.

2. "U.S. Retail Sales Reach $7,040 Billion." *United States Census Bureau.* January 29, 2024. https://www.census.gov/newsroom/press-releases/2024/annual-retail-trade-survey.html.

3. For more on the issues retailers are facing with self-checkout see: Bailey Schulz. "The Downsides of Self-Checkout, and Why Retailers Aren't Expected to Pull Them Out Anytime Soon." *USA Today.* October 24, 2023. https://www.usatoday.com/story/money/2023/10/24/self-checkout-good-bad/71219910007.

4. For many years the largest department store in terms of square footage was Macy's in New York City. However, today the largest store is Shinsegae located in Seoul, South Korea which covers more than 3 million square feet. For more see: "Shinsegae." *Wikipedia.* https://en.wikipedia.org/wiki/Shinsegae.

5. For a list of top franchises see: "Franchise 500 Ranking." *Entrepreneur Magazine.* https://www.entrepreneur.com/franchise500.

6. For the purpose of this discussion, we also include many kiosks under the vending category. To learn more about advanced vending machines or kiosks see: *Kiosk Marketplace.* https://www.kioskmarketplace.com.

7. In recent years, many well-known retailers have fallen on hard times when facing difficult marketing challenges. This has resulted in many retailers filing for bankruptcy. For a listing of retailers that have declared bankruptcy since 2017 see: "The Running List of Major Retail Bankruptcies." *Retail Dive.* https://www.retaildive.com/news/running-list-major-retail-bankruptcies.

8. For more information on RFID tags see: "What is RFID?" *American Barcode and RFID.* https://www.abr.com/what-is-rfid-how-does-rfid-work. Also, to see how it is used to improve retail self-checkout see: Ben Cohen. "The Self-Checkout Even the Haters Will Love." *The Wall Street Journal.* December 16, 2023. https://www.wsj.com/business/retail/uniqlo-self-checkout-rfid-holiday-shopping-fast-retailing-c4287e2f.

9. For more on contactless payments see *Forms of Payment* in Chapter 18.

10. Some retailers experiment with temporary locations under a retail concept called pop-up stores or flash retailing. For examples see: "Pop-Up Shop Ideas: 15 Examples of Successful Shops." *Shopify.* July 27, 2023. https://www.shopify.com/retail/pop-up-shop-ideas.

11. Retailers can often find success for several different reasons such as selling great products (e.g., Apple stores), offering excellent personalized care (e.g., Zappos), attracting customers with low prices (e.g., Walmart), or providing ordering and delivery convenience (e.g., Amazon). However, while these examples of retail success may suggest it is about being great at one key marketing element (e.g., being good at customer service), what all successful retailers have in common is they expend great effort in researching customer needs and in capturing customer data in an effort to fully understand their target market. Thus, we have another example of how the key to marketing success is almost always about knowing and understanding customers through marketing research.

Chapter 10: Wholesaling and Product Movement

As we saw in Chapter 8, it is more the rule than the exception that marketers are not able to handle all distribution activities on their own. Instead, to get products into the hands of customers often requires the assistance of third-party service firms. In addition to retailers, marketers should be aware of others whose expertise in certain facets of distribution can prove quite beneficial.

In this chapter, we first examine another reselling group – wholesalers – and see how they come into play when a marketer attempts to reach the final customer. We show wholesalers exist in many formats, affect a wide range of industries, and offer different sets of features and benefits depending on the markets they serve. In the second half of the chapter, we examine the tasks that must be carried out in order to deliver products to customers. In some cases, the marketer will take on the responsibility of carrying out some functions, while other tasks may be assigned to distribution service providers. Whether handled by the marketer or contracted to others, these functions are crucial to having a cost-effective and efficient distribution system. It is worth noting that while most product movement is concerned with moving tangible products, some of the issues covered here also apply to intangible products, such as services, and to digital products.

WHAT IS WHOLESALING?

Wholesaling is a distribution channel function where one organization buys from supply firms with the primary intention of redistributing to other organizations. A wholesaler is an organization providing the necessary means to: 1) allow suppliers to reach organizational buyers, and 2) allow certain business buyers to purchase products, which they may not be able to purchase directly from suppliers. In the Unitied States, there are over 400,000 wholesale operations employing over 6 million (1) and generating over $11 trillion (2) in annual.

A distinguishing characteristic of wholesalers is they offer distribution benefits for BOTH a supplying party and for a purchasing party. For our discussion of wholesalers, we will primarily focus on wholesalers who sell to other resellers, such as retailers. While many large retailers and even manufacturers have centralized facilities that carry out the same tasks as wholesalers, we do not classify these as carrying out wholesaling operations since these activities only involve purchases and distribution of product for their own use (e.g., Walmart makes purchases to sell in their stores).

It is also important to understand that wholesalers are not limited to distributing only physical products. Wholesalers also exist in such industries as mortgage creation, vacation rentals, and energy distribution. Within the energy industry, one method for distributing electricity is through wholesalers. To be a wholesaler in the electricity market does not require the company be an electricity producer. Instead, an electricity wholesaler can purchase electricity from one supplier and then resell it to others in the electricity supply market. (3)

Benefits of Wholesalers

The benefits wholesalers offer to members of the channel of distribution can be significant and involve most of channel member benefits we discussed in Chapter 8, though specific benefits vary by type of wholesaler. Yet there are two particular benefits – one for their customers and one for their suppliers – that are common to most wholesale operations and are worth further discussion:

◆ Provide Access to Products – Wholesalers are in business to provide goods and services to buyers (e.g., to retailers), who may not be able to make their own purchases for one of the following reasons: 1) the buyer is unable to purchase directly from suppliers because their purchase order quantities are too low to meet suppliers' minimum order requirements, which are often quite high, or 2) the buyer may be able to purchase directly from suppliers but they must pay higher prices compared to other buyers, who obtain better pricing because they purchase in greater quantities. Since wholesalers sell to a large number of buyers, the size of orders they place with suppliers may match those of large retailers, which may allow them to obtain lower prices. Wholesalers can then pass these lower prices along to their buyers, which can enable smaller retailers to remain competitive with larger rivals. In this way, transacting through wholesalers is often the only way certain retailers can stay in business.

◆ Provide Access to Markets – Providing smaller retailers access to products they cannot acquire without wholesaler help offers a benefit for suppliers as well since it opens additional market opportunities for suppliers. That is, suppliers can have their products purchased and made available for sale across a wide number of retail outlets. More importantly, for a company offering a new product, convincing a few wholesalers to stock the product may make it easier to gain traction in the market as the wholesaler can yield power with the smaller retailers by convincing them to order the new product. Considering a wholesaler can serve hundreds of small retail customers, the marketing efforts required to persuade a wholesaler to adopt a new product may be far more efficient compared to efforts needed to convince hundreds of individual store owners to stock the new product.

WAYS TO CLASSIFY WHOLESALERS

In Chapter 9, we showed how retailers can be classified using different characteristics. Wholesalers can likewise be grouped together, though the characteristics are slightly different. For our purposes, we will separate wholesale operations based on four marketing decisions:

◆ Products Carried

◆ Promotional Activities

◆ Distribution Method

◆ Service Level

and one legal factor:

◆ Product Ownership

As we discussed with retailer classifications, these grouping schemes are not meant to be mutually exclusive. Consequently, a wholesaler can be evaluated on each classification.

Products Carried

Similar to how retailers can be classified, wholesalers can also be grouped by the width and depth of the product lines they handle. These groupings include:

◆ General Merchandise – Wholesalers carrying broad product lines fall into the general merchandise wholesaler category. Like general merchandise retailers, the product lines these wholesalers carry may not offer many options (i.e., shallow depth). These wholesalers tend to market to smaller general merchandise retailers, such as convenience or mom-and-pop stores.

◆ Specialty Merchandise – Wholesalers focusing on narrow product lines, but offering deep selection within the lines, fall into the specialty merchandise category. Most specialty merchandise wholesalers direct their marketing efforts to specific industries. For example, specialty wholesalers supply industries such as grocery, electronics, and pharmaceuticals.

Promotional Activities

Wholesalers can be separated based on the importance promotion plays in generating demand for products handled by the wholesaler. Two basic categories exist:

◆ Extensive Promotion – The main job of some wholesalers is to actively locate buyers. This occurs most often when a supplier, such as a manufacturer, hires a wholesaler to find buyers for its products. Extensive promotion can also be part of a wholesaler's plan to aggressively expand its own business by finding new customers. Under these arrangements, the most common promotional activity is personal selling through a sales force, though advertising targeted to business customers may also be used.

◆ Limited Promotion – Nearly all wholesalers engage in some promotional activities. Even in situations where a wholesaler dominates a channel and clients have little choice but to acquire products from it, some promotion will still occur. For instance, at times a wholesaler may use its salespeople to persuade buyers to purchase in larger volume than normal to help the wholesaler clear out inventory or to agree to stock a new product the wholesaler is handling.

Distribution Method

Wholesalers offer distribution options where customers may or may not be able to visit a physical location to acquire their purchases. For the purposes of our discussion, this classification is separated based on whether or not a stationary location exists from which the wholesaler handles the physical movement of products. Options include:

Stationary Location

In most common wholesaler arrangements, the wholesaler has one or more fixed facilities where product handling operations take place. However, while stationary wholesalers share the characteristic of a permanent location, they often differ on whether customers can visit these facilities.

● Customer Accessible – At certain wholesaler locations buyers can shop at the facility. In fact, retail warehouse clubs, such as Costco and Sam's Club, also function as wholesalers for qualifying businesses. In addition to selecting their orders, buyers are responsible for making their own arrangements to transport the items they purchase.

● Not Customer Accessible – Most operations classified as wholesalers do not permit buyers to visit their facilities in order to select items. Rather, buyers place orders over the internet, by phone, or through person-to-person contact with a wholesaler's representative. In more advanced business relationships, the buyer's inventory management system will automatically place orders (see *Ordering and Inventory Management* discussion below). Also, in most cases, the wholesaler takes responsibility for product delivery.

Non-Stationary Location

Not all wholesalers carry inventory at a stationary location. In fact, some do not carry inventory at all. This method of wholesaler distribution includes:

● Mobile – Several specialized wholesalers transport products to the customer's location using vans or trucks. Buyers then have the ability to purchase product by either walking through the mobile facility or ordering from the wholesaler, who then selects the items from the vehicle.

● No Facilities – Some wholesalers do not have physical locations that provide product storage. Instead, these operations rely on others, such as delivery companies, to ship products from one location (e.g., manufacturer) to the buyer's place of business.

Service Level

Wholesalers can be distinguished by the number and depth of services they provide for their customers. Service level categories include:

◆ Full-Service – Wholesalers in this category mainly sell to the retail industry and, in most cases, require a strong, long-term retailer-wholesaler relationship. In addition to basic distribution services, such as providing access to an assortment of products and furnishing delivery, these wholesalers also offer customers many additional services that aid retail store operations. These services often include offering assistance with in-store retail merchandising (see Chapter 9), retail site location decisions (e.g., find best geographic location for a new store), store design and construction, back-end operations (e.g., payroll services), financial support, and many more.

◆ Limited-Service – Compared to full-service wholesalers, buyers dealing with limited-service firms receive far fewer services. Most offer basic services, such as product shipment and allowing credit purchasing, but few offer the number of service options found with full-service wholesalers.

◆ No Service – Some wholesalers follow a business model whose only service is to make products available for sale and only on a cash basis. In these instances, the buyer handles transportation of their purchases.

Product Ownership

Wholesalers can be classified based on whether they do or do not become the owners of the products they sell. By ownership we mean that **title** (i.e., legal ownership) has passed from the party from whom the wholesaler purchased the product (e.g., manufacturer) to the wholesaler. It also means the wholesaler assumes any risk that may arise with handling the product. Ownership options are:

◆ Do Take Title – Wholesalers taking title own the products they purchase.

◆ Do Not Take Title – Wholesalers who do not take title are focused on activities that bring buyers and sellers together. Often these wholesalers never physically handle products.

WHOLESALE FORMATS

Considering the criteria by which wholesalers can be classified, it is not surprising many different wholesale formats exist. Below we discuss ten wholesale formats. While many of these wholesalers also have an online presence, we do not distinguish an "e-wholesaler" as a separate format the way we did with "e-tailers" or online retailers. The reason? While most wholesalers do operate from a brick-and-mortar facility, only a small fraction of wholesale operations permit customer shopping at their facilities.

Consequently, the nature of this industry for many years has been to have customers use communication tools (e.g., phone, fax) to place orders. With the wholesale industry, the internet simply serves as another communication option rather than a significantly different distribution channel.

General Merchandise

These wholesalers offer broad but shallow product lines that are mostly of interest to retailers carrying a wide assortment of products, such as convenience stores, and smaller general merchandise stores, such as those offering closeout or novelty products. Since these wholesalers offer such a wide range of products, their knowledge of individual products may not be strong.

Specialty Merchandise

Many wholesalers focus on specific product lines or industries and, in doing so, supply a narrow assortment of products. However, within the product lines offered there is considerable depth. Additionally, these wholesalers tend to be highly knowledgeable of products they sell and of the markets they serve. (4)

Contractual

In Chapter 8, we introduced the concept of wholesaler-sponsored channel arrangements where a wholesaler brings together and manages many independent retailers. The services of these contractual wholesalers are supplied only to the retailers involved in the contractual arrangement.

Industrial Distributor

The industrial distributor mainly directs its operations to the business customer (e.g., manufacturers) rather than to other resellers. Depending on the distributor, they can carry either broad or narrow product lines.

Cash-and-Carry

A wholesale operation common to the food industry is the cash-and-carry. Historically, this wholesale format involved buyers visiting a wholesaler's facility where they selected their orders, paid in cash, and then handled their own deliveries (i.e., carry) to their place of business. Today many cash-and-carry wholesalers do not limit payment to cash only and instead accept credit card payment. This form of wholesaling has begun to expand outside of the food industry as large wholesale clubs, such as BJ's Wholesale Club, Costco and Sam's Club, allow qualified businesses to purchase products intended for retail sale.

Truck

As the name suggests, truck wholesaling operations are primarily run out of a truck that is stocked with products. These wholesalers often have assigned geographic territories where they regularly visit buyer's locations. In most cases, these wholesalers serve the retail food industry and industrial markets, where they offer specialty product lines. (5)

Rack Jobber

Similar to truck wholesalers, the rack jobber also sells from a truck. However, the main difference is rack jobbers primarily work with retailers where they are assigned and manage space (i.e., racks) within stores. The rack jobber is then responsible for maintaining inventory and may even handle other marketing duties, such as setting product price. This form of wholesaling is most prominent with magazines, candy, bakery, and health-and-beauty products. In some trades, the name rack jobber is being replaced by the name **service merchandiser**.

Drop Shipper

Wholesalers in this category never take physical possession of products, though they do take ownership. Essentially, they are shipping coordinators who receive orders from customers and then place the order with a product supplier. Shipping is then arranged so the supplier ships directly to the drop shipper's customer. Drop shipping is often most useful when large orders are placed so that transportation and product handling costs can be spread over many items (see Box 10-1).

Broker

A far less obvious type of wholesaler is the broker, who is responsible for bringing buyers and sellers together. However, brokers do not take ownership of products and often never handle the product. Brokers are paid based on a pre-negotiated percentage of the sale (i.e., commission) by the side that hires their services. In most cases, the relationship that develops between the broker and the buyer and seller is short-term and only lasts through the purchase. Brokers can be found in the food industry, importing/exporting, and real estate.

Agent

Similar to brokers, agents also bring buyers and sellers together, though they tend to work for clients for an extended period. As with brokers, agents generally are paid on commission. A common type of agent is the **manufacturers' representative**, who essentially assumes the role of a salesperson for a client. Manufacturers' representatives may handle several non-competing product lines at the same time and, during a single meeting with a prospective buyer, may discuss many products from several different companies.

Wholesaling Format Summary

Below in Table 10-1 we summarize each wholesale format by using the five classification characteristics. The characteristics identified for each format should be viewed as the "most likely" case for that format and are not necessarily representative of all wholesalers that fall into this format.

Table 10-1: Wholesaling Format Summary

Format	Products Carried	Promotional Activities	Distribution Method	Service Level	Product Ownership
General Merchandise	general	limited	stationary not accessible	limited	take title
Specialty Merchandise	specialty	limited	stationary may be accessible	full or limited	take title
Contractual	general or specialty	extensive	stationary not accessible	full	take title
Industrial Distributor	general or specialty	limited	stationary may be accessible	limited	take title
Cash-and-Carry	specialty	limited	stationary accessible	no	take title
Truck	specialty	limited	non-stationary mobile	limited	take title
Rack Jobber	specialty	limited	non-stationary mobile	limited	take title
Drop Shipper	specialty	limited	non-stationary no facilities	limited	take title
Broker	specialty	extensive	non-stationary no facilities	limited	do not take title
Agent	specialty	extensive	non-stationary no facilities	limited	do not take title

CONCERNS OF WHOLESALERS

The wholesale industry has served a vital role in the distribution process for well over 100 years. Yet the challenges they face today are raising the stakes as many wholesalers fight to maintain their market position. Some of the most critical issues facing today's wholesalers include:

◆ <u>Disintermediation</u> – The growth of the internet as a communication and distribution channel has led many to conclude that wholesaling will lose its importance as manufacturers and final buyers learn to transact directly. This so called "disintermediation" of marketing channels is a real concern to some wholesalers, especially those that do not function as a dominant party within a distribution channel. For example, assume a retailer operating a gift card store uses a wholesaler only to purchase products from a specific manufacturer. In this situation, if the manufacturer begins to offer direct purchasing to smaller customers the wholesaler may have little leverage in efforts to retain the retailer as a customer. In instances of disintermediation, wholesalers face the challenge of creating greater value for their services with the intention of making the retailer's decision to switch more difficult.

◆ <u>Facility Location</u> – Wholesalers, who are heavily involved in product shipment, may spend considerable time evaluating sites to locate facilities. For organizations needing large facilities, the decision as to where to locate becomes more difficult and more expensive the closer the location is to major metropolitan areas. In fact, land costs in some regions of the world have risen so high that utilizing this space for wholesaling operations may not be feasible. In addition to land costs, facility location is also affected by access to adequate transportation, such as roads, seaports, airports, and rail terminals. Areas with available land often lack the infrastructure needed to support wholesale facilities unless expensive and time-consuming improvements (e.g., build highway, extend rail lines, etc.) are made.

◆ <u>Transportation Costs</u> – For wholesalers involved in transporting products, a history of fluctuating fuel costs has forced a close examination of how they handle product distribution. Transportation expense can represent a significant portion of overall distribution costs and when fuel prices rise these higher costs are often passed on to customers in the form of higher product prices. However, high transportation expense also presents opportunities for wholesalers. For instance, wholesalers have learned to control fuel costs by employing such methods as using equipment and delivery vehicles that are more energy efficient, utilizing computer routing software to determine less costly delivery routes, and offering greater incentives to customers to accept deliveries during less congested times of the day.

◆ <u>Adapting to New Technologies</u> – In addition to technologies to lower fuel costs, other distribution technologies are offering both advantages and disadvantages to wholesalers. New technologies, such as radio frequency identification (RFID) tags placed on shipped products and real-time traffic updates allow wholesalers to maintain tighter control over their distribution activities. However, gaining the benefits associated with these new distribution technologies requires a significant commitment in terms of cost (i.e., purchasing the technologies) and time (i.e., installation and training).

◆ <u>Offering Non-Product Assistance</u> – Wholesalers are finding that offering access to products is not enough to satisfy buyers. Many customers also want wholesalers to offer additional value-added services including employee training (e.g., teach selling skills), promotional support (e.g., financial support for advertising), and assistance in managing their operations (e.g., improve retailer's website). Keeping pace with service demands requires wholesalers to engage in constant research and communication with their customers.

MANAGING PRODUCT MOVEMENT

In addition to enlisting the assistance of retailers and wholesalers to make products available to customers, marketers also face additional concerns when trying to meet distribution objectives. In this section, we examine the tasks that must be carried out in order to physically move products to customers. (6) These tasks include:

◆ Ordering and Inventory Management

◆ Transportation

◆ Product Storage

In some cases, the marketer will take on the responsibility of carrying out some of these functions, while other tasks may be assigned to distribution service providers. Whether handled by the marketer or contracted to others, these functions are crucial to having a cost-effective and efficient distribution system.

ORDERING AND INVENTORY MANAGEMENT

Having products available when customers want to make purchases may seem like a relatively straightforward process. All a seller needs to do is make sure there is product (i.e., inventory) in its possession and ready for the customer to purchase. Unfortunately, being prepared for customer purchasing is not always easy. Having the right product available when the customer is ready to buy requires a highly coordinated effort involving order entry and processing systems, forecasting techniques, customer knowledge, strong channel relationships, and skill at physically handling products.

ORDER ENTRY AND PROCESSING SYSTEMS

The marketer must have a system allowing customers to place orders. This system can be as simple as a consumer walking up to the counter of a small food stand to purchase a few vegetables or as complicated as automated computer systems, where an electronic order is triggered from a retailer to their suppliers (e.g., manufacturer, wholesaler) each time a consumer purchases a product at the retailer's store or when inventory totals reach a minimum level. In either case, the order processing system must be able to meet customers' purchasing needs. In some circumstances, an efficient ordering system can be turned into a competitive advantage. Several years ago, Amazon turned its order handling system into a product feature with the patented "1-click" ordering option that streamlines online ordering by reducing the number of clicks needed to make purchases. (7) It has now gone further by offering an easy voice ordering option using its Alexa app and smart speaker technology. (8)

FORECASTING

Inventory management is often an exercise in predicting how customers will act in the future. By predicting purchase behavior, the marketer can respond by making sure the right amount of product is available. For most large-scale resellers, effective inventory forecasting requires the use of sophisticated statistical tools. These tools take into consideration many variables, such as past purchase history, amount of promotional effort that triggers an increase in customer ordering and other market criteria, to determine how much of the product will be needed to meet customer demand.

CUSTOMER KNOWLEDGE

Inventory management can be fine-tuned to respond to customers' needs. As a marketer learns more about a customer, they begin to observe trends in how and when purchases are made. Combining customer knowledge with forecasting techniques allows the marketer to better estimate product demand and inventory requirements. As we discussed in Chapter 3, a key component for understanding customers is having in place a customer relationship management (CRM) system for tracking and analyzing customer activity.

CHANNEL RELATIONSHIPS

While marketers using channel members to sell consumer products have access to information for their immediate customers (e.g., resellers), they often do not have access to sales and customer behavior information controlled by the party selling to the final consumer (e.g., retailer). Knowing the demand patterns at the final consumer level can give marketers good insight into how resellers order. For marketers, developing relationships with the holder of consumer information (i.e., resellers) can result in information sharing. In fact, as we noted in Chapter 8, some retailers allow marketers direct access to real-time, store-level inventory information so the marketer can monitor how products are selling in stores. This enables them to respond quickly if inventory needs change.

PHYSICAL HANDLING

An often-overlooked area of inventory management involves the actions and skills needed to prepare a product to move from one point to another. Some products require special attention be given to ensure the product is not damaged during shipment. Such efforts must be carefully balanced against increased costs that arise (e.g., need for stronger packaging) in order to provide greater protection to products. Because of this, many marketers will accept the fact that some small level of damage will occur during the distribution process.

TRANSPORTATION

A key objective of product distribution is to get products into customers' hands in a timely manner. While delivery of digital products can be handled in a fairly smooth way by allowing customers to access their purchase over the internet or through an app, tangible products require more careful analysis of delivery options to enable the marketer to provide an optimal level of customer service.

Yet as we noted earlier, "optimal" does not always translate into what a customer may consider is the best method (i.e., may not ship in the fastest way possible). This is particularly the case when companies see an opportunity to expand beyond their own country. When shipping internationally, transportation decisions can become quite complex. Not only are costs higher due to increased distance, but marketers may find transportation options are limited and unreliable. Additionally, the laws and regulations governing transportation may vary for each country. In most cases, when shipping internationally, marketers must enlist the help of third-party distribution partners, who are familiar with the requirements of each foreign market the marketer seeks to enter.

Transportation Features

In terms of delivering products to customers, there are six distinct modes of transportation: air, digital, pipeline, rail, truck, and water. However, not all modes are an option for all marketers. Each mode offers advantages and disadvantages on key transportation features. These features include:

◆ Product Options – This feature is concerned with the number of different products realistically shipped using a certain mode. Some modes, such as pipeline, are extremely limited in the type of products that can be shipped, while others, such as truck, can handle a wide range of products.

◆ Speed of Delivery – This refers to how quickly it takes products to move from the shipper's location to the buyer's location.

◆ Accessibility – This transportation feature refers to whether the use of a mode can allow final delivery to occur at the buyer's desired location or whether the mode requires delivery to be off-loaded onto other modes before arriving at the buyer's destination. For example, most deliveries made via air must be loaded onto other transportation modes, often trucks, before they can be delivered to the final customer.

◆ Cost – Shipping cost is evaluated in terms of the cost-per-item to cover some distance (e.g., mile, kilometer). Often for large shipments of tangible products cost is measured in terms of tons-per-mile or metric-tons-per-kilometer.

◆ Capacity – Refers to the amount of product shipped at one time within one transportation unit. The higher the capacity the more likely transportation cost can be spread over more individual products. This can result in lower transportation cost-per-item shipped (see Box 10-1).

◆ Intermodal Capable – Intermodal shipping occurs when two or more modes can be combined in order to gain advantages offered by each mode. For instance, in an intermodal method called **piggybacking**, truck trailers are loaded onto railroad cars without the need to unload the trailer. When the railroad car has reached a certain destination the truck trailers are off-loaded onto trucks for delivery to a customer's location.

Box 10-1

THE COST ADVANTAGE OF BULK SHIPPING

Transportation expense can represent a significant portion of the final product cost. Because of the high cost of shipping product, suppliers often find it is in the best interest of the distribution channel and the final customer to ship products in bulk quantities. In general, bulk shipping reduces the per-item transportation cost.

For instance, consider what it costs to operate a delivery truck with a shipping capacity of 1,000 boxes. In terms of operational expenses for the truck (e.g., fuel, truck driver's costs, other operational costs), let's assume it costs (US) $1,000 to go from point A to point B. In most cases, with the exception of a little decrease in fuel efficiency, it does not cost that much more to drive the truck whether it is filled with 1,000 boxes of a supplier's product or if it only has 100 boxes. Using this information, it is easy to calculate the transportation cost-per-item:

For the shipment of 100 boxes the transportation cost is:

$$\frac{\$1,000}{100} = \$10 \text{ per-item}$$

For the shipment of 1,000 boxes the transportation cost is:

$$\frac{\$1,000}{1,000} = \$1 \text{ per-item}$$

As this example illustrates, per-item transportation expense can be significantly reduced when marketers use bulk shipping. As we will see in Chapter 18, such advantages are key reasons suppliers offer quantity discounts to encourage large volume orders.

Environmental Benefits

It should be noted that another feature that may soon offer advantages to one or more modes of transportation is the environmental impact a mode may have. For instance, trucks may become a more attractive delivery option as companies involved in shipping increase the number of electric vehicles in their fleets. (9)

Modes of Transportation Comparison

Shown in Table 10-2 are key metrics for freight movement in the U.S. for each mode of transportation that ships physical goods (excludes digital shipments). The metrics indicate that trucks dominate product shipment accounting for nearly 72% of all shipping dollars and more than 71% of weight (measured in tons) shipped. The table also provides insight into intermodal freight traffic (i.e., multiple modes).

Finally, Table 10-3 presents a summary of the six modes compared on each of the key transportation features.

Table 10-2: U.S. Domestic Freight Metrics

Mode of Transportation	Value		Tons Shipped	
	2017 (in USD millions)	Percent of Total	2017 (in thousands)	Percent of Total
All modes	14,517,812	100.0	12,468,902	100.0
Single modes	11,737,969	80.9	11,604,764	93.1
Truck	10,398,910	71.6	8,843,334	70.9
Rail	254,209	1.8	1,251,240	10.0
Water	243,855	1.7	804,392	6.5
Air (a)	496,637	3.4	8,019	.1
Pipeline (b)	344,357	2.4	697,778	5.6
Multiple modes (c)	2,777,749	19.1	770,504	6.2
Other modes	2,095	*	93,634	0.8

a. Includes truck and air
b. Estimates for pipeline exclude shipments of crude petroleum
c. Examples: parcel and U.S. Postal Service, truck and rail, truck and water, rail and water, etc.
* Rounds to zero

SOURCE: U.S. Department of Transportation, Bureau of Transportation Statistics (10)

Table 10-3: Modes of Transportation Summary

Mode	Product Options	Speed	Accessibility	Cost	Capacity	Intermodal Capability
Truck	Very Broad	Moderate	High	Moderate	Low	Very High
Railroad	Broad	Slow	Moderate	Low	Moderate	Very High
Air	Narrow	Fast	Low	Very High	Very Low	Moderate
Water	Broad	Very Slow	Moderate	Very Low	Very High	Very High
Pipeline	Very Narrow	Very Slow	Low	Low	Very High	Very Low
Digital	Very Narrow	Very Fast	Very High	Very Low	Moderate	Very Low

PRODUCT STORAGE

The third key element in product movement concerns storing products for future delivery. Marketers of tangible products, and even digital products (e.g., music apps), may have storage concerns. Storage facilities, such as warehouses, play a vital role in the distribution process for a number of reasons including:

◆ Hold Wide Assortment – As noted in Chapter 8, many resellers allow customers to purchase small quantities of many different products. Yet, as we saw in Box 10-1, to obtain the best prices from suppliers, resellers must purchase in large quantities. In these situations, the need exists for storage facilities that not only hold a large volume of product, but also hold a wide variety of inventory. Additionally, these facilities must be organized in a way permitting sellers to fill orders easily for its customers.

◆ Meet Unanticipated Demand – Holding inventory in storage offers a safeguard in cases of unexpected increases in demand for products. (8)

◆ Needed for Large Shipping Quantities – As we noted in Box 10-1, manufacturers generally prefer to ship in large product quantities in order to more effectively spread per-item transportation cost. This often means manufacturers must create storage areas in which the manufactured goods can build up in the quantities needed for such large shipments to occur.

◆ Offers Faster Response – Additional storage facilities, strategically located in different geographical areas, allow a marketing organization to respond quickly to customers' needs. The ability to respond with quick delivery can be a significant value-added feature since it reduces the buyer's (e.g., retailer) need to maintain a large inventory at its own locations.

◆ Security and Backup – For digital products, additional storage facilities, such as **computer server farms**, are not only needed to offer customers faster access to products (e.g., online content and software), but are also needed to protect against technical glitches and possible security threats.

Types of Warehouses

The physical warehouse is the most common type of storage, though other forms do exist (e.g., storage tanks, computer server farms). Some warehouses are massive structures that simultaneously support the unloading of numerous in-bound trucks and railroad cars containing suppliers' products while at the same time loading multiple trucks for shipment to customers. 11)

Below we discuss five types of warehouses:

Private Warehouse

This type of warehouse is owned and operated by channel members (e.g., suppliers, resellers) and is used for their own distribution activities. For instance, a large, national retail chain may have several regional warehouses or "fulfillment centers" supplying its stores. For instance, Walmart distribution system has over 200 facilities including six that are strategically located to respond to potential emergency situations such as natural disasters. (12))

Public Warehouse

The public warehouse is essentially space that can be leased to solve short-term distribution needs. For instance, retailers operating their own private warehouses may occasionally seek additional storage space if their facilities have reached capacity or if they are making an unusually large purchase but lack additional space in their own facilities. For example, retailers may require extra space to store merchandise in preparation for a special in-store sale or to buy a large quantity of a supplier's specially priced product.

Automated Warehouse

With advances in computer and robotics technology many warehouses now have automated capabilities. The level of automation ranges from a small conveyor belt transporting products in a small area all the way up to a fully automated facility, where only a few people are needed to handle storage activity for thousands of pounds/kilograms of product. In fact, many warehouses use machines to handle nearly all physical distribution activities, such as moving product-filled **pallets** (i.e., platforms that hold large amounts of product) around buildings that may be several stories tall and the length of two or more football fields. And the newest trend in warehouse automation is the use of warehouse robot technology. For instance, many retailers and manufacturers are using small robots for various purposes include moving products around in their storage facilities. (13)

Climate-Controlled Warehouse

Warehouses handle storage of many types of products including those needing special handling conditions, such as freezers for storing frozen products, humidity-controlled environments for delicate products, including produce or flowers, and dirt-free facilities for handling highly sensitive computer products.

Distribution Center

There are some warehouses where product storage is considered a very short-term activity. These warehouses serve as points in the distribution system at which products are received from many suppliers and quickly shipped out to many customers. In some cases, such as with distribution centers handling perishable food (e.g., produce, dairy, meats), most of the product enters in the early morning and is distributed by the end of the day.

REFERENCES

1. "2017 Economic Census for Wholesale Trade." *United States Census Bureau.* https://www.census.gov/data/datasets/2017/econ/economic-census/naics-sector-42.html.

2. "2022 Annual Wholesale Trade Survey." *United States Census Bureau.* January 29, 2024. https://www.census.gov/newsroom/press-releases/2024/annual-wholesale-trade-survey.html.

3. "Market for Electricity." *PJM.* https://learn.pjm.com/electricity-basics/market-for-electricity.aspx.

4. Small retailers, such as neighborhood convenience stores and specialty clothing stores, will often purchase from a variety of wholesalers. For instance, some retailers may look to websites such as Wholesale Central, which provides information on over 1,000 wholesalers listed in over 50 product categories. https://www.wholesalecentral.com.

5. An example of a truck wholesaler is *Snap-on* that provides tools to a variety of industries. For more on this company see: https://www.snapon.com.

6. In some industries, and in particular those in the business market, the tasks involved in the physical movement of products may fall under the purview of departments with names such as logistics and operations. While not directly within the marketing department, these departments coordinate closely with marketing (e.g., marketing alerts logistics of likely increase in demand due to special promotion).

7. Paul Christ. "Patenting Marketing Methods: A Missing Topic in the Classroom." *Journal of Marketing Education.* 27 (1), 2005.

8. For more details see: "Shopping with Alexa." *Amazon.* https://www.amazon.com/gp/help/customer/display.html?nodeId=GHAZNLUYYXSUBA9K.

9. While adoption of electric vehicles (EV) by consumers has been strong, the deployment of EV for commercial use, such as light trucks and vans, has been hampered by production issues. For more see: Neal E. Boudette. "Electric Vans, Delayed by Production Problems, Find Eager Buyers." *New York Times.* May 17, 2023. https://www.nytimes.com/2023/05/16/business/energy-environment/electric-vehicle-delivery-vans.html.

10. "2017 Commodity Flow Survey." *Bureau of Transportation Statistics – U.S. Department of Transportation.* https://www.bts.gov/cfs.

11. For more on the warehouse and product distribution industry see: *Modern Materials Handling.* https://www.mmh.com.

12. For the purposes of this book, Walmart's facilities are labeled as "private warehouses" though the company describes these as "distribution centers." As we note in this section, distribution centers are less about product storage than about continuous product movement with limited storage. For more on Walmart's facilities see: "Our Supply Chain." *Walmart.* https://corporate.walmart.com/about#our-supply-chain.

13. For details on how robots operate in a warehouse setting see: Will Allen. "Guide to Warehouse Robots: Types of Warehouse Robots, Uses, Navigation & More." *6 Rivers Systems.* January 13, 2023. https://6river.com/guide-to-warehouse-robots.

Chapter 11: Promotion Decisions

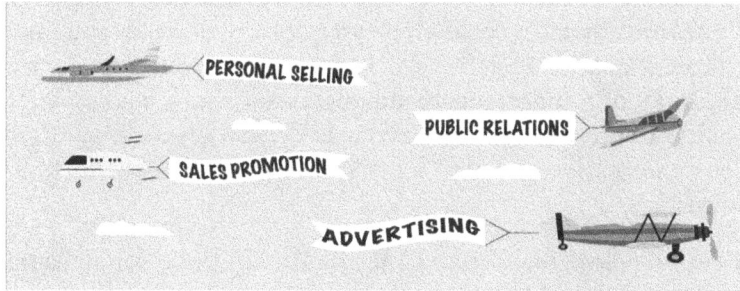

Those unfamiliar with marketing often assume it is the same thing as advertising. Certainly, our coverage so far in **KnowThis: Marketing Basics** has stressed this is not the case. Marketing encompasses many tasks and decisions, of which advertising may only be a small portion. Likewise, when non-marketers hear someone talk about "promotion" they frequently believe the person is talking about advertising. While advertising is the most visible and best understood method of promotion, it is only one of several approaches a marketer can choose.

In this chapter, we begin our discussion of the promotion component of the Marketer's Toolkit. We start by defining promotion, and we show how promotion is used to meet different objectives. Because communication is a key element of promotion, we take an extended look at the communication process. Next, we explore different characteristics of promotion and how different promotional methods stack up to these characteristics. Finally, we discuss factors affecting a marketer's choice of promotional methods.

WHAT IS PROMOTION?

Promotion is the general name given to forms of communication designed to reach a targeted audience with a certain message in order to achieve specific organizational objectives. Nearly all organizations, whether for-profit or not-for-profit, in all types of industries, must engage in some form of promotion. Such efforts may range from multinational firms spending large sums securing a high-profile celebrity to serve as a corporate spokesperson to the owner of a one-person enterprise passing out business cards at a local businesspersons' meeting.

Like most marketing decisions, an effective promotional strategy requires the marketer understand how promotion fits with other pieces of the marketing puzzle (e.g., product, distribution, pricing, target markets). Consequently, promotion decisions should be made with an appreciation for how these affect other areas of the organization. For instance, running a major advertising campaign for a new product without first ensuring there will be enough inventory to meet potential demand generated by the advertising would certainly not go over well with the company's production department (not to mention other key company executives). Thus, marketers should not work in a vacuum when making promotion decisions. Rather, the overall success of a promotional strategy requires input from other functional areas.

In addition to coordinating general promotion decisions with other business areas, individual promotions must also work together. Under the concept of **integrated marketing communication**, marketers attempt to develop a unified and highly coordinated promotional strategy in which a consistent message is presented across many different types of promotional techniques. For instance, salespeople will discuss the same benefits of a product as mentioned in television advertisements. In this way, no matter how customers are exposed to a marketer's promotional efforts they all receive the same information.

Finally, as discussed below, promotion is not limited to the communication of product information to customers. Marketers also use promotional methods to communicate with others who are outside their target market.

Targets of Marketing Promotions

The audience for an organization's marketing communication efforts is not only the marketer's target market. While the bulk of a marketer's promotional budget may be directed at the target market, there are many other groups that could also serve as useful targets of a marketing message including:

◆ Target Market Influencers – There exists a large group of people and organizations with the potential to affect how a marketer's target market is exposed to and perceives a marketer's products. These influencing groups have their own communication mechanisms that reach the target market. With the right strategy, the marketer may be able to utilize these influencers to its benefit. Influencers include news outlets, social media personalities, special interest groups, opinion leaders (e.g., doctors directing patients to purchase a product), and industry trade associations.

◆ Channel Members – Distribution channel members provide services that help the marketer gain access to final customers. Yet in many ways channel members, and particularly resellers, also represent target markets for a marketer's products. While their needs are often very different than those of the final customer, channel members must make purchase decisions when agreeing to handle a marketer's product (see Chapters 9 and 10). Aiming promotion at distribution partners (e.g., retailers, wholesalers, distributors) and other channel members is extremely important and, in some industries, it may represent a higher portion of a marketer's promotional budget than promotional spending directed at the final customer.

◆ Other Organizations – The most likely scenario in which a marketer will communicate with another organization occurs when the marketer is probing the other organization to see if they would have an interest in a joint venture, such as a **co-marketing arrangement**, where both would share marketing costs. Using marketing promotions, such as ads targeted to potential partners, could help create interest in discussing such a relationship. (1)

◆ Other Organizational Stakeholders – Marketers may also be involved with communication activities directed at other stakeholders. This group consists of those who provide services, support, or in other ways impact the organization. For example, an industry group that sets industry standards can affect company products through the issuance of recommended compliance standards for product development or on how other marketing activities are performed. Communicating with this group is necessary to ensure the marketer's views of any changes in standards, and especially those that may negatively impact the marketer, are expressed to these groups.

OBJECTIVES OF MARKETING PROMOTIONS

Many view promotional activities as the most glamorous part of marketing. This may have to do with the fact that promotion is often associated with creative activity undertaken to help distinguish a marketer's products from competitors' offerings. While creativity is a key element in promotion decisions, many times marketers are consumed with developing a highly creative promotion (e.g., humorous advertisement featuring a top Hollywood star) only to see it fail to benefit the organization (i.e., sales do not show a measurable increase).

While creativity is certainly a concern, marketers must first have a deep understanding of how marketing promotions help the organization achieve its objectives before embarking on the creative side of promotion. The most obvious objective marketers have for promotional activities is to convince customers to make a decision benefiting the marketer (of course the marketer believes the decision will also benefit the customer). For most for-profit marketers, this means getting customers to buy a company's product and, in most cases, to remain loyal long-term customers. For other organizations, such as not-for-profits, it means persuading customers to increase donations, utilize more services, change attitudes, or change behavior (e.g., how to eat healthier campaigns).

However, marketers must understand that getting customers to commit to a decision, such as deciding to make a purchase, is only achievable when a customer is ready to make the decision. As we saw in Chapter 4, customers often move through several stages before a purchase decision is made. Additionally, before turning into a repeat customer, purchasers will analyze their initial purchase to see whether they received a good value. In fact, a customer may repeat the full purchasing process several more times before they feel comfortable making repeat purchases.

The type of customer the marketer is attempting to attract, along with the stage of the purchase process a customer is in, will affect the objectives of a particular marketing promotion. And since a marketer often has multiple simultaneous promotional campaigns, the objective of each could be different.

Types of Promotion Objectives

The possible objectives for marketing promotions may include the following:

◆ Building Awareness – New products and new organizations are often unknown to a market, which means initial promotional efforts must focus on establishing an identity. In this situation, the marketer's promotional objectives are to: 1) ensure the message reaches customers, and 2) tell the market who they are and what they have to offer.

◆ Creating Interest – Moving a customer from awareness of the marketer's product to making a purchase can present a significant challenge. As we saw in Chapter 4, customers must first recognize they have a need before they actively start to consider a purchase. The focus on creating messages convincing customers a need exists has been the hallmark of marketing for a long time with promotional appeals targeted at basic human characteristics, such as emotions, fears, sex, and humor.

◆ Providing Information – Some promotion is designed to assist customers in the search stage of the purchasing process. In some cases, such as when a product is so novel it creates a new category of product and has few competitors, the information is simply intended to explain what the product is and may not mention any competitors. In other situations, where the product competes in an existing market, informational promotion, that may include direct comparisons with competitor's products, may be used to help distinguish the marketer's product as part of a product positioning strategy (see *Positioning Products* in Chapter 5).

◆ Stimulating Demand – The right promotion can drive customers to make a purchase. In the case of products, a customer has not previously purchased or has not purchased in a long time, the promotional efforts may be directed at getting the customer to try the product. This is often seen with digital apps, where software companies offer free limited versions of their products. For products with an established customer base, promotion can encourage customers to increase their purchasing by providing a reason to buy products sooner or in greater quantities than they normally do. For example, a pre-holiday newspaper advertisement may remind customers to stock up on beverages for the holiday by purchasing more than they typically purchase during non-holiday periods.

◆ Reinforcing the Brand – Once a purchase is made, a marketer can use promotion to help build a strong relationship that can lead to the purchaser becoming a loyal customer. For instance, many retail stores now ask for a customer's email address so follow-up emails containing additional product information or even an incentive to purchase other products from the retailer can be sent in order to strengthen the customer-marketer relationship.

THE COMMUNICATION PROCESS

Before we venture into an in-depth analysis of promotion, it is necessary to lay additional groundwork by examining how communication works. By understanding the basic concepts of communication, the marketer will have a better idea of what actions should be pursued or avoided to get its message out to its target market.

The act of communicating has been evaluated extensively for many, many years. One of the classic analyses of communication took place in the 1940s and 1950s when researchers, including Claude Shannon and Warren Weaver (2), Wilbur Schramm (3) and others, offered models describing how communication takes place. In general, communication is how people exchange meaningful information. Models that reflect how communication occurs often include the elements shown on Figure 11-1. (4)

Figure 11-1: The Communication Process

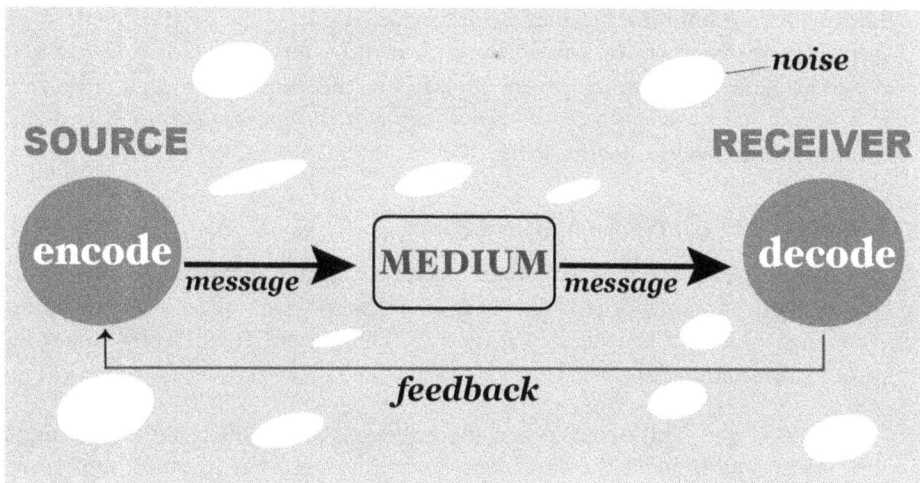

Below we discuss the key elements of the communication process shown in Figure 11-1.

COMMUNICATION PARTICIPANTS

For communication to occur, there must be at least two participants:

- Message Source – The source of communication is the party intending to convey information to another party. In marketing, the message source can be an individual (e.g., salesperson) or an organization (e.g., through advertising). In order to convey a message, the source must engage in **message encoding**, which involves mental and physical processes necessary to construct a message in order to reach a desired goal (i.e., convey meaningful information). This undertaking consists of using sensory stimuli such as imagery (e.g., written words, symbols, images), sound (e.g., spoken word), and scent (e.g., fragrance) to convey a message.

- Message Receiver – The receiver of communication is the intended target of a message source's efforts. For a message to be understood, the receiver must engage in **message decoding** by undertaking mental and physical processes that give meaning to the message. Clearly, a message can only be decoded if the receiver is actually exposed to the message.

COMMUNICATION DELIVERY

Communication takes place in the form of a message exchanged between a source and receiver. A message can be shaped using one or a combination of sensory stimuli working together to convey meaning that meets the objectives of the sender. The sender uses a **transmission medium** to send the message. In marketing the medium may include: the use of information outlets where promotion is only part of the content provided, such as television, websites, apps, radio, and print; promotion-only outlets that only display promotional messages, such as direct mail and billboards; and person-to-person contact outlets where a person presents promotional information directly to another person, such as in-person contact (e.g., salespeople), email, and social media.

Additionally, communication can be improved if there is a two-way flow of information in the form of a **feedback channel**. This occurs if the message receiver is able to respond, often quickly, to the message source. In this way, the original message receiver now becomes the message source, and the communication process begins again.

OBSTACLES TO EFFECTIVE COMMUNICATION

While a message source may be able to deliver a message through a transmission medium, there are many potential obstacles to the message successfully reaching the receiver the way the sender intends. The potential obstacles affecting communication include:

- Poor Encoding – This occurs when the message source fails to create the right sensory stimuli to meet the objectives of the message. For instance, in person-to-person communication, verbally phrasing words poorly, so the intended communication is not what is actually meant, is the result of poor encoding. Poor encoding is also seen in advertisements that are difficult for the intended audience to understand, such as words or symbols lacking meaning or, worse, have totally different meaning within certain cultural groups. This often occurs when marketers use the same advertising message across many different countries. Differences due to translation or cultural understanding can result in the message receiver having a different frame of reference for how to interpret words, symbols, sounds, etc. This may lead the message receiver to decode the meaning of the message in a different way than was intended by the message sender.

- Poor Decoding – This refers to a message receiver's error in processing the message so that the meaning given to the received message is not what the source intended. This differs from poor encoding when it is clear, through comparative analysis with other receivers, that a particular receiver (e.g., other customers) perceived a message differently. Clearly, as we noted above, if the receiver's frame of reference is different (e.g., meaning of words are different) then decoding problems can occur. More likely, when it comes to marketing promotions, decoding errors occur due to personal or psychological factors, such as not paying attention to a full television advertisement, driving too quickly past a billboard, or allowing one's mind to wander while talking to a salesperson.

- Medium Failure – Sometimes communication channels break down and end up sending out weak or faltering signals. At other times, the wrong medium is used to communicate the message. For instance, trying to educate doctors about a new treatment for heart disease using television commercials that quickly flash highly detailed information is not going to be as effective as presenting this information in a print ad, where doctors can take their time evaluating the message.

- Communication Noise – Noise in communication occurs when an outside force, in some way, affects message delivery. The most obvious example is when loud sounds block the receiver's ability to hear a message. Nearly any distraction to the sender or receiver can lead to communication noise. For instance, many customers are overwhelmed (i.e., distracted) by the large number of marketing promotions (e.g., advertising) they encounter each day. Such **promotional clutter** (i.e., noise) makes it difficult for marketers to get their message through to desired customers.

As discussed in Box 11-1, knowledge of the communication process can help marketers avoid these obstacles.

CHARACTERISTICS OF PROMOTIONS

Before we discuss the different types of promotion options available to a marketer, it is useful to gain an understanding of the features that set different options apart. In this section, we isolate eight characteristics on which each promotional option can be judged. While these characteristics are widely understood as being important in evaluating the effectiveness of each type of promotion, they are by no means the only criteria used for evaluation. In fact, as new promotional methods emerge the criteria for evaluating promotional methods will likely change.

For our discussion, we will look at the following characteristics of a promotional method:

1. Intended Audience: Mass vs. Targeted

2. Payment Model: Paid vs. Non-Paid

3. Message Flow: One-Way vs. Two-Way

4. Interaction Type: Personal vs. Non-Personal

5. Demand Creation: Quick vs. Lagging

6. Message Control: Total vs. Minimal

7. Message Credibility: High vs. Low

8. Cost Assessment: Exposure vs. Action

Box 11-1

IMPROVING COMMUNICATION

For marketers, understanding how the communication process works can improve the delivery of their message. Marketers should focus on the following to improve communication with their targeted audience:

Carefully Encode

Marketers should make sure the message they send is crafted in a way that will be interpreted by message receivers as intended. This means having a firm understanding of how their audience interprets words, symbols, sounds, and other stimuli used by marketers. This is particularly beneficial when communicating to target markets that are beyond the marketer's own experiences. For instance, when marketing outside their native country marketers may encounter cultural differences that require adjustments to their advertising message. Marketers, who are not experienced with these differences, may consider using translation software programs to modify their message to fit the native language. However, these programs could present encoding problems as translations are often presented literally and may not be presented in the correct context used within a country. To address these issues, marketers may need to seek help from professionals, who are knowledgeable of a country's culture, customs and social behavior, including understanding the language requirements within local markets.

Allow Feedback

Encouraging the message receiver to provide feedback can greatly improve communication and help determine if a marketer's message was decoded and interpreted properly. Feedback can be improved by providing easy-to-use customer contact options, such as phone numbers and email. Additionally, the creation and management of social media and online forums may also enhance feedback.

Reduce Noise

In many promotional situations, the marketer has little control over interference with its message. However, there are a few instances where the marketer can proactively lower the noise level. For instance, salespeople can be trained to reduce noise by employing techniques limiting customer distractions, such as scheduling meetings during non-busy times, or by inviting potential customers to an environment offering fewer distractions, such as a conference facility. Additionally, advertising can be developed in ways that separate the marketer's ad from others, such as designing magazine ads with a large proportion of whitespace.

Choose Right Audience

Targeting the right message receiver will go a long way to improving a marketer's ability to promote its products. For example, messages are much more likely to be received and appropriately decoded when targeted to those who have an interest in the content of the message (see *Involvement* in Chapter 4).

1. Intended Audience: Mass Promotion vs. Targeted Promotion

Promotions can be categorized based on the intended coverage of a single promotional message. For instance, a single television advertisement for a major sporting event, such as the Olympics, NFL Super Bowl or World Cup, could be seen by millions of viewers at the same time. Such mass promotion, intended to reach as many people as possible, has been a mainstay of marketers' promotional efforts for a long time.

Unfortunately, while mass promotions are delivered to a large number of people, the actual number experiencing the promotion that fall within the marketer's target market may be small. Because of this, many who use mass promotion techniques find it to be an inefficient way to reach desired customers. Instead, today's marketers are turning to newer techniques designed to focus promotional delivery on only those with a high probability of being in the marketer's target market. For example, ad services offered by Google and Microsoft's Bing search engines employ methods for delivering highly targeted ads to customers as they enter terms in each company's search engine. (5) The assumption made by advertisers is that those who enter search terms are interested in the information they have entered, especially if they are searching by entering detailed search strings (e.g., phrases rather than a single word). Following this logic, advertisers, who have the ability to associate relevant words and phrases with their ad, are much more likely to have these displayed to customers within their target market leading to a potentially higher return on their promotional investment. The movement to highly targeted promotions has gained tremendous traction in recent years and, as new and improved targeting methods are introduced, its importance will continue to grow.

2. Payment Model: Paid vs. Non-Paid

Most efforts to promote products requires marketers make direct payments to the transmission medium that is delivering the message. For instance, an organization must pay a magazine publisher to advertise in the magazine. However, there are several forms of marketing promotion that do not involve direct payment in order to distribute a promotional message. While not necessarily "free" since there may be indirect costs involved, the ability to have a product promoted without making direct payment to the medium can be a viable alternative to expensive promotion options.

3. Message Flow: One-Way vs. Two-Way Communication

Promotions can be classified based on whether the message source enables the message receiver to respond with immediate feedback. Such feedback can then be followed with further information being exchanged between both parties. Most efforts at mass promotion, such as television advertising, offer only a one-way information flow that does not allow for easy response by the message receiver. However, many targeted promotions, such as using a sales force to promote products, enable message recipients to respond immediately to information from the message sender.

4. Interaction Type: Personal vs. Non-Personal

Promotions involving real people communicating with potential customers is considered personal promotion. While salespeople are a common and well understood type of personal promotion, another type of promotion, **controlled word-of-mouth promotion**, has evolved as another form of personal promotion. This type of promotion also uses personal contact to spread information about a product. However, unlike the use of salespeople, controlled word-of-mouth promotion is not intended to get a buyer to buy directly from the person who is doing the promoting (see *Controlled Word-of-Mouth Promotion* in Chapter 16).

One key advantage personal promotions have is the ability for the message sender to adjust the message as they obtain feedback from message receivers (i.e., two-way communication). So, if a customer does not understand something in the initial message (e.g., does not fully understand how the product works), the person delivering the message can adjust the promotion to address questions or concerns. Many non-personal forms of promotion, including television and radio advertisements, are inflexible, at least in the short-term, and cannot be easily adjusted to address questions raised by the audience experiencing the ad.

5. Demand Creation: Quick vs. Lagging

As we discussed earlier, the success of promotional activity may not always be measured by comparing spending to an increase in product sales since marketers may use promotion to achieve other objectives. However, when a marketer is seeking to increase demand, certain promotional activities offer advantages in turning exposure to promotion into a quick increase in demand. In general, these activities are most effective when customers are offered a monetary incentive (e.g., save money) or a psychological reason (e.g., improves a customer's perceived group role or status level) to make the purchase.

6. Message Control: Total vs. Minimal

Most promotions are controlled by the marketer, who encodes the message and then pays to have the message delivered. However, no marketer can totally control how the news media, customers, or others talk about a company or its products. Reporters for magazines, newspaper, and news websites, as well as those posting comments on social media, internet forums and retailers' websites, may discuss a company's products in ways that can benefit or hinder an organization's marketing efforts. This is particularly true with non-paid promotions, where a marketer is looking to obtain a free "mention" by an influential message medium, such as a newspaper article, but has little control in getting this to occur (see *Disadvantages of PR* in Chapter 15).

7. MESSAGE CREDIBILITY: HIGH VS. LOW

The perceived control of the message can influence the target market's perception of message credibility. For example, many customers viewing a comparative advertisement, where one product is shown to be superior to a competitor's product, may be skeptical about the claims since the company with the superior product is paying for the advertisement. Yet if the same comparison is mentioned in an article on a news outlet's website it may be more favorably viewed since readers may perceive the author of the story (e.g., reporter) as being unbiased in her/his point-of-view.

8. COST ASSESSMENT: EXPOSURE VS. ACTION

The final characteristic classifies promotions based on the method by which costs are determined for running a promotion. For instance, as we will see in Chapter 12, when it comes to advertising, marketers face numerous costs ranging from promotion creation to message delivery. Costs can be assessed in two main ways: 1) based on general exposure to the promotion; and 2) based on action taken. Box 11-2 provides further insight on these options.

Box 11-2

MEASURES OF PROMOTIONAL EFFECTIVENESS

Whether a promotion is working or not is primarily determined by analyzing the cost of running a promotion versus the results obtained. In general, there are two main methods available for assessing promotional effectiveness:

1. Measurement Based on Exposure

2. Measurement Based on Action

Effectiveness Based on Exposure

With the exposure method, marketers make promotional decisions based on how many people will be exposed to the promotion in relation to the cost of running the promotion. This method has been a mainstay for assessing promotion for a long time primarily because it is easy to calculate. However, the presumption of marketers using this approach is that exposure leads customers to do something, such as make a product purchase. Yet tying exposure to a customer action is not always possible (see *Effectiveness Based on Action* discussion below). Consequently, the exposure approach may be all that is available.

Within the exposure method are two options:

Cost-per-Mille (CPM) – The CPM option evaluates how many people are exposed to a promotion in relation to the cost of the promotion. CPM (also called **cost-per-thousand** as mille is Latin for a thousand) is a commonly used promotional measurement for mass media outlets, such as print and broadcast markets. It is also used in the online advertising industry, though it is generally referred to as **cost-per-impression (CPI)**. CPM calculates how much promotion costs for each 1,000 exposures. For example, if an advertisement costs (US) $10,000 in a city newspaper having a circulation of 500,000 then the CPM for that advertisement is calculated as follows:

$$\textbf{CPM} = \frac{\textbf{\$10,000}}{\textbf{500,000 / 1,000}} = \textbf{\$20}$$

A national or international television advertisement, while expensive to create and broadcast, actually produces a very low CPM given how many people are exposed to the advertisement.

Cost-per-Targeted Exposure (CPTE) – A low CPM can be misleading if a large percentage of the promotion's audience is not within the marketer's target market, in which case the CPTE may be a better metric for gauging promotion effectiveness. The CPTE option looks at what percentage of an audience is within the marketer's customer group and, thus, legitimate targets for the promotion. Clearly, CPTE is higher than CPM, but it offers a better indication of how much promotion is reaching targeted customers.

Effectiveness Based on Action

An even more effective way to evaluate promotional costs is through the **cost-per-action (CPA)** metric. With CPA, the marketer evaluates how many people actually respond to a promotion. Response may be measured by examining purchase activity, website traffic, taps on smartphone advertisements, number of phone inquiries, and other means within a short time after the promotional message is delivered.

Unfortunately, measuring CPA is not always easy and tying it directly to a specific promotion can also be difficult. For example, a customer who purchases a snack product may have first learned about the snack product several weeks before from a television advertisement. The fact that it took the customer some time to make the purchase does not mean the advertisement was not effective in generating sales, though if the CPA was measured within a day or two after the ad was broadcast, this person's action would not have been counted.

However, marketers have at their disposal an ever-growing array of sophisticated customer tracking and analytics techniques, especially for promotions delivered through the internet and mobile networks (see Box 13-2 in Chapter 13). These techniques are continually improving marketers' ability to match exposure to action. Consequently, CPA is bound to one day be the dominant method for measuring promotional effectiveness.

THE PROMOTION MIX

Marketers have at their disposal four main methods of promotion, which taken together comprise the promotion mix. In this section, a basic definition of each method is offered while in the next section a comparison of each method based on the eight characteristics of promotion is presented.

ADVERTISING

This form of promotion involves non-personal paid promotions often using mass media outlets to deliver the marketer's message. While historically advertising has been a one-way form of communication with little feedback opportunity for the customer experiencing the advertisement, rapid developments in information technology and digital networks are presenting customers with more options to provide their opinions on the ads they experience. (6)

SALES PROMOTION

This promotional method covers special short-term techniques, often in the form of incentives, that encourage customers to respond to or undertake some activity. For instance, the use of retail coupons with expiration dates requires customers act while the incentive is still valid.

PUBLIC RELATIONS

Also referred to as publicity, this type of promotion attempts to encourage third-party sources, and particularly the news media and those with a strong online presence, to offer a favorable mention of the marketer's organization and its products. This is accomplished without offering direct payment to the third-party sources.

PERSONAL SELLING

As the name implies, this form of promotion involves personal contact between company representatives and those who have a role in making purchase decisions. For instance, engaging in personal contact with members of a company's buying center (see Box 4-2 in Chapter 4). Often the contact occurs face-to-face, over the telephone, or via online video conferencing.

Each of these methods will be covered in much greater detail in subsequent chapters.

Promotion Mix Summary

Table 11-1 below compares each of the promotion mix options on the eight key promotional characteristics.

Table 11-1: Promotion Mix Summary

Characteristics	Advertising	Sales Promotion	Public Relations	Personal Selling
Intended Coverage	mass targeted	mass targeted	mass	targeted
Payment Model	paid limited non-paid	paid	non-paid	paid
Message Flow	one-way two-way	one-way two-way	one-way	two-way
Interaction Type	non-personal	personal non-personal	non-personal	personal
Demand Creation	lagging	quick	lagging	quick
Message Control	good	good	poor	very good
Message Credibility	low-medium	low-medium	high	medium-high
Cost Assessment	CPM – low CPTE – varies CPA – varies	CPM – medium CPTE – varies CPA – varies	CPM – one CPTE – none CPA – none	CPM – high CPTE – high CPA – high

Evolving Promotional Options

The promotion mix summary presented in Table 11-1 should be viewed only as a general guide, since promotion techniques are continually evolving, and how each technique is compared on a characteristic is subject to change. For instance, the evolution of the internet and mobile technologies are blurring the lines between the promotional categories. This can be seen with the use of social media outlets, such as Facebook, TikTok, and YouTube. As an example, on the surface it would seem a posting by a company on its social media account introducing a new product should be classified as an advertisement since it contains many of the key advertising characteristics. However, most social media postings can be developed without direct payment to a media outlet (i.e., payment to the social media site), which is generally considered a necessary requirement for a promotion to be classified as public relations and not advertising.

Additionally, as we will see in the following chapters, there are several additional aspects of promoting through social media that would place these promotions within other promotional categories. For our discussion, we will continue to place social media promotions within the four existing promotional categories. However, it is likely that as new promotional options using social media continue to evolve, a new promotional category will eventually emerge.

Factors Affecting Promotion Choice

With four promotional methods to choose from, how does the marketer determine which ones to use? The selection can be complicated by the following corporate and marketing decision issues:

CORPORATE ISSUES

- Promotional Objective – As we discussed, there are several different objectives a marketer may pursue with its promotional strategy. Each type of promotion offers different advantages in terms of helping marketers reach their objectives. For instance, if the objective of a subscription-based genealogy website is to get customers to try their service, the use of sales promotion, such as offering a 14-day free trial, may yield better results than simply promoting through a general smartphone app advertisement.

- Availability of Resources – The amount of money and other resources that can be directed to promotion affects the marketer's choice of promotional methods. Marketers with large promotional budgets may be able to spread spending across all promotion options, while marketers with limited funds must be more selective with the promotional techniques they use.

- Company Philosophy – Some companies follow a philosophy dictating where most promotional spending occurs. For example, some companies follow the approach that all promotion should be done through salespeople while other companies prefer to focus marketing funds on product development and hope word-of-mouth communication by satisfied customers helps to create interest in their products.

MARKETING DECISION ISSUES

- Target Market – As one might expect, customer characteristics often dictate how promotion is determined. Characteristics, such as size, location and type of target markets, affect how the marketer communicates with customers. For instance, for a small marketer serving business markets with customers widely dispersed, it may be expensive to utilize a sales force versus using advertising.

- Product – Different products require different promotional approaches. For the consumer market, products falling into the convenience and shopping goods categories are likely to use mass market promotions, such as advertising, while higher-end specialty goods are likely to use personal selling. Therefore, for products that are complex, expensive and take customers extended time to make a purchase decision, person-to-person promotion may be more effective than methods of mass promotion. This is often the case with products targeted to the business market. Additionally, as we discussed in Chapter 7, products pass through different stages in the Product Life Cycle. As a product moves through these stages, the product itself may evolve and promotional objectives may change. This leads to different promotional mix decisions from one stage to the next (see *Planning and Strategy with the PLC* in Chapter 20).

- Distribution – Organizations selling through channel partners can reach the final customer either directly using a **pull promotional strategy** or indirectly using a **push promotional strategy**. The pull strategy is so named since it creates demand for a product by promoting directly to the final customers hoping their interest in the product will help "pull" more product through the distribution channel. This approach can be used when channel partners are hesitant about stocking a product unless they are assured of sufficient customer demand. Alternatively, the push strategy uses promotion to encourage channel partners, often through incentives, to stock and promote the product to their customers. The idea is that by offering incentives to channel members the marketer is encouraging its partners (e.g., wholesalers, retailers) to "push" the product down the channel and into customers' hands (e.g., retailer promotes product to their customers). While most large consumer products companies will simultaneously use both the pull and push strategies, due to the potential high expense of each strategy smaller firms may find they must focus on just one approach.

- Price – Because customers generally need more time and more information when deciding to purchase higher priced products, marketers of these product are more likely to engage in personalized promotion compared to lower priced products that can be marketed using mass promotion.

REFERENCES

1. It should be noted that a co-marketing agreement is not the same as a co-branding agreement that was discussed in Chapter 6. While co-branding utilizes the power of two brands on a new product (e.g., co-branded credit cards), co-marketing does not create a new product but instead companies work together to promote each other's products.

2. Claude. E. Shannon and Warren Weaver. *The Mathematical Theory of Communication*. University of Illinois Press, 1949.

3. Wilbur Schramm. *The Process and Effects of Mass Communication*. University of Illinois Press, 1960.

4. Much of the theory behind the communication process assumes it involves human-to-human contact. Yet as communication methods supported by artificial intelligence continue to evolve it would be expected that the communication process, as it pertains to marketing, will also transform into something that may be different than what is discussed here. However, for the majority of today's marketers this model of the communication process can still be viewed as being highly relevant.

5. For more on their targeted search advertising see: "Google Ads." *Google.* https://adwords.google.com/home and "Microsoft Advertising." *Microsoft.* https://ads.microsoft.com.

6. As we will discuss in Chapter 12, advertisers are now utilizing methods, such as quick response (QR) codes placed within an advertisement, that allow those experiencing the ad to rapidly obtain further information about the product being advertised.

Chapter 12: Advertising

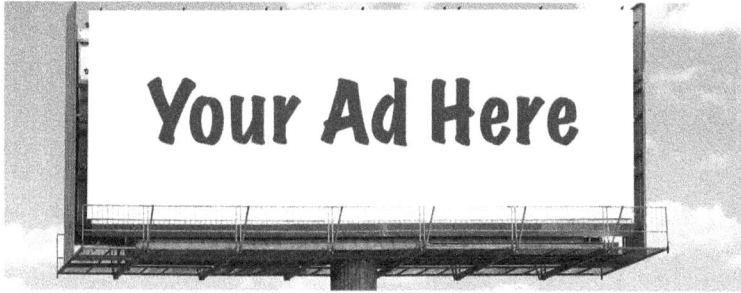

Spending on advertising is huge. While the amount spent on advertising may have dropped significantly during the coronavirus pandemic, organizations still rely heavily on this method of promotion. In fact, it is estimated that around the world marketers spend over (US) $800 billion a year on advertising. (1) This level of spending supports thousands of companies and millions of jobs. In fact, in many countries most media outlets, such as television, radio, websites, social media and print publications, would not be in business without revenue generated through the sale of advertising.

In this chapter, we present the first of a two-part examination of advertising with a discussion of advertising basics. We begin by covering several fundamental issues in advertising including examining what advertising is and why it is important to the marketing organization. We also look at managing the advertising effort by comparing in-house management to that offered by advertising professionals, such as advertising agencies. Finally, we identify different types of advertising and address trends facing the advertising industry.

WHAT IS ADVERTISING?

Advertising is a non-personal form of promotion delivered through selected media outlets that, under most circumstances, requires the marketer to pay for message placement. Advertising has long been viewed as a method of mass promotion in that a single message can reach a large number of people. But this mass promotion approach presents problems since many exposed to an advertising message may not be within the marketer's target market. Because of this, some marketers view advertising as an inefficient use of promotional funds. However, this is changing as new advertising technologies, along with the emergence of new media outlets (see *Type of Media Outlets* in Chapter 13), offer more options for targeted advertising.

Advertising also has a history of being considered a one-way form of marketing communication, where the message receiver (i.e., target market) is not in a position to respond right away to the message. That is, customers cannot immediately seek more information or quickly purchase a product they see advertised. However, this too is changing. For example, many advertisers now include a **quick response (QR) code** on different types of advertisements, including within television ads. The QR codes enable those experiencing the ad to use a mobile device to scan the code to obtain additional advertiser information (e.g., displaying an informational webpage). (2) This development and others suggest that in a few years advertising will move away from a one-way communication model and become one that is highly interactive.

Advantages of Advertising

There are many reasons marketers are attracted to advertising as a method for promoting their products. First, advertising not only has the potential to reach a sizable audience, it can do so in a very short period of time. For instance, while some forms of promotion, such personal selling, reach only a small number at one time, a single advertisement on mass media can be experienced by thousands and even millions of potential customers.

Second, for consumer goods marketers, the inclusion of advertising within a marketing plan may be a convincing factor in gaining the support of resellers (e.g., wholesalers, retailers). While resellers may not be concerned with the creative elements of an advertising campaign (i.e., characters portrayed in an ad), they may feel the marketer is committed to a product's success based on the amount of advertising money being allocated to support a product.

Third, one of the most famous quotes about advertising that is often attributed to Philadelphia retailer John Wanamaker and uttered over 100 years ago says, "Half the money I spend on advertising is wasted; the trouble is I don't know which half." (3) While this statement may still apply to some organizations, newer approaches to advertising offer marketers highly effective methods for targeting customers and also tracking their response. The evolution of advertising to a promotional method that can directly match ad spending to results is making it easier for organizations to allocate funds to advertising methods that are more effective, thus reducing the uncertainty espoused by Wanamaker.

Fourth, as we have noted several times, the internet and mobile technologies have significantly impacted all areas of marketing. One of the most powerful effects these have brought to advertising is the ability to retain advertisements. In this way, an advertisement is no longer restricted to being delivered through a single media outlet (e.g., video ad only on television) or only at a specific time (e.g., single showing of ad during a television program). Instead, with the rise of social media and video sharing sites, such as YouTube, potential customers can still be exposed to an ad even though it is not in the media outlet where it was originally presented. Even better, customer exposure to these ads in other outlets may happen at little or no cost to the marketer.

Finally, advertising is often the best promotional method for responding to serious or sensitive issues, such as addressing a major catastrophe. For instance, advertising is often the best approach for marketers to deliver a heartfelt or explanatory message in response to an issue impacting their customers in local, regional, national, or international markets.

Disadvantages of Advertising

While advertising is often hailed as the best way to promote a product, it does come with several negative issues. First, some forms of advertising are extremely expensive to create and distribute. Consequently, these may not be viable options for many organizations, particularly those marketers operating small businesses. For instance, the production expense for a 30-second advertisement running on a major U.S. prime-time television program may cost well over a half million dollars. Marketers must then factor in the cost of paying a network for advertising time, which can also be a significant expense (see *Television Advertising* in Chapter 13).

Second, the number of exposures to an advertiser's message (i.e., see or hear an ad) that are needed before the message is fully comprehended by the target market appears to be increasing. This is due to a nearly overwhelming number of advertisements customers experience every day. As we will discuss, cutting through the clutter to reach customers may require a large number of exposures that may only occur with heavy spending on advertising (see *Advertising Clutter* in Chapter 13).

Third, for most organizations to be effective using advertising they will need to be highly creative. However, the skills required to be creative may not be the forte of many marketers. In particular, this may be a disadvantage for smaller marketers as bigger organizations are often in a stronger financial position to seek out highly creative people to handle their advertising needs (see *Advertising Agency Functions* discussion below).

Fourth, because of the constant onslaught of advertising across numerous outlets, many customers have taken a negative view and intentionally try to avoid exposure to ads. This can be seen with television streaming services that enable viewers to fast-forward through ads on recorded television programs and with their use of web browsers that block online advertising (see *Ad Skipping and Blocking* discussion below).

Fifth, some forms of advertising have raised environmental concerns. In particular, advertisements posted on telephone poles, buildings, windshields, and other outdoor locations may adversely impact the appearance of neighborhoods and cities. Additionally, if these ads become loose these can increase trash found in public spaces.

Finally, in addition to intentional avoidance of advertising, there is also a heightened level of negative reaction and response to ads. People exposed to ads they dislike are more likely to share their displeasure with a larger group, such as through social media. If such criticism is widely shared, this may harm a marketer's image and force them to expend additional resources to address the issue (see *Market Monitoring* in Chapter 15).

OBJECTIVES OF ADVERTISING

In Chapter 11, we explained five objectives that may be achieved using promotion. Advertising can address all of these, though at different levels of effectiveness.

◆ Building Awareness – The mass communication nature of advertising makes it a particularly attractive promotional option for marketers who are introducing new products and looking to build market awareness. Additionally, advertising can be used to help support a strategy to reposition a product (see *Product*

Positioning in Chapter 5) by creating awareness among a target market to the benefits offered by the product that are new or that may not have been previously known.

◆ Creating Interest – Advertisements are creative productions with the power to capture customers' attention. As we will see in Chapter 13, the large number of methods and media outlets for presenting an advertisement offers marketers ample ways to create appealing ads intended to excite customer interest.

◆ Providing Information – Many forms of advertising expose a targeted market to a message in a brief way and are often not suitable for providing extensive information. However, there are some forms of advertising that can convey a good amount of information. For instance, advertisements sent by direct mail can offer in-depth product information with the inclusion of detailed booklets, links to online videos, and product samples.

◆ Stimulating Demand – Advertising is often used as part of a campaign to encourage a target market to make a purchase. While this certainly seems an obvious usage of advertising, in fact, by itself advertising is not the most effective promotional tool to achieve this objective. Instead, advertisements, that on the surface appear to have the objective of stimulating demand, are generally part of a broader promotional strategy that includes other forms of promotion, most notably sales promotion (see Chapter 14).

◆ Reinforcing the Brand – Repeated use of advertising is often required to support a product. Given the number of ads a target market is exposed to on a regular basis, it almost has become a necessity for marketers to advertise consistently as they fear customers will forget about their product if competitors advertise more frequently. Companies operating in markets where competitors spend heavily on advertising must also spend in order to maintain a consistent **share-of-voice** within the market (i.e., percentage of one marketer's spending on advertising in relation to total spending by all advertisers).

TYPES OF ADVERTISING

If you ask most people what is meant by "type" of advertising, invariably they will respond by defining it in terms of how it is delivered (e.g., television ad, internet ad, etc.). But in marketing, type of advertising refers to the primary "focus" of the message being sent and falls into one of the following categories:

PRODUCT-ORIENTED ADVERTISING

Most advertising spending is directed toward the promotion of a specific good, service, or idea; what we have collectively labeled as an organization's product. In most cases, the goal of product advertising is to promote a specific product to a targeted audience. Marketers can accomplish this in several ways from a low-key approach that simply provides basic information about a product (**informative advertising**) to blatant appeals that try to convince customers to purchase a product (**persuasive advertising**), including using direct comparisons between the marketer's product and its competitor's offerings (**comparative advertising**).

However, sometimes marketers intentionally produce product advertising where the target audience cannot readily see a connection to a particular product. Marketers of new products may follow this **teaser advertising** approach in advance of a new product introduction to prepare the market for the product. For instance, one week before the launch of a new product a marketer may air a television advertisement proclaiming, "*After next week the world will never be the same.*" However, they may do so without any mention of a product or even the company behind the ad. The goal is to create curiosity in the market and interest when the product is launched.

IMAGE ADVERTISING

Image advertising is undertaken primarily to enhance an organization's perceived importance to a target market. Image advertising does not focus on products as much as it presents what an organization has to offer. In these types of ads, if products are mentioned it is within the context of "what we do" rather than a message touting the benefits of a specific product. Image advertising is often used in situations where an organization needs to educate the targeted audience on some issue. For instance, image advertising may be used when a merger has occurred between two companies and the newly formed company has taken on a new name. This type of advertising may also be utilized if a problem has led to negative publicity (e.g., oil spill) and the company wants to let the market know they are about much more than this one issue.

ADVOCACY ADVERTISING

Organizations also use advertising to send a message intended to influence a targeted audience. In most cases, there is an underlying benefit sought by an organization when they engage in advocacy advertising. For instance, an organization may take a stand on a political issue, which they feel could negatively impact the organization, and will target advertisements to voice its position.

PUBLIC SERVICE ADVERTISING

In some countries, not-for-profit organizations are permitted to run advertisements through certain media outlets free of charge if the message contained in the ad concerns an issue viewed as being for the "greater good" of society. For instance, ads directed at social causes, such as teenage smoking, opioid addiction and mental illness, may run on television, radio, and other media without cost to organizations sponsoring the advertisement. Though, in most cases, these ads will air at times when the media outlet does not have a paid advertisement to run.

MANAGING ADVERTISING DECISIONS

Delivering an effective marketing message through advertising requires many different decisions as the marketer develops its advertising campaign. For small campaigns involving little creative effort, one or a few people may handle the bulk of the work. In fact, the internet has made do-it-yourself advertising an easy to manage process and has especially empowered small businesses to control their advertising decisions. Not only can small firms handle the creation and placement of image advertisements appearing on the internet and mobile apps, new services have even made it possible for a single person to create video advertisements. (4)

For larger campaigns, the skills needed to make sound advertising decisions can be quite varied and may not be easily handled by a single person. While larger companies manage some advertising activities within the company, they are more likely to rely on the assistance of advertising professionals, such as those found at advertising agencies (see Box 12-1), to help bring their advertising campaign to market.

TRENDS IN ADVERTISING

Like most areas of marketing, advertising is changing rapidly. Some even argue that changes in the last 20 years have affected advertising more than any other marketing function. The most notable trends to have emerged include:

DIGITAL CONVERGENCE

While many different media outlets are available for communicating with customers, the ability to distinguish between outlets is becoming more difficult due to the convergence of different media types. Digital convergence, which refers to the use of information technology methods to deliver media programming, allows one media outlet to take advantage of features and benefits offered through other media outlets. This can be seen most clearly with television, which in many areas around the world, is broadcast digitally using the same principles of information delivery that are used to allow someone to connect to the internet or mobile networks. This convergence of television opens many potential advertising opportunities for marketers to target customers in ways that were not previously available. For example, the development of **interactive television** is enabling viewers to respond to what appears on their screen in much the same way as can be done when seeing ads on a website. Television advertisements can now encourage viewers to navigate their TV screen (e.g., click using remote control) to acquire more product information, participate in product-related trivia, and even choose a specific version of an ad. (5)

Box 12-1

ADVERTISING AGENCY FUNCTIONS

When marketers look for advertising help, they often turn to advertising agencies. The services offered by an ad agency cover both offline and online methods, and will vary depending on the size and expertise of the agency. For full-service agencies, service offerings will often include:

Account Management

Within an advertising agency, the account manager or account executive handles all key decisions related to a specific client. These responsibilities include locating and negotiating to acquire clients. Once a client agrees to work with the agency, the account manager works closely with the client to develop an advertising strategy. For large clients, an agency may assign an account manager to work full time with only one client and, possibly, with only one of the client's product lines. For smaller accounts, an account manager may manage several different, non-competing accounts.

Creative Team

Agency account managers delegate creative tasks, such as generating ideas, designing concepts and creating the final advertisements, to the agency's creative team. An agency's creative team consists of specialists in graphic design, film and audio production, copywriting, website and mobile app design, and much more.

Researchers

Full-service advertising agencies employ marketing researchers who assess a client's market situation, including understanding customers and competitors, and carrying out tests of creative ideas. For instance, in the early stages of an advertising campaign, researchers may run focus group sessions with selected members of the client's target market in order to get their reaction to several advertising concepts. Following the completion of an advertising campaign, they may use research to measure whether the campaign reached its objectives.

Media Planners

Once an advertisement is created it must be placed in appropriate advertising media outlets. Each advertising media has its own unique methods for accepting advertisements, such as different advertising cost structures (i.e., what it costs marketers to place an ad), different requirements for accepting ad designs (e.g., size of ad), different ways placements can be purchased (e.g., direct contact with media or through a third-party seller), and different time schedules (i.e., time of day an ad will run). Understanding the nuances of different media is the role of media planners, specialists who assist with the development of media strategies including looking for the best media matches and negotiating promotional deals with media outlets.

Other Specialists

In addition to the services listed above, many advertising agencies offer their clients a variety of other services. These include management of social media outlets, expertise in improving a client's position on search engine results (see *Search Engine Optimization* in Chapter 15), and marketing analytics.

Additionally, digital convergence offers advertisers more selective targeting options, such as delivering ads to one household that are different from ads delivered to a neighbor's television even though both households are watching the same program.

The impact of digital convergence is not limited to television. Many media outlets are utilizing technology in creative ways to deliver advertising. Some examples of convergence opportunities that are either currently being pursued or will be in the near future include:

- A media outlet's smartphone application uses GPS technology to trigger a specific advertisement based on a person's physical location.

- A social media site uses information from users' posts and also from a wide range of outside data sources to display advertisements related to specific life events, such as a wedding engagement, new job, and graduation. (6)

- A direct mail postcard carries a different message based on data matching a household's address with television viewing habits.

- An outdoor billboard comes to life when viewed through a mobile app that is powered by **augmented reality (AR)** technology. (7)

The examples cited above represent just a few potential opportunities. The important point for marketers is to pay close attention to developments in this area as these could offer advantages for those who are early adopters.

FOCUS ON AUDIENCE TRACKING

The movement to digital convergence provides marketers with the basic resources needed to monitor users' activity, namely, **digital data**. Any media outlet relying on technology (e.g., internet, mobile, CRM, etc.) to manage the flow of information does so using electronic signals generated by information technology. All digital data has the potential to be captured, stored, and evaluated using data analytics and other software programs.

For media outlets, information delivered in digital form offers the possibility of greater tracking of customers' exposure to specific advertisements. And tracking does not stop with what ads are being delivered; it also works with information being sent from the customer. For instance, as we noted earlier, for certain new advertising formats by clicking on their television screen viewers can obtain information about products they are seeing on their TV. Additionally, advanced advertising technology can allow for cross-channel promotions. This enables marketers to track customer activity across different digital outlets, such as laptops, tablets and smartphones, where customers can be exposed to ads for the same product that appeared on their television. Yet while tracking provides marketers with potentially useful information, this research method has raised many concerns as discussed in Box 12-2.

Box 12-2

AUDIENCE CONCERN WITH TRACKING

While media convergence presents marketers with more options for tracking response to advertisements, such activity also raises ethical and legal concerns, particularly as these relate to customer privacy. (8) Despite these concerns, customer tracking is widely used and newer methods continue to be deployed. Examples of how advertisers monitor and respond to customers include:

Television Viewing

The advent of digitally delivered television allows service providers (e.g., cable, streaming services) to track user activity across media devices and apps. For example, as discussed in Chapter 1, advertisers can track customers and display relevant ads across multiple digital outlets as part of cross-channel marketing promotions. Future innovation will make the user's television experience even more interactive, and consequently open to even more tracking.

Television Recording

Digital television services can track users recording habits and, based on a viewers' past activity, make suggestions for programs viewers may want to record. Additionally, technologies are being developed that can insert advertisements within recorded programs targeted to a particular viewer..

Website Visits

Each time someone accesses a website they leave an information trail that includes how they got to the site, how they navigated through the site, what they clicked on, what was purchased, and much more. When matched to methods of customer identification, such as website login, marketers can track a customer's activity over repeated visits. In fact, one advertising approach, called **remarketing**, follows visitors from one website to another and display ads based on content they viewed on other sites or terms they entered in a search engine (see Box 13-2 in Chapter 13).

Internet Spyware

Downloading games, videos and software, may contain a hidden surprise – spyware. Spyware is the name given to an application that may run in the background of a user's digital devices, and regularly forwards information (e.g., website visits) over the internet to the spyware's owner. The information is then used to gain an understanding of the user's interests or, in the case of adware, may be used to deliver ads based on what is learned about a user's website activity (see Box 1-2 in Chapter 1).

Other Device Tracking

Tracking also occurs on other connected devices including smart speakers. While consumers use these devices for multiple tasks, including creating shopping list, providing reminders and checking the weather, smart speakers can also track customers. For instance, smart speakers can offer shopping recommendations based on shopping list items and, with Amazon, on past purchases.

ADVANCED ADVERTISING RESEARCH

In addition to the research value gained through audience tracking, there is a growing trend to incorporate other highly advanced research techniques as part of advertising decision making. One method that is increasingly gaining marketers' attention is the use of neuro-research techniques. As discussed in Chapter 2, neuro-research utilizes sophisticated brain scanning to learn how people respond to an advertisement. So-called **neuromarketers** believe most processing of advertisements occurs within the unconscious part of the brain and, because of this, many people cannot easily communicate what they actually like or dislike about an ad. By connecting subjects to brain-scanning equipment, neuromarketers feel they can get a much better idea of how people feel about an advertisement. Additionally, eye-tracking devices can be added enabling researchers to match a subject's brain activity with eye movement to determine which parts of an advertisement are drawing the most attention.

AD SKIPPING AND AD BLOCKING

As noted in Box 12-2, advances in television technology offers marketers tremendous insight into viewers' habits and behavior. Yet from the consumer side, streaming television services (e.g., YouTube TV, Hulu) and the digital video recorders (DVR) are changing how people view television by allowing them to watch programming at a time that is most convenient for them. Viewer convenience is not the only advantage of on-demand services. Consumers are also attracted to these services as they often enable viewers to skip over commercials on recorded programs or watch programs that do not contain ads. Ad skipping is particularly an issue for broadcast networks that rely on advertising to pay for programming.

Additionally, advertisers are becoming more concerned when advertising online. In this medium, ad blocking has become a major threat as most web browsers make it easy to install add-on extensions that offer some level of ad blocking capability. These add-ons can be placed on web browsers across all platforms (i.e., computers, tablets, and smartphones).

As more consumers adopt ad skipping and ad blocking features, advertiser's concern with whether they are getting the best value for their television and online advertising money may become a major issue. This may lead them to invest their advertising funds in other media outlets or other promotional methods, where consumers are more likely to be exposed to an advertisement.

CHANGING MEDIA CHOICES

There is a significant cultural shift occurring in how people use media for entertainment, news, and information. Many traditional media outlets, such as newspapers and major television networks, are seeing their customer base eroded by the emergence of new media outlets. The internet and mobile apps have become the principal drivers of this change. In particular, a number of valuable applications tied to the internet and mobile communication are creating new media outlets and drawing the attention of many consumers. Examples include:

- Social Media – Possibly the most significant example of how media usage is changing can be seen with the rapid expansion of social media. Social networking outlets, such as Facebook and X (formerly Twitter), not only offer a venue for social exchange but also, for a growing number of people, these outlets are becoming principal sources for obtaining news and information.

- User-Generated Video Sites – In large part due to the popularity of YouTube and TikTok, what qualifies as video media has now changed. Now anyone can produce videos and post for the world to see. The result is that advertising choices for video production is no longer limited to television programs as marketers can present their ads as part of online video.

- Small Screen Video – While for many years accessing internet video content required the use of computers hardwired to high-speed data networks, today more and more users are streaming online video to small, handheld devices using wireless networks. Nearly all television networks now offer mobile apps to make its programming available in formats suitable for small screen viewing. These new formats also provide marketers with new advertising opportunities. With the number of small screen devices continuing to increase, it is likely this format for advertising will eclipse larger screen advertising within the next few years.

- Mobile Apps – In addition to television networks benefiting from ads viewed within mobile apps, ads on smartphones and tablets are offering rich new ground for all advertisers. In fact, continual improvement in mobile device performance and network data speeds has opened the door for marketers to present advanced advertisements, including "in app" video ads.

- Podcasting – Once considered a small niche within online audio programming, in the last few years podcasting has become an important media outlet. In large part due to highly affordable audio and video equipment, podcasting is quickly evolving into a multi-media entertainment platform. Advertiser have taken notice of these developments and are directing increasingly higher amounts of ad spending to this medium. (9)

- Online Gaming – While gaming systems have been around for some time, gaming accessible over information networks is still evolving. As internet and mobile network connections increase in speed, many gamers have shifted away from games loaded on their local computer and, instead, access games online. This shift is opening new territory for advertisers by enabling marketers to insert special content, including product advertising, within game play.

As these technologies gain momentum and move into mainstream acceptance, marketers may need to consider shifting advertising spending away from more traditional media outlets (e.g., television, print, website, etc.) and toward the newer media options. Marketers should also be aware that new media outlets will continue to emerge as new applications are developed. The bottom line for marketers is they must stay informed of new developments and understand how their customers are using these outlets in ways that may offer advertising opportunities.

GLOBAL SPENDING

When it comes to the location of advertising spending, the U.S. is by far the leader with an estimated 40% of all spending occurring in that market. (10) However, the world's largest companies have recognized that to grow their business they must direct more of their advertising budget to markets that are outside the U.S. While the world's top marketers already spend the majority of their advertising budgets outside the U.S., smaller firms will also need to consider expanding advertising to non-U.S. markets if they want to grow.

For marketers looking to move into foreign markets, the advertising decisions can be quite different compared to their home market. Marketers may find that advertising that works in one country does not work as easily in others. For this reason, marketers new to international marketing should take the time to learn how each market works and, in some cases, enlist the help of experts familiar with nuances of specific international markets (see Box 11-1 in Chapter 11).

REFERENCES

1. "Global Advertising Revenue." *GroupM*. https://www.groupm.com/mid-year-advertising-forecast-2023. It is worth noting that estimates of global advertising spending vary significantly depending on the source and estimation methods used.

2. For more on QR codes in advertising see: "5 Practical Ways to Incorporate QR Codes Into Your Marketing Plan." *Business News Daily*. February 21, 2023. https://www.businessnewsdaily.com/1767-qr-codes-business.html.

3. For more on the background of this retailer see: "John Wanamaker." *Wikipedia*. https://en.wikipedia.org/wiki/John_Wanamaker.

4. There are many options for small businesses to create their own professional looking video ads for placement on websites and apps. For example, Meta, parent company of Facebook, Instagram and others, offers a straightforward approach for creating ads as explained here: "How to Make a Video Ad in Meta Ads Manager." *Meta*. https://www.facebook.com/business/help/247179845697378.

5. For examples of how interactive television advertising works see: "A Suite of Ad Formats for Every Objective." *BrightLine*. https://www.brightline.tv/experience-library.

6. For information on how advertising targeting works on Facebook see: "Ad Targeting: Options to Reach Your Audience Online." *Meta*. https://www.facebook.com/business/ads/ad-targeting.

7. For insights on how augmented reality is used in marketing see: *Aircards*. https://www.aircards.co.

8. For more on issues with tracking see Box 1-2 *Tracking Customers Online and Offline* in Chapter 1.

9. "Podcast Advertising Spending in the United States." *Statista*. https://www.statista.com/statistics/610071/podcast-ad-spending-us.

10. "Magna Advertising Forecasts – June 2023." *Magna*. https://magnaglobal.com/global-ad-market-june-2023-update.

Chapter 13: Managing the Advertising Campaign

An important objective of marketing is to communicate with its target market with the goal of creating interest in an organization's goods and services. A key method for doing this is by engaging in the consistent use of advertising. For many organizations, this entails the development of advertising campaigns, which involves a series of decisions for planning, creating, delivering, and evaluating an advertising effort.

In this chapter, we continue our discussion of advertising by taking a closer look at the decisions involved in creating an advertising campaign. Whether a marketing organization employs a professional advertising agency to handle its advertising campaign or chooses to undertake all advertising tasks on its own, a successful campaign requires a number of critical decisions including: 1) setting the advertising objective; 2) setting the advertising budget; 3) selecting media for message delivery; 4) creating a message; and 5) evaluating campaign results. For leading consumer products companies, that spend large sums to promote their products, each of these decisions is intensely evaluated. Smaller companies with limited budgets may focus what little money they have on fewer decisions, such as message development and selecting media, and give less attention to other areas. No matter the organization's size, knowledge of all advertising campaign decisions is crucial and should be well understood by all marketers.

SETTING THE ADVERTISING OBJECTIVE

As we noted in the Chapter 12, advertising can be used to address several broad promotional objectives including building product awareness, creating interest, providing information, stimulating demand, and reinforcing the brand. To achieve one or more of these objectives, advertising is used to send a message containing information about some element of the marketer's offerings. For example:

◆ Message About Product – Details about the product play a prominent role in advertising for new and existing products. In fact, a large percentage of product-oriented advertising includes some mention of features and benefits offered by the marketer's product. Advertising is also used to inform customers of changes taking place in existing products. For instance, if a beverage company purchases a brand from another company resulting in a brand name change, an advertising message may stress, *"New Name but Same Great Taste."*

◆ Message About Price – Companies that regularly engage in price adjustments, such as running short term sales (see *Markdowns* in Chapter 18), can use advertising to let the market know of price reductions. Alternatively, advertising can be used to encourage customers to purchase now before a scheduled price increase takes place.

◆ Message About Other Promotions – Advertising often works hand-in-hand with other promotional mix items. For instance, special sales promotions, such as contests, may be announced within an advertisement. Also, advertising can help salespeople gain access to new accounts if the advertising precedes the salesperson's attempt to gain an appointment with a prospective buyer. This may be especially effective for a company entering a new market, where advertising may help reduce the uncertainty a buyer may have with setting up an appointment with a salesperson from a new company.

◆ Message About Distribution – Within distribution channels, advertising can help expand channel options for a marketer by making distributors aware of the marketer's offerings. Also, advertising can be used to let customers know locations where a product can be purchased.

SETTING THE ADVERTISING BUDGET

Setting an advertising objective is easy, but achieving the objective requires a well-thought-out strategy. One key factor affecting the strategy used to achieve advertising objectives is how much money an organization has to spend. The funds designated for advertising make up the advertising budget and reflect the amount an organization is willing to commit to achieve its advertising objectives. (1)

Organizations use several methods for determining advertising budgets including:

◆ Percentage of Sales – Under this approach, advertising spending is set based on either a percentage of previous sales or a percentage of forecasted sales. For example, an organization may set their next year's advertising budget at 10 percent of the current year's sales level. One problem with this approach is that the budget is based on what has already happened and not what is expected to occur. If the overall market grows rapidly in the following year, the budget may be well below what is necessary for the company to maintain or increase its sales. Alternatively, companies may consider allocating advertising funds based on a percentage of forecasted sales. In this way, advertising is viewed as a driver of future sales and spending on advertising is linked directly to meeting future sales forecasts. However, since future sales are not guaranteed, the actual percentage spent may be considerably higher than expected if the sales forecast is greater than what actually occurs.

◆ <u>What is Affordable</u> – Often small-sized marketers find spending of any kind to be difficult. In this situation, advertising may be just one of several tightly allocated spending areas with the level spent on advertising varying over time. For these marketers, advertising may only occur when extra funds are available.

◆ <u>Best Guess</u> – Companies entering new markets often lack knowledge of how much advertising will be needed to achieve their objectives. In cases where the market is not well understood, marketers may rely on their best judgment (i.e., executive's experience) of what the advertising budget should be.

SELECTING MEDIA OUTLETS

With an objective and a budget in place, the advertising campaign next focuses on developing the message. However, before effort is placed in developing a message the marketer must first determine which media outlets will be used to deliver its message. The choice of media outlets is crucial as it impacts the type of message that is created, the frequency with which the message will be delivered, the overall cost of the advertising campaign, and several other advertising decisions.

Characteristics of Media Outlets

An advertising message can be delivered via a large number of media outlets. These range from traditional established outlets, such as print publications, radio and television, to newer outlets, including placement within digital apps and podcasts. However, each media outlet possesses different characteristics and presents marketers with certain advantages and disadvantages.

The characteristics by which different media outlets can be assessed include the following seven factors:

1. Creative Options

2. Creative Development Cost

3. Media Market Reach

4. Message Placement Cost

5. Length of Exposure

6. Advertising Clutter

7. Response Tracking

1. CREATIVE OPTIONS

An advertisement has the potential to appeal to four senses – sight, sound, smell, and touch. (It should be noted that promotion can also appeal to the sense of taste but generally these efforts fall under the category of sales promotion, which is discussed in Chapter 14.) However, not all advertising media have the ability to deliver multi-sensory messages. Traditional radio, for example, is limited to delivering audio messages while roadside billboards offer only visual appeal. Additionally, some media may place limits on when particular sensory options can be used. For instance, some websites may only accept certain types of graphical-style advertisements if these conform to a specified minimum size while limiting smaller size advertising to text-only ads (see *Digital Media Advertising* discussion below).

While different media outlets offer different sensory options, these also may present the marketer with different requirements in term of what content is contained within an advertisement. For instance, popular media, such as major television networks and leading magazines, may be more restrictive on the message being conveyed in an ad, while smaller media, such as small websites and specialty mobile apps, may offer fewer content restrictions.

2. CREATIVE DEVELOPMENT COST

The media type selected to deliver a marketer's message also impacts the cost of creating the message. For media outlets that deliver a multi-sensory experience (e.g., television, internet and mobile for sight and sound; print publications for sight, touch, and smell), creative cost can be significantly higher than for media targeting a single sensory experience. But costs for creative advertisements are also affected by the expectation of quality of the media delivering the message. In fact, media outlets may set minimal production standards for advertisements and reject ads not meeting these standards. Television networks, for example, may set high production quality levels for advertisements they deliver. Achieving these standards requires expensive equipment and high-cost labor, which currently may not be feasible for smaller organizations. (2) Conversely, a simple text-only internet advertisement is inexpensive and easy to create.

3. MEDIA MARKET REACH

The number of customers exposed to a single promotional effort within a target market is considered the reach of a promotion. Some forms of advertising, such as national television advertising, offer an extensive reach, while other forms, such as a single roadside billboard on a lightly traveled road, offers limited reach.

The market reach for a media outlet can be measured along two dimensions:

1. Channels Served
2. Geographic Scope

Channels Served

This dimension relates to whether a media outlet is effective in reaching the members within the marketer's channel of distribution. Channels can be classified as:

- Consumer Channel – Does the media outlet reach the final consumer market targeted by the marketer?

- Trade Channel – Does the media outlet reach a marketer's channel partners who help distribute its product?

- Business-to-Business Channel – Does the media outlet reach customers in a business market (i.e., non-consumer market) targeted by the marketer?

Geographic Scope

This dimension defines the geographic breadth of a media outlet and includes:

- International – Does the media outlet have multi-country distribution?

- National – Does the media outlet cover an entire country?

- Regional – Does the media outlet have distribution across multiple geographic regions, within a country such as counties, states, provinces, territories, etc.?

- Local – Does the media outlet primarily serve a limited geographic area?

- Individual – Does the media outlet offer individual customer targeting?

4. MESSAGE PLACEMENT COST

Creative development is one of two principal spending considerations for advertising. The other cost is for media placement, which includes the purchase of time, space, or location from media outlets delivering the message. Advertising placement costs vary widely from extremely small amounts for certain online advertisements to highly expensive rates for advertising on major television programs (see Box 13-1). For example, in the United States the highest cost for advertising placement occurs with television ads shown during the National Football League's Super Bowl championship game, where ad rates for a single 30-second advertisement exceed (US) $7 million. (3) By contrast, ads placed through online search engines may cost less than (US) $5.

5. LENGTH OF EXPOSURE

Some products require customers be exposed to just a small amount of information in order to build customer interest. For example, the features and benefits of a new snack food can be explained in a short period of time using television or radio commercials. However, complicated products need to present more information for customers to understand the full concept. Consequently, advertisers of these products will seek media formats that allot more time to deliver the message.

Media outlets vary in how much exposure they offer to their audience. Print publications provide opportunities for longer exposure times since these media types can be retained (i.e., keep old print magazines) or are otherwise accessible (i.e., access previous issues online) by the audience, while exposure on television and radio are generally limited to the length of time the ad is broadcast.

Box 13-1

FACTORS IN SETTING ADVERTISING RATES

Media outlets set advertising rates using several factors, though the most important are the following:

Audience Size

The first factor refers to the number of people who experience the media outlet during a particular time period. For example, for television outlets audience size is measured in terms of the number of program viewers, for print publications audience is measured by the number of readers, and for websites audience is measured by the number of visitors. In general, the more people who are reached through a media outlet, the more the outlet can charge for ads. However, actual measurement of the popularity of media outlets is complicated by many factors to the point where media outlets are rarely trusted to give accurate figures reflecting their audience size. To help ensure the validity of **audience measurements**, nearly all leading media outlets have agreed to be audited by third-party organizations and most marketers rely on these auditors to determine whether the cost of ad placement in a specific media outlet is justified given the audited audience size. (4)

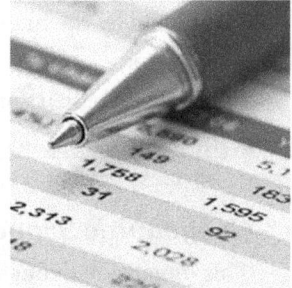

Audience Type

When choosing a media outlet, selection is evaluated based on the outlet's customer profile (i.e., viewers, readers, listeners, website visitors, app users) and whether this matches the characteristics of the marketer's desired target market. The more selectively targeted the audience, the more valuable this audience is to advertisers. This is because advertisements are being directed to those with the highest potential to respond to the advertiser's message. The result is that media outlets, whose audience possess similar characteristics (e.g., age, education level, political views, etc.) sought by certain advertisers, are in a position to charge higher advertising rates than media outlets that do not appeal to such a targeted group.

Characteristics of the Advertisement

Media outlets also charge different rates based on creative characteristics of the message. Characteristics that create ad rate differences include:

♦ Run Time – such as a 15-second versus a 30-second television advertisement

♦ Size – such as a few lines of text versus a full-page internet advertisement

♦ Print Style – such as a black-and-white versus a color postcard

♦ Location in Media – such as placement on the back cover versus placement on an inside page of a magazine

6. ADVERTISING CLUTTER

In order to increase revenue, media outlets often include a large number of ads within a certain time, space, or location. For instance, television programs may contain several ads inserted during the scheduled run-time of a program, including many presented as 15-second or shorter commercials. A large number of advertisements delivered through a growing number of different media outlets (e.g., smartphones, digital billboards, etc.) create an environment of advertising clutter, which makes it difficult for those in the targeted market to recognize and remember particular advertisements.

To break through the clutter, advertisers may be required to increase the frequency of their advertising efforts (i.e., run more ads). Yet greater **advertising frequency** increases advertising expense. Alternatively, advertisers may seek opportunities offering less clutter, where an ad has a better chance of standing out from other promotions. This can be seen with certain podcasts where one or a small number of "sponsors" may run just a few ads over the course of an hour-long program.

Some marketers also address clutter by placing ads in venues where placement has not been common, including such public spaces as school buses, parking meters, and public restrooms. While marketer say such placement offers the potential for greater advertising awareness, critics have characterized this as **ad creep** and say it strengthens their argument that marketers are continually invading personal privacy.

7. RESPONSE TRACKING

As we noted in Chapter 12, marketers are embracing new technologies making it easier to track audience response to advertisements. Newer media outlets developed using internet and mobile network technologies offer effective methods for tracking audience response compared to traditional media. But newer media is not alone in providing response tracking. Other advertising outlets, such as advertising by mail and television **infomercial** programming (i.e., long-form commercials), also provide useful measures of audience reaction.

Type of Media Outlets

Today's marketers must be well-versed in a wide range of media options. Advertising options that were once limited to just a few media outlets have dramatically expanded with the evolution of communication technology, including the continued developments in digital technology. This has changed how consumers and businesses are exposed to advertising messages. For example, many consumers will be simultaneously exposed for several media options as they sit in front of their television. With mobile phones, tablets, laptops and other devices readily present, a consumer's attention is easily taken away from television advertisements. Consequently, reaching a target market requires marketers to consider advertising through a variety of media outlets.

Below we discuss the leading media outlets used for advertising.

TELEVISION ADVERTISING

Television advertising offers the benefit of reaching large numbers in a single exposure. Yet because it is a mass medium capable of being seen by nearly anyone, television lacks the ability to deliver an advertisement to highly targeted customers compared to other media outlets. However, television networks are attempting to improve their targeting efforts. In particular, networks operating in the pay-to-access arena, such as those with channels on cable and TV streaming services, are introducing more narrowly themed programming designed to appeal to selective audiences. Despite these efforts, television remains an option that is best for products targeted to a broad market.

The geographic scope of television advertising ranges from advertising within a localized area (e.g., small town) using fee-based services offered by cable and fiber optic services, to advertising nationally using major broadcast networks.

As noted in Chapter 12, television advertising, once viewed as the pillar of advertising media outlets, is facing numerous challenges from alternative media (e.g., internet, wireless networks) and from the invasion of technology devices, such as digital video recorders (DVR), that have empowered viewers to be more selective when choosing ads to view. To combat this, many networks and local television stations now accept a broader range of advertising. For instance, while in the past the length of television ads were primarily 30 or 60 seconds, today ads appear with shorter run-times (e.g., 15-second ads), longer run-times (e.g., 30-minute infomercial), or even overlayed while a program is still broadcasting.

Yet for marketers, traditional television outlets, such as cable and fiber optic networks, are losing a significant number of customers. These customers, often referred to as cord cutters, are turning to newer internet-connected options, such as streaming services and specialized apps, to obtain their television content. (5) As noted in the *Digital Media Advertising* discussion below, many of these programming services offer tracking and targeting features not available with traditional television outlets. These newer services also offer interactive advertising that enables viewers to gain more information on a product presented in an advertisement by clicking a button on their remote control (see Digital Convergence in Chapter 12). When this is done, data is collected and customer response can be measured. For advertisers, streaming services may also offer the added benefit of blocking viewers ability to fast forward through ads. (6).

DIGITAL MEDIA ADVERTISING

The fastest growing media outlets for advertising are through those accessible on digital devices that utilize internet and wireless network technologies. Digital media advertising principally includes ads presented on computers, tablets, and "smart" devices, such as smartphones and smart TVs. (7) Compared to spending in other media, the rate of spending for digital media advertising has experienced tremendous growth. In fact, by some estimates, global spending on digital media is now the largest advertising medium as total expenditure now exceed television ad spending. (8) Digital media advertising's influence continues to expand and each year more major marketers shift a larger portion of their promotional budget to this medium. Two key reasons for this shift rest with the digital media's ability to: 1) narrowly target an advertising message; and 2) track user response to the advertiser's message. For advertisers, digital media offers several advertising options including:

- Website Advertising – When visiting a content-focused website (i.e., a website that primarily delivers informative content rather than selling products), there is a good chance visitors will be exposed to advertisements. Whether the website is viewed on a large screen or a small mobile device, ads are an omnipresent feature of most users' online experience. (9) When creating website advertising campaigns, marketers have a large number of options to consider. These include:

  - Multiple creative types including video, image-only, text-only, 360-degree, and virtual reality

  - Multiple ad sizes, including full-screen, various fixed designs (e.g., long and narrow, small square box), ads that open in a new browser window, and flexible ads that adjust to screen size

  - Multiple user involvement options including users exposed to an ad without needing to interact (e.g., ad appears on the top of the screen), users viewing and having to wait before viewing content (e.g., wait 10 seconds before watching a video), and users having to act (e.g., click) in order to remove the ad

  - Multiple general targeting options including displaying ads based on viewer demographics, geographic location, and time of day

  - Multiple specific targeting options including displaying ads based on user's input such as words entered in a search engine, displaying ads based on the content of a webpage (i.e., **contextual advertising**), and displaying ads based on user's previous experience on a particular website (see Box 13-2)

  - Selective ad placement options including displaying ads on specific websites, displaying ads in specific locations on a website (e.g., top of page), and presenting ads that appear to be part of the regular content of a site but are, in fact, advertisements (a.k.a., **native advertising**)

- Digital App Advertising – The growth in advertising on smartphones and other smart devices is being fueled by technological advances occurring with computing power as well as significant gains in speed of data delivered over wireless networks. This has resulted in rapid growth within the digital advertising industry. Not only are advertisements displayed when a user's digital device views certain internet sites, advertisements are also embedded within specialized apps that run on these devices. For example, many apps that make money by charging for access to a full-featured app will offer a "free" downloadable version that offers fewer features and also displays ads. Or a television network may market a free smart TV app that will allow access to ad-supported programming. Also, social media apps offer unique ways for inserting advertisements within users' postings. For instance, social media has embraced the use of augmented reality (AR) particularly for retailers selling clothing and personal care products that enable users to see how they may look when outfitted with these products. (10)

Box 13-2

HOW REMARKETING WORKS

As discussed in Chapter 12, a powerful promotional technique that has become a must-use strategy for digital marketers is remarketing. At its core, remarketing (also called **retargeting**) involves sending reminder messages to customers to get them to reconsider an action they did not take. For example, an e-commerce website can remarket to customers who visited the site but did not complete an online purchase. Targets of remarketing can range from customers, who only viewed a single page and then left the site, to situations of "**shopping cart abandonment**," where customers placed product in their online shopping cart only to not go forward with the purchase.

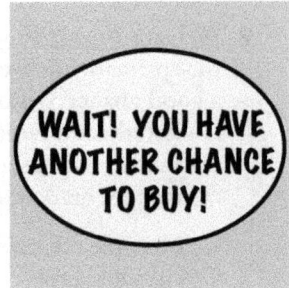

There are many ways remarketing can take place, but for simplicity purposes we will separate these as being either externally managed or internally managed. Externally managed remarketing occurs after customers leave a marketer's website or app. Prior to leaving, computer code is installed on the customer's digital device. Through the use of customer tracking methods, the code is recognized and remarketing can provide specific product reminder messages, typically in the form of advertisements, while customers are visiting other digital outlets. Message delivery is generally handled by a third-party provider, such as Google and other major advertising networks. For example, let's assume a customer visits Amazon and searches for a particular product, such as bird feeders. But after viewing a few product options, the customer leaves Amazon without making a purchase. Using remarketing techniques, Amazon can follow the customer to other websites, where an ad for bird feeders may appear, thus offering Amazon another chance to persuade the customer to make a purchase.

Internally managed remarketing is where the marketer provides their own reminders while the customer remains on the site. For instance, a visitor to a clothing website may have looked at several jackets but then shifted their search to view shirts. As the visitor examines shirts, a pop-up notice may remind them about the jackets they were previously investigating. Additionally, if the visitor is already a customer and has been identified when they came to the site, the website may also be able to remarket through the use of reminder emails.

While remarketing offers tremendous benefits for marketers, not everyone supports this marketing method. In particular, privacy advocates are at odds with remarketing techniques, claiming that most customers are not aware of the tracking that occurs. Additionally, for those who are aware, there is often no easy way to opt-out of being tracked. However, internal remarketing would appear to be somewhat less intrusive than externally managed remarketing, especially if someone is already an existing customer of the organization doing the remarketing. Yet for proponents of stronger privacy policies, tracking is still tracking no matter how it is done, so expect methods of remarketing to remain a contentious issue. (11)

- Email Advertising – Using email to deliver an advertisement affords marketers the advantage of low distribution cost and potentially high reach. In situations where the marketer has a highly targeted list, response rates to email advertisements may be quite high. This is especially true if those on the list have agreed to receive email, a process known as opt-in marketing. Email advertisement can take the form of a regular email message or be presented within the context of more detailed content, such as a newsletter. However, there is a significant downside to email advertising due to highly publicized issues related to abuse (i.e., spam).

- In-Text Advertising – This type of digital advertising ties ads to text found within a marketer's digital material, such as specific words or phrases contained in articles or other online content. For example, when placed on websites, text is formatted to be distinct from surrounding information (e.g., underlined words) and an ad will be triggered in the form of a pop-up box when visitors move their cursor over the text.

RADIO ADVERTISING

Promotion through radio has been a viable advertising option for 100 years. Radio advertising is mostly local to the broadcast range of a radio station, though, at least three options exist offering national and, potentially, international coverage. First, in many countries there are radio networks using many geographically distinct stations to broadcast simultaneously. In the United States, some networks, such as Bloomberg (business programming) and ESPN (sports programming), broadcast nationally either through a group of company-owned stations or through a **syndication arrangement** (i.e., business agreement) with partner stations. Second, the emergence of radio programming delivered via satellite (e.g., SiriusXM) has become an option for national advertising. Finally, the potential for national and international advertising has become more attractive as many radio stations now broadcast over the internet and through smartphone applications.

In many ways, radio suffers the same problems as traditional television, namely, it's a mass medium that is not highly targeted and offers little opportunity to track responses. Yet unlike television, radio presents the additional disadvantage of limiting advertisers to audio-only advertising. For some products, advertising without visual support is not effective. However, the restriction that radio is limited to audio-only advertising is changing. This can primarily be seen in the form of internet access and apps that not only allow radio stations to be heard but also enable audio ads to be supported by visual messages that appear on the screen of the device that is streaming the radio station.

It is important to note that commercial radio is not the only outlet for audio advertising. As previously discussed, podcasts have become highly popular (see *Changing Media Choices* in Chapter 12) and this has led many advertisers to place ads in these outlets. Additionally, advertisements can be embedded within audio content played on websites. Such website audio placements have become relatively easy with audio streaming services, such as SoundCloud.

PRINT PUBLICATION ADVERTISING

Print publications include magazines, newspapers, and special issue publications. The geographic scope of print publications varies from locally targeted community newspapers to internationally distributed magazines. Magazines, especially those targeting specific niches or specialized interest areas, are more narrowly focused compared to broadcast media. Additionally, magazines offer the option of allowing marketers to present their message using high quality imagery (e.g., full color), and can also offer tactile (e.g., inserted material to be touched) and scent (e.g., perfume) experiences (see Box 13-3). And as previously noted, print publications can offer the target market longer exposure to an ad.

Newspapers, while also presenting advertisers with color advertisements, offer the advantage of targeting national (e.g., USA Today, The Wall Street Journal) or local (e.g., small town publication) markets. **Special issue publications**, which appear in both magazines and newspapers, can offer highly selective targeting since these often focus on extremely narrow topics (e.g., auto buying guide, vacation guides, college and university ratings, etc.).

The downside of traditional print publications is that readership has dropped consistently over the last few decades. Again, the emergence of the internet and mobile networks is a key reason for the decline. Newspapers are particularly vulnerable and there are many who question the future of printed news as a viable media outlet. In fact, most print publications have recognized they need to change and have migrated their content to digital media (e.g., mobile apps).

DIRECT MAIL ADVERTISING

This method of advertising uses postal and other delivery services to ship advertising materials (e.g., postcards, letters, brochures, catalogs, flyers) to a physical address of targeted customers. Direct mail is most effective when it is designed in a way that makes it appear to be special to the customer. For instance, a marketer using direct mail can personalize mailings by including message recipients' names on the address label or by inserting their names within the content of the advertisement.

Direct mail can be a highly cost-effective method of advertising. This is due to cost advantages obtained by printing in high volume. For most printing projects, the majority of printing costs are related to initial print machine set up to run a print job and not because of the quantity of material printed. Therefore, the total cost of printing 50,000 postcards is only slightly higher than printing 20,000 postcards, but when the total cost is divided by the number of cards printed, the cost per-card drops dramatically as more pieces are printed. Obviously, there are other costs involved in direct mail, primarily postage expense.

While direct mail offers the benefit of low-cost production for each distributed piece, the actual cost-per-exposure can be quite high as large numbers of customers may discard the mailing before reading. This has led many to refer to direct mail as **junk mail** and, due to the name, some marketers view the approach as ineffective. However, direct mail, when well-targeted, can be an extremely effective promotional tool.

SIGNAGE ADVERTISING

The use of signs to communicate a marketer's message places advertising in geographically identified areas in order to capture customer attention. The most obvious method of signage advertising (also called **out-of-home advertising**) is through **billboards**, which are generally located in high traffic areas. Outdoor billboards come in many shapes and sizes, though the most well-known are large structures located near transportation points intending to attract the interest of people traveling on roads or public transportation. Indoor billboards are often smaller than outdoor billboards and are designed to attract the attention of foot traffic (i.e., those moving past the sign). For example, smaller signage in airports, train terminals, and large commercial office space fit this category.

While billboards are the most recognizable example of signage advertising, the Outdoor Advertising Association of America identifies over thirty formats (12) as falling under this method of advertising including:

● Airborne or plane banners, where large signs are pulled behind an airplane

● Mobile billboards, where signs are placed on vehicles, such as buses and cars, or even carried by people

● Wall murals, where ads are painted directly on buildings or other structures

● Fully wrapped buses, where ads are designed to cover the entire exterior

PRODUCT PLACEMENT ADVERTISING

Product placement is an advertising approach that intentionally inserts products into entertainment programs, such as movies, television programs, and video games. Placement can take several forms including:

● Visual imagery with a product appearing as a background element

● Actual product use by an actor in an entertainment program

● Words spoken by an actor that include the product name

Product placement is gaining acceptance among a growing number of marketers for two main reasons. First, in most cases the placement is subtle so as not to divert significant attention from the main content of the program or media outlet. This approach may lead the audience to believe the product was selected for inclusion by program producers and not by the marketer. Consequently, this may heighten the credibility of the product in the minds of the audience since their perception, whether accurate or not, is that the product was selected by an unbiased third-party. Second, as we discussed in Chapter 12, entertainment programming, such as television, is converging with other media, particularly with digital media outlets. And as we discussed, some television advertisers are placing QR codes on their ads that enable viewers to request information. It is expected that soon viewers will be able to purchase products that appear in a program by simply pointing at an on-screen item with a TV remote control As this technology emerges and as marketers continue to explore other placement options (see Box 13-3), product placement opportunities could become an attractive promotional method for many marketers.

Box 13-3

OTHER SENSORY PRODUCT PLACEMENT

Product placement is not limited to movies and television. Other options are currently in use, especially in the gaming world, and more are being actively explored. Some additional product placement options include:

Musical Product Placement

Music or other audio integrated into entertainment programming has afforded musical artists with product placement opportunities for many years. (13) More recently, musical placement has found new options in the electronic gaming market. For many of today's gamers, their gaming system includes not only the gaming unit attached to a screen but also includes connections to an advanced audio system. Game developers have taken advantage of the enhanced gaming environment by populating their software with numerous songs from genres aimed at younger players. Most songs are up-tempo tunes that help create an atmosphere of excitement while players battle on the screen. After playing a game for many weeks, the gamer may be exposed to a song well over 100 times. In fact, for avid gamers, they will hear the song much more while playing video games than through other musical outlets (e.g., music streaming services). The result is that many new artists have benefited from this intense exposure, and the placement of their songs within an electronic game can be a key factor in helping to launch a successful musical career.

Scent Product Placement

The intentional inclusion of scent as a promotional aid has garnered much attention and could lead to a number of product placement opportunities. Olfactory elements have been used for several years at amusement parks to enhance customers' experience at shows and on rides. A broader consumer market will almost certainly develop with gaming most likely being the first to explore this sensory product placement option. As scent becomes a recognized sensory experience for media programming, there is little doubt scent-related product placements will follow. For instance, a bathroom scene in a movie may one day result in the smell of brand name room deodorizer wafting through the theater.

Tactile Product Placement

Touch or feel sensations may also be a product placement opportunity. Today's gamers utilize feel devices to heighten the experience by way of such items as vibrating controllers and motion chairs. Sometime soon a television viewer may experience a program from several sensory angles including a tactile one. For example, a television show may not only show the visual product placement of a certain brand of automobile, but also the inclusion of tactile placement which could suggest the smooth ride one might get from being in the real thing.

SPONSORSHIP ADVERTISING

A subtle method of advertising is an approach in which marketers pay, or offer resources and services, for the purpose of being seen as a supporter of an organization's event, program, or product offering (e.g., section of a website). Because sponsorships are less blatantly promotional compared to other forms of advertising, these may be appealing for marketers looking to establish credibility with a particular target market.

There are numerous local, regional, national, and international sponsorship opportunities ranging from a local not-for-profit art center to the Olympics. Exposure opportunities include signage, printed handouts, sponsored receptions, and much more. However, many sponsorship options lack the ability to tie spending directly to customer response. Additionally, the visibility of the sponsorship may be limited to relatively small mentions, especially if the marketer is sharing sponsorship with many other marketers.

It is important to note, that in the digital world sponsorship advertising is considered to be different than native advertising (see *Digital Media Advertising* discussion above). As mentioned, sponsorship advertising is generally subtle and, in most situations, the advertiser does not have influence over the content which they are sponsoring. On the other hand, the information contained in native advertising is controlled by the marketer and presents not so subtle references to a specific product. Native advertising may also provide a "call to action" for how someone can learn more about the product, while sponsorship advertising generally does not.

OTHERS

While the advertising outlets discussed above represent the overwhelming majority of advertising methods, there are several more including:

- Advertising on professional sports team uniforms (e.g., name of advertiser on front of jersey)

- Advertising using telephone recordings (e.g., political candidate's messages)

- Advertising via fax machine (though in the U.S. such methods are limited by Federal law)

- Advertising through inserted material in product packaging (e.g., within the envelope containing credit card bill)

- Advertising imprinted on retail receipts (e.g., cash machine receipt)

- Advertising placed on or around another product (e.g., imprinted on plastic bags used to protect newspapers)

CREATING A MESSAGE

In our discussion of the communication process in Chapter 11, we saw that effective communication requires a message source create (encode) a message that can be interpreted (decode) by the intended message receiver. In advertising, the act of creating a message is often considered the creative aspect of carrying out an advertising campaign. And because it is a creative process, the number of different ways a message can be generated is limited only by the imagination of those responsible for developing the message. (14) In doing so, the marketer must take into consideration a number of issues. The primary issues are:

GENERAL MESSAGE CREATION FACTORS

When developing the message, the marketer must consider several factors that affect how the message is created including:

- Characteristics of the Target Audience – Important features of the target market (e.g., age, location, attitudes, etc.) impacts what is conveyed in the message.

- Type of Media Used – The media outlet (e.g., television, digital, print, etc.) used to deliver the message impacts the way a message will be created.

- Product Factors – Products that are highly complex require a different message than simpler products. Additionally, the target market's familiarity with a product affects what is contained in a message. For instance, a new product attempting to gain awareness in the market will have a message that is much different than a product that is well known.

- Overall Advertising Objective – As mentioned, the objective of the advertising campaign can affect the type of ad that is designed. For example, an advertisement with the objective of stimulating immediate sales for an existing product will have a different message than an advertisement seeking to build initial awareness of a new product.

KEY MESSAGE ELEMENTS

Most advertising messages share common elements within the message including:

- The Appeal – This refers to the underlying idea that captures the attention of a message receiver. Appeals can fall into such categories as emotional, fearful, humorous, and sexual.

- Value Proposition – The advertising message generally contains a reason for customers to be interested in the product, which often means the ad will emphasize the benefits obtained from using the product.

- Slogan – To help position the product in a customer's mind and distinguish it from competitors' offerings, advertisements will often contain a consistent phrase or group of words marketers include within their promotional message that is repeated across several different messages and different media outlets.

MESSAGE TESTING

Before choosing a message, marketers running large advertising campaigns will want to have confidence in their message by having potential members of the targeted audience provide feedback. The most popular method of testing advertising used by marketers (or used by its advertising agency) is to conduct focus groups. At these sessions, several advertising messages are presented to the members of the focus group, who then discuss and offer their evaluation of each advertisement. For digital media outlets, technology allows for testing of ads by randomly exposing website visitors or app users to different ads and then measuring their response.

EVALUATING CAMPAIGN RESULTS

The final step in an advertising campaign is to measure the results of carrying out the campaign. In most cases, the results measured relate directly to the objectives the marketer is seeking to achieve. Therefore, whether a campaign is judged as being successful is not always tied to an increase in product sales. Rather, campaign effectiveness may be evaluated on other measures. For example, when the advertising objective is to build product awareness, a key measurement of a successful campaign may be reflected in how many more people are now aware of the product.

In order to evaluate an advertising campaign, it is necessary for two measures to take place. First, there must be a pre-campaign or **pre-test measure** that evaluates conditions prior to campaign implementation. For instance, prior to an advertising campaign for Product X a random survey may be undertaken of customers within a target market to see what percentage are aware of Product X. Once the campaign has run, a second post-campaign or **post-test measure** (e.g., another survey) is undertaken to see if there is an increase in awareness.

The time between the pre-test measure and the post-test measure is determined by the marketer and also by the type of campaign being run. For television advertising campaigns, the time frame between measures may be several weeks or months. However, the post-test measure for digital advertising campaigns may occur just a few days after the pre-test measure due to the rapid availability of customer tracking data (see Box 1-2).

Of course, not all marketers have the resources to carry out in-depth campaign analysis. This is especially the case when the measures require personal contact (e.g., interviewing members of the target market). However, for online marketers there exists a number of relatively inexpensive campaign testing tools, such as Google Ads service. (15)

REFERENCES

1. For a listing of leading U.S. advertisers and the estimated yearly amount spent on advertising see: "Ad Age Leading National Advertisers 2023." *Ad Age.* https://adage.com/lna2023. (Note: Access may require providing personal information.)

2. Of course, the evolution of artificial intelligence (AI) has the potential to dramatically reduce the cost of message development.

3. For a graphical view of how the price of 30-second Super Bowl ads have changed in recent years see: "Super Bowl Average Costs of a 30-Second TV Advertisement." *Statista.* https://www.statista.com/statistics/217134/total-advertisement-revenue-of-super-bowls.

4. For more details on the auditing of media outlets and the value these services provide see: *Alliance for Audited Media.* https://auditedmedia.com.

5. Delivery of ads using digital technology also occurs in other ways, such as through billboards; however, for the purpose of distinguishing different types of media outlets these are not included within digital media advertising but under other relevant outlets.

6. For a summary of television streaming services features see: James K. Willcox. "Guide to Streaming Services." *Consumer Reports.* https://www.consumerreports.org/electronics-computers/streaming-media/guide-to-streaming-video-services-a4517732799.

7. Video devices accessing content via the internet, for instance a smart TV or streaming device such as Roku and Apple TV, are often labeled as connected TV (CTV) devices. The content delivered to a CTV, including streaming services such as YouTube TV and Netflix, are often called over-the-top (OTT) services.

8. Sara Labow. "Digital Ad Spend Worldwide to Pass $600 Billion This Year." *eMarketer.* July 14, 2023. https://www.insiderintelligence.com/content/digital-ad-spend-worldwide-pass-600-billion-this-year.

9. As mentioned in the *Ad Skipping and Ad Blocking* discussion in Chapter 12, methods are now available for blocking website advertisements. As a result, a certain percentage of users' experience with content-focused websites may not include being exposed to ads.

10. For examples of how augmented reality (AR) advertising is used on Facebook see: "Facebook Augmented Reality Ads." *Facebook.* https://www.facebook.com/business/success/categories/augmented-reality-ads.

11. As was noted in Chapter 2, the General Data Protection Regulation (GDPR) instituted by the European Union has impacted marketers' ability to track customers. Consequently, this has made remarketing a more challenging advertising technique in EU countries.

12. "Media Formats." *Out of Home Advertising Association of America.* https://oaaa.org/resources/media-formats.

13. For more on how music product placement works see: "Music Placement Companies." *Bart Day Law.* https://bartdaylaw.com/music-placement-companies.

14. AI also has the potential to expand the number of creative ways to develop a message.

15. "Google Ads." *Google.* https://ads.google.com.

Chapter 14: Sales Promotion

Rewards   **Loyalty Programs**

-70%
-50%
-20%

Free Product   **Coupons**

CASHBACK

In a time when customers are exposed daily to a nearly infinite number of promotional messages, many marketers are discovering advertising alone is not enough to move members of a target market to take action, such as convincing them to try a new product. In addition, some marketers are finding certain characteristics of their target market (e.g., small but geographically dispersed) or characteristics of their product (e.g., highly complex) make advertising a less attractive option. Still for other marketers, the high cost of advertising may drive many to seek alternative, lower cost techniques to meet their promotion goals. For these marketers, better results may be obtained using other promotional approaches and may lead to directing much of their promotional spending to non-advertising promotions.

In this chapter, we continue our discussion of promotion decisions by looking at a second promotional mix item: sales promotion. Sales promotion is used widely in many industries, especially by marketers selling to consumers. We show that the objectives of sales promotion are quite different than advertising and are specifically designed to encourage customer response. Coverage includes a detailed look at promotions aimed at consumers, channel partners, and business-to-business markets. Finally, we will look at the trends shaping the sales promotion field.

WHAT IS SALES PROMOTION?

Sales promotion describes promotional methods using special short-term techniques to persuade members of a target market to respond or undertake certain activity. As a reward, marketers offer something of value to those responding or undertaking certain activities. These rewards are generally in the form of lower cost of ownership for a purchased product (e.g., lower purchase price, money back), or the inclusion of additional value-added material (e.g., something more for the same price).

Sales promotion is used by a wide range of organizations in both the consumer and business markets, though the frequency and spending levels are much greater for consumer products marketers. Unfortunately, considering the number of different methods that can be classified as sales promotion, it is difficult to measure the yearly amount spent on this promotional method, though it is likely on par with what is spent yearly on advertising.

Sales Promotion vs. Advertising

Sales promotion is often confused with advertising. For instance, a television advertisement mentioning a contest that will award winners with a free trip to a Caribbean island may give the contest the appearance of advertising. While the delivery of the marketer's message through television media is certainly labeled as advertising, what is contained in the message, namely the contest, is considered a sales promotion. The factors that distinguish between the two promotional approaches are:

♦ <u>Evidence of Time Constraint</u> – Sales promotion involves a short-term value proposition where an advertisement does not. In general, if there is a limited time period within which action must be taken then it most likely qualifies as a sales promotion. In our contest example, a stated entry deadline would indicate a time constraint.

♦ <u>Customer Action Required</u> – Sales promotion requires customers to perform some activity in order to be eligible to receive the value proposition. For instance, in our Caribbean trip example, customers may need to complete an online form to make them eligible to be entered in the contest.

The inclusion of BOTH a timing constraint and an activity requirement is a hallmark of sales promotion. While an advertisement may be used to communicate the elements of the sales promotion, the promotional method that rewards the customer is considered a sales promotion.

Advantages of Sales Promotion

Sales promotion can prove useful for marketers in several ways. First, sales promotion offers a number of a highly effective methods for exposing customers and business partners to new products. These methods can be particularly effective in moving customers to take an action, such encouraging consumers to sample a new product or getting retail outlets to test a new product in their stores.

Second, at the consumer level, sales promotion helps to strengthen customer involvement and loyalty as it is often the primary mechanism organizations use to interact with their customers. As we will discuss, customers often feel a stronger connection to an organization when sales promotion rewards them for being good customers.

Third, some sales promotions can be quickly created and made available within a market. For instance, unlike an advertisement, which may take weeks or months to develop, some methods of sales promotion, such as an email coupon (see *Coupons* discussion below), can be produced and distributed very quickly. Additionally, information about a company's sales promotions can often spread rapidly to targeted customers, particularly by word-of-mouth and social media. The result is that a large number of customers can become aware of a new promotion within a very short time frame.

Fourth, sales promotion is often used as a supporting feature of other methods of promotion. For example, salespeople may be provided with certain promotional items that they can then pass on to sales prospects (see *Promotional Products* discussion below). Also, a sales promotion is often tied to company advertising as a way of enhancing the message and encouraging customer action (e.g., ad mentions a "money back" offer).

Finally, sales promotion can be used to rapidly reduce inventory in situations where product replacement is needed. For instance, marketers may utilize a sales promotion that lowers price (see *Promotional Pricing* discussion below) to quickly move perishable products that are getting close to an expiration date or clearing inventory of older models so that new models can be stocked.

Disadvantages of Sales Promotion

While the benefits of sales promotion are very attractive to a marketer's promotional plan, there are downsides to this type of promotion. First, repeated use of sales promotion may condition customers to wait until a product promotion is available before making their next purchase. This, in turn, may result in the marketer not maximizing a product's revenue potential as many customers will not pay full price or, if full price is paid, the marketer may face other promotional costs in order to receive the full price (e.g., need to offer other free products).

Second, along with the potential for having customers delay purchase until a promotion is available, the overuse of some sales promotions can lead customers to lower their perception of a product's quality and its overall image. This is especially the case when frequent short-term price reductions are used as customers may become conditioned to believe the lower price is the regular price. This may cause them to believe the product's quality is not comparable to similar competitors' products that offer less frequent or no price reductions.

Third, while in the same way an advertisement competes with other ads for customers' attention (see *Advertising Clutter* in Chapter 13), so too do sales promotions. This is especially an issue with promotions delivered to customers via email, postal mail, and printed media as these may also include numerous offerings from other marketers. As with advertising, promotional clutter associated with sales promotion is expected to become even more significant in the next few years.

Finally, some sales promotions targeted to consumers (see *Consumer Sales Promotions* discussion below) require the assistance of distributors, such as retailers, for the promotion to work. However, not all distributors may accept a consumer sales promotion, especially if the promotion requires the distributor to perform extra work. For instance, an organic beverage company may provide a grocery store chain with free product to sample in their stores. However, the grocery chain may not accept this promotion if dispensing the free product must be managed by the retailer's own employees rather than by representatives of the beverage company.

OBJECTIVES OF SALES PROMOTION

Sales promotion is a tool used to achieve most of the five main promotional objectives discussed in Chapter 11:

◆ <u>Building Awareness</u> – Several sales promotion techniques are highly effective in exposing customers to products for the first time and can serve as a crucial promotional component in the early stages of new product introduction. Additionally, several techniques have the added advantage of capturing customer information at the time of exposure to the promotion. In this way, sales promotion can serve as a useful customer information gathering tool (e.g., capture customers' email address), which can then be used as part of follow-up marketing efforts.

◆ <u>Creating Interest</u> – Marketers find sales promotion has the potential to be extremely effective in creating interest in a product. In fact, creating interest is often considered the most important use of a sales promotion. In the retail industry, an appealing sales promotion can significantly increase customer traffic to retail outlets. Digital marketers can use similar approaches to bolstering customer traffic to websites and to using shopping apps. Another important way to create interest is to move customers to experience a product. Several sales promotion techniques offer the opportunity for customers to try products for free or at low cost.

◆ <u>Providing Information</u> – Generally, a sales promotion is designed to move customers to some action and are rarely simply informational in nature. However, some sales promotions do offer customers access to product information. For instance, a promotion may allow customers to try a fee-based online service for free for several days. This free access may include receiving product information via email.

◆ <u>Stimulating Demand</u> – Next to creating interest, the most prominent use of sales promotion is to build demand by convincing customers to make a purchase. Special promotions, especially those lowering the cost of ownership to the customer (e.g., price reduction), are often employed to stimulate sales.

◆ <u>Reinforcing the Brand</u> – Once customers have made a purchase, a sales promotion can be used to encourage additional purchasing and used to reward purchase loyalty (see *Loyalty Programs* discussion below). Many companies, including airlines and retail stores, reward good or "preferred" customers with special promotions, such as notification of "exclusive deals" sent by email or surprise price reductions mentioned when the customer is at the in-store checkout counter.

CLASSIFICATION OF SALES PROMOTION

A sales promotion can be classified based on the primary target audience to whom the promotion is directed. These include:

◆ Consumer Market Directed – Possibly the most well-known methods of sales promotion are those intended to appeal to the final consumer. Consumers are exposed to numerous sales promotions nearly every day and, as discussed later, many buyers are conditioned to look for sales promotions prior to making purchase decisions.

◆ Trade Market Directed – Marketers use various sales promotions to target a variety of customers, including partners within their channel of distribution. Resellers, who are often referred to as trade partners, are targets for the majority of such spending. Trade promotions are initially used to entice channel members to carry a marketer's products and, once products are stocked, marketers utilize promotions to strengthen the channel relationship.

◆ Business-to-Business Market Directed – A smaller subset of sales promotion is targeted to the business-to-business (B-to-B) market. While these promotions may not carry the glamour associated with consumer or trade promotions, B-to-B promotions are used in many industries.

In the next few sections, we discuss each classification in more detail.

CONSUMER SALES PROMOTIONS

Consumer sales promotions encompass a variety of short-term promotional techniques designed to induce customers to respond in some way. The most popular consumer sales promotions are directly associated with product purchasing. These promotions are intended to enhance the value of a product purchase by either reducing the overall cost of the product (i.e., get same product but for less money) or by adding more benefit to the regular purchase price (i.e., get more for the money).

While tying a promotion to an immediate purchase is a key use of a consumer sales promotion, it is not the only one. As we noted above, sales promotion techniques can be used to achieve other objectives, such as building brand loyalty or creating product awareness. Such promotions can also be used as part of a pull promotional strategy where increased customer demand may encourage channel members (e.g., retailers) to stock a product. As discussed below, there are wide assortment of consumer promotions:

COUPONS

Most consumers are quite familiar with this form of sales promotion, which offers purchasers price savings or other incentives when the coupon is redeemed at the time of purchase. Coupons are short-term in nature since most (but not all) carry an expiration date. Also, coupons require consumer involvement in order for value to be realized. In most cases, involvement consists of the consumer making an effort to obtain the coupon (e.g., access coupon on smartphone app) and then presenting it (e.g., scanning coupon) at the time of purchase. Customers are exposed to coupons in many different ways as explained in Box 14-1. (1)

Box 14-1

HOW COUPONS ARE OBTAINED

Coupons are used widely by marketers across many retail industries and reach consumers in a number of different delivery formats including:

Free-Standing Inserts (FSI)

The traditional approach to distributing coupons is to insert these within printed media, such as newspapers and direct mail. The FSI method may require customers to remove coupons from surrounding material (e.g., cut out) in order to use.

Merchant Printed

A delivery method common in many food and drug stores is to present coupons at the end of a purchase. These coupons, which are often printed either at the bottom of the customer's receipt or produced as a separate printout, are intended to be used for a future purchase and not for the current purchase which triggered the printing.

Customer Generated

Coupons falling within this format require the customer undertake efforts to produce the coupon. An example would be coupons customers print from a manufacturer's website or email. However, the fastest growing way to obtain coupons is for customers to select and load **digital coupons** via apps on mobile devices. These coupons generally appear along with a barcode image that is then scanned by an electronic reader when the customer makes a purchase.

Coupon Codes

The internet and mobile networks are also where customers can access non-printable coupons redeemable during online purchases. These digital coupons, commonly known as promotion codes or promo codes, are redeemed when the customer enters a designated coupon code during the purchase process.

Product Display

Some coupons are nearly impossible for customers to miss as these are located close to the product. In some instances, coupons may be contained within a coupon dispenser fastened to the shelf holding the product, while in other cases coupons may be attached to a separate display (see *Point-of-Purchase Displays* discussion below) and customers can remove (e.g., tear off) and use at the checkout counter.

Customer Loyalty Coupons

Retailers with loyalty programs (see *Loyalty Programs* discussion below) often permit customers to add coupons to their accounts. These coupons may be manually "clipped" by customers from the retailer's website, app or email, or coupons may be automatically added to a customer's account based on their purchase history. Coupons in a customer's account can then be redeemed when she/he enters loyalty program information during the purchasing process (e.g., scans app loyalty card image during checkout).

Cross-Product

This involves the placement of coupons within or on other products. For example, a sports drink marketer may imprint a coupon for its product on the package of a high-energy snack. Also, this delivery approach is used when two marketers have struck a **cross-promotion** arrangement, where each agrees to undertake certain marketing activity for the other.

REBATES

Rebates, like coupons, offer value to purchasers typically by lowering the customer's final cost for acquiring the product. While rebates share some similarities with coupons, they differ in several key aspects. First, rebates are often handed or offered (e.g., accessible on the internet) to customers after a purchase is made and cannot be used to obtain immediate savings in the way coupons are primarily used. (So-called **instant rebates**, where customers receive price reductions at the time of purchase, have elements of both coupons and rebates; however, we will classify these as coupons based on the timing of the reward to the customer.)

Second, rebates often request the purchaser to submit personal data in order to obtain the rebate. For instance, customer identification, including name, address, phone and email contact information, is usually required to obtain a rebate. Also, the marketer may ask those seeking a rebate to provide additional data, such as indicating the reason for making the purchase.

Third, unlike coupons that always offer value at the time of a purchase (assuming it is accepted by the retailer), receiving the value of a rebate only occurs if the customer takes action after the purchase. Marketers know that not all customers will respond to a rebate they have received. Some will misplace or forget to submit the rebate while others may submit after a required deadline. In fact, marketers will factor in an estimated **non-redemption rate** as they attempt to calculate the cost of the rebate promotion.

Finally, compared to coupons, rebates tend to be used as a value enhancement for higher-priced products. For instance, rebates are a popular sales promotion for automobiles and appliances, where large amounts of money may be returned to the customer.

TRADE-IN PROMOTIONS

Trade-in promotions allow consumers to obtain lower prices by exchanging something the customer possesses, such as an older product that the new purchase will replace. While the idea of gaining price breaks for trading in another product is most frequently seen with automobile sales, these promotions are used in other industries, such as smartphones, where the customer's exchanged product can potentially be refurbished and resold by the marketer in order to extract value.

PROMOTIONAL PRICING

One of the most powerful sales promotion techniques is the short-term price reduction or, as known in some areas, "on-sale" pricing. Lowering a product's selling price can have an immediate impact on demand, though marketers must exercise caution since the frequent use of this technique can lead customers to anticipate the reduction, and consequently withhold purchase until the price reduction occurs again.

As we will see in in Chapter 18, promotional pricing is also considered within the framework of price setting. More on this promotional method will be provided as part of that discussion.

LOYALTY PROGRAMS

Promotions offering customers a reward, such as price discounts and free products, for frequent purchasing or other activity are called loyalty programs. These promotions have been around for many years but expanded in popularity when introduced in the airline industry as part of frequent-flier programs. Today loyalty programs (also known as **rewards programs**) are used by marketers in nearly all retail markets. In many of these markets, such promotions may be known as **club card programs** since members often must display a verification card or loyalty program app as evidence of enrollment in the program.

Many loyalty programs have become ingrained as part of the value offered by a marketer. That is, a retailer or marketing organization may offer loyalty programs as general business practice. Under this condition, because the loyalty program is always offered, it does not qualify as a sales promotion since it does not fit the requirement of offering a short-term value. However, even within a loyalty program that is part of a general business practice, a sales promotion can be offered, such as a special short-term offer that lowers the number of points needed to acquire a free product.

SAMPLES AND FREE TRIALS

Enticing members of a target market to try a product is often easy when the trial comes at little or no cost to the customer. The use of samples and free trials may be the oldest of all sales promotion techniques dating back to when society advanced from a culture of self-subsistence to a culture of trade.

Samples and free trials give customers the opportunity to experience products, often in small quantities or for a short duration, without purchasing the product. Today, these methods are used in almost all industries and are especially useful for getting customers to try a product for the first time. Sampling can take place at a person's home (e.g., included with a direct mail ad), in-store (e.g., through a product sampling table), and out-of-home (e.g., handouts on college campuses).

EXPERIENTIAL MARKETING EVENTS

While the idea of getting people to try something before they buy it is far from being new, the use of so-called experiential marketing methods, designed to immerse potential customers in a product prior to making a purchase commitment, have increased. Unlike old-style product giveaways, experiential marketing is as much about the environment and the interaction as it is about the products being sampled. One of the most common experiential marketing approaches is to attract a large number of people to a specific location, where products are then consumed as part of a social event. To do this, brands may engage an experiential marketing specialist to coordinate one or many events held on the same day. (2)

FREE PRODUCT

Some promotional methods offer free products but with the condition that it cannot be obtained until a purchase is made. The free product may be in the form of additional quantities of the same purchased product (e.g., buy one, get one free) or specialty packages (e.g., value pack) that offer more quantity for the same price as regular packaging.

PREMIUMS

Another form of sales promotion involving free merchandise are premiums or "give-away" items. Premiums differ from samples and free product in that these often do not consist of the actual product, though there is generally some connection. For example, a smartwatch manufacturer may offer access to free downloadable apps for those purchasing the watch.

CONTESTS AND SWEEPSTAKES

Consumers are often attracted to promotions where the potential benefit obtained is unusually high. Under these promotions, only a few lucky consumers receive the value offered in the promotion. Two types of promotions offering high value are contests and sweepstakes.

Contests are special promotions awarding value to winners based on skills they demonstrate compared to others. For instance, a baking company may offer free vacations to winners of a baking contest. Contest award winners are often determined by a panel of judges.

Sweepstakes or drawings are not skill based, but rather based on luck. Winners are determined by random selection. In some situations, the chances of winning may be higher for those who make a purchase if entry into the sweepstakes occurs automatically when a purchase is made. But in most cases, anyone is free to enter without the requirement to make a purchase.

A subset of both contests and sweepstakes are **games**, which come in a variety of formats, such as scratch-off cards and collection of game pieces. Unlike contests and sweepstakes, which may not require purchase, to participate in a game, customers may be required to make a purchase. In the United States and several other countries, where eligibility is based on purchase, games may be subjected to rigid legal controls and may actually fall under the category of lotteries. In the U.S., a promotion is considered to be a **lottery** if it contains three elements: 1) an award or prize; 2) won by chance; and 3) the requirement that those entering must pay for the chance. Such promotional methods are tightly controlled and may be illegal in several U.S. states.

PRODUCT DEMONSTRATIONS

Many products benefit from customers being shown how products are used through a demonstration. Whether the demonstration is experienced in-person or via video form, such as a YouTube video, this promotional technique can produce highly effective results. Unfortunately, demonstrations are often expensive to arrange. Costs involved in delivering demonstrations may include paying for the demonstrator, which can be high if this person is well-known (e.g., nationally known chef), equipment, staging and other setup expenses, and payment for the space where the demonstration is given.

PERSONAL APPEARANCES

An in-person appearance by someone of interest to the target market, such as an author, sports figure or celebrity, is another form of sales promotion capable of generating customer traffic to a physical location. However, in much the same way as product demonstrations, a personal appearance promotion can be costly since the marketer normally must pay a fee and possibly travel expenses for the person to appear.

TRADE SALES PROMOTIONS

As noted in Chapter 11, certain promotions can help "push" a product through the channel by encouraging channel members to purchase and promote the product to their customers. For instance, a trade promotion designed for retailers may encourage them to instruct their employees to promote a marketer's brand over competitors' offerings. With thousands of products competing for limited shelf space, spending on trade promotion is nearly equal to the amount spent on consumer promotions.

Many sales promotions aimed at building relationships with channel partners follow similar designs as those directed to consumers, including promotional pricing, contests, and free product. In addition to these, several other promotional approaches are specifically designed to appeal to trade partners including:

POINT-OF-PURCHASE DISPLAYS

Point-of-purchase (POP) displays are specially developed materials intended for placement in retail stores. These displays allow products to be prominently presented, often in high customer traffic areas (e.g., near front entrance), and thereby increase the probability the product will stand out. POP displays come in many styles, though the most popular are ones allowing a product to stand alone, such as in the middle of a store aisle or sit at the end of an aisle (i.e., **end cap promotion**).

For channel partners, POP displays can significantly increase product sales compared to sales levels experienced at the product's normal shelf position. Also, many marketers will lower the per-unit cost of products in the POP display as an incentive for retailers to agree to include the display in their stores.

ADVERTISING SUPPORT PROGRAMS

In addition to offering promotional support in the form of physical displays, marketers can attract channel members' interest by offering financial assistance in the form of advertising money. These funds are often directed to retailers, who then include the company's products in their advertising. In certain cases, the marketer will offer to pay the entire cost of advertising, but more often the marketer offers partial financial support known as **co-op advertising** funds.

SHORT-TERM TRADE ALLOWANCES

This promotion offers channel partners price breaks and other incentives for agreeing to stock a product. In most cases, the allowance is not only given as encouragement to sell the product but also as an inducement to promote the product in other ways. For instance, it may be used for: obtaining more attractive shelf space (e.g., placement on an eye-level shelf); securing a high-traffic store location (e.g., placement on end cap at the front of store); highlighting the product in company-produced advertising, on website display, or within a retailer's app (e.g., featured product); or agreeing to have the retailer's sales personnel "talk-up" the product to customers.

Allowances can be in the form of price reductions, also called **off-invoice promotion**, where the price is lowered based on the quantity purchased, and **buy-back guarantees**, where a manufacturer agrees to accept fully refunded returns for product that does not sell within a certain time frame.

SALES INCENTIVES

When the main objective of a sales promotion is to stimulate demand and increase sales, a marketer may be able to use promotion techniques that are aimed at those in a channel member's organization who also affect sales. Primarily, marketers may offer sales promotions to its resellers' sales force and customer service staff as incentives to help sell more of the marketer's product. Sometimes called **push money**, these promotions typically offer employees cash or prizes, such as trips, for those that meet certain sales levels.

PROMOTIONAL PRODUCTS

Among the most widely used methods of trade sales promotions is the promotional product; products labeled with the brand or organization name that serve as reminders of the actual product. For instance, companies often hand out free calendars, coffee cups, and pens that contain the product logo. Table 14-1 presents one estimate of the top 10 categories for promotional products. (3)

Table 14-1: Top 10 Promotional Products

Product	Percentage
T-Shirts	17.1
Drinkware	9.9
Polos	9.7
Caps/Headwear	8.8
Bags	6.8
Wearables (non-shirts)	6.8
Writing Instruments	4.6
Shirts - Other	4.0
Flags/Banners	3.6
Desk/Office/Business Accessories	3.4

TRADE SHOWS

One final type of trade promotion is the industry trade show. Trade shows are organized events that bring industry buyers and sellers together in one central location. In most cases this is a physical environment (e.g., convention center), though **virtual trade shows** are also presented over the internet. (4)

While the cost of participating in trade shows is often quite high, marketers are attracted to this promotional method since it offers the opportunity to reach a large number of potential buyers in one convenient setting. At these events, most sellers attempt to capture the attention of buyers by setting up a display area to present their product offerings and meet with potential customers. These displays can range from a single table covering a small area to erecting specially built display booths that dominate the trade show floor.

BUSINESS-TO-BUSINESS SALES PROMOTIONS

The use of sales promotion is not limited to consumer products marketing. In business markets, sales promotion is also used as a means of moving customers to action. However, the promotional choices available to the B-to-B marketer are not as extensive as those found in the consumer or trade markets. For example, most B-to-B marketers do not use coupons. Rather, the techniques more likely to be utilized include:

- Price Reductions
- Free Product
- Trade-In
- Promotional Products
- Trade Shows

Of the promotions listed, trade shows are the mostly widely used sales promotion within the business-to-business market. Trade shows, also called **trade fairs**, are especially critical for firms looking to expand into global markets. In many global markets, especially in Europe, trade fairs have a long history of being one of the most cost-effective ways to promote products. The largest B-to-B trade fair is Hannover Messe held annually in Germany. The fair, which contains multiple industry trade shows, attracts thousands of exhibitors from over 70 countries and over 225,000 visitors.

TRENDS IN SALES PROMOTION

Marketers who employ sales promotion as a key component in their promotional strategy should be aware of how the climate for these types of promotions is changing. The important trends in sales promotion include:

CUSTOMERS' EXPECTATIONS

The onslaught of sales promotion activity over the last several decades has eroded the value of the short-term requirement for customers to act on sales promotions. Many are now conditioned to expect a promotion at the time of purchase, otherwise they may withhold or even alter their purchase if a promotion is not present. For instance, food shoppers are inundated on a weekly basis with such a wide variety of sales promotions that their loyalty to certain products has been replaced by their loyalty to current value items (i.e., products with a sales promotion). For marketers, the challenge is to balance the advantages offered by short-term promotions versus the potential of eroding loyalty to the product.

COMMUNICATION AND DELIVERY

Traditionally consumers became aware of sales promotions in passive ways. That is, most customers obtained promotions not through an active search but by being a recipient of a marketer's promotion activity, such as receiving coupons in the mail or being presented with a loyalty card at a store. Today the internet and mobile technologies have changed how customers become aware of many promotions. In addition to websites and apps offering access to coupons, social media and community forum sites enable customers to learn how to obtain sales promotions. Monitoring these sites may offer marketers insight into customers' attitudes about certain promotions and may even suggest ideas for future promotions. Additionally digital technologies are presenting marketers with a number of new delivery options. For example, the combination of mobile devices and GPS technology permits marketers to target promotions to a customer's physical location. This allows retailers and other businesses to issue sales promotions, such as sending digital coupons to a customer's mobile device when they are near the location where the coupon can be used.

TRACKING

As we discussed in our coverage of advertising, tracking customer response to marketers' promotional activity is critical for measuring the success of an advertisement. In sales promotion, tracking is also used. For instance, grocery retailers whose customers are in possession of loyalty cards, have the ability to match customer sales data to coupon use. This information can then be sold to coupon marketers, who may use the information to get a better picture of the buying patterns of those responding to the coupon. This may include using the information to generate instant coupons at the checkout counter.

CLUTTER AND NEED FOR CREATIVITY

As previously noted, sales promotion shares similar problems with advertising when it comes to promotional clutter (see *Disadvantages of Sales Promotion* discussion above). The rise of clutter in sales promotion is expected to become more problematic as more marketers increase their sales promotion spending. To stand out, marketers must find creative ways, including new types of sales promotion, that will separate their promotions from those of their competitors.

REFERENCES

1. For more information on the coupon industry in the U.S. including data and analytics information see: "U.S. Coupon Market Trends - Statistics & Facts." *Statista*. https://www.statista.com/topics/1156/coupon-market-trends-in-the-united-states.

2. For examples of experiential marketing events see: Branden Becker. "13 Examples of Experiential Marketing Campaigns That'll Give You Serious Event Envy." *HubSpot*. https://blog.hubspot.com/marketing/best-experiential-marketing-campaigns.

3. C.J. Mittica. "SOI 2023: Products – Apparel Comes Out Ahead." *The Advertising Specialty Institute*. August 2, 2023. https://www.asicentral.com/news/web-exclusive/august-2023/soi-2023-products-apparel-comes-out-ahead.

4. For more on trade shows see: Kelly Murphy. "Trade Show Statistics: Benchmarking Success in the Industry." *ConferenceSource*. https://conference-source.com/trade-show-statistics.

5. *Hannover Messe*. https://www.hannovermesse.de.

Chapter 15: Public Relations

Of the four promotional mix options available to marketers, public relations (PR) is probably the least understood, and consequently often receives the least amount of attention. Many marketers see public relations as only handling rudimentary communication activities, such as issuing press releases and responding to questions from the news media. But in reality, in a time when customers are inundated with thousands of promotional messages every day, public relations offers powerful methods for cutting through the clutter.

In this chapter, we investigate how public relations is growing in importance as a marketing tool and is now a critical element in helping marketers reach their objectives. We look at both the advantages and disadvantages of using PR for promotion. We see that PR uses a variety of tools to enhance the relationship between an organization and its target audience. And we show how, when handled correctly, PR can allow a marketer's message to stand out compared to other promotional methods.

WHAT IS PUBLIC RELATIONS?

Public relations involves activities that are intended to cultivate positive relations with key organizations and groups through the use of a variety of communications channels and tools. Traditionally, this meant an organization's public relations team would work with members of the news media and other media groups to publicize the organization and/or its products in an attempt to gain favorable stories in print and broadcast media. However, today the role of public relations is much broader and includes:

◆ Closely monitoring numerous media sources and other outlets for public comment about an organization and its products.

◆ Communicating with targeted customers by offering useful and timely information about an organization and its products.

◆ Building goodwill among an organization's customers, business partners, local community, and others by conducting special programs and events.

◆ Managing crises that threaten the image of an organization or its product.

In this chapter, most of our focus is on how public relations supports marketing by helping to shape the image (sometimes referred to as **publicity**) of a product and organization as perceived by customers and business partners. Yet it should be noted, there are other stakeholders an organization reaches via the public relations function, such as employees and non-target market groups (see *Targets of Marketing Promotion* in Chapter 11). Favorable media coverage about a company or its products often reaches these audiences as well and may offer potential benefit to the marketer.

It is also worth noting that in most large organizations there are other aspects to public relations which are not necessarily marketing related. Specifically, **investor relations (IR)** or **financial public relations** focus on financial issues facing organizations. These areas are guided by specific legal disclosure regulations. However, coverage of this type of PR will not be provided here. (1)

Advantages of PR

Public relations offers several advantages not found with other promotional options. First, PR is often considered a highly credible form of promotion. One of PR's main points of power rests with helping to establish credibility for a product, organization, or person (e.g., CEO) in the minds of targeted customer groups by capitalizing on the influence of a third-party — the media. Audiences view their preferred media outlets as independent sources that are unbiased in their coverage, meaning the decision to include the name of the company and the views expressed about the company is not based on payment (i.e., advertisement), but on the media outlet's judgment of what is newsworthy. For example, a positive story about a new product in the business section of a local newspaper may have a greater impact on readers than a full-page advertisement for the product since many readers perceive the newspaper as presenting an impartial perspective of the product. (2)

Second, a well-structured public relations campaign can provide the target market with more detailed information than they receive with other forms of marketing promotion. For instance, media sources often have more time (e.g., a segment on local television morning show) or more space (e.g., online story) to offer a fuller explanation of a product or organization than is available with 30-second television advertisements. While other PR tools, such as special events (see *Special Events* discussion below), offer marketers extended time with members of a targeted group.

Third, depending on the media outlet, a story mentioning an organization may be picked up by a large number of additional media resulting in a single story spreading to many other outlets. For instance, a story posted on a major newspaper's website can spread rapidly as bloggers and social media users provide links to the story.

Fourth, in many cases, public relations objectives can be achieved at low cost when compared to other promotional efforts. This is not to suggest public relations is not costly; it may be especially when a marketer hires PR professionals to handle the work. Yet when compared to the direct cost of other promotions, in particular advertising, the return on promotional expense can be quite high.

Disadvantages of PR

While public relations holds many advantages for marketers, there are also concerns when using this promotional technique. First, while media-directed public relations (see *Media Relations* discussion below) uses many of the same print, digital and broadcast media outlets as advertising, it differs significantly from advertising in that marketers do not have direct control over whether a message is delivered. For instance, a marketer may spend many hours talking with a magazine writer, who is preparing an industry story, only to find that her company is never mentioned in the article.

Second, while other promotional messages are carefully crafted and appear in a predetermined media vehicle exactly as the marketer prepared it (e.g., advertisement on a search engine), public relations generally conveys information to a member of the media (e.g., reporter), who then "re-crafts" the information for use in the media's content (e.g., news story, online posting). This may result in a final message that may not be precisely what the marketer planned.

Third, while a PR campaign has the potential to yield a high return on promotional expense, it also can have the opposite effect. For example, a PR campaign may feature a well-known speaker, who is paid a considerable sum by a marketer to speak to attendees at an industry trade show. However, if only a few people attend the talk, this may be judged as being an ineffective use of promotional funds. There is also the chance that an intended message of a PR campaign is misunderstood or is viewed negatively by members of a target market. (3)

Fourth, with public relations there is always a chance a well-devised PR content item, such as arranging to have an organization's president interviewed on air at a major cable news network, will get "bumped" from planned media coverage because of a more critical breaking news story, such as a significant event (e.g., earthquake), severe weather, or serious international situation.

Finally, marketers accustomed to handling many of their own tasks may find that public relations requires a different skill set than other types of promotion. As explained in Box 15-1, for many marketers, because of the complex nature of this field, some PR functions may be better left to seasoned PR professionals.

Box 15-1

THE BENEFITS OF PUBLIC RELATIONS PROFESSIONALS

While do-it-yourself public relations is certainly undertaken by many marketers, gaining satisfactory results can often prove difficult for those who have little experience in this promotional area. Instead, most marketers are better served by seeking the assistance of PR professionals, who understand all aspects of this diverse field. Skilled PR professionals offer many advantages for marketers with the two most prominent being:

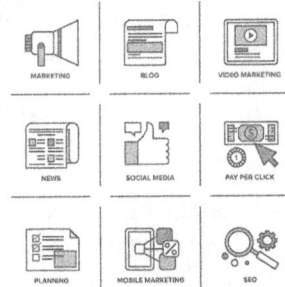

Understand the Importance of Media Content

A critical tool for PR is the development of media relations (see *Media Relations* discussion below). Public relations professionals are trained to unearth good information about a company and its products, which can then be presented to the media (see Box 15-2) in the form of content ideas (e.g., suggest an article featuring the company, suggest an on-air interview with a company representative). Public relations professionals are skilled at presenting content ideas in ways that capture the interest of members of the media.

Know the Media

Knowledge of the media's market may place PR professionals in a better position to match content ideas with the type of information sought by specific media members. Their skill at targeting the right media may prove to be a more efficient use of promotional resources than would occur if a marketer, who has little understanding of media needs, attempted to handle this on their own. This skill is especially valuable for organizations looking to do PR beyond their home market. Unlike advertising, where a standardized message can often work across different countries and cultures, the message presented through PR must often be adjusted for individual countries and, in some cases, subcultures within countries. For this reason, many organizations find that undertaking PR in the global market is better left to experienced professionals, who possess greater knowledge of a particular foreign market.

OBJECTIVES OF PUBLIC RELATIONS

Like other aspects of marketing promotion, public relations is used to address several broad objectives including:

◆ <u>Building Awareness</u> – When introducing a new product or relaunching an existing product, marketers can use a PR element to generate customer attention and awareness, particularly through media placements, social media announcements, and special events.

◆ Creating Interest – Any positive attention PR can generate among media outlets, whether it results in an in-depth story or just a brief mention, can help entice interest within a target audience. For example, around important holidays, a new festive holiday food may receive PR support with promotional releases sent to the food media or through a free sampling event that may attract local television coverage.

◆ Providing Information – Public relations can be used to provide customers with detailed information about goods and services. Through organization-produced materials, such as online video tutorials, customer newsletters, social media postings and other useful material, PR delivers information to customers that can help them gain understanding of a product or an organization.

◆ Stimulating Demand – While not as effective as sales promotion for moving customers to make a purchase, PR can still be a useful technique for building demand. For instance, a positive story about a product in a major media outlet can lead to a discernible increase in product sales.

◆ Reinforcing the Brand – In many organizations, the public relations function is also involved with brand reinforcement by maintaining positive relationships with targeted audiences and thereby aiding in building a strong image. Today it is crucial for organizations and brands to build a favorable image. A strong image helps the marketer grow its business and may also help protect the organization in times of crises.

PUBLIC RELATIONS TOOLS

Whether handling PR internally or hiring professionals (see Box 15-1), marketers should be familiar with the key tools available for public relations. These tools are discussed in detail below.

MEDIA RELATIONS

Historically, the core of public relations has been media relations, which includes efforts to gain the attention of members of the press (e.g., TV, online news websites, radio, newspaper, magazine) and other influential voices (e.g., specialty websites, bloggers, podcasters). In particular, PR professionals attempt to have information associated with an organization (e.g., new product introduction) appear in the media outlet's content. This is done by developing engaging and relevant story angles, or other content ideas that are pitched to the media. It is necessary to understand that media placements only come when content ideas are of interest to the media and that no direct payment is made to the media for placements. In fact, in order to maintain the highest level of credibility, many news organizations bar reporters and writers from accepting even the smallest gifts (e.g., free pencils with product logo) from organizations.

For marketers, it is essential to know that many content items mentioning an organization or its products that appear in a media outlet often start with a suggestion from a PR person. This may occur through one of the media building techniques discussed in Box 15-2 or through direct conversations with the content creators (e.g., journalists). If things work out, a content creator will, at best, produce a positive content item with the organization/product as a key feature or, at a minimum, include the organization or product name somewhere within a wider industry-focused piece.

In addition to reaching out to journalists, PR also targets segments of the media market that are not part of an established news organization including TV program producers, independent bloggers and podcasters, and influential social media personalities (see *Trends in Public Relations* discussion below). Within some markets, these voices have attracted a large and loyal following. Public relations campaigns targeting these groups are rapidly gaining favor and represent media outlets that may carry significant influence within a target market. (4)

Box 15-2

TECHNIQUES FOR BUILDING MEDIA RELATIONS

While the objective of media relations is to obtain favorable mentions for an organization or product without direct payment to a media outlet, the process for accomplishing this is by no means free. Public relations professionals **"pitch"** story ideas to reporters, news editors, and other influential opinion leaders by using a variety of techniques that can be expensive. These techniques include:

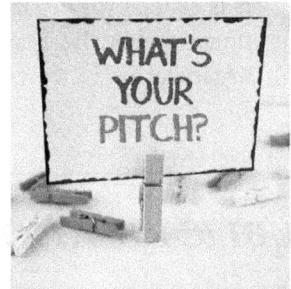

News Releases

One of the most frequently undertaken tasks of public relations professionals is the preparation of a news release (a.k.a., press release). A news release is a prepared message (e.g., print, video, audio) intended to highlight one or more issues facing an organization. For instance, a news release is often used to announce a new product, indicate changes occurring with existing products, and to introduce new company personnel. Organizations can distribute news releases on their own (e.g., post on website, send out by email, provide link on social media), or by using a paid news distribution service.

Social Media

It can be argued the evolution of social media has affected public relations more than any other marketing area (see *Trends in Public Relations* discussion below). With the advantage of being both a broadcast communication platform and an interactive one-on-one platform, many in PR now view social media as the best method for engaging media outlets. However, it should be understood, the effectiveness of social media will depend on whether media outlets actually follow an organization's communications. In fact, as more organizations direct more of their PR efforts to social media, the task of getting media outlets to follow their messages is likely to become more challenging.

Press Kits

This is the name given to prepared materials, such as organization background, biography of a firm's executives and spokespersons (see *Media Tour* discussion below) and other supporting materials (e.g., product videos), that provide information useful to media outlets. Such kits can be sent to media outlets via package delivery services or accessible on an organization's website. As more organizations utilize press kits, the design and content options have expanded in an effort to capture more media attention. For instance, press kits delivered to media outlets can be packaged in uniquely detailed containers such as bags, pouches, plastic cases, and cardboard tubes.

Matte Release

Some media outlets, especially small local newspapers, may accept articles written by an organization as filler material when their publications lack sufficient content. Public relations professionals submit a matte release (a.k.a., mat releases) through **syndicated news services** (i.e., services that supply content to many media outlets) or directly to targeted media via email.

Industry Articles

Many industry websites and print publications allow companies to submit articles authored by company personnel, such as a CEO or Marketing Manager. Depending on the media outlet, the articles can cover specific happenings at a company or may be written with the intention of addressing a business issue. In either case, PR professionals may have significant input into the creation of the article even though they are not identified as the author.

Online Press Room

Finally, to address the needs of media outlets, the public relations staff often manage an online "press room" section within the organization's website. This area caters to the needs of media outlets including providing easy access to news releases, digital press kits, list of company contacts, links to various organizational social media platforms, information request forms, and more.

MEDIA TOUR

Some new products can be successfully publicized when launched with a media tour. On a media tour a company **spokesperson** travels to selected cities to introduce a new product. This is often done by having the spokesperson booked on TV and radio talk shows, conducting interviews with print and internet news reporters, or discussing the product with others that may impact the target market (e.g., bloggers, podcasters, social media influencers). The spokesperson can be a company employee, or someone hired by the company, perhaps a celebrity or "expert" who has credibility with the target audience. A media tour may also include personal appearances with targeted customers through such events as public appearances, speaking engagements, live online video interview, or autograph signing opportunities. (5)

NEWSLETTERS AND INFORMATIONAL EMAIL

Marketers, who have captured names and addresses of customers and potential customers, can use detailed content in the form of newsletters or informational email as a way to build stronger relations. Marketers using newsletters and informational email are effective when they strive to provide content of interest to their targeted audience. For instance, a bookstore may include reviews of new books, information on book author speaking engagements, and details on in-store or online promotions. A food manufacturer may include seasonal recipes, descriptions of new products, and coupons. Online newsletters and email also offer the opportunity to include clickable links to retail outlets carrying the marketer's product and to videos offering additional product information.

SPECIAL EVENTS

These run the gamut from receptions to elegant dinners to stunts to special appearances. Special events can be designed to reach a narrow audience, such as a dinner with a guest speaker targeted to individuals interested in college savings plans, or aimed at a large group, such as a strawberry festival designed to promote state tourism and targeted to a large geographic area. Stunts, such as building the world's largest ice cream sundae during National Ice Cream month, capture the attention of an audience in the immediate area. Stunts can also attract the attention of mass media, such as TV news, newspapers, and social media. Finally, special appearances of a recognizable symbol of an organization can draw the interest of the target market and media outlets. For instance, in the U.S., the Oscar Mayer Wienermobile is a classic example, providing a recognizable icon that travels the United States garnering attention wherever it visits. As with all PR programs, special event planners must work hard to ensure an event conveys the correct message and image to the target audience.

SPEAKING ENGAGEMENTS

Speaking before industry conventions, trade association meetings, and other groups provides an opportunity for an organization's experts to demonstrate their knowledge to potential customers and business partners. Typically, these opportunities are not explicitly used to promote an organization or its products. Rather, speaking engagements are a chance to talk on a topic that appeals to an interested group and serve to highlight the speaker's expertise in a particular field. Often the only mention of the sponsoring organization or the products associated with the speaker is found in the speaker's biography. Nevertheless, the right speaking engagement, in front of an appropriate target audience, offers opportunities for generating customer interest.

EMPLOYEE COMMUNICATIONS

For many companies, communicating regularly with employees is essential for keeping them informed of developments, such as new products, sales incentives, personnel issues, and other changes. Companies use a variety of means to communicate with employees, including email, newsletters, and social media. In larger firms, an in-house PR department often works in conjunction with the Human Resources Department to develop employee communications.

COMMUNITY RELATIONS AND PHILANTHROPY

Organizations often realize positive results by fostering strong relations with important and potentially influential audiences, such as members of their regional community. Programs that are supportive of the community include: sponsoring local organizations and institutions (e.g., arts organizations, community activities, parks); conducting educational workshops (e.g., for teachers and parents); and donating product or money in support of community events. Effective community relations can help a company weather bad publicity or a crisis situation that can unexpectedly arise due to such issues as problems with a product, perceived service shortcomings, unethical behavior by management, and false rumors. Some companies also make an effort to contribute to charitable groups, especially organizations that have some relationship to the company's mission or to a person at the company.

ADDITIONAL PUBLIC RELATIONS ACTIVITIES

While the PR tools discussed above are primarily used to help achieve specific marketing objectives (e.g., increase sales), public relations may also undertake additional activities aimed at maintaining a positive image for an organization. These activities include:

MARKET MONITORING

Monitoring public comment about an organization and its products is becoming increasingly necessary, especially with the growth of digital media outlets. Today monitoring not only includes watching what is written and reported in traditional print and broadcast media, it requires attention be paid to discussions occurring on social media, news websites, discussion forums, blogs, podcasts, and other public messaging areas. Marketers must be prepared to respond quickly to erroneous information and negative opinions as these can spin out of control very quickly (see *Crisis Management* discussion below). Failure to correct misinformation can be devastating to a product or an organization's reputation.

There are many specialized monitoring services that help keep track of news and comments about an organization and its products. These services can be used to measure the effectiveness of PR campaigns, such as indicating how many times a company is mentioned in various media outlets. Many larger organizations have their own customized software systems for monitoring public comment. Today many of these systems are built with the underlying support of artificial intelligence (AI), which enables organizations to quickly learn about items of interest (e.g., mentions of its products) made across most digital media outlets. Smaller companies, can also monitor relevant news and comments by utilizing fee-based software (6), although there are several no-cost monitoring options that are also available. For example, Google offers a free "alerts" service, that will email a listing each time a keyword, such as a company or product name, is mentioned in news articles, blog posts, and certain social media. (7)

CRISIS MANAGEMENT

Marketers need to be prepared to respond quickly to negative information about their organization. When a problem with a product arises, whether real or driven only by rumor, a marketer's investment in a product can be in serious jeopardy. Today, with the prevalence of digital media, negative information can spread rapidly. Using monitoring tools marketers can track the issues and respond in a timely fashion. Additionally, to manage response effectively, many companies, led by their public relations staff, have a crisis management plan in place that outlines steps to take when responding to a situation, including indicating who is authorized to speak on behalf of the company should a crisis event occur.

TRENDS IN PUBLIC RELATIONS

Until recently most public relations activity involved person-to-person contact between PR professionals and members of the media, such as journalists and television news reporters. However, within the last few years several developments have altered the tasks performed and skills needed by PR people. In most cases, these changes are the result of evolving digital media technologies.

The important trends in public relations include:

SOCIAL MEDIA

By far the most significant development to affect public relations in the last 30 years is the impact played by social media. While those responsible for such functional areas as distribution and personal selling may use social media in a general way, such as sending out announcements, there are other areas of marketing where social media has significantly transformed how things are done. And maybe the most impacted area is public relations.

In a matter of just a few years, social networks have created opportunities for monitoring and communicating that are quickly raising these methods to the top of the list of PR tools. In fact, many journalists and other media members find social media to be a more convenient way to acquire information, particularly if they want to monitor happenings in a specific industry. By following relevant social media postings, members of the media have information delivered to them, rather than having to spend time searching for it. Consequently, marketers had little option but to move more of their PR function in this direction.

Marketers should also understand that the term "social media" is a catch-all term that includes much more than just the well-known outlets such as Facebook, LinkedIn, and X (formerly Twitter). In fact, there are many subcategories that fall under the social media umbrella, including media sharing (e.g., Instagram, Snapchat, TikTok, YouTube), discussion forums (e.g., reddit), product review (e.g., TripAdvisor), bookmarking (e.g., Pinterest), and many more.

While social media offers tremendous PR advantages across many outlets with a posting potentially moving rapidly across a targeted group (i.e., message going "viral"), it also poses significant threats. As noted earlier, one of the most pressing issues is that social media often requires PR professionals to respond rapidly to negative or misleading information. In effect, social media is turning PR into a 24-hour, 7 days-a-week job, particularly for global companies.

Also, the time required to monitor and respond to the growing number of social media outlets is forcing some companies to place less emphasis on traditional public relations tasks, such as the creation of press kit materials. However, since social media continues to evolve as a PR tool, it is unclear if shifting workload to social media will carry the same return on investment as what is offered with traditional PR tools. (8)

CHANGING SKILL SETS

As we have discussed, public relations is becoming much more involved in creating content and strategies for the social media platforms of their own organizations or for clients. This has led to PR careers for not only those possessing traditional PR skills, such as strengths in communications, graphic design and journalism, but also those with certain high-tech skills, including being familiar with AI tools, and marketing research expertise. This is evident in the need for people who can interpret the information provided by online "listening tools" that PR professionals are using to monitor what is going on in the social media world (see *Market Monitoring* discussion above).

Additionally, PR is quickly moving to video-driven content as its main form of communicating with media outlets. This will also present public relations employment opportunities both in front of the camera (e.g., content presenters) and behind the camera (e.g., video editors).

SEARCH ENGINE OPTIMIZATION

A crucial task of publicity is convincing media outlets to mention the name of a product, company, or person. For several years, internet marketers have recognized the importance of getting their company information listed in what has become an influential media outlet – internet search engines. Using methods dubbed search engine optimization (SEO), marketers employ specific techniques in an effort to attain higher rankings for relevant search queries. For instance, an online clothing retailer may attempt to be one of the first websites listed when someone enters the search phrase "men's suits." If the retailer's website meets the search engine's criteria for ranking, then the website could appear at the top of the search results page, without cost to the retailer.

While, at first glance, SEO may not seem like a responsibility of public relations, it would appear to contain the main characteristics for making it so, namely getting a third-party media outlet (i.e., search engine) to mention the company (i.e., search rankings) at no direct cost the company (i.e., no payment for ranking). And, just as PR people can use methods to affect coverage within traditional media, optimizing a website can work to influence results in search engines by using content techniques (e.g., use of specific **keywords**) along with technical improvements (e.g., loading speed) that allow a website to fit within ever-changing search engine ranking criteria. In this way, SEO does what PR professionals do by obtaining good placement in third-party media outlets. (9)

REFERENCES

1. For more on investor relations and how it differs from public relations see: Evan Tarver. "Investor Relations (IR)." *Investopedia*, May 23, 2023. https://www.investopedia.com/terms/i/investorrelations.asp.

2. It should be noted that while some have argued media outlets are not unbiased, those presenting these arguments are generally associating these with issues related to politics and governing, rather than issues within the business realm, such as mentions of a marketer or its products.

3. The issue of negative response to a PR message can be seen with an Anheuser-Busch promotion for its Bud Light beer that featured a transgender social media influencer. For more see: Amanda Holpuch. "Behind the Backlash Against Bud Light." *New York Times*. September 18, 2023. https://www.nytimes.com/article/bud-light-boycott.html.

4. If an organization is paying someone to mention a product (e.g., blogger, social media influencers), U.S. law requires such payment be identified by those being paid. For more on this advertising endorsement law see: "Truth in Advertising – Advertisement Endorsements." *Federal Trade Commission*. https://www.ftc.gov/news-events/topics/truth-advertising/advertisement-endorsements.

5. When media tours are undertaken virtually through TV, radio or internet, these are often called satellite media tours. For more see: "What is a Satellite Media Tour?" *Lyons Public Relations*. https://www.lyonspr.com/what-is-a-satellite-media-tour.

6. Many products are available offering companies of all sizes the ability to monitor social media for mentions of their company, products, industry, and much more. Most of these products are fee-based services. For a listing of services see: "Best Social Media Marketing Tools." *G2*. https://www.g2.com/categories/social-media-monitoring.

7. "Google Alerts." *Google*. https://www.google.com/alerts.

8. While social media is a well-understood element in public relations for consumer products marketers, nearly all types of organizations, including those primarily in the business-to-business market, are also finding benefits. For examples see: Katie Woods. "Making Waves: Unexpected Industries Innovating on Social." *SproutSocial*. February 8, 2023. https://sproutsocial.com/insights/boring-industries-social.

9. For more on search engine optimization see: "What Is SEO / Search Engine Optimization?" *Search Engine Land*. https://searchengineland.com/guide/what-is-seo.

Chapter 16: Personal Selling

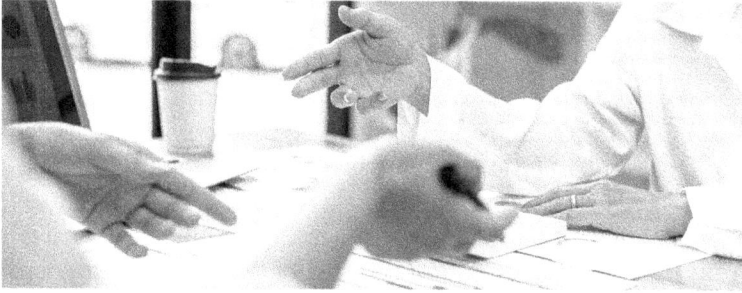

In the past few chapters, we discussed how marketers can use advertising, sales promotion, and public relations to reach a large number of customers. Unfortunately, advertising and sales promotion share one significant disadvantage: these are primarily non-personal forms of communication. While public relations contains elements of personal communication through use of such methods as social media, email and special events, it often lacks the relationship-building advantages found when communicating face-to-face with a potential customer. And whether an organization is in retailing or manufacturing, sells goods or services, is a large multinational or a local startup, or is out to make a profit or is a not-for-profit, in all probability at some point they will need to rely on face-to-face, personal contact with customers. In other words, they will need to promote their product offerings using personal selling.

In this chapter, we define personal selling, look at the advantages and disadvantages, and see how it fits within an organization's promotional strategy. We also see there are a variety of different selling roles available to the marketing organization, including some whose objectives are not tied to getting customers to buy. Finally, we examine several trends facing the personal selling field.

WHAT IS PERSONAL SELLING?

Personal selling is a promotional method in which one party (e.g., salesperson) uses skills and techniques to build personal relationships with another party (e.g., those involved in a purchase decision) resulting in both parties obtaining value. In most cases, the "value" for the salesperson is realized through the financial rewards of the sale while the customer's "value" is realized from the benefits obtained from consuming the product. However, as we will discuss, getting a customer to purchase a product is not always the objective of personal selling. For instance, selling may be used for the purpose of simply delivering information. Because selling involves personal contact, this promotional method often occurs through face-to-face meetings, telephone conversation, video conferencing, or online chat.

Among marketing jobs, more people are employed in sales positions than any other marketing-related occupation. In the United States alone, the U.S. Department of Labor estimates that over 13 million people, or about 9% of the overall labor force, are directly involved in selling and sales-related positions. (1) Worldwide this figure may be closer to 100 million. Yet these figures vastly underestimate the number of people who are actively engaged in some aspect of selling as part of their normal job responsibilities. While millions of people can easily be seen as holding sales jobs, the promotional techniques used in selling are also part of the day-to-day activities of many who are usually not associated with selling. For instance, top corporate executives, whose job titles include CEO or COO, are continually selling their companies to major customers, stock investors, government officials, and many other stakeholders. The techniques they employ to gain benefits for their organizations are often the same ones used by frontline salespeople as they sell to their customers. Therefore, our discussion of the promotional value of personal selling has implications beyond marketing and sales departments.

Advantages of Personal Selling

One key advantage personal selling has over other promotional methods is that it is a two-way form of communication. In selling situations, the message sender (e.g., salesperson) can adjust the message as they gain feedback from a message receiver (e.g., customer). Consequently, if a customer does not understand the initial message (e.g., does not fully understand how the product works), the salesperson can make adjustments to address questions or concerns. Many non-personal forms of promotion, such as a radio advertisement, are inflexible, at least in the short-term, and cannot be easily adjusted to address questions that arise from the audience experiencing the ad.

A second advantage is that the interactive nature of personal selling also makes it the most effective promotional method for building relationships with customers, particularly in the business-to-business market. This is especially the case for companies selling expensive products, as such purchases may take a considerable amount of time to complete and may involve the input of many people at the purchasing company (see Box 4-2 in Chapter 4). In these situations, sales success often requires the marketer to develop and maintain strong relationships with members of the purchasing company.

Building relationships is also a critical part of the personal selling process when doing business internationally. Business cultures in such area as Asia and Latin America are often built on personal relationships between buyer and seller rather than on seeking the best business deal. While building closer business relationships may take time, salespeople, who are able to cultivate such relationships, often find greater success compared to competitors who sell on price alone. (2)

Finally, personal selling is the most practical promotional option for reaching customers who are not easily reached through other methods. The best example lies in selling to the business market where, compared to the consumer market, advertising, public relations, and sales promotions are often not as effective.

Disadvantages of Personal Selling

Possibly the biggest disadvantage of personal selling is the degree to which this promotional method is misunderstood. At some point in time, nearly everyone can recall an unpleasant experience with a salesperson, who they believed was overly aggressive or even downright annoying. But as we discuss in Box 16-1, while there are certainly many salespeople that fall into this category, the truth is salespeople are most successful if they focus their efforts on satisfying customers over the long term and not focusing on their own selfish interests for the purpose of making a quick sale.

A second disadvantage that exists with personal selling relates to numerous expenses organizations face when utilizing this method of promotion. Costs incurred in personal selling include:

◆ <u>High cost-per-action (CPA)</u> – As noted in Chapter 11, CPA can be a key measure of the success of promotion spending. Since personal selling involves person-to-person contact, the money spent to support a sales staff can be steep. For instance, in some industries it costs well over (US) $300 each time a salesperson contacts a potential customer regardless of whether a sale is made. These costs include compensation (e.g., salary, commission, bonus), providing support materials (e.g., product literature, product samples), allowances for entertainment spending, travel expenses, office supplies, digital devices, telecommunication, and much more. With such high cost for maintaining a sales force, this is often not a practical option for selling products in which a single purchase does not generate a large amount of revenue.

◆ <u>Training Costs</u> – Most forms of personal selling require extensive training of the sales staff on such issues as product knowledge, industry information, and selling skills. At most companies, training occurs for both new hires (e.g., training on company policy, selling methods, products, etc.) and for experienced employees (e.g., training before the launch of new products). For companies that require their salespeople to attend formal training programs, the cost of training can be quite high and include such expenses as travel, hotel, meals, and training equipment. Additionally, while salespeople are in training, an organization is most likely also paying certain fixed costs including the trainee's salary, health care, and other expenses.

A third disadvantage of personal selling is that this form of personal promotion is not for everyone. Job turnover in sales is generally much higher than it is for other marketing positions. For companies that assign their salespeople to handle certain customer groups (e.g., handle all customers in a geographic territory), turnover may leave a company without representation in a customer group for an extended period of time while the company recruits and trains a replacement.

Box 16-1

A MISUNDERSTOOD FIELD

Here is a quick question: Which of the following five mental images comes closest to what you think about when you hear that someone's job involves "selling"?

1. Someone who is highly extroverted and quick with stories that keep everyone laughing.

2. Someone on a used car lot who makes every car sound like a gem.

3. Someone in a clothing store who corrals customers when they first enter and then will not leave them alone.

4. Someone calling at dinner time trying to get the "head of the household" to buy a home security system.

5. A knowledgeable, hard-working and highly trained professional, who uses finely honed communication techniques to fully understand and satisfy the needs of her/his customers.

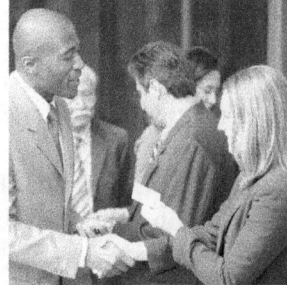

If you chose one of the first four options, don't feel bad, you're in tremendous company. Lots of people share the view that selling is something done by people who are manipulative, arrogant, aggressive, greedy, and only concerned about getting the sale. While there certainly are some salespeople that fit these descriptions, today the most successful salespeople are ones who work hard to understand their customers' needs with the ultimate goal of ensuring the customer is satisfied at a high level.

Additionally, to understand customers, the most important characteristic of a good salesperson is not their ability to carry on a conversation, but their ability to listen to the customer.

Also, personal selling holds a key role in the promotional activities of a large number of organizations. In fact, in the business market, where one company sells products to another company, money spent to support the selling function far exceeds spending on advertising.

Thus, while many people have experienced annoying and possibly unethical salespeople, the truth is selling is one of the most powerful methods for building customer relationships and those successful at selling are much more likely to reflect the description presented in #5. (3)

OBJECTIVES OF PERSONAL SELLING

Personal selling is used to meet the five objectives of promotion in the following ways:

◆ Building Awareness – A common task of salespeople, especially when selling in the business markets, is to educate customers on new product offerings. In fact, salespeople serve a vital role at industry trade shows, where they discuss products with show attendees. But building awareness using personal selling is also important in consumer markets. For instance, the advent of controlled word-of-mouth promotion (see Box 16-2) is leading to personal selling becoming a useful mechanism for introducing consumers to new products.

◆ Creating Interest – The fact personal selling involves person-to-person communication makes it a natural method for getting customers to experience a product for the first time. In fact, creating interest goes hand-in-hand with building product awareness as sales professionals can often accomplish both objectives during the first encounter with a potential customer.

◆ Providing Information – When salespeople engage customers a significant amount of the conversation focuses on product information. Consequently, most marketing organizations provide their sales staff with extensive sales support, including slide presentations, brochures, research reports, online videos, and many other forms of informational material.

◆ Stimulating Demand – The most fundamental objective of personal selling is to convince customers to make a purchase. As we will see below in our discussion of selling roles, getting customers to buy is the prime function of a large segment of selling roles.

◆ Reinforcing the Brand – Most personal selling is intended to build long-term relationships with customers. A strong relationship can only be built over time and requires regular communication with a customer. Meeting with customers on a regular basis enables salespeople to discuss their company's products and, by doing so, helps strengthen customers' knowledge of what the company has to offer.

CLASSIFYING SELLING ROLES

Worldwide millions of people have careers that fit in the personal selling category. However, the actual functions carried out by someone in sales may be quite different. Below we discuss the four main types of selling roles: order getters, order takers, order supporters, and sales supporters. It should be noted that these roles are not mutually exclusive and that a salesperson can perform more than one and possibly all roles.

Order Getters

The role most synonymous with selling is a position in which the salesperson is actively engaged in using his/her skills to obtain orders from customers. Such roles can be further divided into:

NEW BUSINESS DEVELOPMENT

A highly challenging, yet potentially lucrative, sales position is one where the main objective is to find new customers. Sales jobs in this category are often in fields that are intensely competitive but offer high rewards for those who are successful. The key distinguishing factor of these positions is that, once a sale is made, new business salespeople will generally pass customers on to others in their organization who handle account maintenance. These sales roles include:

- Business Equipment Sales – These salespeople are often found in industries where company profits are generated primarily through the sale of supplies and services that come after an initial equipment purchase. The key objective of business equipment salespeople is to get buyers to purchase the main piece of equipment for which a large number of supplies and services are needed. For instance, traditionally in the photocopier industry, business equipment salespeople focus on establishing new accounts. However, once a photocopier sale is made, they pass along the account to other sales personnel, who then handle sales of supplies and maintenance contracts.

- Telemarketing – This category includes product sales transacted over the phone, whether aimed at businesses or consumers. While in the U.S. some laws restrict unsolicited phone selling (4), the practice is still widely used in both consumer markets and business markets. (5)

- Consumer Selling – Certain companies are extremely aggressive in their use of salespeople to sell products to consumers. These include: retailers selling certain high-priced consumer products, including furniture, electronics, and clothing; sellers of housing products, including real estate, security services, and building replacement products (e.g., windows); and in-home product sellers, including those selling door-to-door, and products sold at "**home party**" events, such as cosmetics, kitchenware, and decorative products.

ACCOUNT MANAGEMENT

Most people engaged in sales are not only involved in gaining the initial order but work to build and maintain long-term relationships with their clients. Salespeople involved in account management are found across a broad range of industries. Their responsibilities involve all aspects of building customer relationships from initial sale to follow-up account servicing. These include:

- Business-to-Business – These salespeople sell products for business use with an emphasis on follow-up sales. In many cases, business-to-business salespeople present several different items to their customers (i.e., broad and/or deep product line), rather than a single product. Consequently, while the initial sale may only result in the buyer purchasing a few products, the potential exists for the buyer to purchase many other products as the buyer-seller relationship grows.

- Trade Selling – Sales professionals working for consumer products companies normally do not sell to the final user (i.e., consumer). Instead, their role is focused on first getting distributors, such wholesalers and retailers, to handle their products. Once this is accomplished, they help distributors sell their products by offering ideas for product advertising, in-store displays, and sales promotions.

Order Takers

Selling does not always require a salesperson use methods designed to encourage customers to make a purchase. In fact, the greatest number of people engaged in selling are not order getters, rather they are considered order takers. In this role, salespeople primarily assist customers with a purchase in ways that are much less assertive than how order getters handle their role. As might be expected, compensation for order takers is generally lower than order getters. Among those serving an order taker role are:

◆ Retail Assistants – While some retail salespeople are involved in new business selling, the vast majority of retail employees handle order taking tasks ranging from directing customers to product locations to handling customer checkout.

◆ Industrial Distributor Assistants – Industrial purchase situations also have personnel to handle customer purchases. For instance, distributors of building products often operate a facility where contractors shop for supplies. The person handling these transactions would likely fit the order taker role.

◆ Customer Service Representative – Order taking is also handled in situations that are not face-to-face. Usually this occurs via phone conversations or through online chat between buyers and customer service personnel.

Order Supporters

Some salespeople are not engaged in direct selling activity at all. That is, they do not actively sell to the person who is the ultimate customer for their product. Examples of order support salespeople include:

◆ Missionary – These salespeople are used in industries where customers make purchases based on the advice or requirements of others. In this role, the salesperson concentrates on selling activities that target those who influence purchases made by the final customer. Industries in which missionary selling is commonly found include: pharmaceuticals, where salespeople, known as **product detailers**, discuss products with doctors (influencers) who then write prescriptions for their patients (final customer); and higher education, where salespeople discuss textbooks with college professors (influencers) who then assign these to their students (final customer).

◆ <u>Controlled Word-of-Mouth Promotion</u> – As discussed in Box 16-2, another type of order supporter specializes in word-of-mouth promotion. This method of promotion, which also is known by such terms as **buzz marketing** and **advocacy marketing**, is similar to missionary selling as salespeople do not actively look to make a sale. However, it differs from missionary selling in that salespeople will talk to the eventual purchaser of the product.

Box 16-2

CONTROLLED WORD-OF-MOUTH PROMOTION

One of the most influential forms of promotion occurs when one person speaks highly of a product to someone else, particularly if the message sender is considered an unbiased source of information. Until recently, marketers have had little control over person-to-person promotion that did not involve salespeople (i.e., a biased source).

However, marketers are now using methods of promotion that strategically take advantage of the benefits offered by word-of-mouth promotion. Unlike salespeople who often attempt to obtain an order from customers, controlled word-of-mouth promotion uses real people, such as social media influencers, to help spread information about a product but do not directly elicit customer orders.

With controlled word-of-mouth promotion, a marketer hires people to spread positive information about a product. They are often trained to do so in a way that does not make it obvious that they are being paid to intentionally convey positive information. This technique is especially useful when building a high level of awareness for a new product. For example, a brewer may form a team of word-of-mouth marketers that visits local taverns and night spots, or actively post on social media. As part of their job, these marketers may "talk up" a new beer sold by the brewer and even purchase the product for some customers. Yet they may carry out their task without directly disclosing that they are being compensated for their efforts.

While controlled word-of-mouth has received a great deal of marketer interest, this form of promotion has also been subjected to negative publicity due to potential legal issues it raises. In particular, in the U.S. someone who is hired to "act" as if they are interested in an organization's product and is compensated for their efforts (e.g., social media influencers), is required to fully disclose this relationship to those receiving the message. Failure to do so may lead to government action again them. (6)

Sales Supporters

A final selling role involves those who assist mostly with the selling activities of other sales professionals. These include:

◆ <u>Technical Specialists</u> – When dealing with the sale of technical products, particularly in the business market, salespeople may need to draw on the expertise of others to help with the process. This is particularly the case when the buying party consists of a buying center. In Chapter 4, we indicated that, in business selling, many people from different functional areas are involved in the purchase decision. If this buying center includes technical people, such as scientists and engineers, a salesperson may seek assistance from members of her/his own technical staff to help address specific questions.

◆ <u>Office Support</u> – Salespeople also may receive assistance from their company's office staff in the form of promotional materials, setting up sales appointments, finding sales leads, arranging meeting space, or organizing trade show exhibits.

TRENDS IN PERSONAL SELLING

While the basic premise of personal selling, building relationships, has not changed much since the evolution of the marketing concept (see Box 1-1 in Chapter 1), there are a number of developments impacting this method of promotion including:

CUSTOMER INFORMATION SHARING

Possibly the most dramatic change to occur in how salespeople function on a day-to-day basis involves the integration of customer relationship management (CRM) systems into the selling arena. As we discussed in Chapter 3, CRM is the name given to both the technology and the philosophy that drives companies to gain a better understanding of their customers with the goal of building stronger long-term relationships. The essential requirement for an effective CRM system is the need for all customer contact points (e.g., salespeople, customer service, websites) to gather information to share with others in the organization.

Yet when first introduced, CRM faced some rough times within the sales force for the exact reason it is important: salespeople must share their information. Salespeople historically have been highly effective at developing relationships and learning about customers, but often loathed sharing this with others since possessing detailed customer information was often viewed as an important element in what made a salesperson valuable. In the minds of some salespeople, letting go of the information reduced their importance to the company. For example, some salespeople felt sharing all they know about a customer would make them expendable since a company could simply insert someone new into their role who will have access to the customer information collected by the salesperson who was replaced.

While this attitude toward CRM often made implementation difficult in many organizations, most salespeople now understand that it is not going away. CRM and information sharing have proven to be critical in maintaining strong customer relations and salespeople have learned to adapt to it.

RELIANCE ON MOBILE TECHNOLOGY

The move to an information sharing approach is most effective when salespeople have ready access to CRM and other information sources. With mobile communication available almost anywhere, such access allows salespeople to retrieve needed information at any time. For instance, if a salesperson takes a customer to lunch, he/she can quickly access their company website or specialized software to respond to customer questions, such as how long it may take to receive a product if an order is placed. The implication is that salespeople are now truly mobile as nearly all of their software applications are accessible from almost anywhere.

Additionally, the proliferation of mobile apps provides an abundance of options for increasing sales force productivity. For instance, apps can be used to: deal with customers (e.g., take notes, store business cards); manage business files (e.g., scan documents; access online files); prepare for meetings (e.g., update a slide presentation, finding meeting spots); and much, much more.

USE OF SOCIAL MEDIA

The sales forces' adoption of mobile technologies has made it easier for them to explore the use of social networks for building business relationships. While salespeople actively use consumer-oriented social media such as Facebook and Instagram, the most popular social network for building sales relationships is LinkedIn, since it is primarily aimed at businesspeople. Consequently, the contacts found through LinkedIn tend to be of higher quality than contacts found through other social networks.

SALES PRESENTATION TECHNOLOGIES

Technology also plays a key role in how sales professionals engage existing and potential customers. These tools offer salespeople practical and cost-effective alternatives to in-person selling. Options including:

- Video Conferencing – A widely used method of electronic sales presentations is one delivered through video conferencing. Aside from its nearly universal use for all customer contact during the coronavirus pandemic, many salespeople regularly use video conferencing in the first stage of the sales process as it can greatly lower the initial cost of reaching sales prospects (e.g., reduces travel expense). Yet anyone who has an internet or mobile network connection knows that communicating via video can, at times, be a trying experience as the image and sound quality may appear to be slow and jittery. However, current leading video conferencing applications such as Zoom, FaceTime and Skype, have addressed many of these concerns and offer a generally reliable real-time video conferencing experience that can satisfy the needs of most salesperson-buyer virtual meetings.

- Online Text Chat – Online chat allows for real-time communication between multiple participants. While this form of buyer-seller communication may not be highly effective at getting someone to make a purchase, it has proven beneficial in building initial customer interest. For example, potential customers visiting a website may use the chat feature to ask a few questions about the company's products. Engaging customers this way can then lead to the customer agreeing to a phone call from a salesperson to discuss the product further.

- Virtual Trade Shows – As noted in Chapter 14, in business-to-business marketing, industry trade shows are a convenient promotional method for reaching many potential buyers in a short period of time. Unfortunately, trade shows can be quite expensive to attend for both buyers and sellers. Yet the value trade shows possess for generating sales leads has persuaded many organizations to explore other meeting options, including online or virtual trade shows. These meetings take place through special "venues" created on the internet, which allow participants to attend while sitting in front of their computer. (7)

SALES TRAINING TECHNOLOGIES

Developing the skills and techniques needed to be successful at selling requires the individual seller and the seller's organization to be fully committed to sales training. Sales training is the hallmark of professional selling. If there is one characteristic separating the truly successful salesperson from those who are not successful, it is the amount of training and preparation they receive.

Most organizations employing a sales force offer new salespeople an extensive formal in-person training program, often held at dedicated training facilities. The length of training programs ranges from a few days to many months depending on the industry. But once a salesperson has moved on to selling to customers, training does not stop. Those involved in selling must continue to stay abreast of their products, customers, markets, and competitors. While many companies continue to deliver ongoing training using the same in-person methods used when they first trained their salespeople, most firms are finding that training can be just as effective using technology options. In particular, many organizations have invested heavily in a customized **learning management system (LMS)**, which allows their salespeople to obtain training remotely through computers, tablets, and smartphones. Additionally, the use of an LMS offers salespeople the flexibility to train at times that work best for them. (8)

While feedback using technology-based training is not as personal as in-person training, sophisticated programs are effective in educating and testing trainees' knowledge. Also, a real trainer can be available via email, online chat, social media, or by phone if a question does arise. Additionally, compared to paper-based materials, digital delivery of training materials is low cost and can be made available to the entire sales force in a short time frame. Also, the use of messaging services (e.g., text message), specialized apps, and email enables salespeople to be immediately notified when new material is published. This is useful when the sales force must be made aware of new information, such as a price change or new information on a competitor's product.

USE OF CUSTOMER SALES TEAMS

As we noted in our discussion of technical specialists, salespeople may require the assistance of others in their organization in order to deal effectively with prospects. In fact, many companies are moving away from the traditional sales force arrangement, where a single salesperson handles nearly all communication with an account, in favor of a team approach where multiple personnel are involved. Teams consist of individuals from several functional areas, such as marketing, manufacturing, distribution, and customer service. In some configurations, all members share bonuses and other incentives if the team meets sales goals. Clearly to be effective a team approach will require the implementation of a strong customer relationship management (CRM) system.

REFERENCES

1. "National Occupational Employment and Wages Estimates United States." *Bureau of Labor Statistics – U.S. Department of Labor*. May 2022. https://www.bls.gov/oes/current/oes_nat.htm#41-0000.

2. For more on the need for building trust in international business relationships see: Jeanne M. Brett and Tyree Mitchell. "How to Build Trust with Business Partners from Other Cultures." *Harvard Business Review*. January 31, 2020. https://hbr.org/2020/01/research-how-to-build-trust-with-business-partners-from-other-cultures.

3. For a discussion on the history of personal selling see: Rolph E. Anderson, Alex H. Cohen, Paul F. Christ, Rajiv Mehta, and Alan J. Dubinsky. "Provenance, Evolution, and Transition of Personal Selling and Sales Management to Strategic Marketing Channel Management." *Journal of Marketing Channels*. 26 (1), 2020.

4. The U.S. government has produced detailed rules governing telemarketing sales. For more see: "Complying with the Telemarketing Sales Rule." *U.S. Federal Trade Commission*. https://www.ftc.gov/business-guidance/resources/complying-telemarketing-sales-rule.

5. For an interesting look at bad telemarketing see: Mark Fairlie. "10 Worst Telemarketing Calls Ever." *Business News Daily*. October 2, 2023. https://www.businessnewsdaily.com/11268-worst-telemarketing-experiences.html.

6. For more on the requirements to disclose these types of promotion see: "Part 255: Guides Concerning the Use of Endorsements and Testimonials in Advertising." *Federal Trade Commission - National Archives*. July 26, 2023. https://www.ecfr.gov/current/title-16/chapter-I/subchapter-B/part-255.

7. For more on how virtual trade shows exhibitors use technology for developing content see: "The Future of Content Creation for Virtual Trade Shows." *AIContentfy*. August 11, 2023. https://aicontentfy.com/en/blog/future-of-content-creation-for-virtual-trade-shows.

8. Like most marketing functions, sales and especially sales training is also benefiting from the evolution of artificial intelligence (AI) as discussed here: Prabhakant Sinha, Arun Shastri, and Sally E. Lorimer. "How Generative AI Will Change Sales." *Harvard Business Review*. March 31, 2023. https://hbr.org/2023/03/how-generative-ai-will-change-sales.

Chapter 17: Pricing Decisions

What do the following words have in common? Fare, dues, tuition, interest, rent, and fee. The answer is that each of these is a term used to describe what one party must pay to acquire benefits from another party. More commonly, most people simply use the word price to indicate what it costs to acquire a product. For marketers, the pricing decision can be complex as many factors must be considered when arriving at the final selling price for a product.

In this chapter, we begin a two-part discussion of the pricing component of the Marketer's Toolkit. We start by defining price and see how it has a different meaning for different parties to a transaction. We next look at why price is essential to marketing and to an organization. Finally, considerable attention is given to the internal and external factors that influence pricing decisions.

WHAT IS PRICE?

In general terms, price is a component of an exchange or transaction that takes place between two parties and refers to what must be given up by one party (i.e., buyer) in order to obtain something offered by another party (i.e., seller). Yet this view of price provides a somewhat limited explanation of what price means to participants in the transaction. In fact, price means different things to buyers and sellers in an exchange:

◆ Buyers' View – For those making a purchase, such as final customers, price refers to what must be given up to obtain benefits. In most cases, what is given up is financial consideration (e.g., money) in exchange for acquiring access to a good or service. But financial consideration is not always what the buyer gives up. Sometimes in a **barter** situation a buyer acquires a product by giving up his/her own product. For instance, two farmers may exchange cattle for crops. Also, as discussed in Box 17-1, a buyer may also give up other things to acquire the benefits of a product that do not involve direct financial payment, such as personal time required to learn how to use the product.

◆ Sellers' View – To the selling organization, price reflects the revenue generated for each product sold and is an essential factor in determining profit. For those responsible for marketing decisions, price serves as a marketing tool and is a key element in marketing promotions. For example, most retailers highlight product pricing in their advertising campaigns.

Price is commonly confused with the notion of **cost** as in, "*I paid a high cost for buying my new smartwatch.*" Technically these are different concepts. Price is what a buyer pays to acquire products from a seller. Cost concerns the seller's investment (e.g., manufacturing expense) in the product exchanged with a buyer. For marketing organizations seeking to make a profit, the hope is a product's price will exceed its cost so the organization can see financial gain from a transaction.

Finally, while product pricing is a main topic for discussion when a company is examining its overall profitability, pricing decisions are not limited to for-profit companies. Not-for-profit organizations, such as charities, educational institutions and industry trade groups, also set prices. For instance, charities seeking to raise money may set different "target" levels for donations that reward donors with increases in status (e.g., name in newsletter), gifts, or other benefits. While a charitable organization may not call it a "price" in their promotional material, in reality these donations are equivalent to price since donors are required to give a contribution in order to obtain something of value.

Box 17-1

WHAT PRICE MEANS TO CUSTOMERS

When faced with a purchase decision, most customers will evaluate the entire marketing offering and will not simply make a decision based solely on a product's monetary price. In fact, price is one of several variables customers evaluate when they mentally assess a product's overall value.

As we discussed in Chapter 1, value refers to the perception of benefits received for what someone must give up. An easy way to see this is through a **value equation**:

$$\text{Perceived Value} = \frac{\text{Perceived Benefits Received}}{\text{Perceived Price Paid}}$$

For marketers, it is necessary to recognize that the price paid in a transaction is not only financial, it can also involve other things a buyer may be giving up. For example, in addition to paying money, a customer may have to spend time learning to use a product, pay to have an old product removed, close down current operations while a product is installed, or incur other expenses.

Consequently, while the monetary price is a crucial marketing decision, marketers must also take into consideration many other issues that can affect what customers view as the perceived price.

IMPORTANCE OF PRICE

When marketers talk about what they do as part of their responsibilities for marketing products, the tasks associated with setting price are often not at the top of the list. Marketers are much more likely to discuss activities related to promotion, product development, marketing research, and other tasks that are considered to be the more appealing and exciting parts of the job. One reason for the lack of attention paid to pricing is that many believe price setting is a mechanical process requiring utilization of financial tools, such as spreadsheets, to build the marketer's case for setting price levels. While pricing may not tap into a marketer's creative skills to the same degree that other marketing activities do, it is important to understand that pricing decisions can have significant consequences for an organization. Therefore, the level of attention given to pricing is just as important as the attention given to more recognizable marketing tasks.

Some reasons why attention to pricing is critical include:

Most Flexible Marketing Decision

For marketers, price is the most adjustable of all marketing decisions. Unlike product and distribution decisions, which can take months or years to change, or some forms of promotion, which can be time-consuming to alter (e.g., creating a new television advertisement), price can be changed very rapidly. The flexibility of pricing decisions is particularly relevant in times when the marketer seeks a quick way to stimulate demand or to respond to competitor price actions. For instance, a marketer can agree to a field salesperson's request to lower price for a potential buyer during a phone conversation. Likewise, a marketer in charge of online operations can raise prices on hot selling products with the click of a few on-screen buttons. (1)

Need for Setting the Right Price

Pricing decisions made hastily without sufficient research, analysis, and strategic evaluation can lead the marketing organization to lose revenue. Prices set too low may mean the company is missing out on additional profits that could be earned if the target market is willing to spend more to acquire the product. Additionally, attempts to raise an initially low-priced product to a higher price may be met by customer resistance if they feel the marketer is attempting to take advantage of its customers. Prices set too high can also impact revenue if it prevents interested customers from purchasing the product. Setting the right price level takes considerable market knowledge and, especially with new products, may require testing of different pricing options.

Trigger of Early Perception

Oftentimes, customers' perceptions of a product are formed as soon as they learn the price, such as when a product is first seen in a store with a price tag attached. While the final decision to make a purchase may be based on the value offered by the entire marketing offering (i.e., actual and augmented product), it is possible the customer will not evaluate a marketer's product at all based on price alone. For example, customers may form impressions of a product if they consider the price to be too high (e.g., *"that product can't be worth that price"*) or too low (e.g., *"for that price that product must not be very good"*). It is necessary for marketers to know if customers are more likely to dismiss a product when all they know is the price. If so, pricing may become the most important of all marketing decisions if it can be shown that customers are avoiding learning more about the product because of the price.

Important Part of Sales Promotion

Many times, price adjustments are part of a sales promotion that lowers price for a short term to stimulate interest in the product. However, as we noted in our discussion of promotional pricing in Chapter 14, marketers must guard against the temptation to adjust prices too frequently. Continually increasing and decreasing price can lead customers to be conditioned to anticipate price reductions. Consequently, they may withhold purchase until a price reduction occurs again.

Affects Demand for Other Products

How a company prices one product can affect the overall demand for other products. This is especially the case where the demand for other products is directly tied to the demand for a main product. In particular, marketers making the bulk of their profits from the sale of goods and services used to support the main product must take this into consideration. For example, operators of gambling casinos often entice customers by offering very low hotel room rates knowing they can generate higher revenue in other ways when customers visit the casino (e.g., revenue from gaming, food, special shows, etc.). The hotel must be mindful of increasing hotel room rates as doing so could have an impact on revenue that comes from these other sources.

FACTORS AFFECTING PRICING DECISIONS

For the remainder of this chapter, we look at factors that affect how marketers set price. The final price for a product may be influenced by many factors, which can be categorized into two main groups:

◆ Internal Factors – When setting price, marketers must take into consideration several factors, which are the result of organizational decisions and actions. To a large extent, these factors are controlled by the marketer and, if necessary, can be altered. However, while the organization may have control over these factors, making a quick change is not always realistic. For instance, product pricing may depend heavily on the productivity of a company's manufacturing facilities (e.g., how much can be produced within a certain time frame). The marketer knows increasing productivity can reduce the cost of producing each product, which potentially allows the marketer to lower the product's price. But increasing productivity may require substantial changes at the manufacturing facility that take time (and are potentially costly) and will not translate into lower price products for a considerable period of time.

◆ External Factors – There are a number of influencing factors, which are not controlled by the company but will impact pricing decisions. Understanding these factors requires the marketer conduct research to monitor what is happening in each market the organization serves since the effect of these factors can vary by market.

Below we provide a detailed discussion of both internal and external factors.

Internal Factors

The pricing decision can be affected by factors that are controlled by the marketing organization including:

MARKETING OBJECTIVES AND STRATEGY

Marketing decisions are guided by the objectives established by the leaders of the organization. While we will discuss this in more detail when we cover *Marketing Planning and Strategy* in Chapter 20, for now it is necessary to understand that all marketing decisions, including price, are impacted by the strategy formulated to meet marketing objectives. For instance, marketers whose objective is to be known as an affordable alternative to high-end products would be expected to have a marketing strategy that includes having a product's price set at or below the price of most direct competitors.

It should be noted, not all companies view price as a key selling feature, and consequently it may not play a major role in helping the marketer meet its objectives. Some firms, for example those seeking to be viewed as market leaders in product quality, de-emphasize price and concentrate on a strategy highlighting non-price benefits (e.g., quality, durability, service, etc.). Such non-price competition can help the company avoid competing against new products that sell for a lower price. It can also protect against potential **price wars** that often break out between competitive firms that follow a market share objective (discussed in Chapter 20) and use price as a key selling feature. (2)

COSTS

For many for-profit organizations, the starting point for setting a product's price is to determine first how much it will cost to get the product to their customers. Obviously, whatever price customers pay must exceed the cost of producing a good or delivering a service, otherwise the company will lose money.

When analyzing cost, the marketer will consider all costs needed to get the product to market including those associated with production, marketing, distribution, and company administration (e.g., office expense). These costs can be divided into two main categories:

Variable Costs

These costs are directly associated with the production and sale of products, and may change as the level of production or sales changes. Typically, variable costs are evaluated on a per-unit basis since the cost is directly associated with individual items. Most variable costs involve costs of items that are either components of the product (e.g., parts, packaging) or are directly associated with creating the product (e.g., electricity to run an assembly line). However, there are also marketing variable costs, such as certain promotional expenses (e.g., cost of redeemed coupons) that could fluctuate based on sales volume.

For marketers selling physical products, variable costs, especially for product components, tend to decline as more units are produced. This is due to an organization's ability to receive discount pricing for large quantity purchases from component suppliers (see *Quantity Discounts* in Chapter 18).

Fixed Costs

Also referred to as **overhead costs**, these represent costs the marketing organization incurs that are not affected by level of production or sales. For example, for a manufacturer of writing instruments that has just built a new production facility, whether they produce one pen or one million they will still need to pay the monthly commercial mortgage for the building.

From the marketing side, fixed costs may also exist in the form of such expenditures as fielding a sales force, carrying out an advertising campaign, and paying a service to host the company's website. These costs are fixed because there is a level of commitment to spending that is not affected by production or sales levels. While fixed costs are normally not associated with either level of production or sales volume, marketers still must factor these into their price, though, as discussed in Box 17-2, doing so is not always easy.

OWNERSHIP OPTIONS

An important decision faced by marketers as they are formulating their pricing strategy deals with who will have ownership of the product (i.e., holds legal title) once an exchange has taken place. There are two basic options available:

- <u>Buyer Owns Product Outright</u> – The most common ownership option is for the buyer to make payment and then obtain full ownership. Under this condition, the price is generally reflective of the full value of the product.

- <u>Buyer Has Right to Use but Does Not Have Ownership</u> – Many products permit customers to make payment in exchange for the right to use a product but not to own it. This is seen in the form of usage, rental, or lease payment for such goods and services as automobiles, manufacturing equipment, music streaming services, and internet cloud data storage. In most cases, the price paid by the customer is not reflective of the full value of the product compared to what the customer would have paid for full ownership of the product. It should be noted, under some lease or rental plans there may be an option for customers to buy the product outright (e.g., car lease), often requiring a large final payment.

> **Box 17-2**
>
> ## WHAT'S THE REAL COST?
>
> When selling a product, determining the cost for an individual unit can be a complicated process. While variable costs are often determined on a per-unit basis, applying fixed costs to individual products is often less straightforward. For example, if a company manufactures five different products in one manufacturing plant how should it distribute the plant's fixed costs (e.g., mortgage, insurance, utilities, etc.) over the five products?
>
> In general, an organization assigns fixed costs to individual products if it can clearly associate the costs with the product. For instance, it may assign the cost of operating production machines based on how much time it takes to produce each item or assign advertising expense to the specific product an advertising campaign is promoting.
>
> Alternatively, some firms may instruct the marketing department to add a certain percentage of the variable cost as a way to cover fixed costs. For example, final cost for products may be determined by adding an additional 20 percent on top of the per-unit variable cost.
>
> Finally, if it becomes too difficult to associate costs to specific products, a company may simply allocate total fixed costs by general category of product and assign it on some percentage basis. As an example, for a discount retailer's website that sells many products, the cost of operating the website may be distributed among product categories (e.g., books, hardware, women's clothing, etc.) based on such metrics as percentage of user traffic in relation to total website traffic, percentage of category sales in relation to overall sales, or some other measure. With this approach, individual products may not see a fixed cost allocation, though the overall product category will.
>
> No matter which method is used, setting price based only on the cost of the materials and labor needed to produce a product may significantly underestimate the true costs incurred. As we will see in Chapter 18, product cost is only one of many considerations that go into determining the final price.

External Market Factors

The pricing decision can be affected by factors that are not directly controlled by the marketing organization. These factors include:

ELASTICITY OF DEMAND

Marketers should never rest on their marketing decisions. They must continually use marketing research and their own judgment to determine whether marketing decisions need to be adjusted. When it comes to adjusting price, the marketer must understand what effect a change in price is likely to have on the target market's demand for a product. Understanding how price changes impact the market requires the marketer have a firm understanding of the concept economists call elasticity of demand, which relates to how purchase quantity changes as prices change.

Elasticity is evaluated under the assumption that no other changes are being made (i.e., "all things being equal") and only price is adjusted. The logic is to see how price alone will affect overall demand. Obviously, the chance of nothing else changing in the market but the price of one product is often unrealistic. For example, competitors may react to the marketer's price change by changing the price of their product. Despite this, elasticity analysis does serve as a useful tool for estimating market reaction.

Elasticity deals with three types of demand scenarios:

- Elastic Demand – Products are considered to exist in a market that exhibits elastic demand when a certain percentage change in price results in a larger and opposite percentage change in market demand. For example, if the price of a product increases (decreases) by 10% the demand for the product is likely to decline (rise) by greater than 10%.

- Inelastic Demand – Products are considered to exist in a market that exhibits inelastic demand when a certain percentage change in price results in a smaller and opposite percentage change in market demand. For example, if the price of a product increases (decreases) by 10%, the demand for the product is likely to decline (rise) by less than 10%.

- Unitary Demand – This demand occurs when a percentage change in price results in an equal and opposite percentage change in market demand. For example, if the price of a product increases (decreases) by 10%, the demand for the product is likely to decline (rise) by 10%.

For marketers, the pivotal issue with elasticity of demand is to understand how it impacts company revenue. In general, the following scenarios apply to making price changes for a given type of market demand, though it should be clear these effects will only apply to relatively small changes in price:

- For Elastic Markets – Increasing price lowers total revenue, while decreasing price increases total revenue.

- For Inelastic Markets – Increasing price raises total revenue, while decreasing price lowers total revenue.

- For Unitary Markets – There is no change in revenue when price is changed.

COMPETITOR PRICING

Marketers will undoubtedly look to competitors for indications of how price should be set. For many consumer products marketers, researching competitive pricing is relatively easy, particularly with the help of internet search engines, searching retailers' websites, or **price comparison apps**. However, price analysis can be somewhat more complicated for products sold in the business market. This is because final price may be affected by a number of factors including whether competitors allow customers to negotiate the final price.

Almost all marketing decisions, including pricing, will include an evaluation of competitors' offerings. The impact of this information on the actual setting of price depends on the competitive nature of the market. For example, products that dominate markets and are viewed as market leaders may not be heavily influenced by competitor pricing, since they are in a commanding position to set prices as they see fit. On the other hand, in markets where a clear leader does not exist, the pricing of competitive products will be carefully considered. Yet marketers must not only limit research to competitive prices. They must also pay close attention to how these companies will respond to the marketer's pricing decisions. For instance, in highly competitive industries, such as gasoline or airline travel, companies may respond quickly to competitors' price adjustments, thereby reducing the effect of such changes.

While gathering pricing information on products offered by competitors is research that most marketers are accustomed to performing, there is other product pricing that may also affect marketers. In some cases, pricing decisions may be impacted by products that are not considered direct competitors. Here are two examples:

Related Product Pricing

Products offering new ways for solving customer needs may look to pricing of products that customers are currently using, even though these other products may not appear to be direct competitors. For example, a marketer of a new online golf instruction service that allows customers to access golf instruction via their computer or smart device may look at prices charged by local golf professionals for in-person instruction to gauge where to set its price. While, on the surface, online golf instruction may not be a direct competitor to an in-person golf instructor, marketers for the online service can use the cost of in-person instruction as a reference point for setting price.

Primary Product Pricing

As we discussed in Chapter 6, marketers may sell products viewed as complementary to a primary product. For instance, wireless Bluetooth earbuds are considered complementary to a primary product, such as smartphones. The pricing of complementary products may be affected by pricing changes made to the primary product, since customers may compare the price for complementary products based on the primary product price. To illustrate, companies selling accessory products for the Apple iPad may do so at a price that is only 10 percent of the purchase price of the iPad. However, if Apple decided to drop the price dramatically, for instance by 50 percent, the accessory at its present price would now be 20 percent of the of iPad price. This may be perceived by the market as a doubling of the accessory's price. To maintain its perceived value, the accessory marketer may need to respond to the iPad price drop by also lowering the price of the accessory.

CUSTOMER AND CHANNEL PARTNER EXPECTATIONS

Possibly the most obvious external factor influencing price setting concerns what customers and channel partners expect from products they are considering for purchase. As we discussed, when it comes to making a purchase decision, customers assess the overall "value" of a product much more than they assess the price alone. When deciding on a price, marketers need to conduct customer research to determine what **price points** are acceptable. Pricing beyond these price points could discourage customers from purchasing.

When determining price, marketers must also consider firms in their channels of distribution. Channel partners expect to receive financial compensation for their efforts, which usually means they receive a percentage of the final selling price. The percentage or margin between what channel members pay the marketer to acquire products and the price they charge their customers must be sufficient to cover costs and earn a desired profit (see Box 18-1 in Chapter 18).

CURRENCY CONSIDERATIONS

Marketers selling internationally must be acutely aware of how monetary exchange rates can affect the price of its products in foreign markets. Depending on fluctuations in currency rates, a product's price in the importing country's currency can be significantly different from what the marketer has planned, which can have notable marketing implications (see Box 17-3). For instance, a company seeking to be a low-price market leader may find this strategy works when selling in its home market but when selling in an importing country with a weak currency the product's price may be at a mid-price level compared to competitive products. This could dramatically impact the perceived value of the product by customers in this market. Alternatively, if the currency of the marketer's country is weak compared to the currency in the buyer's market, a product could sell at a price that is much lower than what the marketer expects. This could lead customers in the importing country to perceive the product to be of lower quality compared to similar products selling at higher prices.

Additionally, in some situations, currency issues may not even permit a buyer and a seller to negotiate an exchange. This is likely to occur when a country's currency is not widely recognized or when a currency's value is fluctuating rapidly. Under these conditions, a seller from one country may refuse to accept the currency offered by a buyer from another country. To overcome this, the two parties may agree to an exchange arrangement that does not involve currency. The primary method for carrying out this exchange is through the use of one or more bartering techniques, collectively called **countertrade**, where a seller ships product to a buyer and in exchange receives the buyer's product. As an example, a U.S. marketer of chemical products may negotiate a trade with an African mining company whose currency is not stable. The exchange may involve the U.S. company trading fertilizer in exchange for minerals mined by the African firm. While the value of countertrade occurring is not easily measured, it is believed to be quite significant and is an essential trading option used by many companies around the world.

Box 17-3

THE EFFECT OF EXCHANGE RATES ON PRICING

To see the impact currency has on pricing, consider what may happen to a U.S. company selling its products in Germany. For these examples, assume the initial exchange rate is 1 Dollar = .9 Euro. Under the current exchange rate, if the company sells a product for $10 in the U.S. the equivalent price to customers in Germany will be €9. But what might happen if the exchange rate changes?

Using a simplified example, assume a product's selling price in a foreign market is based on the U.S. price. However, let's assume it is not a set price but fluctuates based on exchange rates. Let's see what may happen as rates change under the following conditions:

Weaker Dollar – Stronger Euro

If the exchange rate moves from $1= €.9 to $1 = €.8, the rate is becoming weaker for the U.S. dollar but stronger for the Euro. This means it will now take fewer Euros to purchase the same product. In our example, where it previously required €9 to purchase the product, with a stronger Euro it now requires €8. Thus, customers in Germany perceive the product as becoming less expensive.

Stronger Dollar – Weaker Euro

If the exchange rate moves from $1= €.9 to $1 = €.1.0, the rate is becoming stronger for the U.S. dollar but weaker for the Euro. This means it will now take more Euros to purchase the same product. In our example, where it previously required €9 to purchase the product, with a weaker Euro it now requires €10 Euros. Thus, customers in Germany perceive the product as becoming more expensive.

It is essential to understand that with these examples the change in the exchange rate alone is affecting product pricing. Because exchange rates are not controllable by the marketer, companies selling internationally need to pay close attention to currency fluctuations to ensure the price customers pay in their local markets is consistent with the company's marketing strategy.

GOVERNMENT REGULATION

Marketers must be aware of regulations impacting how price is set in the markets in which their products are sold. These regulations are primarily government enacted meaning that there may be legal ramifications if the rules are not followed. Price regulations can come from any level of government and vary widely in their requirements. For instance, in some industries, government regulation may set a **price ceiling** (how high prices may be set), while in other industries there may be a **price floor** (how low prices may be set).

A regulation related to price ceilings and floors is the concept of **resale price maintenance**. As we will see in Chapter 18, in the U.S. marketers selling to retailers and other distributors often indicate a minimum or **manufacturer's suggested retail price (MSRP)** at which products are sold. Yet, for many years, retailers ignored this and, instead, determined the final price in ways they saw fit, which could be lower or higher than the MSRP. However, in 2007 the U.S. Supreme Court ruled that manufacturers have the right to set suggested prices that retailers must follow. (3) Today this remains a contentious issue as several U.S. states support retailers in their efforts to set their own prices.

Additional areas of potential pricing regulation of concern to marketers include such issues as:

- <u>Deceptive Pricing</u> – When the method of pricing misleads customers into believing the price is lower than what they actually pay. (4)

- <u>Price Discrimination</u> – When a seller deliberately charges some customers a different price than other customers without a valid reason for doing so.

- <u>Predatory Pricing</u> – When a seller intentionally sets price low to drive competitors from the market (see Box 18-3 in Chapter 18).

- <u>Price Fixing</u> – When two or more parties (e.g., competitors) agree on a price to charge within a market for similar products.

Finally, when selling beyond their home market, marketers must recognize that local regulations may make pricing decisions different for each market. This is particularly a concern when selling to international markets where failure to abide by regulations can lead to severe penalties. For example, countries may institute **tariffs** on products shipped into the country. Often these tariffs are intended to protect domestic industries by raising the final selling price of products for the importing company. Consequently, marketers must have a clear understanding of regulations in each market they serve.

REFERENCES

1. Changing price can also be a highly automated process in which computer programs evaluate multiple variables and then instantly alter the price. This method is best represented by ridesharing service Uber and its surge pricing method. For more, see *Dynamic Pricing* in Chapter 18.

2. An example of a price war can be seen with Tesla's marketing strategy in China where they have repeatedly dropped price in an attempt to broaden their market share. For more see: Selina Cheng. "Tesla Cuts Prices in China as Price-War Truce Fails." *The Wall Street Journal*. August 17, 2023. https://www.wsj.com/business/autos/tesla-cuts-prices-in-china-as-price-war-truce-fails-60af6d4d.

3. "Leegin Creative Leather Products vs. Psk Inc." *United States Supreme Court*, June 28, 2007. https://www.loc.gov/item/usrep551877.

4. For more on laws impacting deceptive pricing in the U.S. see: *United States Code of Federal Regulations, Title 16 Subchapter B - Part 233*. https://www.ecfr.gov/current/title-16/chapter-I/subchapter-B/part-233

Chapter 18: Setting Price

In Chapter 17, our coverage centered on understanding the impact pricing decisions have on marketing strategy, and how internal and external factors are likely to affect price setting. With this groundwork laid, we now turn our attention to the methods marketers use to determine the price they will charge for their products.

In this chapter, our primary emphasis is to look at pricing as a five-step process. The process takes into consideration many different decisions before the marketer arrives at a final selling price. We will examine this process by first assessing how price fits into the organization's overall marketing objectives. Next, we look at several approaches for setting the initial product price. For many marketers, the initial price is not the final price and adjustments must be made. In the next step, we consider situations where marketers must make changes to their initial price and the various methods that are available for doing this. We conclude the five-step process by looking at payment options marketers can choose when selling their product. We complete the discussion of pricing by examining two additional methods, auction and bid pricing, and see how these fit within pricing strategy.

STEPS IN THE PRICE SETTING PROCESS

For some marketers, more time is spent agonizing over price than any other marketing decision. Many times, this is due to a lack of understanding of the important factors that should be considered when faced with a pricing decision. To address this, we take the approach that price setting consists of a series of decisions or steps the marketer makes. The steps include:

1. Examine Objectives

2. Determine an Initial Price

3. Set Standard Price Adjustments

4. Determine Promotional Pricing

5. State Payment Options

While this process serves as a useful guide for making pricing decisions, not all marketers follow this step-by-step approach. Many marketers may choose to bypass Steps 3 and 4 altogether. Additionally, it is necessary to understand that finding the right price is often a trial-and-error exercise, where continual testing is needed.

Like all other marketing decisions, marketing research is critical to determining the optimal selling price. Consequently, the process laid out here is intended to open the marketer's eyes to the options to consider when setting price and is in no way presented as a guide for setting the "perfect" price.

It is also important to understand that, just like many other marketing areas, technology serves a key role in pricing. For example, companies in such industries as retailing, travel, and insurance have turned to computerized methods for helping set the right price. In particular, marketers are using **price optimization software**, that is built using advanced mathematical modeling (see *Dynamic Pricing* discussion below). These software programs take into consideration many of the internal and external pricing factors discussed in Chapter 17 along with other variables, such as sales history, in order to arrive at an ideal price. Marketers should know that much of what is discussed in this chapter are also essential elements of these price setting programs.

STEP 1: EXAMINE OBJECTIVES

As we discussed in Chapter 17, pricing decisions are driven by the objectives set by the management of the organization. These objectives come at two levels. First, the overall objectives of the company guide all decisions for all functional areas (e.g., marketing, production, human resources, finance, etc.). Guided by overall company objectives, the marketing department will set its own objectives. Marketing department objectives may include financial objectives, such as **return on investment (ROI)**, cash flow and maximize profits, or non-financial marketing objectives such as a percentage of market share, level of product awareness, and increase in store traffic, to name a few.

Pricing decisions like all other marketing decisions are used to help the marketing department meet its objectives. For instance, if the marketing objective is to build market share it is likely the marketer will set the product price at a level that is at or below the price of similar products offered by competitors.

Additionally, the price setting process looks to whether pricing decisions are in line with the decisions made for the other marketing areas (i.e., target market, product, distribution, promotion). For instance, if an organization with a strong brand name targets high-end consumers with a high-quality, full-featured product, the pricing decision would follow the marketer's desire to have the product be considered a high-end product. In this case, the price would be set high relative to competitors' products that do not offer as many features or do not have an equally strong brand name.

STEP 2: DETERMINE AN INITIAL PRICE

With the objectives in Step 1 providing guidance for setting price, the marketer next begins the task of determining an initial price level. We say initial because, in many industries, this step involves setting a starting point from which further changes may be made before the customer pays the final price.

Sometimes called **list price** or **published price**, marketers often use this as a promotional or negotiating tool as they move through the other price setting steps. For companies selling to consumers, this price also leads to a projection of the recommended selling price at the retail level or manufacturer's suggested retail price (MSRP). The MSRP may or may not be the final price for which products are sold. For strong brands that are highly sought by consumers, the MSRP may, in fact, be the price at which the product will be sold. (1) But in many other cases, as we will see, the price setting process results in the price being different based on adjustments made by the marketer and others in the distribution channel (see Box 18-1).

Marketers have at their disposal several approaches for setting the initial price. These approaches include:

◆ Cost Pricing

◆ Market Pricing

◆ Competitive Pricing

Cost Pricing

Under cost pricing, the marketer primarily looks at product costs (e.g., variable and fixed) as the key factor in determining the initial price. This method offers the advantage of being easy to implement as long as costs are known. But one significant disadvantage is that it does not take into consideration the target market's demand for the product. This could present considerable problems if the product is operating in a highly competitive market where competitors frequently alter their prices.

There are several types of cost pricing methods including:

MARKUP PRICING

This pricing method, often utilized by resellers who acquire products from suppliers, uses a percentage increase on top of what is paid for the product to arrive at an initial price. A leading general retailer, such as Walmart, may apply a set percentage for each product category (e.g., women's clothing, automotive, garden supplies, etc.) making the pricing consistent for all like-products. Alternatively, the predetermined percentage may be a number that is identified with the marketing objectives (e.g., required 20% ROI).

Box 18-1

PRICING AND THE DISTRIBUTION CHANNEL

Some marketers utilize multiple channel partners or resellers to handle product distribution. For marketers selling through resellers, the pricing decision is complicated by resellers' need to earn a profit and marketers' need to have some control over the product's price to the final customer. In these cases, setting price involves more than only worrying about what their direct customers are willing to pay (e.g., the price retailers will be charged). They must also be concerned with the pricing decisions resellers will make when they turn around and sell the product to their customers (e.g., the price final consumers will be charged).

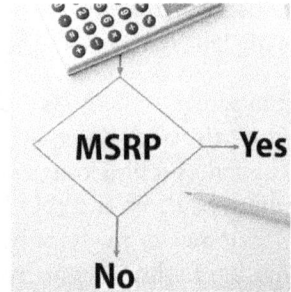

When resellers are involved, marketers must recognize that all members of the channel will seek to profit when a sale is made. If a marketer wants to sell the product at a certain retail price (e.g., MSRP), then the price charged to the first channel member to handle the product can potentially influence the final selling price. And in some situations, this may create problems causing the reseller to sell the product at a price that differs from what the marketer is expecting.

To see how problems arise, assume a marketer sets an MSRP of (US) $1.99 for a product selling through a distribution channel. This channel consists of wholesalers, who the marketer charges $1.89 to purchase the product, and retailers who in turn buy the product from wholesalers. In this example, it is unlikely the retailer will sell the product at the MSRP since the wholesaler will add to the $1.89 purchase price to increase their profit. The retailer in turn will add to the price it pays to the wholesaler when selling to consumers. In this scenario, it is possible the retailer's price to the final consumer will be closer to $2.99 than the $1.99 MSRP.

As this example shows, marketers must take care in setting price so that all channel partners feel it is worth their effort to handle the product (see *Trade Allowances* discussion below). Clearly sales can be dramatically different from what the marketer forecasts if the selling price to the final customer differs significantly from what the marketer expects. As noted in Chapter 17, the seller could claim the retailer is violating the resale price maintenance law (see *Government Regulation* in Chapter 17), though doing so may force the retailer to balk at handling a marketer's product altogether if they are forced to charge a retail price that is either much greater than what they believe customers are willing to pay or lower than what is profitable.

The lesson here is that marketers must consider all members of the distribution channel as well as the final customer when making pricing decisions. (2)

For resellers that purchase thousands of products (e.g., retailers), the simplicity inherent in markup pricing makes it a more attractive pricing option compared to other methods which may be more time-consuming to implement. However, the advantage of ease of use is sometimes offset by the disadvantage that products may not always be optimally priced resulting in products that are priced too high or too low given customer demand for the product.

As discussed in Box 18-2, markup can be done as either a percentage of cost or a percentage of selling price.

Box 18-2

DIFFERENT WAYS TO CALCULATE MARKUP

Resellers differ in how they use markup pricing with some using the Markup-on-Cost method and others using the Markup-on-Selling-Price method. We demonstrate each using an item that costs a reseller (US) $50 to purchase from a supplier and sells to customers for (US) $65.

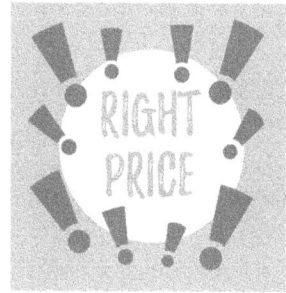

Markup-on-Cost

Using this method, markup is reflected as a percentage by which initial price is set above product cost as shown in the following formula:

$$\frac{\text{Markup Amount}}{\text{Item Cost}} = \text{Markup Percentage}$$

$$\frac{\$15}{\$50} = 30\%$$

The calculation for setting initial price using Markup-on-Cost is determined by simply multiplying the cost of each item by a predetermined percentage then adding the result to the cost:

$$\text{Item Cost} + (\text{Item Cost x Markup Percentage}) = \text{Price}$$
$$\$50 \quad + \quad (\$50 \times .30) \quad = \$65$$

Markup-on-Selling-Price

Many resellers, and in particular retailers, discuss their markup not in terms of Markup-on-Cost but as a reflection of price. That is, the markup is viewed as a percentage of the selling price and not as a percentage of cost, as it is with the Markup-on-Cost method. For example, using the same information as was used in assessing the Markup-on-Cost, the Markup-on-Selling-Price is reflected in this formula:

$$\frac{\text{Markup Amount}}{\text{Selling Price}} = \text{Markup Percentage}$$

$$\frac{\$15}{\$65} = 23\%$$

The calculation for setting initial price using Markup-on-Selling-Price is:

$$\frac{\text{Item Cost}}{(1.00 - \text{Markup Percentage})} = \text{Price}$$

$$\frac{\$50}{(1.00 - .23)} = \$65$$

Why Two Methods?

So why do some resellers use Markup-on-Cost while others use Markup-on-Selling-Price? The answer to this lies more with promotion than with pricing. In particular, Markup-on-Selling-Price is believed to aid promotion, especially for resellers who market themselves as low-price leaders. This is because the amount a reseller makes in percentage terms is always lower when calculated using Markup-on-Selling-Price than it is with Markup-on-Cost.

For example, in the Markup-on-Cost example where the markup is 30%, the gross profit is $15 ($65-$50). If the reseller using Markup-on-Selling-Price received a gross profit of $15 its markup would only be 23 percent ($50/[1.00-.23] = $65). Consequently, a retailer's advertisement may say: *"We Make Little, But Our Customers Save a Lot"* and back this up by saying they only make a small percentage on each sale. When in reality, how much they make in monetary terms may be equal to another retailer who uses Markup-on-Cost and reports a higher markup percentage.

COST-PLUS PRICING

In the same way markup pricing arrives at the price by adding a certain percentage to the product's cost, cost-plus pricing also adds to the cost by using a fixed monetary amount rather than percentage. For instance, a contractor hired to renovate a homeowner's bathroom will estimate the cost of doing the job by adding his/her total labor cost to the cost of the materials used in the renovation. The homeowner's selection of ceramic tile to be used in the bathroom is likely to have little effect on the labor needed to install it whether it is a low-end, low-priced tile or a high-end, premium-priced tile. Assuming most materials in the bathroom project are standard sizes and configuration, any change in the total price for the renovation is a result of changes in material costs while labor costs are likely to remain constant.

BREAK-EVEN PRICING

Break-even pricing is associated with **break-even analysis**, which is a forecasting tool used by marketers to determine how many products must be sold before the company starts realizing a profit. Like the markup method, break-even pricing does not directly consider market demand when determining price. However, it does indicate the minimum level of demand that is needed before a product will show a profit. From this the marketer can then assess whether the product can realistically achieve these levels.

The formula for determining the break-even point takes into consideration both variable and fixed costs (discussed in Chapter 17) as well as price, and is calculated as follows:

$$\frac{\text{Fixed Cost}}{\text{Price} - \text{Variable Cost per Unit}} = \text{Break-Even in Number of Units}$$

For example, assume a company operates a single-product manufacturing plant that has a total fixed cost (e.g., purchase of equipment, commercial mortgage, etc.) per year of (US) \$3 million and the variable cost (e.g., raw materials, labor, electricity, etc.) is \$45.00/unit. If the product is sold directly to customers for \$120, it will require the company sell 40,000 units to reach the break-even point.

$$\frac{\$3,000,000}{\$120 - \$45} = 40,000 \text{ units}$$

Again, it must be emphasized that marketers must determine whether the demand (i.e., number of units needed to reach the break-even point) is realistically attainable. Simply plugging in a number for price without knowing how the market will respond to this price is not an effective way to approach this method of price setting. (3)

Note: A common mistake when performing this analysis is to report the break-even point in a monetary value such as in dollars (e.g., results reported as \$40,000 instead of 40,000 units). The calculation presented above is a measure of units that need to be sold. Clearly, it is easy to turn this into a revenue break-even analysis by multiplying the units needed by the selling price. In our example, 40,000 units x \$120 = \$4,800,000.

Market Pricing

A second method for setting initial price is market pricing. Under the market pricing method, cost is not the main factor driving pricing decisions. Rather, initial price is based on analysis of marketing research in which customer expectations are measured. The main goal is to learn what customers in an organization's target market are likely to perceive as an acceptable price. Of course, this price should also help the organization meet its marketing objectives.

Market pricing is one of the most common methods for setting price, and the one that seems most logical given marketing's focus on satisfying customers. So, if this is the most logical approach why don't all companies follow it? The main reason is that using the market pricing approach requires a strong marketing research effort to measure customer reaction. For many marketers, it is not feasible to spend the time and money it takes to do this right. Additionally, for some products, especially new high-tech products, customers are not always knowledgeable enough about the product to know what an acceptable price level should be. Consequently, some marketers may forego market pricing in favor of other pricing approaches.

For those marketers who use market pricing, the options include:

◆ Backward Pricing

◆ Psychological Pricing

◆ Price Lining

BACKWARD PRICING

In some marketing organizations, the price the market is willing to pay for a product is an important determinant of many other marketing decisions. This is likely to occur when the market has a clear perception of what it believes is an acceptable level of pricing. For example, customers may question a product carrying a price tag that is double that of a competitor's offerings but is perceived to offer only minor improvements compared to the other product. In these markets, it is essential to undertake research to learn whether customers have mentally established price points for products in a certain product category. The marketer can learn this by surveying customers with such questions as, *"How much do you think these types of products should cost you?"*

In situations where a certain price level is ingrained in the market, the marketer may need to use this price as the starting point for many decisions and work backwards to develop product, promotion, and distribution plans. For instance, assume a company sells products through retailers. If the market is willing to pay (US)$199 for a product but is resistant to pricing that is higher, the marketer will work backwards factoring out the profit margin retailers are likely to want (e.g., $40) as well as removing the marketer's profit (e.g., $70). From this, the product cost will remain ($199-$40-$70= $89). The marketer must then decide whether they can create a product with sufficient features and benefits to satisfy customers' needs at this cost level.

PSYCHOLOGICAL PRICING

For many years, researchers have investigated customers' response to product pricing. Some of the results point to several intriguing psychological effects price may have on customers' buying behavior and their perception of individual products. (4) We stress that certain pricing tactics "may" have psychological effects since the results of some studies have suggested otherwise. But enough studies have shown effects exist making this topic worthy of discussion.

Methods of psychological pricing include:

Odd-Even Pricing

One effect, dubbed "odd-even" pricing, relates to how customers may perceive a significant difference in product price when pricing is slightly below a whole number value. For example, a product priced at (US) $299.95 may be perceived as offering more value than a product priced at $300.00. This effect can also be used to influence potential customers as those who have bought may mention the price to others as being lower than it actually is. This may be due to the buyer mistakenly recalling the price being "well below" the even number or the buyer wants to impress others with their success in obtaining a good value. For instance, in our example a buyer who pays $299.95 may tell a friend they paid "a little more than $200" for the product when, in fact, it was much closer to $300.

Prestige Pricing

Another psychological effect, called prestige pricing, points to a strong correlation between perceived product quality and price. The higher the price, the more likely customers are to perceive it as higher quality compared to a lower priced product. (Although, there is a point at which customers will begin to question the value of the product if the price is too high.) In fact, the less a customer knows about a product the more likely she/he is to judge the product as being higher quality based on only knowing the price (see *Trigger of Early Perception* in Chapter 17). Prestige pricing can also work with odd-even pricing as marketers, looking to present an image of high quality, may choose to price products at even levels (e.g., $10 rather than $9.99).

Reference Pricing

As we discussed in Chapter 4, the process involved in making purchase decisions can be quite complex. But for most customers, the purchase decision will involve a comparison of one product to another with price being a critical evaluative criterion. Because of this, marketers, who believe they have a price advantage, will create an arrangement where customers can easily compare one product to another. As an example, a retail grocery store may price its store brand coffee slightly below a leading premium brand and then place the store brand right beside the premium brand. With effective packaging and labeling, shoppers may feel the store brand is of similar quality but sells for less. In this way, the store hopes customers use the premium brand as a reference point, which will then present the store's brand as being more attractive in terms of price.

PRICE LINING

As we have discussed many times, marketers must appeal to the needs of a wide variety of customers. The difference in the "needs set" between customers often leads marketers to the realization that the overall market is really made up of a collection of smaller market segments (see Chapter 5). These segments may seek similar products but with different product features, such as different models whose product components (e.g., different quality of basketball sneakers) or service options (e.g., different hotel room options) will vary between markets.

Price lining or **product line pricing** is a method that primarily uses price to create a separation between different models. With this approach, even if customers possess little knowledge about a set of products, they still may perceive products are different based on price alone. The key is whether prices for all products in the group are perceived as representing distinct price points (i.e., enough separation between each). For instance, a marketer may sell a base model, an upgraded model, and a deluxe model each at a different price. If the differences in features for each model are not readily apparent to customers, such as differences that are inside the product and not easily viewed (e.g., difference between digital cameras), then price lining will help the customer recognize that differences do exist as long as the prices are noticeably separated.

Price lining can also be effective as a method for increasing profitability. In many cases, the cost to the marketer for adding different features to create different models or service options does not alone justify a significant price difference. For example, an upgraded model may cost 10 percent more to produce than a base model but using the price lining method the upgraded product price may be 20 percent higher, thereby, making it more profitable than the base model. The increase in profitability offered by price lining is one reason marketers introduce multiple models. Offering more than one model allows the company to satisfy the needs of different segments. It also presents an option for a customer to "buy up" to a higher priced and more profitable model.

Competitive Pricing

The final approach for setting initial price uses competitors' pricing as a key marker. Clearly when setting price, it makes sense to look at the price of competitive offerings. For some, competitor pricing serves as a central reference point from which they set their price. In certain industries, particularly those in which there are a few dominant competitors and many small companies, the top companies are in the position of holding price leadership roles where they are often the first in the industry to change price. Smaller companies must then assume a price follower role and react once the top companies adjust their price.

When basing pricing decisions on how competitors are setting their price, organizations may follow one of the following approaches:

◆ Below Competition Pricing – A marketer attempting to reach objectives that require high sales levels (see *Market Share Growth* in Chapter 20) may monitor the market to ensure its price remains below competitors.

◆ <u>Above Competition Pricing</u> – Marketers using this approach are likely to be perceived as market leaders in terms of product features, brand image, or other characteristics that support a price that is higher than what competitors are charging for their products.

◆ <u>Parity Pricing</u> – A simple method for setting the initial price is to price the product at the same level at which competitors price their product.

STEP 3: SET STANDARD PRICE ADJUSTMENTS

With the first round of pricing decisions now complete, the marketer's next step is to consider whether there are benefits to making adjustments to the list or published price. For our purposes, we will consider two levels of price adjustments – standard and promotional. The first level adjustments are those we label as "standard" since these are consistently part of the marketer's pricing program and not adjustments that appear only occasionally as part of special promotions (see *Step 4: Determine Promotional Pricing* discussion below).

In most situations, standard adjustments are made to reduce the list price in an effort to: 1) stimulate interest in the product; or 2) indirectly pay channel partners for the services they offer when handling the product. In some circumstances, the adjustments go the other way and leads to price increases in order to cover additional costs incurred when selling to different markets (e.g., higher shipping costs).

It should be noted, that given certain circumstances, organizations may not make adjustments to their list price. For instance, if the product is in high demand, the marketer may see little reason to lower the price. Also, if the marketer believes the product holds sufficient value for customers at its current list price, then they may feel reducing the price will lead buyers to question the quality of the product (e.g., *"How can they offer all those features for such a low price? Something must be wrong with it."*). In such cases, holding fast to the list price allows the marketer to maintain some control over the product's perceived image.

For organizations that do make standard price adjustments, their options include:

◆ Quantity Discounts

◆ Trade Allowances

◆ Special Segment Discounts

◆ Geographic Pricing

◆ Early Payment Incentives

Quantity Discounts

This adjustment offers buyers an incentive of lower per-unit pricing as more products are purchased. Most quantity or volume discounts are triggered when a buyer reaches certain purchase levels. For example, a buyer may pay the list price when they purchase between 1-99 units but receive a 5 percent discount off the list price when the purchase exceeds 99 units.

Options for offering price adjustments based on quantity ordered include:

Discounts at Time of Purchase

The most common quantity discounts exist when a buyer places an order exceeding a certain minimum level. While quantity discounts are used by marketers to stimulate higher purchase levels, the rationale for using these often rests in the cost of product shipment. As discussed in Box 10-1 in Chapter 10, shipping costs per unit tend to decrease as volume shipped increases. This is because the expenses (e.g., truck driver expense, fuel cost, road tolls, etc.) required to transport product from one point to another do not radically change as more product is shipped. Consequently, the transportation cost per item drops as more are ordered. This allows the supplier to offer lower prices for higher quantity.

Discounts on Cumulative Purchases

Under this method, the buyer receives a discount as more products are purchased over time. For instance, if a buyer regularly purchases from a supplier, they may see a discount once the buyer has reached predetermined monetary or quantity levels (e.g., once 1,000 units are purchased the price drops on the next purchase). The key reason to use this adjustment is to create an incentive for buyers to remain loyal and to continue to purchase again.

Trade Allowances

Manufacturers relying on channel partners to distribute their products (e.g., retailers, wholesalers) offer discounts off of list price called trade allowances. These discounts function as an indirect form of payment for a channel member's work in helping to market the product (e.g., keep product stocked, talk to customers about the product, provide feedback to the manufacturer, etc.).

Essentially, the difference between the trade allowance price paid by a reseller and the price the reseller charges its customers is the reseller's profit. For example, in a grocery store situation, let's assume the maker of snack foods sells a product to retailers that carries a stated MSRP of (US) \$2.95, but offers resellers a trade allowance price of \$1.95. If the retailer indeed sells the product for the MSRP, the retailer will realize a 33% markup-on-selling-price (\$1.95/(1-.33) = \$2.95). Obviously, this percentage will be different if the retailer sells the product at a price that does not match the MSRP. However, the crucial point to understand is that marketers must factor in what resellers expect to earn when they are setting trade allowances. This amount needs to be sufficient to entice the reseller to handle and possibly promote the product.

Special Segment Pricing

In some industries, distinct classes of customers within a target market are offered pricing that differs from the rest of the market. The main reasons for doing this include building future demand by appealing to new or younger customers, improving the brand's image as being sensitive to customers' needs, and rewarding long-time customers with price breaks.

For instance, many companies, including movie theaters, fitness facilities and pharmaceutical firms, offer lower prices to senior citizens. Some marketers offer not-for-profit customers lower prices compared to that charged to for-profit firms. Other industries may offer lower prices to students or children.

Another example used by service organizations is to offer pricing differences based on convenience and comfort enjoyed by customers when experiencing the service, such as higher prices for improved seat locations at sporting or entertainment events.

Geographic Pricing

The sale of some products may require marketers pay higher costs due to the geographic area in which a product is sold. This may lead the marketer to adjust the price to compensate for the higher expense. The most likely cause for charging a different price rests with the cost of transporting a product from the supplier's distribution location to the buyer's location. If the supplier is incurring all costs for shipping, then they may charge a higher price for products in order to cover the extra transportation expense. For instance, for a manufacturer located in Los Angeles, the transportation cost for shipping products by air to Hawaii is likely much more than it would be to ship the same amount of product by truck to San Diego. In this situation, since the manufacturer is incurring the shipping cost, they may set a different product price for Hawaiian purchasers compared to buyers in San Diego.

Transportation expense is not the only geographic-related cost that may raise a product's price. As noted in Chapter 17, special taxes or tariffs may be imposed on certain products by local, regional, national or international governments, which a seller may pass along in the form of higher prices.

Early Payment Incentives

For many years, marketers operating primarily in the business market (see *Business Market* in Chapter 5) offered incentives to encourage their customers to pay early. Typically, business customers are given a certain period of time, normally 30 or 60 days, before full payment is due. To persuade faster payment that enables the seller to obtain the money quicker, marketers have offered early payment discounts often referred to as **cash terms**. This discount is expressed in a form indicating how much discount is being offered and in what time frame. For example, the cash terms 2/10 net 30 indicate that if the buyer makes payment within 10 days of the date of the bill, then they can take a 2 percent discount off the invoice, otherwise the full amount is due in 30 days.

While this incentive remains widely used, its effectiveness in getting customers to pay early has diminished. Instead, many customers, especially large volume buyers, simply remove the discount from the bill's total and then pay within the required "net" time frame (or later!). For this reason, many companies are discontinuing offering this discount.

STEP 4: DETERMINE PROMOTIONAL PRICING

The final price may be further adjusted through promotional pricing. Unlike standard adjustments, which are often permanently part of a marketer's pricing strategy and may include either a decrease or increase in price, promotional pricing is a temporary adjustment that only involves price reductions. In most cases, this means the marketer is selling at a price that significantly reduces the profit it makes per unit sold.

As one would expect, the main objective of promotional pricing is to stimulate product demand. But as we noted back in our discussion of sales promotion in Chapter 14, marketers should be careful not to overuse promotional programs that temporarily reduce the selling price. If promotional pricing is used too frequently, customers may become conditioned to anticipate the reduction. This results in buyers withholding purchases until the product is again offered at a lower price. Since promotional pricing often means the marketing organization is making very little profit off of each item sold, consistently selling at a low price could jeopardize the marketer's ability to meet its financial objectives.

The options for promotional pricing include:

◆ Markdowns

◆ Loss Leaders

◆ Sales Promotions

◆ Bundle Pricing

◆ Dynamic Pricing

Markdowns

The most common method for stimulating customer interest using price is the promotional markdown method, which offers the product at a price that is lower than the product's normal selling price. There are several types of markdowns including:

Temporary Markdown

Possibly the most familiar pricing method marketers use to generate sales is to offer a temporary markdown or **on-sale pricing**. These markdowns are normally for a specified period of time, the conclusion of which will result in the product being raised back to the normal selling price.

Permanent Markdown

Unlike the temporary markdown, where the product will eventually be raised back to a higher price, the permanent markdown is intended to move the product out of inventory and not to be returned. This type of markdown is used to remove old products that are perishable and close to being out of date (e.g., day-old donuts), older models that must be sold to make room for new models (e.g., cars), or products the marketer no longer wishes to sell.

Seasonal Markdown

Products that are primarily sold during a particular time of the year, such as clothing, gardening products, sporting goods and holiday-specific items, may see price reductions at the conclusion of their prime selling season.

Loss Leaders

An important type of pricing program used primarily by retailers is the loss leader. Under this method, a product is intentionally sold at or below the cost the retailer pays to acquire the product from suppliers. The idea is that offering such a low price will entice a high level of customer traffic to visit a retailer's physical store, e-commerce website, or shopping app. And once there, customers will easily make up for the profit lost on the loss leader item by purchasing other items that are not following loss leader pricing. For instance, many convenience stores, that also provide gasoline, may use gas pricing as a loss leader. Their hope is that the low price, which is often displayed on large roadside signage, will not only generate traffic to the gas pumps but also to the inside of the store, where customers will purchase regularly priced products, such as food and drinks.

While loss leader pricing is a useful option for generating customer interest, marketers should be aware of potential legal issues as explained in Box 18-3.

Box 18-3

LEGAL CONCERNS WITH LOSS LEADER PRICING

Marketers should be aware that some governmental agencies view loss leaders as a form of predatory pricing and, therefore, consider it illegal. As noted in Chapter 17, predatory pricing occurs when an organization is deliberately selling products at or below cost with the intention of driving competitors out of business. Of course, this differs from our discussion, in which loss leader pricing is considered a form of promotion and not a form of anti-competitive activity.

In the U.S., several state governments have passed laws under the heading Unfair Sales Act (sometimes referred to as Minimum Markup Laws), which prohibit the selling of certain products below cost. (5) The main intention of these laws is to protect small firms from below-cost pricing activities of larger companies. States that enforce such laws primarily do so for specific product categories, such as gasoline and tobacco.

Sales Promotions

As we noted in Chapter 14, marketers may offer several types of pricing promotions to stimulate demand (i.e., sell more products). While we have already discussed "on-sale" pricing as a technique to build customer interest, there are other sales promotions that are designed to lower price. These include rebates, coupons, trade-in and loyalty programs. To manage these promotions, marketers often utilize **campaign management software** that incorporates customer identification and tracking to determine the best opportunities for offering special promotions.

For online retailers, identifying and tracking customers may be relatively easy if customers have previously purchased and their login information is retained by their web browser or on the retailer's mobile app. In situations where customers are not easily identified, a retailer may place a small data file (i.e., cookie) or other device identifiers on a visitor's computer or mobile device (see *Privacy Concerns and Customer Cooperation* in Chapter 1). These identifiers enable retailers to monitor users' behavior, such as how often they visit a website, how much time they spend on the site, what information they access, and much more. For example, the marketer may offer a special promotion if a visitor has come to the site at least five times in the last six months but has never made a purchase.

At brick-and-mortar retail stores, campaign management software is also used to offer customers price reductions or other incentives. For example, a sales promotion may be triggered when customers use a store loyalty card. If a customer's characteristics match requirements in the software program, they may be offered a special incentive, such as 10 percent off if they also purchase another product.

Bundle Pricing

Another pricing adjustment designed to increase sales is to offer discounted pricing when customers purchase several different products at the same time. Termed bundle pricing, the technique is often used to sell products that are complementary to a main product. For buyers, the overall cost of the purchase shows a savings compared to purchasing each product individually. For example, a camera retailer may offer a discounted price when customers purchase both a digital camera and a high-end camera case that is lower than if both items were purchased separately. In this example, the retailer may promote this as, *"Buy both the digital camera and the durable camera case and save 25%."*

Bundle pricing is also used by marketers as a technique that avoids making price adjustments on a main product for fear that doing so could affect the product's perceived quality level (see *Step 3: Set Standard Price Adjustments* discussion above). Rather, the marketer may choose to offer adjustments on other related or complementary products. In our example, the message changes to, *"Buy the digital camera and you can get a durable camera case for 50% less."* With this approach, the marketer is presenting a price adjustment without the perception of it lowering the price of the main product.

Dynamic Pricing

The concept of dynamic pricing has received a great deal of attention in recent years due to its prevalent use by airlines, hotels, and ridesharing services. But the basic idea of dynamic pricing has been around since the dawn of commerce. Essentially, dynamic pricing allows for point-of-sale (i.e., at the time and place of purchase) price adjustments to take place for customers meeting certain criteria established by the seller.

The most common and oldest form of dynamic pricing is **haggling**, the give-and-take that takes place between buyer and seller as they settle on a price. While the word haggling may conjure up visions of transactions taking place among vendors and customers in a street market, the concept is widely used in business-to-business markets as well, where it carries the more reserved label of **negotiated pricing**.

However, technological advances offer a new dimension for the use of dynamic pricing. Unlike haggling, where the seller makes price adjustments based on a person-to-person discussion with a buyer, dynamic pricing uses sophisticated price optimization software to adjust price. It achieves this by combining customer data (e.g., who they are, how they buy, when they buy) with pre-programmed price offerings. If a customer meets certain criteria, then special pricing may be offered. Compared to campaign management software (see *Sales Promotion* discussion above), which is primarily focused on stimulating greater product sales (i.e., sell more units), price optimization is intended to maximize revenue per unit sold (i.e., make more for each unit sold).

As noted, dynamic pricing is also widely used in the service sector where travel services, such as airlines and hotels, will offer different pricing for the same service. For instance, airline ticket pricing will vary based on such criteria as type of customer (e.g., business vs. leisure traveler) and date of purchase. Additionally, in some industries, dynamic pricing is used to respond to changes in demand. Known as **surge pricing**, pricing software may increase prices from a regular level to a higher level as demand increases. For example, surge pricing is used by ridesharing services, such as Uber (6) and Lyft, to adjust prices higher during times of peak demand. While surge pricing may be best associated with the service industry, online retailers, such as Amazon, also deploy this approach when pricing products. (7)

STEP 5: STATE PAYMENT OPTIONS

With the price decided, the final step for the marketer is to determine in what form a payment may be received, the methods used for handling a payment, and in what time frame a customer will make a payment. As one would expect, payment is most often in a monetary form, though in certain situations, the payment may be part of a barter arrangement in which goods or services are exchanged.

Form of Payment

The monetary payment decision can be a complex one. One issue marketers face is deciding in what form payments will be accepted. These options include cash, debit card, check, money orders, credit card, online and mobile payment systems (e.g., PayPal), and **digital currency** (e.g., Bitcoin). For international purchases, currency issues and other uncertainties may require the use of alternative payment options including bank drafts, letters of credit, and international reply coupons, to name a few. (8)

Handling of Payment

Marketers must also decide how the actual payment will be handled. For instance, in a retail setting it would seem that common forms of payment, including cash, debit card and credit card, are obvious choices for most transactions. However, some retailers may limit forms of payment, including those that do not take cash and some that do not accept certain credit cards. Additionally, in many business-to-business transactions payment may only take place in the form of bank transfers.

While in the retail environment traditional payment options still represent a significant percentage of consumer purchases, the use of contactless payments is growing. Contactless payments allow customers to make purchases by simply holding a credit card, debit card, or mobile device (e.g., smartphone) near an electronic payment reader. (9) Nearly all major credit card companies offer contactless cards while payments using apps on mobile devices, also called **mobile payments**, are offered by the leading smartphone companies including Apple, Google, and Samsung. Additionally, a number of other payment apps, such as Venmo, make it easy to send payments when buying online or when buying directly. (10)

Time Frame of Payment

One final pricing decision considers when payment will be made. Many marketers find promotional value in offering options to customers for the date when payment is due. Such options include:

◆ Immediate Payment in Full – Requires the customer make full payment at the time the product is acquired.

◆ Immediate Partial Payment – Requires the customer make a certain amount or percentage of payment at the time the product is acquired. Most commonly this is in the form of a down payment. Subsequent payments will occur either in one lump sum or at agreed intervals (e.g., once per month) through an installment plan option.

◆ Future Payment – Provides the buyer with the opportunity to acquire use of the product with payment occurring sometime in the future. Future payment may require either payment in full or partial payment.

OTHER PRICING METHODS

Two pricing approaches that do not fit neatly into the price setting process we've described are auction and bid pricing. Both follow a model in which one or more participants in a purchasing transaction make offers to another party. The difference exists in terms of which party to a transaction is making the offer.

AUCTION PRICING

Auction pricing is a pricing method where the buyer, in large part, sets the final price. This pricing method has been around for hundreds of years, but today it is most well-known for its use in the auction marketplace business models, such as eBay and business-to-business marketplaces. While marketers selling through auctions do not have control over the final price, it is possible to control the minimum price by establishing a price floor or **reserve price**. In this way, the product is only sold if a bid is at least equal to the floor price.

BID PRICING

Bid pricing typically requires a marketer compete against other suppliers by submitting its selling price to a potential buyer who chooses from the submissions. From the buyer's perspective, the advantage of this method is that suppliers are more likely to compete by offering lower prices than would be available if the purchase was made directly without competitive offers. Bid pricing occurs in several industries, though it is a standard requirement when selling to local, state, national, and many international governments.

In a traditional bidding process, the offer is sealed or unseen by competitors. It is not until all bids are obtained and unsealed that the marketer is informed of the price listed by competitors. The fact that marketers often operate in the dark in terms of available competitor research makes this type of pricing one of the most challenging of all price setting methods.

However, many purchase situations are now adopting an auction method, called **reverse auction**, to make the bidding process more transparent. Reverse auctions are typically conducted on the internet and, in most cases, limited to business-to-business purchasing. With a reverse auction, a buyer informs suppliers of its product needs and then identifies a time when suppliers may bid against each other. Usually the time is limited and suppliers can often see what others are offering.

In either traditional bidding or reverse auction, the marketer's pricing strategy depends on the projected winning bid price, which is generally the lowest price. However, price alone is only the deciding factor if the bidder meets certain qualifications; thus, the low bidder is not always guaranteed to win.

REFERENCES

1. Automobile dealers routinely quote a vehicle's MSRP in their advertisements, though only in cases where a vehicle is in extremely high demand does anyone pay this amount. Instead, dealers set their final price based on other factors as explained here: : Elizabeth Rivelli. "Car MSRP vs. Invoice: Everything You Need to Know." *Car and Driver*. February 3, 2023. https://www.caranddriver.com/auto-loans/a31874008/car-msrp-vs-invoice.

2. Following the coronavirus pandemic and subsequent economic slowdown, economies around the world experienced tremendous growth. In the U.S., many companies responded by raising prices resulting the highest level of inflation since the 1980s. However, by 2023 large retailers felt the price increases were too much and pressured their suppliers to reduce their product costs. For more see: Liz Young. "Big Retailers are Looking to Reassert Leverage in Supply Chains to Rein in Costs." *The Wall Street Journal*. March 15, 2023. https://www.wsj.com/articles/supplier-buyer-relations-are-shifting-again-as-pandemic-strains-ease-f7121226.

3. There are several free online tools for calculating break-even if fixed cost, variable cost, and price can be estimated. For one of these calculators see: "Break-Even Calculator." *Bplans*. https://www.bplans.com/business-calculators/break_even_calculator.

4. For insight into how customers perceive prices and the impact this may have on the marketer see: Sandeep Heda, Stephen Mewborn, and Stephen Caine. "How Customers Perceive a Price Is as Important as the Price Itself." *Harvard Business Review*. January 03, 2017. https://hbr.org/2017/01/how-customers-perceive-a-price-is-as-important-as-the-price-itself.

5. For an example see: "Unfair Sales Act." *State of Wisconsin*. https://datcp.wi.gov/Pages/Programs_Services/UnfairSalesAct.aspx.

6. For more on Uber's pricing see: "How Surge Pricing Works." *Uber*. https://www.uber.com/us/en/drive/driver-app/how-surge-works.

7. Some feel surge pricing will soon be common among a wide range of products in part due to the power of AI. For more see: Oliver Barnes, Philip Georgiadis and Laura Onita. "The Rise of Surge Pricing: 'It Will Eventually Be Everywhere'." *Financial Times*. September 15, 2023. https://www.ft.com/content/d0e3bcb5-b824-414e-bfac-4c0b4193e9f0.

8. For more information on other methods of payment for international trade see: "Methods of Payment." *Export.gov*. https://www.trade.gov/methods-payment.

9. For more information on contactless payments see: Casey Bond. "What is a Contactless Credit Card." *U.S. News & World Report*. July 19, 2023. https://money.usnews.com/credit-cards/articles/what-is-a-contactless-credit-card.

10. The use of contactless payments grew sharply during the coronavirus pandemic. For a summary of key statistics on the use of contactless payments see: Mary King. "22 Contactless Payment Statistics." *Fit Small Business*. May 23, 2023. https://fitsmallbusiness.com/contactless-payment-statistics.

Chapter 19: Managing External Forces

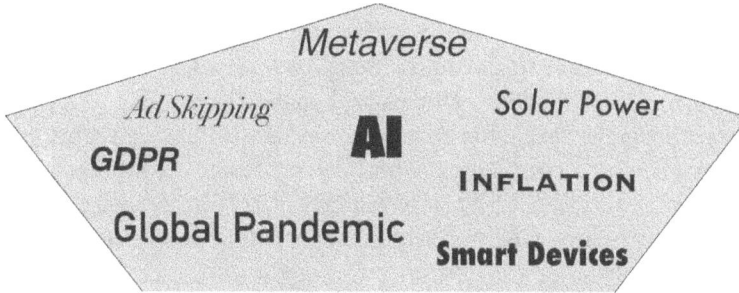

The bulk of material covered in the first 18 chapters is intended to give those new to marketing a basic understanding of the decisions marketers make as they work to satisfy customer needs. Our focus has largely centered on decisions marketers control, such as product design, promotional message, type of distribution, setting price, etc. Now that we have laid out the Marketer's Toolkit, we begin a new section examining additional issues facing marketers as they manage their marketing efforts.

In this chapter, we explore factors outside of marketers' control but that play a vital role in shaping an organization's marketing strategies and tactics. As we will see, external forces present both opportunities and threats. Each force holds the potential to alter how an industry conducts its business and how individual marketing organizations make decisions. Our coverage includes an in-depth evaluation of seven key external forces: demographics, economic conditions, governmental environment, influential stakeholders, cultural and societal change, innovation, and competitors.

WHAT ARE EXTERNAL FORCES?

The daily routine for most marketers sees them engaging in activities related to the key marketing decisions contained within the Marketer's Toolkit we introduced in Chapter 1, namely selecting target markets, creating products, establishing distribution, developing promotions, and setting price. These decisions are considered to be controllable by the marketer, who has the final say on the attributes for each.

Unfortunately, while decisions in the Toolkit are largely directed by the marketer, these decisions can be strongly affected by external forces that are beyond the direct control of the marketing organization. By "direct control" we mean marketers lack the power to determine the direction and intensity of a change in these forces. Instead, marketers must treat external forces as something to monitor and respond to when necessary. Certainly, there is no better example of the impact external forces can have on marketers (and nearly everyone else in the world!) than with the speed with which the coronavirus pandemic spread catching nearly all organizations unprepared. And more recently, the emergence of artificial intelligence (AI) has likewise surprised many organizations. (1)

While the pandemic and AI may seem like extreme examples of an uncontrollable events affecting marketers, less dramatic external forces can also have wide-ranging impact. For instance, it is not inconceivable to see the day when **driverless vehicles** are a popular transportation option for both consumers and businesses. Many believe the advance technologies built into driverless vehicles will make these safer to operate compared to human-controlled vehicles. This advancement in automotive technology could have implications for insurance companies, who may see fewer customers choosing broader and more expensive coverage. Driverless vehicles could also pose a threat to auto shops as these vehicles may be involved in fewer accidents, thus requiring fewer repairs. (2)

While marketers lack direct control over external forces, in some cases, they can exercise a small amount of influence over these factors. For instance, advances in mobile devices have played a pivotal role in changing how consumers acquire information. But while mobile device manufacturers are credited with being the catalyst for changing a social behavior (an external force), they represent just one of several organizational groups (e.g., software developers) and individuals (e.g., social media users), whose actions were necessary for behavior to change across a large group. Consequently, while one company can market goods and services with the intention of changing how a target market behaves, it is nearly impossible for one company alone to control the change.

For marketers, the key to dealing with most external forces is to engage in continual marketing research. For larger organizations, this may involve assigning research personnel to watch these factors as part of their day-to-day responsibilities. A research staff dedicated to monitoring external forces may offer marketers the ability to predict changes and respond well in advance of changing conditions. For example, researchers may be able to offer predictions on how the economy (an external force) may change over the next one to two years. The marketer can then consider these predictions and decide whether it is in the organization's best interest to respond (e.g., introduce new products, lower prices, etc.).

For small organizations that do not have the luxury of an in-house marketing research staff, monitoring change is difficult and often means they react after a change has occurred. However, new marketing research tools (see Chapter 2) are making the monitoring task much easier allowing small organizations to respond quicker than they have in the past.

THE KEY EXTERNAL FORCES FACING MARKETING

For our discussion, we highlight seven fundamental external forces. Each external force is described in detail though these are not presented in order of importance. In fact, the importance of each force may vary depending on the marketing organization and the industry in which they compete. For instance, a company manufacturing technology products may feel innovative forces are more important than demographic changes, while a financial services firm may feel their attention is better directed at aggressively monitoring and reacting to economic conditions.

Demographics

Demographics involves the evaluation of characteristics of a population and how these change over time. The characteristics that are of most interest to marketers fall into two categories:

◆ Total Population – These characteristics take a broad view of the population as a whole in terms of size (e.g., number of people, number of businesses) and location (e.g., geographic region).

◆ Personal Variables – These characteristics look at how the population is changing based on individual factors such as gender, age, income, level of education, family situation (e.g., single, married, cohabitation), sexual preference, ethnicity, occupation, and social class.

We saw in Chapter 5, demographics is a key variable used to segment both consumer and business markets. In particular, demographic variables are an essential component in creating customer profiles. These profiles are based on both demographic and non-demographic (e.g., customer behavior, attitudes, lifestyles) factors and are used for grouping customers into definable market segments from which a marketer then selects its target markets. Since demographics is tied directly to identifying target markets, monitoring how demographics change is critical for making marketing decisions.

Most demographic shifts do not occur rapidly. Consequently, marketers will not see dramatic changes in a short period of time in the manner that other external forces can impact an organization (e.g., impact of a new government regulation). However, over the long term, demographics can reshape a target market requiring organizations to rework their marketing strategy in an effort to appeal to a changing market.

ADJUSTING TO DEMOGRAPHIC TRENDS

While demographic change occurs slowly, marketers can begin to see indicators of potential change by identifying small trends that may suggest a larger shift over time. By paying close attention to these trends, organizations can prepare a long-term marketing strategy in the event the shift becomes more apparent.

To illustrate how a marketer may respond, consider the demographic characteristic birthrate. In some countries, the overall birthrate is declining, while the average age of the population is increasing (i.e., people living longer). For a company targeting the youth market with sporting products, this trend may suggest, that in coming years, it will see shrinkage in demand for its products as the youth market population declines. On the other hand, demographic data may signal to the company that another market (i.e., older consumers), which was not previously targeted, may hold potential for new products. If it is predicted the shift will occur over several years, the sporting products company can slowly move into the new market by offering products geared toward older adults. (3)

Economic Conditions

Since most marketers are engaged in activities designed to entice customers to spend their money, it makes sense that economic conditions represent a powerful external force. Economic analysis looks at how a defined group produces, distributes, and consumes goods and services. These groupings can range from those defined broadly (e.g., country) to those defined narrowly (e.g., small town).

Of course, the production, distribution, and consumption of products are also of high interest to marketers and, in fact, many leading scholars of marketing first studied economics before moving to marketing. In simple terms (and with apologies to both marketers and economists), the key difference between the marketer and the economist is that marketers are engaged in activity that make things happen to individual customers (e.g., create demand for products), while economists are engaged in activity showing the effects marketers' decisions have on a group (e.g., how much is being spent by certain groups on marketers' products).

Additionally, economists whose job it is to study a group may use hundreds of economic variables when assessing how a group is responding. Marketers tend to evaluate far fewer economic variables preferring to concentrate on those variables that affect spending behavior of consumers and businesses they target. For marketers, the economic variables of most interest include:

◆ Income – how much is being earned

◆ Spending – what consumers and businesses are doing with their money

◆ Interest Rates – the cost of borrowing money

◆ Inflation – how prices for goods and services are changing

◆ Cost of Living – the financial requirements of living in a certain geographic area

◆ Employment Rates – the percentage of employable people who are working

◆ Exchange Rates – how the value of currencies changes between countries and regions

IMPORTANCE OF ECONOMIC CONDITIONS

For many marketers, there is a relationship between level of sales and how customers are doing financially. For most products, this relationship is a direct one – as customers' financial condition improves so will selling opportunities for the marketer. A clear example of this can be seen with the sale of luxury products, where marketers are likely to see their sales grow as the target market's economic condition improves. However, other products may see improvement as economic conditions decline. For instance, during weak economic conditions marketers of career preparation services, such as those offering personal resume development and job search assistance, may see increased interest by workers who are unemployed or who fear their job may not be stable.

Whether an organization benefits from improving or declining economic conditions, it is necessary to monitor changes occurring in the economy in which the organization's target markets are located. In particular, marketers should watch for changing patterns in customer spending, which may indicate that a long-term change in the economy is occurring.

Changes extending over a long period (more than six months) may be part of the **business cycle** of an economy. A business cycle is presented as a series of up (economic expansions) and down (economic contractions) measures. During expansion, an economy grows, and this generally leads to more jobs, higher income, and increased customer spending. However, an economy growing too quickly can present problems of **inflation**, where product prices grow too quickly. In this situation, even though customers have higher incomes, purchasing may be lower since product prices have increased. Such situations are a main reason an economy will contract or see customer spending decrease. If this decrease is severe, this can lead to marketers seeing a significant reduction in sales, which may indicate the presence of an economic **recession** (i.e., economic decline).

Governmental Environment

Marketing decisions must be made with an understanding of how these are impacted by international, national, regional, state, and local laws and regulations. For marketers, laws (i.e., acts passed by governmental ruling bodies) and regulations (i.e., requirements put in place by governmental agencies) identify rules and procedures that guide certain marketing activities. Failure to conform to requirements established by governments and their agencies may result in fines, sanctions, or other legal action (see Box 19-1).

The governmental environment is a difficult external force to monitor for two key reasons. First, the number and variety of laws and regulations can be overwhelming even for the most seasoned marketer. For instance, in the U.S. alone there are potentially hundreds of laws and regulations that are either directly or indirectly targeted to marketing decisions. Table 19-1 provides a sampling of the issues covered by U.S. laws and regulations, and the primary marketing decision areas these affect. (4)

Because the legal and regulatory environment may be different within each market targeted by an organization, businesses seeking to establish a global presence may be selective as to which geographic markets they will pursue. For example, a small start-up pharmaceutical company, that has developed its first product, may initially look to market their product in countries that have less restrictive testing and research requirements compared to countries were approval for marketing a drug is much more involved. In this way, the company can begin to generate revenue while also gathering the needed information for entry into other, more controlled markets.

The second reason the governmental environment proves difficult is due to the complexity inherent in understanding laws and regulations, which often makes it impossible for marketers to handle these issues on their own. Seeking legal assistance is necessary (and often costly) for most marketers no matter their size.

Box 19-1

MARKETERS VS. THE GOVERNMENT

As noted in Chapter 11, a sizable hurdle marketers face when promoting their products is the need to be heard above the "noise" created by competitors. Because customers constantly are bombarded with promotional messages, marketers often seek ways to stand out so those in the target market will pay attention.

There are several options for doing this. One technique is to increase the frequency of advertising in hopes repetitiveness will eventually get customers to pay attention. Another option is to create promotions that are very different from what the market is used to experiencing. For instance, Apple's classic "1984" NFL Super Bowl ad is often used as an example of an ad countering advertising norms. (5)

Yet sometimes in their quest to rise above the noise, creativity gets the best of a marketer resulting in a far different outcome than what was envisioned. For example, a company well-known for producing humorous advertisements may find customers are far less responsive if their advertising shifts to a creative approach that now addresses serious subject matter. Or worse, when fighting to rise above the noise, marketers become too creative to the point where their message is not even supported by the facts. While such messages may initially capture the attention of the target market, eventually these people will be put off by what the advertiser is offering. And if these ads are glaringly misleading, the marketer's messages may also draw attention from another interested group – legal authorities.

Over the years, many organizations have faced U.S. government scrutiny for their marketing promotions. In most cases, the government claims the promotions are not just slightly misleading but are intentionally deceptive. In other words, the marketer behind the promotion is aware that what is being said is purposely twisting the truth. For serious cases, an organization confronted by government claims of false promotion must decide between accepting that they are doing something wrong or fight the claims in court. History tells us that most will eventually settle with the government. Over the years such well-known companies and brands as Volkswagen, Walmart, Kellogg, Red Bull, and L'Oreal have all faced government scrutiny for promotions that contain false or misleading information, and eventually settled their issues, often paying a steep fine to do so. (6) More recently, the U.S. Federal Trade Commission issued warning letters to nearly 700 companies, including many large firms, regarding deceptive marketing practices. (7)

Table 19-1: Examples of Laws and Regulations in Marketing

Decision Area	Coverage
General	unfair competition, restraint of trade, environmental
Target Market	discrimination, online registration, privacy
Product	product safety, labeling, intellectual property, warranties
Promotion	deceptive and misleading claims, advertising to children, telemarketing, email spam, promotional giveaways, endorsments
Distribution	tying contracts, exclusive dealerships, transportation safety
Pricing	price discrimination, deceptive pricing, predatory pricing, consumer credit purchasing, price maintenance

DEALING WITH THE GOVERNMENT

In addition to seeking legal assistance, organizations may find value by engaging in either direct discussion with government personnel or indirect discussion through firms hired to serve as a representative for the marketing company, such as consultants and lobbyists. Representatives are particularly beneficial when selling internationally, where existing relationships between governments and hired representatives can effectively reduce bureaucratic red tape.

In situations where proposed legislation is likely to impact an entire industry, communication with the government may occur through a marketer's participation in an **industry trade group** or trade association. These groups perform many tasks on behalf of their members, including maintaining relations with governmental groups to ensure the industry's voice is heard with regard to pending legislation affecting the industry.

Finally, marketers should not view the governmental environment as always erecting obstacles. In many cases, laws and regulations present marketing opportunities. For example, in response to U.S. Federal Government rules limiting the size of liquid, gel, and aerosol products that may be carried aboard an airplane, several personal care products companies (e.g., shaving cream, hair care, toothpaste, etc.) viewed this as an opportunity to market their products in new packaging that they promote as approved for airline travel.

Influential Stakeholders

Besides dealing with the government, marketers must also pay close attention to other groups that can affect marketing activity. The most important of these groups are those that have an interest or stake in the organization. While such groups may not carry the same power as governmental agencies, stakeholders can still command a great deal of influence, especially in terms of swaying public opinion. If their voice is strong enough, this can then lead to governmental action.

Influential stakeholders can be divided into two categories:

Connected Stakeholders

These stakeholders consist of groups that regularly interact with the marketing organization and often perform key activities that help the marketer succeed. Examples include supply and distribution partners (e.g., distributors, material suppliers), industry standards groups, and support companies (e.g., advertising agencies). To address concerns raised by these groups often requires direct communication by management with their connected stakeholders.

Peripheral Stakeholders

These stakeholders consist of groups that may not routinely impact the marketer unless a specific issue arises that draws their attention. Examples include religious organizations, community activists, and cause supporters. To address concerns and to communicate with these peripheral stakeholders, marketers often seek the help of public relations professionals. Depending on the circumstances, the PR strategy may involve initiating contact prior to an issue becoming public (i.e., **preemptive strategy**) or the strategy may be to take a wait-and-see approach before taking action (i.e., **responsive strategy**).

Cultural and Societal Change

Society is made up of many different cultural groups. As we note in Chapter 4, members of a cultural group share similar values and beliefs, which are learned and reinforced by others within the same cultural group. These shared values and beliefs lead members of a cultural group to behave in similar ways (e.g., customs, traditions, likes/dislikes, attitudes, perceptions, etc.).

Cultural groups can be viewed on several levels. At a broad level, a cultural group consists of a very large number who share basic values (e.g., ethnicity, religious affiliation). While looking at the broad level can offer some insight into how a general cultural group behaves, marketers are much more concerned with examining cultural groups at narrower levels. Such analysis of cultural groups leads to the study of subcultures, which consist of individuals sharing values and beliefs that revolve around specific interests. For instance, a large subcultural group may exist in a certain region of a country. While collectively they share basic cultural values with others in their country (e.g., sense of patriotism), they may also share special values with those in their local region that are not shared consistently throughout the country (e.g., work ethic, taste in food, etc.).

But what is often of even more interest to marketers is the identification of smaller subcultures (e.g., type of shopper, music preference, online gaming enthusiast, etc.). Members of smaller subcultures, who share similar values, are also likely to have similar needs and, as we discussed in Chapter 5, this suggests that subcultures are natural for market segmentation. For marketers, it is important to recognize that a single consumer may belong to many different subcultures. Fully understanding the structure and key values of a subculture can offer marketers valuable clues for reaching these customers.

EVOLUTION OF CULTURAL CHANGE

Cultural values and beliefs are not stagnant, rather these evolve and change. However, the pace of change differs depending on the level examined. At the broad cultural level changes often evolve slowly. For instance, consider how people in the United States and Switzerland view the importance of saving money. People in the United States are more inclined to spend their earned income than they are to save resulting in a low household savings rate for Americans. Those living in Switzerland are more concerned with saving and show a high household savings rate. (8) The difference in values toward savings has been consistent for many years and no one expects consumers from either country to alter their values in the near future.

While broad cultures tend to shift values and beliefs slowly, changes within subcultures can occur relatively quickly. This can be seen within the music industry, which often experiences rapid shifts as a subculture of music enthusiasts discovers new artists and musical styles. The key for marketers targeting subcultures is to maintain close contact with these groups through regular marketing research in order to see how different subcultures behave. In doing so, marketers may be able to spot trends, which they can capitalize on through new marketing tactics, such as creating new products, opening new sales channels, or offering more value to their customers.

Innovation

Arguably the external forces with the greatest potential for changing how marketers and industries compete are those associated with innovation. When most people think of innovation, they immediately assume it has to do with computers, robotics, and other high-tech equipment. While today the majority of innovative new products rely in some way on information technology, it is not a requirement for something to be regarded as innovative. Instead, an innovation is viewed as anything new that solves needs by offering a significant advantage (e.g., more features, more convenient, easier to use, lower cost, etc.) over existing methods. For example, an airline may devise a new way to load passengers using existing products (no new technologies). The impact of this new method is that it decreases the amount of time needed to fill a plane and improves the airline's on-time performance rate. If this new method is viewed positively by customers, governmental groups, and the media it may gain widespread acceptance by other airlines, who will make similar changes to their loading procedures.

As noted in the above example, for an innovation to be truly influential it must be widely adopted within a targeted group (e.g., within an industry, by a target market). Once adopted an innovation becomes significant if it leads to behavioral changes including changing how consumers and businesses satisfy their needs. These changes present both opportunities and threats to marketers.

Because of the potential innovation has in affecting products and industries, it is no surprise that many marketing organizations direct significant funds to researching this external force. In fact, in many industries, such as pharmaceuticals and software development, spending on technological research and development represents a significant portion of an organization's overall budget. (9)

INNOVATION IN MARKETING

Marketers in many industries know that innovation through new product development is vital to remain competitive. But product decisions are not the only marketing area affected by new developments. As we've discussed throughout this book, innovation can affect almost all marketing elements as outlined in Table 19-2.

Table 19-2: Innovation in Marketing

Marketing Area	Effect of Innovation
Marketing Research	Creates new ways to conduct research, including more sophisticated methods for monitoring and tracking customer behavior and analyzing data.
Targeting Markets	Allows for extreme target marketing where micro marketing is replacing mass marketing. For customer service, technology makes it easier to manage relationships and allows for rapid response to customers' needs.
Product	Creates new digital goods/services. Incorporates innovation into existing good/service which enhances value by offering improved quality, features, and reliability at a lower price.
Promotion	New techniques (e.g., AI driven methods) allow better matching of promotion to customers' individual characteristics, activity, and location. Makes it easier for sellers to offer product suggestions and promotional tie-ins.
Distribution	Creates new channels for product distribution and customer transaction (e.g., purchasing with mobile apps). Allows more control over inventory management, increased delivery speed, and closer monitoring of product shipments.
Pricing	Enables the use of dynamic pricing methods.

Many of the benefits shown in Table 19-2 are driven by the evolution of information technology, including the internet, mobile devices and more recently, artificial intelligence (AI). These technologies are transforming how all functional areas within an organization perform work. However, it can be argued that no functional area has been more affected by these developments than marketing. Over the next decade, it is expected that innovation in information technologies will continue to significantly impact marketing, and marketers are well served to embrace it (see Box 19-2).

Box 19-2

THE MESSAGE TO RETAILERS: INNOVATE OR DIE

As we have noted many times in this book, the internet, mobile and AI technologies are altering how nearly all business is done. While it is certainly debatable as to which industries have been affected the most, certainly the impact e-commerce shopping has had on retailing is at the top of the list. Whether this is because technology allows customers to choose from a virtually unlimited number of items or offers the convenience of rapid delivery or makes it easy for customers to gain information and place an order, shopping has been transformed.

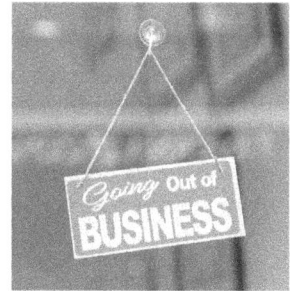

Yet the benefits customers obtain from retail technology is just one of many changes retailers are facing. For example, changes include such things has millennials moving from suburban to urban areas, which impacts the location of physical stores. Also, there is greater emphasis on health and fitness, which is changing the types of products customers seek. And, of course, the increased sharing of information among fellow shoppers, such as through social media and rating websites, is making it necessary for retailers to communicate in more detail and with a greater sense of urgency.

A good example of how retailing is changing can be seen in the grocery industry. The nature of grocery stores is to operate on very low profit margins, which means attracting a large number of customers is critical. With increased competition coming from such powerhouse retailers as Amazon and Walmart, to remain competitive means traditional grocery stores need to innovate or face a very uncertain future.

For instance, grocery stores need to not only address issues of location, food choice and customer communication, but they also need to become more tech-savvy. While leading grocers have adopted many technologies in recent years (e.g., enhanced shopping apps, scan-and-go purchasing), to stay competitive they will need to stay abreast of evolving innovations. For example, future technologies may include home delivery using driverless vehicles and drones, voice-activated ordering (e.g., such as that offered by smart speaker and smart display devices), and robot-assisted stocking of store shelves. (10)

Competitors

For many marketers, the competitive external force is the one most relevant to immediate day-to-day decision making. While the other external forces we've discussed tend to be examined periodically (or in some cases rarely), monitoring competitor activity is often a daily undertaking.

Monitoring competitors can offer insights in three key dimensions:

Competitors as Threats

The most obvious reason to monitor the competition is to see how they are responding in the same markets in which the marketer operates. Many larger companies, recognizing the importance of keeping tabs on their competition, have created specific positions, and even departments, focusing on gathering and analyzing competitor data.

These **competitive intelligence** programs mainly employ high-tech methods to locate information about competitors, such as news reports, government filings (e.g., patents, stock reports), AI software, social media postings, and changes to competitors' websites. Even small-sized marketers can track competitors' actions. For instance, as we noted in Chapter 15, there are several news and information services that will alert a marketer (usually via email) when a competitor is mentioned in the news.

Competitors as Partners

While many may consider competitors as the enemy, there are situations where competitors can present opportunities. This happens often to large companies that offer a broad product line serving many target markets. In some markets, a company may compete aggressively with another firm, but in other markets it may make more sense for both to work together.

This can be seen in the U.S. retail industry where department store chain Kohl's has engaged in a partnership arrangement with e-commerce powerhouse Amazon. The agreement allows Amazon customers to return their purchases to Kohl's locations. Even though Amazon sells many of the same products that are also sold at Kohl's, the retail chain views this deal as an opportunity to attract more customers to their stores even if these customers did not make their purchase at a Kohl's location.

Competitors of Tomorrow

In many industries and, in particular technology-focused industries, the most dangerous competitors are the ones that have yet to emerge. Because technology-dependent industries, such as high-tech, consumer electronics and pharmaceuticals, rely heavily on innovative new products, serious competitors can appear quickly from what seems to be out of nowhere.

For instance, as discussed throughout this book, artificial intelligence (AI) has in a short time gone from being primarily a tool for high-tech users to now being utilized everyday by millions of people. For example, leading search engines including Google and Bing incorporate AI within their search options while other products, such as ChatGPT and DALL-E, give anyone the power to accomplish such tasks as gaining in-depth knowledge on almost any topic, quickly writing detailed reports, and creating professional-style images. Of course, while these tools are benefiting the regular user, there is growing concern these will potentially impact many existing jobs and businesses that offer similar products and services, such as freelance writers, graphic designers, and financial analysts. (11)

The key lesson to be learned from our examination of external factor is that marketers must constantly be aware of what is happening in the external environment, whether anticipated or unexpected (see Box 19-3), and to be prepared to take action if the need arises. As discussed in Chapter 15, if an uncontrollable factor is negatively impacting the organization, then it is imperative to have contingency plans in place in case a response is needed. But if these factors present opportunities then, as we will see in Chapter 20, having a responsive marketing planning process could offer the organization an advantage in being quick to pursue the opportunity.

Box 19-3

PREPARING FOR THE UNEXPECTED

While the seven factors cited above represent the key external variables facing an organization, there are certainly many others that hold the potential to impact the marketing function. Of course, as was discussed earlier, the widespread global pandemic the world experienced beginning in 2020 is an extreme case of an uncontrollable external factor. While situations such as the pandemic are extremely rare, others are more common. For instance, uncontrollable weather events, such as hurricanes and blizzards, can dramatically affect a marketer's ability to sell (e.g., retail store closures), distribute (e.g., roads impassable), and even promote their products (e.g., loss of electricity prevents potential customers from watching a scheduled television advertisement).

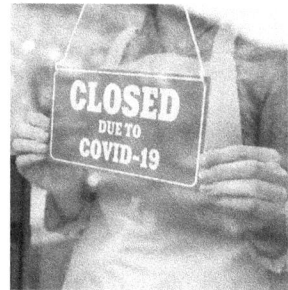

Marketers may also be negatively impacted based on perceived association rather than on the reality of a situation. This can be seen when customers associate all organizations in an industry with problems experienced by other organizations. For example, large-scale customer data breaches, including to such large firms as Microsoft, Facebook and Equifax, have led many customers to question the security of any information they provide online. Consequently, many customers now refuse to provide detailed information. (12) Whether these perceptions are true or not, all organizations in an affected industry have little choice but to immediately take action and shift resources to focus attention on such unexpected event.

REFERENCES

1. For insight on potential issues organizations may face with AI see: "Your Employer is (Probably) Unprepared for Artificial Intelligence." *The Economist*. July 16, 2023. https://www.economist.com/finance-and-economics/2023/07/16/your-employer-is-probably-unprepared-for-artificial-intelligence.

2. For insight into the potential affect driverless vehicles may have as an external force see: "Impact of Self-Driving Cars." *Wikipedia*. https://en.wikipedia.org/wiki/Impact_of_self-driving_cars.

3. An example of how sports marketers have begun targeting the older customer market can be seen with the growth of pickleball. For more see: Jaclyn Peiser. "Pickleball Craze Drives Major Shifts in Retail Landscape." *Washington Post*. September 4, 2023. https://www.washingtonpost.com/business/2023/09/04/pickleball-craze-is-big-score-business.

4. For more information on U.S. legal and regulatory issues facing marketers see: "Advertising and Marketing." *Federal Trade Commission*. https://www.ftc.gov/business-guidance/advertising-marketing.

5. For more details on Apple's "1984" ad see: "1984 (Advertisement)." *Wikipedia*. https://en.wikipedia.org/wiki/1984_(advertisement).

6. For details on the issues facing these companies see: John Harrington and Grant Suneson. "Cigarettes and Supplements Are Among the 42 Most Outrageous Product Claims of All Time." *USA Today*. May 11, 2019. https://www.usatoday.com/story/money/2019/05/11/43-most-outrageous-product-claims-of-all-time/39451953.

7. "FTC Warns Almost 700 Marketing Companies That They Could Face Civil Penalties if They Can't Back Up Their Product Claims." *Federal Trade Commission*. April 13, 2023. https://www.ftc.gov/news-events/news/press-releases/2023/04/ftc-warns-almost-700-marketing-companies-they-could-face-civil-penalties-if-they-cant-back-their.

8. "Household Savings Forecast." *Organization for Economic Cooperation and Development*. https://data.oecd.org/hha/household-savings-forecast.htm.

9. Each year the Massachusetts Institute of Technology (MIT) lists the top technologies of the year. For more see: *MIT Technology Review*. https://www.technologyreview.com.

10. For more on how AI may impact grocery retailers see: Aaron Ricadela. "Transforming Supermarkets and Grocery Stores with AI." *Oracle*. September 5, 2023. https://www.oracle.com/retail/grocery/grocery-ai.

11. For the potential threats to employment posed by AI see: "Which U.S. Workers Are More Exposed to AI on Their Jobs?" *Pew Research Center*. July 26, 2023. https://www.pewresearch.org/social-trends/2023/07/26/which-u-s-workers-are-more-exposed-to-ai-on-their-jobs.

12. For a list of major data breaches see: Kyle Chin. "Biggest Data Breaches in US History." *UpGuard*. July 18, 2023. https://www.upguard.com/blog/biggest-data-breaches-us.

Chapter 20: Marketing Planning and Strategy

In reviewing the material covered in the first 19 chapters, one conclusion can be easily drawn – marketing is a complex field. To achieve long-term success, marketers must not only consider decisions for each of the components contained in the Marketer's Toolkit, they must also understand how these elements work together to achieve the goal of creating value for customers and the organization.

In our final chapter, we see that the key for ensuring the marketing components work together is to have a full understanding of the marketing planning process. We begin with a discussion of the importance of planning and show why the development of a Marketing Plan is a necessary undertaking for nearly all marketers. As part of this discussion, we distinguish between strategies and tactics, and examine the role these play in the planning process. Next, to aid in our understanding of planning, we explore how the Product Life Cycle (PLC) offers valuable guidance for marketing decisions. We cover in detail the circumstances marketers face as their products move through the PLC and why marketing decisions must be continually fine-tuned to adjust to these changes. Throughout this discussion, we see how the PLC can offer insight into what challenges marketers may face as the market for their product continues to evolve.

IMPORTANCE OF PLANNING

As we have seen throughout this book, marketers consider many factors when making decisions. Of course, the main factors are those directly associated with how customers respond to an organization's marketing efforts, such as how they react to changes in a product, new advertisements, special pricing promotions, etc. But when making decisions, marketers face other concerns that are not directly customer related. For instance, we have discussed how marketing decisions (e.g., lowering price) may place pressure on other areas of the organization (e.g., production, shipping). Other examples of how marketing decisions may have an impact include:

◆ Marketers must be aware of how their decisions fit with the overall objectives of the organization. For example, a company whose goal is to be the low-price leader may have concerns if the company's marketing department wants to market a high-end product since this would go against the reputation and core strengths of the company.

◆ Marketing decisions also directly affect an organization's financial condition. Marketers' efforts generate the funds (i.e., sales) needed for the organization to survive but do so while using the organization's resources. Controls must be put in place to make sure the results of what the organization spends through marketing meet expectations (e.g., meets return on investment goals).

◆ Outside the organization, marketers' decisions may affect peripheral stakeholders (see Chapter 19), who are not directly connected to the marketing organization but have the potential to impact the organization if issues arise that draw their attention.

Because marketing decisions have both internal and external impact, marketers are wise to make their decisions only after engaging in careful and disciplined planning. In marketing, planning is a deliberate process in which the marketer looks to gain a full understanding of current circumstances and then use this knowledge to prepare for future events. For marketers, planning is an essential task that must be continually undertaken. As we will see, shifting market conditions, including changing customer needs and competitive threats, often lead marketers to discover that what worked in the past will not work in the future. This requires organizations to respond with revisions in how a product is marketed.

Marketing planning is also necessary since it is often a prerequisite for obtaining funding. Whether one is a marketer in a large corporation seeking additional money for her or his department, or is part of a small startup company looking for initial funding, requests for money almost always necessitates the presentation of a supporting plan.

Finally, it is risky for marketers to make hasty, off-the-cuff decisions without regard to the potential implications. Instead, with proper planning, marketing decisions can be made with consideration to the affect these have both inside and outside the organization.

THE MARKETING PLAN

The central point in planning for marketing decisions is the development of a Marketing Plan. We define the Marketing Plan as a well-researched marketing analysis that attempts to explain what has happened in the past and outlines steps that will be taken by the marketer in the future.

The scope of the Marketing Plan depends on the organization and the industry. For instance, a small technology company may have a less elaborate plan that has a short time frame enabling the company to be highly flexible and quickly adaptable to meet the needs of a rapidly changing market. A more established marketing organization, such as a large consumer products firm, may create a highly structured plan that clearly identifies all activities taking place over a 12-month period.

For companies operating separate units in different international markets, a different Marketing Plan is often needed for each market even though the same product is sold in each location. This is often necessary since the conditions for one market may be significantly different than another market and, because of this, require a different marketing approach.

Whether the marketer is creating a short plan intended to cover just a few months or a full-blown document that guides it for a year or more, nearly all plans require the undertaking of significant marketing research to gain stronger insight on the market. With knowledge of the market, the marketer can then begin to build the plan, which will include the following six components (1):

1. SITUATION ANALYSIS

The situation analysis is designed to take a snapshot of where things stand at the time the plan is developed. This part of the Marketing Plan is extremely important and quite time consuming as it looks at the current situation in terms of: 1) the components of the Marketer's Toolkit (target markets, product, distribution, promotion, and pricing); 2) the competition; 3) the financial conditions facing the organization; and 4) external forces.

2. MARKETING OBJECTIVES

The ultimate purpose of a Marketing Plan is to lead to actions that will help the organization meet a goal. The goal is reflected in one or more objectives the organization expects to achieve with its marketing efforts. The objectives flow from the top of the organization down to the marketing department. Objectives can be in the form of: 1) financial goals, such as profits; 2) sales volume or return on investment; or 3) marketing goals, such as achieving a certain level of **market share** (i.e., percentage of market held by an organization) or a certain number of visitors to an online store.

3. MARKETING STRATEGY

Achieving objectives requires the marketer engage in marketing decision making indicating where resources (e.g., marketing funds) are directed. However, before spending begins on individual marketing decisions (e.g., where to advertise), the marketer needs to establish a general plan of action summarizing what will be done to reach the stated objectives. The information produced at this stage of the planning process helps guide the development of specific tactical programs (see *Strategy and Tactical Programs* discussion below).

4. TACTICAL MARKETING PROGRAMS

Marketing strategy sets the stage for specific actions that take place. **Marketing tactics** are the day-to-day activities marketers undertake and involve the major marketing decision areas. As would be expected, this is the key area of the Marketing Plan since it explains exactly what will be done to reach the organization's marketing objectives. Of course, the majority of what is covered in this book deals with these decisions.

5. FORECASTS AND MARKETING BUDGET

Carrying out marketing tactics almost always means that money must be spent. The marketing budget lays out the spending requirements needed to implement marketing tactics. While the marketing department may request a certain level of funding they feel is required, in the end, it is upper management that will have the final say on how much financial support is offered. In most cases, such requests must be justified by showing what is expected to happen if the money is allocated. For this, marketers must develop forecasts that may include estimates of sales volume, number of customer visits, level of product awareness, coupon usage rates, and many others.

6. IMPLEMENTATION AND ANALYSIS

This part of the Marketing Plan identifies how and by whom the tactical programs are carried out. In many cases, a timeline is presented showing when tasks will occur and who will be responsible. Additionally, the Marketing Plan shows how and when success will be measured. For instance, a large retailer that introduces a new line of products may undertake sales analysis once per week to see whether the tactical marketing programs for this line are working to meet sales expectations.

STRATEGY AND TACTICAL PROGRAMS

As noted above, one of the most crucial components of the marketing planning process is the need to develop a cohesive marketing strategy that guides tactical programs for the marketing decision areas. In marketing, there are two levels to strategy formulation: General Marketing Strategies and Decision Area Strategies.

GENERAL MARKETING STRATEGIES

These set the direction for all marketing efforts by describing, in general terms, how marketing will achieve its objectives. There are many different General Marketing Strategies, though most can be viewed as falling into one of the following categories:

Market Expansion

This strategy looks to grow overall sales in one of two ways:

- Grow Sales with Existing Products – With this approach, the marketer seeks to increase the overall sales of products the company currently markets. This can be accomplished by: 1) getting existing customers in current markets to buy more; 2) getting potential customers in current markets to buy (i.e., those who have yet to buy); or 3) selling existing products in new markets.

- Grow Sales with New Products – With this approach, the marketer seeks to achieve its objectives through the introduction of new products. This can be accomplished by: 1) introducing updated versions or refinements to existing products; 2) introducing new products that are extensions of existing products; or 3) introducing new products not previously marketed.

Market Share Growth

This strategy looks to increase the marketer's overall percentage or share of the market. In many cases, this can only be accomplished by taking sales away from competitors. Consequently, this strategy often relies on aggressive marketing tactics.

Niche Market

This strategy looks to obtain a commanding position within a certain segment of the overall market. Usually, the niche market is much smaller in terms of total customers and sales volume than the overall market. Ideally, this strategy aims at positioning the product so it is viewed by customers as being different than products marketed by organizations targeting the larger market. (2)

Status Quo

This strategy looks to maintain an organization's current position in the market, such as maintaining the same level of market share.

Market Exit

This strategy looks to remove the product from the organization's product mix. This is most often accomplished by: 1) selling the product to another organization; or 2) eliminating the product. (3)

DECISION AREA STRATEGIES

These involve the decisions within key marketing areas (target marketing, product, distribution, promotion, pricing) that are guided by the General Marketing Strategy. For example, a General Marketing Strategy centering on entering a new market with new products may be supported by Decision Area Strategies that include:

- Target Market Strategy – employ segmenting techniques

- Product Strategy – develop new product line

- Distribution Strategy – use methods to gain access to distribution partners that service the target market

- Promotion Strategy – create a plan that can quickly build awareness of the product

- Pricing Strategy – create price programs that offer lower pricing versus competitors

Achieving the Decision Area Strategies is accomplished through development of a detailed Tactical Programs for each area. For instance, to meet the Pricing Strategy that lowers price below competitors, the marketer may employ such tactics as quantity discounts, trade-in allowances, or sales volume incentives to distributors.

PLANNING AND STRATEGY WITH THE PLC

As we have seen, there are many components to consider within the marketing planning process. In fact, for many marketers creating the Marketing Plan represents one of the most challenging and burdensome tasks they face. Fortunately, over the years marketing academics and professionals have put forth theories, models, and other tools to aid planning. Possibly the most widely used planning tool within marketing is the Product Life Cycle (PLC) concept, which we introduced in Chapter 7. The PLC suggests a product goes through several stages of "life" (Development, Introduction, Growth, Maturity, and Decline) with each stage presenting the marketer with different circumstances to which they must react.

As we will see, the PLC helps the marketer understand that marketing planning must change as a product moves from one stage to another. For example, marketers will find what works when appealing to customers in the Introduction stage is different than marketing methods used to attract customers during the Growth stage.

For the rest of this chapter, we offer a detailed look of how the PLC can aid marketing planning. The discussion is presented using the following assumptions and techniques:

◆ The chief scope of analysis is at the product form level, where many companies offer products with similar benefits. In Chapter 7, we suggested that electric cars would be an example of a product form (see Box 7-1). In most cases, a product form is a market with certain characteristics that change over time.

◆ We break down each stage and discuss market characteristics in terms of the following key internal and external factors:

- Level of Competition
- Nuances of the Target Market
- Available Product Options
- Price Level
- Promotional Focus
- Distribution Strategy
- Total Industry Profits

◆ While, at the general level, the PLC is divided into five main stages, we view most stages as consisting of substages that result from noticeable changes in market characteristics.

◆ While market characteristics are evaluated for the product form, we offer strategy guidance for individual brands that compete within these specific markets.

◆ The PLC is tightly linked to the Diffusion of Innovations discussed in Chapter 7. It is necessary to keep in mind the five adopter categories: Innovators, Early Adopters, Early Majority, Late Majority, and Laggards.

◆ While the examples presented in our PLC discussion focus mainly on marketing situations facing for-profit businesses, it should be understood that not-for-profit businesses are confronted with similar situations. Thus, being aware of the issues faced in the PLC will also strengthen the marketing efforts of many of these organizations.

Development Stage

The Product Life Cycle begins long before a product is brought to market. While technically sales do not start until the next stage, in the initial Development stage marketers must address many of the same issues they will face once the product is launched. Much of what happens follows our discussion of New Product Development in Chapter 7, where marketing research is the key element in planning. Most of what occurs in this stage is experienced only by companies that are on the forefront of innovation of a new product form rather than just a new brand (see Box 7-1).

In our discussion, the Development stage is divided into two distinct substages: Early Development, with characteristics outlined in Table 20-1; and Late Development, with characteristics outlined in Table 20-2.

EARLY DEVELOPMENT STAGE

For firms developing a new product form, this stage (see Table 20-1) is primarily concerned with marketing research. This stage is equivalent to the *Concept Development and Testing* step (see Chapter 7) for new product development. Customers and distribution partners are only involved to aid in information gathering, often through focus group research. Because the product form is still in early development, the marketer has yet to determine whether the company will move forward with a full product launch.

Table 20-1: Early Development Stage

Key Factors	Market Characteristics
Competition	No real competition exists since the product is in early development, much of which is in-house and not readily viewable to competitors. However, from a research perspective, competitors are now being identified.
Target Market	The target market exists only in marketing research terms. Possibly a small number of target customers are used to assist with research.
Products	The product exists only in the form of ideas and prototypes. Inventory is not yet available.
Prices	Pricing is non-existent unless a company charges its research customers a fee to be part of early product testing.
Promotion	Promotion has yet to occur as companies continue to refine their products and build their marketing plans.
Distribution	Mostly limited to internal analysis of possible distribution alternatives, though there may be some communication with a limited number of distribution partners in order to gauge interest.
Industry Profits	At this stage, there are costs only.

LATE DEVELOPMENT STAGE

Products that have moved to the late stage of development (see Table 20-2) have done so because marketing research suggests there is strong potential for success. By this point, a marketer has a real product (not just ideas) and is in the position to test it in the market. Consequently, this stage matches the *Market Testing* step for new product development. Firms electing to test their product in real "test markets" will do so using all of their marketing tools.

Table 20-2: Late Development Stage

Key Factors	Market Characteristics
Competition	While a marketer may not face competition in terms of sales, they may face competitive pressure from companies developing similar products, such as competition to acquire materials or technologies for product development, competition to line up product evaluators, and competition to get the early word out about the product to the media and other influencers. Additionally, competition may exist in the form of other types of products that potential customers currently use to satisfy needs targeted by this new product form. If these competitors are aware that a new product form is being developed, they may increase efforts to sell their products with the intention of reducing the market's need for the new product.
Target Market	Companies may test market the product among a small group of customers or within a selected geographic market.
Products	Companies researching the product form begin to produce small quantities of the product, primarily for testing or to build initial awareness (e.g., for display at trade shows).
Prices	Initial market price is discussed and if there are active test markets the company may be testing different price levels.
Promotion	Promotion often begins prior to product launch as marketers prepare the market for the product's arrival. Emphasis may be on public relations in an attempt to encourage the media to discuss the product prior to launch. If a real test market is used, companies may be testing several promotional options, including advertising and sales promotion.
Distribution	For a product sold through distributors, the groundwork is being laid to build the distribution network. In some cases, distributor education and training will start prior to the product launch.
Industry Profits	A small amount of revenue may be generated if real test markets are used but, for the most part, marketers continue to experience substantial costs.

Introduction Stage

This stage represents the launch of the new product form by one or more companies. It is done only after the marketer has created a detailed Marketing Plan. In many cases, tactical marketing decisions (target marketing, product, distribution, promotion, pricing) have been adjusted as the product has gone through the Development stage.

The Introduction stage is divided into two distinct substages: Early Introduction, with characteristics outlined in Table 20-3; and Late Introduction, with characteristics outlined in Table 20-4.

EARLY INTRODUCTION STAGE

For the early entrants in the market, a crucial goal is to create awareness for the product form. If customers can see that the product form holds similar characteristics to existing products then the marketer's task is easier since their job becomes one of convincing customers that this new product form is better than what they are currently using (e.g., *"This new style running shoe offers performance and comfort features not found with traditional running shoes."*).

However, if the product form is significantly different from existing products, then the marketer's job may be far more difficult. Under these conditions (see Table 20-3), marketers must not only make customers aware of the new product, but they must also fully explain what the product is, how it works, and what benefits are derived from its use. For some products, such as technology products, conveying this message can prove difficult as customers may not fully understand how the product works, and consequently not see a need for the product.

Another issue that often confronts new technology products is that companies selling competing products may do so by employing different and often incompatible technologies. Such products often confuse consumers as they fear one technology may ultimately win the battle and leave purchasers of other products with a product that may not be supported in the future. A possible example of this may be found within the rapidly evolving field of augmented reality (AR), which was first discussed in Chapter 12. In very general terms, AR represents technologies that insert digital information (e.g., imagery) within a person's real-world environment. An example are the digital lines that appear on a television screen to represent a first down line in American football. The AR industry has attracted many firms, including Apple, Google and Meta, who see great potential in this field, including developing specialize hardware and apps. As AR develops, what is now a crowded market is likely to see the emergence of only one or two top products, with all others eventually being displaced.

Whether customers understand the product or not, the Early Introduction stage requires promotional spending directed to addressing the need for customer education and building awareness. Also, education and awareness alone are not enough; customers must often be enticed to try a product through special promotional efforts (e.g., free trials).

Table 20-3: Early Introduction Stage

Key Factors	Market Characteristics
Competition	In many cases, when two or more companies are working to be first to market with a new product form, one company will be out ahead and for a period of time have the market to itself. However, this does not mean there is no competition. The company launching the product still faces competition from existing products customers previously purchased to satisfy their needs.
Target Market	To establish interest in the market for a new product form, marketers will initially target Innovators and, to a larger extent, Early Adopters.
Products	From the target market's perspective, product options are limited, since only one or a very small number of companies are selling products. Because of the uncertainty of whether the product will be accepted by a larger market and because of the expense involved in producing products in small volume (primarily due to low demand), there are few product options available.
Prices	In most cases, marketers follow a pricing strategy, called **price skimming**, in which price is set at a level that is much higher than can be sustained once competitors enter the market. Price skimming allows the company to recover development and initial marketing costs before the onslaught of competitors inevitably force prices lower.
Promotion	For products considered to be a leap ahead of existing products, early marketers may have some difficulty explaining how the product satisfies customers' needs. This is particularly an issue with high-tech products. In this situation, the marketer must engage in a promotional campaign designed to educate the market on the general product form and not necessarily focus only on promoting a specific brand. Additionally, sales promotion may be used to encourage product trials. Also, the sales force may begin a strong push to acquire distributors.
Distribution	Upon product launch, marketers continue efforts to build their distribution network. As we saw in the Development stage, the focus of marketers is to find distributors committed to handling the product.
Industry Profits	Marketers often experience low profits or, most likely, a loss as the cost of acquiring customers (i.e., advertising, free trials) is high. Additionally, marketers may need to pay back development expense to the corporation or to other investors.

LATE INTRODUCTION STAGE

Early entrants continue to create awareness and educate customers, but their promotional orientation may shift to a "buy-our-brand" approach if more companies enter the market. Thus, at this stage (see Table 20-4), marketers begin to position their products with the intention of separating themselves from the competition.

In many ways, this stage is where the real competition begins and aggressive marketing tactics are likely to be the norm in the very near future. However, those selling in this market must understand, that because the mass market (i.e., Early Majority) has yet to purchase in large numbers, there is still a high level of uncertainty as to whether the product form will be successful. This is especially the situation with high-tech products. As noted in the *Criticisms of the PLC* discussion Chapter 7, for technology products a chasm may appear that clearly separates buyers in this stage from potential buyers in the Growth stage. Overcoming this may require a significant change in the marketing effort that may include redesigning the product to make it much easier to use.

Table 20-4: Late Introduction Stage

Key Factors	Market Characteristics
Competition	By this stage, any company that was alone in launching the new product form is alone no longer, as it is highly likely at least one competitor (and likely more) has entered the market.
Target Market	Marketers are now engaged heavily in getting a high percentage of Early Adopters to accept the product.
Products	With competitors entering the market, choices available to customers expand, though the differences between competitors' offerings are often not significant.
Prices	Product pricing remains high, though any competitors entering at this stage may attempt to compete with the early entrants by offering a lower relative price.
Promotion	The promotional message is still one designed to educate the market on the benefits of this new product form, yet with more competition there is a noticeable increase in the use of advertising that highlights a company's brand. Also, personal selling and sales promotion have increased, especially for targeting the channel of distribution as entrants attempt to secure distributors.
Distribution	The number of distributors continues to increase with many now offering products from several market entrants (which at this point may still be only a few).
Industry Profits	Losses continue to mount due to high marketing costs and the need to recover development expense. Losses may be even higher than anticipated if the target market adopts slower than forecast or if more companies enter than were expected.

Growth Stage

The Growth stage is characterized by product sales increasing, often at an extremely rapid rate. This is often marked by large percentage sales increases over previous periods (e.g., 50 percent increase in sales from one quarter to the next). This is an indication the product has advanced beyond Early Adopters and is now being purchased by the mass market (i.e., Early Majority). It is also the stage when early entrants begin to realize profits, though the fact the market is now profitable invariably leads to increased competition. It is also the time when competitors use aggressive techniques to position their brand in a way that will separate it from the rush of new entrants. (4)

For many products, the Growth stage is represented by three distinct substages: Early Growth, with characteristics outlined in Table 20-5; Middle Growth, with characteristics outlined in Table 20-6; and Late Growth, with characteristics outlined in Table 20-7.

EARLY GROWTH STAGE

In the early part of the Growth stage (see Table 20-5), marketers are seeking to expand the market beyond the Early Adopters and into the mass market. They do this by using Market Expansion strategies (see *Strategy and Tactical Programs* discussion above) including: 1) Grow Sales with Existing Products by getting new market segments to buy the product; and 2) Grow Sales with New Products by introducing new models containing different sets of features. The latter strategy is used not only to appeal to new customers but also to encourage repeat purchasing by existing customers.

Additionally, greater emphasis is placed on using promotion to continue building awareness and driving interest in the product form. This is due to: 1) the need to reach a broader market; and 2) the need to maintain an effective **share of voice** (i.e., percentage of all promotions in the market), so the marketer's message is not lost among the increased promotional spending by competitors.

MIDDLE GROWTH STAGE

In the middle part of the Growth stage (see Table 20-6), the objective is to continue a Market Expansion strategy. The most likely strategy is to seek out new market segments that have not been targeted. Sometimes this can be done using the same products previously introduced, though in most cases entering a new market will require revisions to existing products.

This stage is also a time to focus on product positioning. The idea is to use marketing decisions to affect customers' perceptions of a brand by trying to either: 1) separate a brand from other products (i.e., differentiate); or 2) bring a brand closer to competitors' offerings (i.e., equivalency). For the **product differentiation approach**, marketers use promotional methods showing why their brand is different, while the **product equivalency approach** suggests how the brand is equal to other brands but offers notable advantages, such as a lower price.

Table 20-5: Early Growth Stage

Key Factors	Market Characteristics
Competition	Only a few competitors are in the market as others wait to see whether the mass market will adopt the product. However, competitors, who sell products customers previously purchased to satisfy needs now addressed by the new product form, may be getting very aggressive in their marketing tactics as they sense the new product form to be a threat.
Target Market	Continued focus is on Early Adopters but marketers begin to identify new market segments containing the Early Majority.
Products	A basic product sold to the Early Adopters remains but plans are underway to introduce products with different configurations, such as more options (e.g., advanced model) and fewer options (i.e., stripped-down model). This is needed in order to satisfy many different potential segments of the mass market.
Prices	The average selling price may remain high, especially in cases where market demand is strong but only a few competitors exist.
Promotion	Promotions are broadened with more emphasis on mass advertising and sales promotions to encourage product trial. Also, personal selling and sales promotions to distributors continue as marketers attempt to make inroads into distributors that target the mass market.
Distribution	Marketers look for new channels that enable the product to begin to reach the mass market. For instance, consumer products may look to gain distribution in large discount retailers.
Industry Profits	The early market entrants may begin to experience profits as early development costs have been covered and overall demand is gaining steam.

Late-to-market competitors may use a **penetration pricing approach** to establish a position in the market. Penetration pricing intentionally sets a price that is below long-term pricing in order to capture a large share of the market. In many cases, the firm will raise price once the product is established. (5)

Finally, some marketers also determine that it is time to focus on specific segments of the market by employing a niche marketing strategy. In this way, they may be shielded from competition that exists in the larger generally market, especially if the niche market is much smaller than the general market and is not likely to attract the interest of larger brands.

Table 20-6: Middle Growth Stage

Key Factors	Market Characteristics
Competition	More competitors are attracted to the market as they see the potential for high profits. Competitors selling products customers previously purchased to satisfy needs may be extremely aggressive (may be entering the Maturity stage of their product form's PLC) resulting in substantial price reductions.
Target Market	The Early Majority sector of the mass market begins to purchase in higher volume and, depending on the product, existing customers (i.e., Early Adopters) may be purchasing again. Those in the Late Majority are becoming customers.
Products	Companies increase the number of product offerings in order to differentiate themselves from competitors. In most cases, new product offerings improve on the performance or benefits offered by earlier products. However, the target market may begin to feel burdened by too many choices.
Prices	As more competitors enter with more product options, prices may begin to fall, though the effect may not be felt as strongly if demand remains high. Pricing may be somewhat more competitive if large companies, with strong financial backing, are now entering. It may also be competitive in smaller segments, where multiple companies are trying to establish a niche.
Promotion	Emphasis has shifted away from building awareness of the general product form to heavy advertising and sales promotions centered on promoting individual brands. Heavy selling and sales promotions continue with distributors.
Distribution	Distribution reaches saturation levels as nearly all possible channels are now handling the product.
Industry Profits	Marketers, who were early entrants, may begin to see high profits as demand is increasing while the pricing levels remain fairly strong. Depending on the product, unit cost of production may be dropping as manufacturing levels increase.

LATE GROWTH STAGE

Many marketers find this to be the most difficult part of the PLC. The late Growth stage (see Table 20-7) is a turbulent time with firms fighting to survive as market growth slows. This is not to say that overall sales are declining but that the percentage of growth from one period to the next is declining. For instance, sales over a three-year period may show an overall increase, but it is occurring at a decreasing rate compared to previous years (e.g., 20%, 15%, 10%). While this example evaluates decline in terms of year-over-year change, for products in fast changing markets, such as high-tech products, the measure may be better examined by comparing a shorter time frame, such as a three-month quarter-over quarter comparison.

The key objective for a marketer is to remain competitive by maintaining an overall market power position (e.g., promote product as being a trusted leading brand) or by achieving an insulated position within a niche market segment (e.g., promote product as offering strong benefits not offered by leading brands). Brands may use various marketing tactics that keep existing customers happy (e.g., earned points programs, improved customer service) while also enticing new customers to try the product (e.g., rebates, extended payment, try-before-you-buy). The marketer may encourage distribution partners to remain loyal by offering such incentives as attractive pricing, promotional assistance, and customized packaging.

Table 20-7: Late Growth Stage

Key Factors	Market Characteristics
Competition	The market begins to see slower growth and companies find themselves in a highly competitive market. Fierce battles may occur on some fronts, such as within segments where demand is falling faster than in other segments.
Target Market	The overall market is still growing in terms of sales volume, especially as the product spreads to the Late Majority. But there is some evidence that, while sales are increasing, overall growth is occurring at a decreasing rate compared to previous time periods.
Products	With so many competitors offering numerous product options, customers may be overwhelmed and confused by the choices available. In cases where customers do not fully understand the product (e.g., technology product), they may feel more comfortable purchasing only the top brands or products sold at leading distributors (e.g., top retailers), who may offer a generous product return policy
Prices	The average price is falling rapidly as market growth begins to slow and competitors struggle to maintain their market share. Price wars may break out.
Promotion	There is heavy spending on advertising and especially on sales promotions offering purchase and repurchase incentives.
Distribution	With demand beginning to slow, some distributors cut back on the number of products they stock. They may even threaten to stop carrying products if leading product marketers do not offer additional incentives.
Industry Profits	Marketers begin to see a leveling off of profits as overall revenue flattens due to slowing demand and falling prices. However, marketing costs still remain high.

Maturity Stage

At some point in time, sales begin slowing down for the product form. Instead of double-digit growth from one period to the next, the industry limps along with low, single digit sales increases or worse. There are two key reasons why this occurs. First, the market has become saturated and a large majority of potential customers has already purchased the product. In the case of products that have a long **buy-cycle** (i.e., time between repeat purchases), the infrequency of repurchase results in slow sales for some time. (6)

Second, customers have moved on to purchase other products that are seen as replacements for this product form. In this situation, the growth of the product form may have been interrupted with the introduction of a new product form (e.g., standard thermostats being replaced by internet-connected smart thermostats).

The slowing of market growth is a signal the product form may have reached the Maturity stage of the PLC (see Box 20-1). In our discussion, the Maturity stage is divided into two distinct sub-stages: Early Maturity, with characteristics outlined in Table 20-8, and Late Maturity, with characteristics outlined in Table 20-9.

Box 20-1

WHEN MARKET GROWTH SLOWS

Reaching the Maturity stage in the PLC means that marketers can no longer count on the growth in the overall market as the trigger for increased company sales. This can be best explained by examining the data presented in the table below, which shows company sales over three consecutive periods (e.g., quarters, years).

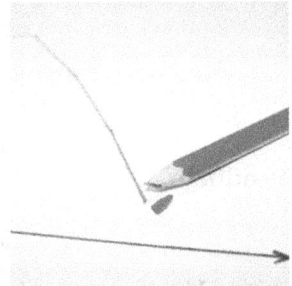

As shown, during the PLC Growth stage (Period 1 to Period 2) a marketer may see product sales increase without the need for an increase in market share. Under this market condition, the marketer can still do well without having to grow its percentage of the market. In fact, if its market share dropped to 6 percent in Period 2 the marketer would still realize an overall sales increase compared to the previous period (200,000 x 6% = 12,000 units). But in Period 3 overall market sales have leveled off and maintaining the same level of market share no longer leads to increased growth. This situation makes for a very competitive market as firms fight to increase sales by increasing their market share.

Period	Market Size	Market Share	Company Sales
1	100,000	10%	10,000 units
2	200,000	10%	20,000 units
3	200,000	10%	20,000 units

EARLY MATURITY STAGE

In the early part of the Maturity stage (see Table 20-8), the key objective is to enact strategies that enable a product to survive in the face of strong competition driven by decreasing demand. In fact, marketers may be happy following a Status Quo strategy intended just to maintain their market position. Unfortunately, this may prove quite difficult as this stage (often called the **shakeout stage**) leads to many products failing or being absorbed by competitors (i.e., companies merge with competitors, companies sell products to competitors).

In order to survive, marketers may need to resort to tactics designed to "steal customers" from their competitors, which often involves significant price promotions (e.g., heavy discounting) or strong promotions intended to improve image or solidify a niche. Marketers, who have avoided competing on price, may be in a better position to weather the storm if they have convinced the market their product contains unique features that few other products offer. This can be the case if they have successfully established a strong position in a niche market.

A more likely scenario for companies at this stage is to employ new tactics to regrow their market in an effort to extend the Growth stage of the PLC. The use of so-called **resurgence tactics** includes such measures as:

- Changing how customers use the product including: encouraging more frequent use or more consumption per usage (e.g., consume two units at a time instead of one unit); suggesting new benefits that can be obtained from using the product (e.g., has added health benefits not previously promoted); or suggesting new uses for the product with promotional messages, such as: *"Did you know our product can also do this?"*

- Finding new markets not previously targeted, such as moving beyond the consumer market into business markets or expanding to global markets.

- Developing new product options (i.e., product line extensions) that offer more or better features (e.g., easier to use, safer, more attractive) that may get existing customers to re-purchase more quickly than they would normally.

- Heightening interest by changing the product's perceived image through such methods as heavy promotion and package redesign.

- Competing with lower priced brands by offering an alternative low-price product through private branding arrangement with distribution partners (see *Private Label or Store Branding* discussion in Chapter 6).

Table 20-8: Early Maturity Stage

Key Factors	Market Characteristics
Competition	By far the fiercest competition takes place at this stage as marketers move to grab customers from weakened competitors. At this stage, many competitors fail or merge with others.
Target Market	Little or no growth is occurring as the market is saturated or the target market looks to other products to satisfy its needs. Laggards may start buying but only if they can no longer purchase products they previously purchased to satisfy their needs.
Products	Many products are still marketed though some level of **product standardization** has occurred. Any new models introduced do not lead to significant improvement in product performance. At best, the new models offer minor, incremental improvements.
Prices	The average price continues to fall possibly below cost as competitors attempt to remain in the market. Price wars occur in many segments.
Promotion	Heavy competitive advertising and extensive promotions take place with the objective of getting existing customers to switch (for their repeat purchases). The same occurs in the distribution channel as marketers try to encourage distributors not to drop the product from their inventory.
Distribution	Distributors continue to reduce their inventory and promotional expense for the product form. They also become extremely selective on the products they will carry. At the retail level, shelf space begins to decline for the product form.
Industry Profits	Industry profits fall rapidly and many firms lose money as they increase spending in hopes of remaining in the market.

LATE MATURITY STAGE

If companies have failed to extend the PLC in the early part of the Maturity stage, there is a low probability the product form will experience growth again (see Box 20-2 for how growth may still occur). Instead, companies will continue to market the product, albeit with little effort other than making it available to customers who have been purchasing it for some time.

By the late part of the Maturity stage (see Table 20-9), marketers that are still selling may no longer consider the product to be important for the future of their organization. However, this does not mean the product no longer holds value. In fact, for some brands, particularly those that were market leaders, the product may be extremely valuable for the profit it continues to generate (a.k.a. **cash cow**), which is then used to fund new products. Consequently, some attention is still paid to the product but only to ensure that it is still available for those who want to purchase.

Table 20-9: Late Maturity Stage

Key Factors	Market Characteristics
Competition	The competitive landscape has stabilized. The only survivors remaining are a few market giants and several small niche firms.
Target Market	The market has very few first-time buyers and almost all companies now focus on getting existing customers to remain loyal.
Products	There is a significant reduction in the introduction of new models. Any new models focus mostly on just a few minor performance enhancements and stylistic improvements.
Prices	Overall prices stabilize and may rise due to limited competition.
Promotion	Large competitors begin to cut back on expensive promotions designed to attract new customers and focus on reminder promotions to loyal customers.
Distribution	Overall, distribution has stabilized with few new distributors agreeing to handle the product. For products sold through retail stores, only a small amount of shelf space is devoted to the product.
Industry Profits	Companies see profits recover as demand stabilizes, prices rise, and marketing expenditure to support the product declines.

Decline Stage

A product form has reached the Decline stage when it becomes clear the market is no longer able to sustain itself, unless something unexpected or unusual occurs in the market (see Box 20-2). Similar to the Maturity stage, the Decline stage may last for an extended period of time, especially for products that have been adopted by a large percentage of the market, who are not inclined to purchase a different product to satisfy their needs (i.e., those considered to be Laggards). (7)

Since the end of the product form is seen as inevitable, there are no substages here. In fact, marketers are faced with Market Exit strategies when they reach the Decline stage (see Table 20-10). There are two ways marketers can address this. First, companies may consider a **milking strategy** that involves getting the most out of the product in terms of sales without spending any additional funds to support the product. This strategy works best if a sizable market remains that is loyal to the product and not particularly price sensitive. A customer base with these characteristics allows a marketer to ride through the Decline stage for some time while earning sizable profits.

Second, companies may look to sell off or divest the product. In some situations, this can be done by making a small investment to slightly improve the product in order for it to be more attractive to companies interested in acquiring the product.

However, discontinuing a product does not mean a marketer no longer earns revenue from the product form. Many discontinued products, especially those used in business and industrial settings, will continue to earn money through support services, such as selling supplies and service/repair contracts. (7)

Table 20-10: Decline Stage

Key Factors	Market Characteristics
Competition	As time goes on firms drop out until ultimately there is no one producing the product.
Target Market	Mostly consists of Laggards, who have been loyal to this type of product for a long time and have not moved on to newer products.
Products	No new improvements are introduced and some models are discontinued.
Prices	Prices may be rising as competitors drop out and companies still in the market have little incentive to engage in price competition. Also, there may be a large, loyal market that may not be sensitive to price increases. However, some companies looking to get out of the market but that have existing inventory may drastically markdown the product to encourage rapid sales.
Promotion	Companies limit promotions to occasional reminders directed at loyal customers, though overall little is spent.
Distribution	With declining demand distributors are removing products. The marketer may even make the decision to remove the product from unprofitable distributors. Sales may shift to online-only distribution or via other non-traditional channels.
Industry Profits	For companies remaining, profits may be stable and possibly significant if this stage takes a long time to play out.

Box 20-2

THE UNUSUAL CASE OF VINYL RECORDS DEFYING PRODUCT LIFE CYCLE THEORY

There is a good chance that most individuals who are under 35 years old have likely never had the experience of placing a vinyl record onto a turntable. Possibly in a club they have observed a DJ using this musical format but that may be as close as they have come. For this generation, and even for many people over 35 years old, vinyl records and turntables are old technologies, which many believe, has been replaced with the convenience of digital recordings.

Since it has been such a long time since vinyl recordings were the main form of listening to music (35 or more years at this point), most people would assume this product form has long ago left the Maturity stage of the Product Life Cycle and must now rests deep within the bowels of the Decline stage.

Well, maybe that is not quite what is happening. Sure, there is a large number of Laggards that still prefer the sound of vinyl recordings over digital, but PLC strategy suggests when products reach the Decline stage of the PLC, companies have little incentive to innovate or invest in the product form and, thus it is destined to die. That is, unless the product form experiences a reawakening that attracts new users.

This appears to be the situation with vinyl records. The interest in this old technology is growing and not just with old folks. Customers are demanding these products mostly because they believe the quality of sound recording on vinyl is superior to other audio formats, though others appreciate the "physical interaction" that is required to listen to records. (8)

For marketers, the problem is whether this is a trend that is sustainable and not just a fad. Companies producing vinyl are in a tough spot as most of the equipment used to press records (i.e., the term for how records are manufactured) is quite old and replacement parts are expensive. Yet if demand continues to grow, it is possible we can see a very unusual example of how a product that is all but dead, defies PLC theory and once again becomes a growth product.

REFERENCES

1. While these six concepts represent the main parts of the Marketing Plan, other items may also be included. For detailed explanation on creating a Marketing Plan see the "How to Write a Marketing Plan" tutorials found on *KnowThis.com*, the support website for this book. https://www.knowthis.com.

2. Many small businesses are successful by focusing their marketing strategy on niche markets. For more see: Alexandra Sheehan. "Start Selling in a Niche Market Today: 9 Examples." *Shopify*. December 12, 2022. https://www.shopify.com/blog/niche-markets.

3. Large organizations regularly undertake a review process to assess the future viability of products. For instance, Amazon removed 27 of its 30 private label clothing brands in an effort to reduce costs, though some experts believe it was also a move to reduce government scrutiny of the company's business practices. For more see: Dana Mattioli. "Amazon Cuts Dozens of House Brands as It Battles Costs, Regulators." *The Wall Street Journal*. August 10, 2023. https://www.wsj.com/articles/amazon-cuts-dozens-of-house-brands-as-it-battles-costs-regulators-3f6ad56d.

4. Television streaming is an example of an industry entering the PLC Growth stage and has attracted a number of major media players. For a summary of this industry and the competition see: "List of Streaming Media Services." *Wikipedia*. https://en.wikipedia.org/wiki/List_of_streaming_media_services.

5. However, as was noted in Box 18-3 in Chapter 18, setting a price that is intentionally low with the purpose of driving out competitors is likely to be viewed as predatory pricing and is considered illegal in many countries.

6. An example of a product struggling in the maturity stage due to a long buy-cycle can be seen with the Instant Pot multicooker. Because a large part of the target market has already purchased this or similar competitors' products, sales have dropped significantly from peak levels. This was a major reason Instant Pot's parent company was forced to declare bankruptcy as explained here: Jesus Jiménez. "The Instant Pot Was Beloved. Now Its Maker Has Filed for Bankruptcy." *New York Times*. June 15, 2023. https://www.nytimes.com/2023/06/15/business/instant-brands-bankruptcy.html.

7. Some products can reach the Decline stage in a very short period of time due to the products failing to be accepted by the market. This means these products experienced a very quick trip through the PLC. For examples of products with a short PLC see: Ben Gilbert and Lakshmi Varanasi. "33 of the Biggest Failed Products from the World's Biggest Companies." *Business Insider*. August 4, 2023. https://www.businessinsider.com/biggest-product-flops-in-history-2016-12.

8. For metrics showing the growth of vinyl records in the U.S. see: Marie Charlotte Götting. "Retail Value of LP/EP Shipments in the United States." *Statista*. March 28, 2023. https://www.statista.com/statistics/186814/value-of-non-cd-album-shipments-in-the-us-music-industry-since-1999.

Marketing Case Studies

ATHLETES ATTIRE

Summary

A small clothing company, focused on athletic sportswear for women and men, must find ways to respond to slowing sales. While the company's founder does not see a need for major changes, the marketing staff may have different ideas.

Situation

Athletes Attire is a manufacturer and marketer of products in the active sportswear market. Their products consist of women's and men's workout pants and shirts. Designs for both the women's and men's products are similar, though these differ slightly to address differences between the body features of each gender. Both the women's and men's line of workout pants consist of a single style (traditional long leg with elastic waist) that are available in two colors (light gray and dark blue) and four sizes (small, medium, large, and extra-large). For the women's workout shirt line there are two styles (short-sleeve and sleeveless), four colors (light blue, pink, white, and black) and four sizes (extra small, small, medium, and large). While the men's workout shirts are sold in two styles (short sleeve and sleeveless), two colors (white and dark blue) and three sizes (medium, large, and extra-large).

Although the number of styles and colors is small compared to their competitors, Athletes Attire feels limited selection provides certain benefits. First, they concentrate their styles and colors on traditional offerings that are slow to go out of fashion. By doing this, Athletes Attire feels consumers are more likely to wear the outfits longer and, consequently, may feel they are obtaining more value for their money. Second, fewer styles and colors help the firm reduce product costs since less raw materials are needed and production runs are maximized. Third, the company believes their distributors (retailers) do not like to handle many different styles since it requires the retailers to devote more space on their store shelves. Finally, Sue Bradley, the company's president, feels strongly that to remain competitive her firm must spend more of its time and money improving operations (e.g., production) rather than trying to set fashion trends. She often tells her staff: *"Let the other guys set the fashion trends with new designs, and we will set the sales trends with lower costs and lower prices."*

Athletes Attire has been in business for over 20 years. Bradley created the company when she became frustrated with the product selections she found in her local clothing and sporting goods stores. *"I went to the stores looking to buy simple clothing that I could use when I exercise. But fashion-wise, the clothing I saw was just over-the-top and very expensive. I created these designs myself, and I think these are pretty good for addressing the needs of those looking for something basic."* When asked to elaborate on how the company knows how customers view their products, Bradley responded: *"Not really sure. We don't spend much time asking customers what they think. If they contact us by email or by phone, we may ask how they like our products, but otherwise we base customers' opinions on how sales are going."*

The company's marketing staff consists of two full-time employees, who share a wide range of duties, including dealing with retail customers (i.e., stores that sell the company's products), developing and executing promotional strategy, and attending a few industry trade shows. As one employee noted: *"Most of our time is spent talking with retailers about orders they placed or products they want to return. We do occasionally try to attract new retailers through things like trade shows, but the president feels we are better off having retailers contact us instead of us spending a lot of time trying to sell to retailers."* The marketing department also hires a part-time college intern, who works for four months. Over the course of a year, the department will have three interns - one for the spring, one for the summer and one for the fall. Interns are primarily responsible for updating Athletes Attire's website and occasionally posting information to social media. The intern is also responsible for finding news reports that discuss competitors and passing this information on to the full-time staff. As a marketing employee noted: *"I would say the information we get from the interns is how we learn the most about our competitors. We cannot really afford to do much marketing research, so we need to rely on what our interns find."*

In the past, Athletes Attire has limited their consumer advertising to occasional ads in a few family-oriented magazines including Family Circle and Redbook. These ads have not changed much in the last five years because, *"Our ads are simple and to the point, and we think people get the message,"* says Bradley. Recently, to help conserve their promotional resources, Athletes Attire has cut back on the number of ads they place, and they are also now running these in black-and-white rather than color.

Athletes Attire sells its clothes mainly through a few discount clothing stores, including national chains Marshalls and Ross, and regional chains, such as Boscov's. Typically, these retailers carry products from several clothing manufacturers. They also may carry their own line of sportswear, which is normally priced below brand name products.

In the last few years, Athletes Attire has seen sales decline. No one is quite sure why, but Bradley thinks it is a short-run problem that can be attributed to several chain retailers closing a number of their locations. *"Things will turn around soon. All we need to do is to get our retailers to work a little harder."* Others in the company are not so sure and think lower sales may be a symptom of deeper problems. Says one employee, "*Our distributors are beginning to pinch us for every penny we have. They claim the market for this product is just not as great as it used to be. I think we have real problems that our company needs to address very soon.*"

Concern is growing within the marketing staff that Bradley is too ambitious when she recently stated at a staff meeting: "*I think if we get creative we can grow sales by a minimum of 15% in the next 12 months. We just have to be smart about it since we really cannot afford to spend more on marketing next year.*" Bradley has instructed the marketing department to review the "*entire marketing program and report back to me with appropriate recommendations for reaching our sales goal.*" She also made it clear she would be willing to "*listen to any and all ideas you have to get us to our target goal.*"

Issues to Consider

1. How do you feel about the circumstances Athletes Attire is facing? Should Bradley be concerned with the direction the company is heading? If so, offer reasons why this is the case. If not, explain why you feel Bradley should not be overly concerned.

2. Assume you are the head of marketing for Athletes Attire. Discuss what you would do to increase company sales. Make sure to include any ramifications your plan will have on the company's current business. Also, explain how you would present your results to Bradley. What will it take to be convincing in your presentation?

3. Assess the comments made by Bradley. What is your sense of Bradley as a manager and her vision for the company?

4. What do you think of Athletes Attire distribution strategy? If you feel this strategy is not working, then suggest what can be done to improve it. If you believe the company is following the right distribution strategy, then suggest what can be done to encourage their retailers to sell more.

5. Research the sportswear industry and identify companies that would "likely" be viewed as competitors to Athletes Attire. Justify your reasons for selecting these companies.

6. Discuss how Athletes Attire's market has changed over the last 10 years. Where do you see this market heading in the next 10 years?

THE ALWAYS-ON-TIME DELIVERY COMPANY

Summary

A regional package delivery company must consider several marketing issues as it makes plans to expand into the overnight delivery market. Prior to presenting the plan to senior management, vice-president of marketing, Bill Carson, has called a department meeting to evaluate the plan one last time.

Situation

"I think we have a real shot at taking some of their business away," said Bill Carson during a department meeting. *"I think they are very vulnerable to our strategy."* Bill Carson is vice-president of marketing for The Always-On-Time (AOT) Delivery Company, a regional shipper of packages. He is talking about a new overnight delivery service his company is considering. Although overnight shipment has long been dominated by big name players, such as FedEx and UPS, Carson believes AOT has one significant advantage over its competitors: price. *"If we can convince people that our service is just as good as what our competitors offer but is cheaper, we are bound to capture a good chunk of the overnight shipping market."*

AOT, which is headquartered in central Pennsylvania, has been in the package delivery business for ten years. The company only handles business-to-business package delivery. AOT's main shipping area encompassing the Northeast region of the United States. Their shipping area covers most deliverable addresses from the middle of Virginia to Massachusetts. Unlike their bigger competitors, which operate throughout the world, AOT has chosen a strategy that is summed up in their advertising slogan, *We Don't Want The World's Business, We Only Want Your Business!*

Currently, AOT provides a guarantee of 2-day delivery on all packages shipped within their coverage area. AOT uses a pricing model where shipping cost is calculated based on distance and weight. Examples of the pricing structure are shown in the table below. Total shipping cost is calculated by first identifying the distance range and then multiplying the package weight by the cost-per-pound and adding the minimum shipping charge. For example, shipping a 30-pound package 150 miles will cost $17.50 ($7.00 + [30lbs. x $ .35]).

Distance (miles)	Minimum Shipping Charge	Cost per Pound
< 50	$5.00	$.30
50 - 99	$6.00	$.33
100 - 200	$7.00	$.35
> 200	$8.00	$.38

While customers can place pickup orders through the AOT website, the most profitable customers are those who fall under the "locked in" category. "Locked in" customers receive special shipping rates and are provided with a regularly scheduled pick-up time when an AOT vehicle will come to their location. Schedules vary from daily pickup to twice-a-week pickup (AOT does not offer their "locked in" customers pickup that is less than two times in a week.) As part of the "locked in" program, customers agree to have packages to ship on the designated pickup day. If a customer does not have packages when the AOT vehicle arrives, the "locked in" agreement states that AOT can charge a $10 Inconvenience Fee. But as Carson notes, "*We rarely enforce the Inconvenience Fee. Yes, some customers may take advantage of us and regularly do not have packages to ship, but the fact we can include them as being a customer when we talk to other potential customers makes up for the times they do not have a package.*"

Most "locked in" customers are recruited by a small two-person sales force. These salespeople spend about 50% of their time finding new customers. They primarily cold call customers over the phone, though at least one day a week they do travel to locations within their assigned territories.

In addition to its headquarters, AOT has additional distribution locations in upstate New York and southern Delaware. The company picks up packages at customers' business locations and delivers these to one of its distribution centers, where packages are sorted, loaded on an outbound vehicle, and then shipped. AOT does not use aircraft to ship packages. Instead, the company maintains a fleet of trucks, vans, and SUVs to handle product delivery. As Carson explains, "*Having a fleet of aircraft is extremely expensive to operate. We feel that we can provide the same level of service as our competitors but at a lower price since we do not have the high overhead costs that our competitors likely have.*"

Carson believes AOT's current distribution system is sufficient for handling a new overnight service. He feels all that is needed to handle the new service is a few more drivers and vehicles. "*Seventy-five percent of our current business is done in an area that spans 300 miles north-to-south by 50 miles east-to-west along the Interstate 95 corridor. We believe that a package given to us by noon can be delivered to its destination by ten o'clock the next day using just our transportation fleet. We realize some packages may miss this delivery time, but the overwhelming majority should make it there on time.*"

Carson believes the time is right to introduce the overnight service for three reasons:

1. Research indicates the overall market for shipping business packages in the Northeast region has grown at a rate of 8% per year for the last 3 years. Though that number is derived from all types of shipping and not just overnight shipping.

2. Carson believes the major shippers are too consumed with being the biggest rather than being the best. Because of this, he feels competitors cannot develop strong customer relationships the way AOT believes it can.

3. In conversations with a few customers, Carson feels customers are interested in a lower priced shipper for overnight delivery. *"Clearly there is a void, and we think we are the best at filling it."*

In discussions with AOT's senior management and with his marketing staff, Carson has set a goal of generating $3 million in revenue from the overnight shipping in the first year. Carson is budgeting $75,000 for advertising and $20,000 for increased sales force expense. Additionally, AOT anticipates it will need to spend up to $300,000 for new vehicles, equipment, and to hire and train additional drivers.

Carson knows that getting the message out will take some time. Since the company's clients are mainly small-to-medium size businesses, Carson believes promotion should start with existing customers. He feels a postcard campaign introducing the service along with updates to the website and an email blast will help spread the word. Also, he wants the sales force to spend more time in the field letting existing customers know about the overnight delivery service. However, he is adamant when it comes to promotional spending: *"We are positioning ourselves as a low-cost alternative to the bigger guys. Because we offer lower prices, we must be very conservative with our promotional spending."*

Though Carson is saying the company's overnight delivery service will be priced lower than competitors, he has suggested the price will not be that much lower. *"Even if we are just a few cents lower we can still boast that we are the low-price provider. We just need to make sure that is the case."*

Before a final decision is made to introduce the overnight delivery service, Carson must once again present the plan to AOT's senior management. His presentation is in a few hours, and he wants to make sure he has all the information needed to address any questions members of AOT's senior management may raise. At a final department meeting to go over the plan, Carson says: *"I think the plan looks good. Do you see anything that is missing or that we really need to discuss with this plan?"*

Issues to Consider

1. What do you think of Carson's plan to enter the overnight package delivery market? What do you see as the key advantages and disadvantages of this plan? As part of your evaluation, consider the plan in terms of important marketing issues related to understanding customers, marketing research, and marketing mix decisions.

2. Evaluate the three reasons Carson cites for why he believes the time is right for entering the overnight shipping business. Are there any issues Carson may be overlooking with the reasons he has stated? If so, suggest how these may impact what Carson already believes.

3. How do you feel about Carson's explanation regarding not charging "locked in" customers the Inconvenience Fee if they do not have packages to ship?

4. Assess Carson's promotional plan for introducing overnight delivery.

5. Research the 2-day ground delivery pricing rates for FedEx and UPS. How does AOT's pricing compare? Carson claims AOT's key advantage in the package delivery market is pricing. How can AOT be assured they are the low-price shipper?

6. Assuming AOT introduces overnight delivery, what pricing model should they follow? How would the pricing model you have developed compare to AOT's main competitors?

CALIFORNIA PLAYSETS

Summary

Ralph Fallows is looking to extend his streak of successful retail businesses with a new venture targeting the play equipment market. Based in California, Ralph wants to have stores across the U.S. within two years and international locations within four years. To reach this goal, he believes his company will need to engage in aggressive word-of-mouth promotion and intense personal selling.

Situation

Ralph Fallows is a man who has become highly successful investing in different retail concepts. While still in college, with the help of funds from his parents, he bought a food truck from an owner who was retiring. Ralph ran the food truck for a year, but after he had issues with where the city would allow him to park his truck, he sold his business for a small profit. After he had graduated, Ralph saw opportunity in pizza retailing. He bought a small pizzeria store and within two years had opened four additional locations. Despite several run-ins with local government food inspectors, Ralph's Pizza became a popular spot. It caught the attention of a bigger pizza chain, which offered to buy out Ralph's stake. He felt the offer was too good to pass up, so he sold and decided to move on.

His next venture was in frozen yogurt. He again bought an existing operation, this one with two stores. He grew his California-based company to 40 locations in four U.S. states. However, as the chain expanded Ralph became frustrated with what he considered to be "stupid stuff." For instance, he disliked dealing with some workers who he regarded as constant complainers and not team players. *"I realize I sometimes do things that are not always understood by my people, but that is why we have become successful,"* he once told an industry magazine. After a five-year run with the frozen yogurt business, Ralph again decided to sell the business, and he is now considering a new challenge.

Ralph has thought long and hard about a new opportunity and believes he has finally come up with it: children's playsets. Ralph thinks this is a viable market. He also suspects a company devoted to the sale and installation of play equipment has tremendous potential. He supports this by telling his new staff:

1. *"Many parents, who are dual income couples, can afford expensive playsets. And, they are not only buying these to please their kids, but they may also be buying so they can show off to their neighbors."*

2. *"It is pretty clear that parents are recognizing the importance of physical activity in their children's daily routine and are encouraging them to play outdoors more often."*

3. *"More children are populating states in the south and west where outdoor activities are more likely to be all year round. There is no doubt this part of the U.S. offers great potential."*

4. *"Daycare is an exploding industry, and play equipment is in high demand. That is the one market that may be the easiest to enter."*

Ralph feels the time is right to target the play equipment market. To his knowledge, there are only a few firms catering strictly to this market. He would like to launch his operation in California within the next six months and hopes the company will have a national presence within two years. And, if all goes well, he envisions international expansion within four years.

The current plan is to start with a limited number of products. Ralph's idea is to pay a professional designer to create initial product designs. He is also considering outsourcing product manufacturing, at least until demand grows to a level that will make it economical to hire his own manufacturing unit. Ralph plans to expand product offerings once the company has established locations throughout the U.S.

In Ralph's mind, the company will initially sell three levels of playsets. The levels differ in terms of the size and design of the base structure, which become larger as the product levels increase. Additionally, as levels increase so will the price. Though prices have not been determined, Ralph feels the base structures will range from $2,000 to $6,000. While the base structures provide general play equipment features, such as swings and a basic sliding board, the company will also sell add-on products, such as circular tube slides, tot swings, and climbing walls.

Ralph believes establishing a successful business in the play equipment market requires excellence in two methods of promotion: active word-of-mouth and strong personal selling. For word-of-mouth, Ralph predicts significant postings to *"sharing outlets,"* including social media, product review websites and discussion forums, will help to quickly build awareness and interest. He expects to *"be creative and maybe a little over the top"* in the use of these outlets. In discussing his word-of-mouth ideas, Ralph feels customers are so dependent on sharing outlets they often trust what they experience on these outlets more than what they experience with product advertisements. He imagines his company's marketing department hiring several engagement officers, who spend nearly all their time communicating on sharing outlets. *"In today's world, advertising is not the way to get to people, we need to directly engage them,"* Ralph tells his staff.

Ralph has suggested many times that engagement does not always mean being an obvious company representative. *"Many companies have staff members post comments even without indicating they are part of the company they are discussing. I don't see a big issue with doing this as long as we are not overtly negative about our competitor's products. People want information, and if we give them the right information, then I don't feel we always need to identify who we are."*

To Ralph, engaging people on sharing outlets will be the key to generating customer traffic. Once prospective customers are in the store, Ralph believes closing a sale will require his salespeople be exceedingly friendly and somewhat aggressive. In Ralph's mind, selling play equipment is much like selling automobiles in that customers *"come to the store knowing they want something, they just are not sure what that something is that they want."* To convince customers to make a purchase, Ralph is planning to build a sales force that is highly trained and able to handle different types of customers. He also believes offering high commissions will provide a strong incentive for the sales force to work hard. The initial plan is to offer a standard 15% commission for selling the base units while selling add-on features will result in a 20% commission.

Once purchased, the playset will be shipped to the buyer's location. During the sales process, the sales force will encourage buyers to have their playset installed by the company (for a fee), though customers may opt to handle their own installation. In addition to offering commissions to their salespeople, Ralph also is considering offering incentives to the installation team. These employees can earn additional money if they can persuade buyers to purchase add-on products after a playset has been delivered.

For Ralph, this business concept seems like a sure winner. He is convinced the combination of strong products and aggressive promotion is perfect for the play equipment market. He believes parents, who are buying for their children, will not be too concerned with price since *"many parents will want their kids to have the best playset in the neighborhood."* And business buyers, such as daycare facilities and summer camps, will want high-end, sturdy products that will be functional for many years. Ralph is confident his approach to this market is the right way to go. To him, the task is straightforward: *"If we can just get these people in the door, I am sure we can sell them a great product. It is all about making sure we get the word out, so people know who we are."*

Issues to Consider

1. Review the statements Ralph has made regarding the viability of this market. Is his assessment a good one? What are some issues he may not be considering? Is Ralph realistic in hoping to have locations nationwide within two years and international locations in four years?

2. Evaluate what Ralph likely experienced while building his first three businesses. What advantages and disadvantages does this suggest for the likelihood of being a successful company in the play equipment market?

3. What do you think about Ralph's declaration that the keys to being successful in the play equipment market are word-of-mouth promotion and personal selling? Are there other marketing or business issues that may hold equal or greater importance?

4. How do you feel about Ralph's statement regarding company employees not identifying who they are when posting to sharing sites? Are there any ethical concerns with this form of promotion?

5. What is your view of Ralph's statement that customers shopping for playsets can be compared to customers shopping for automobiles? What are the similarities and differences between each? Also, does Ralph's statement apply to both parents and business buyers, such as daycare facilities, camps, and schools?

6. How do you feel about the way Ralph plans on using "sharing outlets" to build customer interest? What issues may he not be considering with the tactics he is suggesting?

7. Assume Ralph has delegated all marketing decisions to you with the understanding that your ideas may be different than his. Lay out a marketing plan for this company indicating your suggestions for addressing target market, product, distribution, promotion, pricing and other relevant decisions.

SNAPPY SNACKS

Summary

Molly Smith, product manager for a manufacturer and marketer of spicy snack products, must decide how to address sluggish sales of a newly introduced product. Potentially complicating the situation are Molly's assistant product managers, who appear to have different ideas on what needs to happen to improve sales.

Situation

Molly Smith had heard the commotion before she entered the conference room. *"Push"* said Sarah Martin in a loud tone. *"Pull"* shouted back Kirk Jenkins even louder. Molly is a product manager for Snappy Snacks, a U.S. manufacturer of consumer snack foods. Snappy Snacks' products are distributed primarily in grocery stores throughout the U.S. and in 12 countries. Within the snack food industry, Snappy Snacks is considered a niche brand with a focus on marketing mostly spicy flavored products. This niche approach has served the company well. The Snappy Snacks brand name is often one that consumers mention when asked to list companies that come to mind when they hear the phrase "spicy snack food."

Currently, Snappy Snacks product mix includes both traditional snack foods and specialty snack products. Traditional snacks consist of various types of spicy flavored potato chips, tortilla chips, and pretzels. Specialty snacks consist of products that fall into one of three categories: 1) products that are not distributed widely (e.g., products for regional tastes); 2) products considered to be seasonal (e.g., summer snacks); and 3) so-called "stand alone" products that Snappy Snacks sells in only one product form (e.g., a single popcorn product).

Because of their niche approach, most Snappy Snacks products tend to be priced somewhat higher than leading mass-market snack brands. When explaining this pricing strategy to retailers and other distributors, the Snappy Snacks sales force is trained to present research demonstrating how consumers are willing to pay extra for the unique flavors that Snappy Snacks' products provide.

Smith, who is responsible for the company's specialty line, has called a meeting to review results of their newest snack product, Hot Sauce Flavored Potato Skins (HSFPS). As the name states, HSFPS are made from the outer layer of potatoes that are cooked with a spicy sauce and then dried. Once cooked and dried, preservatives are added. The HSFPS are then packaged in either a 24-ounce "party size" bag or a smaller individual 6-ounce bag. Product packaging follows the same design layout as other Snappy Snacks products except for the addition of a large graphic showing several potato skins after these have been cooked.

The HSFPS product is like many other Snappy Snacks products in that it is intended to be a fun food. As Smith has stated many times to her staff: *"This snack line is not about promoting healthy diets. It's a social food that is best shared. In other words, our foods are about having a good time."* In fact, the target market for HSFPS has been described as relatively young (ages 16-25), urban-suburbanites who are not overwhelmingly concerned about eating healthy. They are high consumers of junk food and often purchase these products on impulse. A survey Smith's staff undertook to learn about consumer purchasing found that many in this target market are influenced to make a purchase because they observed others consuming the product. Typical of responses to the purchase influence question is this one from a 20-year-old who said, *"I saw a video of this guy eating it on YouTube. It seemed different, so I picked up a bag."*

Because it is a specialty product, Snappy Snacks has set a premium price for HSFPS compared to the company's traditional line of snack products. For instance, in many stores, Snappy Snack's 24-ounce bag of regular spicy potato chips has a suggested retail price of $5.39 while the same size bag of HSFPS is priced at $5.99. Despite the difference in suggested retail price, the price retailers and distributors pay is the same at $2.59.

The HSFPS product, which was launched only in the U.S. six months ago with great fanfare and high hopes, was thought by many Snappy Snacks executives to be a sure winner. Extensive marketing research, including full-scale test markets in Sacramento and Memphis, suggested the product had the potential to be a strong seller. However, once rolled out in all markets, sales have been extremely sluggish.

As Smith enters the meeting room, she remains silent as Sarah and Kirk continue asserting their positions. For Molly, it was common to hear her assistant product managers argue. In fact, she often encourages debate because, in Smith's mind, the best ideas come from this type of discussion. After a few minutes of listening, Molly interrupts and says: "*Ok, what's the problem.*"

The problem, explains Sarah, is how the company should promote the new HSFPS snack. "*I think we should be using more of a push strategy and Kirk thinks we need to employ more pull methods.*" Molly listens but does not immediately react as experience has taught her that being silent for few seconds can calm down her team. Finally, Smith takes over the meeting saying: "*Okay, before we tackle the push/pull issue, let's get a handle on where we are right now. Kirk why don't you fill us in on what has happened so far.*"

For the next twenty minutes, Jenkins provides an encapsulation of HSFPS's rocky journey. He begins by discussing product sales. He states that for the first six months HSFPS has generated $3 million in total sales. "*However, these figures are well below what we had forecasted. We were predicting at least $5 million in the first six months. The low sales number probably has several causes, but certainly we can point to our distribution numbers as a key issue.*" Jenkins explains that while Snappy Snacks has established a sizable distribution network with its niche products, their extensive distribution network is not benefiting their new product. Jenkins goes on to explain that the company's sales force is reporting great difficulty in getting retailers and distributors to handle "*more silly new products.*" Jenkins suggests distributors "*...are just being overloaded with new products and they are telling our people that enough is enough.*" He estimates that only 35% of their existing distribution network has agreed to handle HSFPS.

Next Jenkins reviews the impact of the HSFPS promotional plan. He notes that for the first six months following product launch, the firm spent nearly $5 million on promotion. Much of the promotional budget was directed to the development and broadcast of television advertisements that appeared on sporting events, cable television networks, such as the Food Network, AMC and MTV, and some reality television programs. The money not spent on television was mostly directed to online advertising with ads targeting websites popular with Millennials. Despite the money spent on promotion, a recent product awareness study shows a low level of recognition for HSFPS. *"The ads do not seem to be capturing the target market's attention, at least not so far,"* says Jenkins.

When Jenkins completed his assessment, Smith spoke. *"I agree we have a problem that needs immediate attention. I don't think the company is going to allow us much more time in getting this product to work. We still have another two million dollars or so in the budget, and maybe six more months. We need to evaluate this thoroughly and come up with a new plan of attack. Now let's put our heads together and get to work."*

Molly then asks Sarah and Kirk to explain why their approach is the one that will work.

Issues to Consider

1. What reasons can be cited for the slow growth of this product? Of these reasons, which ones seem to be the most critical and need to be immediately addressed?

2. What exactly are Sarah and Kirk arguing about? Side with one of the assistant product managers and explain why you support their position. Also, explain what the risks may be for the position you select.

3. Evaluate the Snappy Snacks' niche strategy for marketing products. What are the advantages and disadvantages of marketing only spicy flavored products?

4. Consider the premium pricing decision for HSFPS from the point-of-view of Snappy Snacks' distribution network. How do retailers and wholesalers benefit and suffer from this pricing approach?

5. Lay out a detailed Marketing Plan intended to increase sales within the six-month time frame that Molly mentioned.

6. How do you feel about Molly's statement that Snappy Snacks products are not about being healthy but about having fun?

7. Research the snack food industry and identify companies that would "likely" be viewed as competitors to Snappy Snacks. Justify your reasons for selecting these companies.

THE SLEEK SKIER

Summary

A marketer of high-end skiing attire has seen its business expand rapidly in just five years. However, consumer research indicates there may be much more potential than is being realized. The company's president has instructed the marketing staff to analyze their business and develop a new plan with the goal of doubling sales within two years.

Situation

The Sleek Skier is a five-year-old manufacturer and marketer of upscale snow skiing attire. To this point in its growth, the company has limited its product offerings to ski pants and jackets. The Sleek Skier has earned a reputation within the skiing community for marketing stylish clothing that is durable, comfortable, and lightweight. Customers often rave about the company on social media and discussion forum sites focused on skiing and other outdoor activities.

Since its inception, the firm's sales have risen from $70,000 in year one to nearly $8 million in the most recent year. Ninety-five percent of sales for The Sleek Skier's products come through purchases made on its website. Depending on when a purchase is made and in what geographic region a buyer resides, customers usually receive their order within five business days when standard shipping is selected. Two-day express shipping is also available, though customers will pay a premium for this service. Buyers have 15 days to return products, though they are encouraged to first contact customer service before making a return. Customer service is available Monday through Friday by phone or online chat during the company's 9 am to 5 pm business hours.

In addition to selling online, The Sleek Skier operates a small outlet store at its headquarters in Boulder, Colorado. The outlet store's inventory is primarily comprised of products customers have returned, closeouts of older clothing styles, and products containing small defects. The outlet store is only open on Friday, Saturday, and Sunday from mid-October through mid-April, mainly for the convenience of weekend skiers heading to Colorado ski areas.

Each of the company's product categories - pants and jackets - consist of multiple styles. For instance, the most recent year's line of ski jackets features the following three styles:

- *Active* - This is The Sleek Skier's base product targeted to the occasional skier who would like a ski jacket that also functions as a general winter jacket. The list price for this product is $300.

- *3-in-1* - This is a durable, two-part jacket targeted to the more frequent skier. It consists of both a tighter fitting insulated inner jacket and an outer shell jacket. Each can be worn separately or combined into a single jacket. The list price for this product is $450.

- *Alpine* - An extremely lightweight jacket that is targeted to avid skiers. The list price for this product is $400.

All jackets are made with advanced waterproof materials, have removal hoods, and contain multiple inside storage pockets. All jackets are also tailored with slight differences for men and women. Each style is available in two color designs.

The Sleek Skier's line of ski pants follows a similar segmenting approach as seen with the jackets, however, the color designs are more extensive, especially for women's styles. Pricing for ski pants ranges from $200 to $275.

The market for The Sleek Skier's products is worldwide with 50% of online sales coming from the U.S., 20% from Canada, 20% from Europe, and 10% from other locations. While overall sales are spread across many countries and regions, demand for specific products can be more localized. For example, while in the U.S. sales of men's ski jackets are nearly equal for each style, that is not the case outside the U.S. For instance, in Europe the Alpine style far outsells the other styles. The Sleek Skier's marketing team has wondered why this is the case but has yet to find a clear reason why Alpine is more popular.

Despite most sales coming via their online store, The Sleek Skier has yet to invest heavily in website and e-commerce analytics. Currently, the marketing team has access to only basic website data, such as site page views and general visitor information, including visitor's location, length of visit, and visitor traffic sources. This information indicates that 60% of visitors arrive on The Sleek Skier's website through advertisements that are displayed based on certain queries made on major search engines. However, tracing the activity of visitors arriving this way shows that few are making purchases after clicking on an ad. Instead, from what the marketing team can determine, more purchases occur from organic search engine traffic (i.e., clicks on non-paid links that appear for a user's search inquiry), or when the company's website URL is directly entered into a web browser. While the marketing team is aware of the value derived from organic search traffic, they also know The Sleek Skier only appears on the first page of search results for very detailed search phrases. For direct URL entry, the team is not entirely sure where new customers are finding the website URL but surmise it is from comments on social media, other online mentions, or in the company's print ads.

Basic website analysis is also indicating an increasing number of visitors are viewing the website on mobile devices, such as smartphones and tablets. For The Sleek Skier this is creating some concern as their website, while designed to be a mobile-friendly site, tends to load slowly on mobile devices.

The Sleek Skier promotes its products in several ways. For the previous year, the company's promotional budget was $500,000 of which 60% was directed to internet and mobile advertising, 20% for advertisements placed in skiing and outdoor-oriented magazines, 10% for direct mail sent to U.S. customers who had previously purchased, and 10% for other promotions, including sponsoring events at several ski resorts.

For sales promotion, The Sleek Skier uses coupons contained in direct mail promotions. Coupon offers vary and have included such incentives as free express shipping, 10% off an entire order, and discounts off select ski resort lift tickets. For the past year, to qualify for a coupon offer, customers were required to spend a minimum of $500. Additionally, when placing an online order, they had to enter a valid coupon code. Analysis of this promotion shows that coupons were used by 10% of purchasers.

Executives at The Sleek Skier recently conducted a consumer research study to learn more about customers' perception of their products. The research was gathered online following the completion of a purchase. One of the most interesting results indicates that 75% of customers surveyed said they would only consider The Sleek Skier when they need to purchase ski clothing. This response caught the company's executives by surprise. Although they knew they had good products, they didn't think customers would react this favorably. With such strong feedback the company's president wondered why sales were less than $8 million. *"Look if people like us so much why are we such a small player in this industry?"* The president was referring to the fact that in a billion-dollar industry (i.e., ski apparel), The Sleek Skier is barely noticed. The president began to wonder if selling almost exclusively online was the best approach for the company to become more visible and to grow.

The president also had a straightforward message for the marketing team: *"Put your thinking caps on and tell me what you think we should do. We have good products that our customers love. And I'm sure that more people will love it too. Now I want you to come up with a plan that will increase our sales to $15 million within the next two years. However, you must realize that we are not a big company that can afford to spend zillions of dollars on promotion. We need a plan that will attract more customers without requiring excessive promotional spending. So, while I am increasing your promotional budget to $700,000, you need to spend this in a smart way. I also want you to improve our analytics tools so we can better understand who our customers are and how they are interacting with us."*

Issues to Consider

1. Assume you are the marketing director for The Sleek Skier. Describe the changes the company will need to make to its marketing strategy to achieve the president's objective of doubling sales in two years. Additionally, discuss any ramifications your suggested changes will have on the company's current business.

2. The Sleek Skier's CEO appears to be concerned with the company selling its products almost exclusively online. Offer reasons why the president may have these concerns.

3. Evaluate The Sleek Skier's promotional strategy. How do you feel they should allocate the currently budgeted promotional funds? Explain your reasons.

4. How can customer research and online analytics be used to improve the company's marketing effort? Also, how can these be used to determine why the Alpine style of ski jackets outsells other styles in European markets?

5. What should be done to address the issues with the website when it appears on mobile devices? How would any changes potentially impact the company's marketing effort?

6. What do you think of the way The Sleek Skier addresses customer service? In particular, how can their approach to customer service impact sales to international buyers?

7. Research the ski clothing industry and identify companies that would "likely" be viewed as competitors to The Sleek Skier company. Justify your reasons for selecting these companies.

USERS SPEAK

Summary

A social media start-up focused on health care services is facing a crucial point as it tries to establish a niche in a market dominated by well-known competitors. Nearly two years after entering the market, the company's founders are concerned. While the company has spent heavily on promotion, the number of users joining this new social media outlet have lagged. With funds running low and their financial backers growing restless, the company founders have limited time to grow their business.

Situation

The exterior of Lisa and Jason Wilson's office does not give a true impression of the nature of their business. Housed in a 19th century farmhouse, the Wilsons' company, Users Speak, is a social media start-up where people can share their insights on health care services, such as doctors, hospitals, and outpatient services. While similar topics are often discussed on other social networks, Users Speak promotes its business as the *"main outlet for communicating what people really feel about health care services."*

The Wilsons started the company nearly three years ago when they believed social sharing sites were becoming too large and less focused on specific topics. As Lisa Wilson explained it, *"We felt a more targeted approach primarily directed at the health care industry could not only be of value to consumers but also potentially profitable."* After a little more than one year of development and with the backing of several venture capitalists, Users Speak was launched with aggressive and expensive promotion, including local television advertisements in 10 large cities in the U.S. and Canada. The company also advertised on search engines, other social media outlets, and thousands of websites via online advertising brokers. The Wilsons spent aggressively because they *"wanted to hit the ground running and quickly build market awareness."*

Within six months of launching, customer interest and user registration on Users Speak was strong. Some of this can be attributed to a special promotion tied to the advertising. This promotion was a contest offering five randomly selected registered users the opportunity to win $25 for every comment they posted on Users Speak during a month-long sales promotion. Additionally, the more comments users made the more opportunities they had of being selected. For instance, someone posting 50 comments during the month would have their name entered 50 times and if they won, they would win $1,250.

Initially, the month-long promotion seemed like a good idea as it achieved its goal of building customer interest as over 15,000 new accounts were created and the number of postings increased significantly. However, it soon became apparent that a high volume of comments came from a relatively small group of registered users. In fact, about 400 users, almost all of whom were newly registered, commented 500 or more times. By the end of the promotion, the Wilsons believed that possibly the wrong message was sent with the contest. They surmised that posting quantity seemed to far outweigh posting quality. That is, some posters were primarily commenting for the chance of making money and not for the services being offered by Users Speak. This proved to be especially troublesome for the company as two winners of the contest each won over $20,000 while total payout for all winners was nearly $45,000. In contrast, during the contest period total advertising revenue generated by Users Speak was less than $20,000. The Wilsons and their team, which currently consists of ten employees and a few part-time consultants, had not counted on this. While a small start-up company often struggles financially in the beginning, this unexpectedly large payout combined with the large amount spent on advertising has placed serious constraints on Users Speak's finances.

In addition to the financial issues resulting from the contest, Users Speak also experienced problems handling the large volume of posted comments resulting in a significant slowdown in the company's social media app. The Users Speak website also suffered during this time and, at one point, was offline for five hours. Predictably this led users to be critical in postings they made to Users Speak. In fact, responses became so critical that users' discussion of the company and its service were removed until Users Speak was able to recover to full-service levels.

Despite these issues, Users Speak has general received positive reviews from customers and even from a few media outlets. One major U.S. television network news program, which profiled social networking outlets including Users Speak, supported the company's assertion that well-known social media platforms have grown *"too large and too fragmented and, consequently, are not able to offer quality discussion of specific topics, such as health care services."* While Jason Wilson believes such statements reinforce what his company is trying to achieve, he was critical of the news program telling his staff, *"They spent too much time analyzing the big guys and very little time was spent on quality sites like ours."*

To date, the only source of revenue for Users Speak has been from advertisements placed on its app and website. Currently, Users Speak's advertising revenue per user (ARPU) is about 40 cents/month. The Wilsons feel that ARPU will increase as more users are added and advertisers see greater value in placing ads on Users Speak. However, Lisa Wilson feels that for the company to really grow it will have to identify additional revenue streams. For example, a user subscription program, where paid customers gain access to additional benefits, such as one-on-one help finding health care services, has been considered. However, Lisa Wilson is not sure the time is right to explore other revenue sources. *"We think about new ways of building revenue all the time. But we first need to get our platform under control before we start investing in other revenue opportunities."*

From a technology perspective, Users Speak has also faced challenging times. In addition to the technical issues experienced during the month-long promotion, Users Speak customers have also encountered service outages at other times. While most downtimes are short and often limited to certain geographic areas, many customers have posted comments expressing irritation with the downtimes. Like the reaction to the contest, highly negative comments were removed. At one point, Jason Wilson posted a *"note to all Users Speak customers"* message that addressed the technical problems, though users' comments to his message were not permitted.

Other technical issues have arisen with the Users Speak mobile app. As mobile platforms are updated, such as when a mobile phone manufacturer upgrades the phone's underlying operating system, app software developers often must update their products to be compatible with the mobile platform upgrade. Users Speak, like many small companies, can find upgrades challenging as they have a limited number of technical workers and upgrading existing software can take time away from developing new product features.

As previously noted, Users Speak attempts to distinguish its product from other social media outlets by concentrating on the health care service sector. Upon registering for an account, users are asked to identify up to five health care services for which they have the most interest. While many services are listed, the nutrition and healthy eating category has been the most active with over 20% of all users indicating this as one of their five health care services. While not listing a specific health care service does not prevent users from posting comments in an unselected health care service, users are only able to initiate a new conversation in one of the five services they initially selected. The Wilsons reason that limiting users in this way improves the quality of Users Speak as the initiator of a discussion has greater passion for the topic, and, consequently, it will be of more interest to other users.

For all users, topics can be filtered in numerous ways (e.g., by geographic area, subspecialties, specific institutions, etc.) and users can be alerted via the app when new comments are posted within a filtered topic area or a specific topic. For instance, a user can be alerted when a new comment is posted regarding a specific service offered at a specific hospital (e.g., cancer treatment).

As they near the two-year anniversary of the product launch, the Wilsons find Users Speak at a crossroads. Aside from the month-long sales promotion that resulted in a large number of new user accounts, account creation has only averaged about 6,500 new users per month. Additionally, those who create accounts tend to be enthusiastic participants for the first ninety days and then their participation wains. Also, for those who have had accounts for more than one year, less than 25% continue to participate. To get these users involved more often, Users Speak uses frequent email reminders.

While it is not unusual for technology products to face difficult decisions after just a short time on the market, the Wilsons feel that what they decide to do in the next few months could ultimately determine whether the company can attain long-run success. To assess where the company is now and where it may be going, the Wilsons have convened a staff meeting in the dining room of the farmhouse, which serves as the company's conference room. The Wilsons want to hear the staff's thoughts on what should be done to increase the number of users and the level of users' engagement with the platform. In turn, they hope this will help increase advertising revenue.

Lisa Wilson tells the staff the company must grow users by at least 10,000 per month for the next twelve months or their financial backers may no longer fund this venture. In those twelve months, the company has about $400,000 to spend for technological developments and marketing. While the Wilsons do not expect Users Speak to be profitable in the near future, they are hoping the cash flow generated from advertising will be enough to cover employee expense (salaries and benefits) as well as any expenses for outsourcing services to contractors. They believe monthly advertising revenue of $70,000 should be sufficient to pay expenses and keep the company afloat through the next year.

Issues to Consider

1. What value does Users Speak actually provide? How does this compare to other social media outlets? Is there really a niche market for this type of social media outlet?

2. What do you think of Users Speak initial strategy for engaging in heavy promotion in order to quickly gain market awareness? What are the pros and cons of spending so heavily in the early stages of entering a market?

3. The Wilsons believe the wrong message was sent with the sales promotion. Do you agree with this considering that it accomplished the goals of increasing the number of user account creations?

4. How should the sales promotion have been handled and how could Users Speak have protected itself against those who are only out to win the contest? What other types of sales promotion could be useful for increasing the number of users?

5. In what ways can Users Speak increase the advertising revenue per users (ARPU)? Also, what other revenue options could Users Speak pursue? What effect would these have on employee workload?

6. Research how other social media companies faced difficult times in their early growth. Evaluate how companies that survived handled these difficult times. Also discuss companies that were not able to survive.

7. Should Users Speak have removed or blocked users' negative comments about the company? Are there ethical issues with removing or blocking users' comments?

8. What are the advantages and disadvantages to limiting users to just five categories for creating comments? Should users be allowed to start conversation in more than five selected services?

9. Develop a plan designed to encourage users to get more involved after their first 90 days with the service?

THE PERFECT PASTA PRODUCERS OF PITTSBURGH

Summary

A regional supplier of pasta products is facing declining sales despite a 60-year history of offering affordable products that appeal to working and middle-class families. The head of marketing, Denise Alexander, believes a complete review of the firm's marketing strategy is required and that both short-term and long-term plans are needed to address the situation.

Situation

The Perfect Pasta Producers of Pittsburgh (4Ps) company has been in business for over 60 years manufacturing and selling various dry packaged pasta throughout the Midwest region of the United States. For many years, the company was perceived as a reliable producer of an established brand found in many households. While 4Ps has been on store shelves for many years, sales have been slowly declining for the last three years. In an attempt to understand what may be causing the decline, the head of 4Ps marketing department, Denise Alexander, hired a consulting firm to conduct a consumer research study. The study was undertaken in one week over five afternoons (Monday through Friday) outside three supermarkets in the Chicago area. The researchers asked consumers leaving the store several questions about pasta products including asking them to list the two brands of pasta which they most preferred. For this study, a store's own branded pasta products were included in the count. Four-hundred and ten consumers took part in the study. Of the respondents only 25 listed 4Ps as one of their top two brands. The 25 that responded rated 4Ps as follows:

First Place = 12

Second Place = 13

For the top pasta brands question, each brand was assigned a score. The brand score was based on the following formula: 2 points for first place and 1 point for second place. Thus, all brands listed by respondents obtained a total point value determined by the number of mentions it received for each of its top two placements. For 4Ps, their total was 37 points while the top brand in the study received 400 points.

Alexander is very concerned with the results of the consumer survey. She wonders whether there is an inherent problem with 4Ps marketing strategy. She has decided a complete review of the company's strategy is needed. She begins by looking at the key decision areas.

TARGET MARKET

4Ps views their target market as primarily head of households within working and middle-class families. The company does not position its products to appeal to consumers whose preference is for fine pasta. Instead, the company sees their market as consumers who view pasta as an easy and cost-efficient way of feeding a family. Targeting those responsible for "feeding a family" has served the company well for many years. It has been particularly useful within Midwestern industrial cities, where the company once garnered a sizable market share. While 4Ps believes its market share is still relatively stable in these cities, overall its market share has slipped.

PRODUCTS

While 4Ps top competitors offer a more diverse product mix containing a number of different product lines, including complementary products such as sauces, 4Ps markets only dry packaged pasta. On several occasions, Alexander has presented senior management with ideas for moving into other product lines. However, despite showing competitive analysis to support her position, Alexander's product line expansion ideas are often met with the well-known refrain *"that is not who we are."*

While 4Ps pasta is made from all-natural ingredients, these ingredients are not considered to be the highest quality compared to more expensive competitors. The management of 4Ps prefers to obtain the best ingredients for its money, which often means making deals for lower priced and slightly above average quality products. The firm offers eight traditional types of pasta products including spaghetti, manicotti, rigatoni, linguine, etc. The last new product to be introduced was nearly fifteen years ago when conchiglie (pasta shells) was marketed.

Within the pasta types, 4Ps offers different options. For instance, for spaghetti, the company markets three types: regular, thin, and thick. Overall, the company produces 20 different types of products. All products fall under the 4Ps brand name (e.g., 4Ps Spaghetti, 4Ps Rigatoni, 4Ps Linguine, etc.). The products are packaged in plain white cardboard boxes with green and blue lettering. Labeling is limited to the company logo, product name, ingredients listing, company contact information (address, phone number, website URL, social media logos) and UPC code.

PROMOTION

As Alexander explains it, 4Ps' promotional strategy is a "controlled" approach designed to make the best use of funds. Because the brand has been around for so long, the company believes excessive expenditure on promotion is likely to yield only "marginally useful results." Consequently, 4Ps' promotional spending is less than several of their competitors.

4Ps primary form of advertising is through television commercials. For instance, a new 4Ps television advertisement depicts a multi-generational family gathered around a large table enjoying a pasta meal. The voice-over message, which has been the company's slogan for over 50 years, says: *"The Right Choice for a Real Family Meal."* This ad, like many previous ads, conveys a message of family and loyalty to 4Ps products.

4Ps supports a sales force of six field salespeople and one major accounts salesperson. Most of the salespeople have been with the company for at least ten years. Each salesperson is assigned a geographic territory. A salesperson's principal responsibilities are: 1) to maintain existing accounts, including gathering information and improving display position on store shelves; and 2) to sell to new outlets that may open in their territory. Of these two responsibilities, much more time is spent on managing existing accounts than on locating new accounts.

The major accounts salesperson focuses on relationships with buyers for larger grocery chains and with the major wholesalers, who sell to smaller chains and individually-owned stores. The key responsibilities of this salesperson are: 1) to deal with existing customers, including convincing them to stock more of 4Ps' products and accept promotional programs; and 2) to expand distribution by finding new accounts.

Other promotional methods used by 4Ps are primarily limited to sales promotions, though the firm limits sales promotions to occasional coupons and co-op advertising with retailers. (Co-op advertising is where the manufacturer agrees to pay some or all of the cost of a retailer's advertisement for a product.)

Excluding the expenses associated with the sales force, the company has a yearly budget of $2,000,000 for promotion for all pasta products.

DISTRIBUTION

The 4Ps products are sold to wholesale and retail accounts in eight states within the Midwestern region. Products are sold exclusively in supermarkets and are not available in other retail outlets. Most supermarkets in which 4Ps products are found are part of a regional chain or are individually-owned stores. Most recent information suggests 4Ps products are distributed in 40% of the supermarkets in their targeted areas. However, less than 5% of these stores carry more than ten different 4Ps products.

PRICE

Products are priced on the lower end. Prices tend to be slightly above retailers' own pasta store brand but at least 10-15% below higher quality competitors. Although pricing is relatively low, 4Ps still makes a profit due to low costs of raw materials, marketing, and administrative expenses. They also have recently started producing products from a new high-tech manufacturing facility that has lowered product costs. There has been some talk of further lowering the price to compete against a store's own private label brand, but the sales force has suggested retailers and wholesalers may view this negatively.

Twice a year, the company offers promotional pricing that lowers prices across all products. The promotion lasts for one week and coincides with the National Football League Super Bowl game and the 4th of July holiday. The amount of price reduction varies by product but, in general, prices are reduced by 15%. In doing so, 4Ps is primarily offering their distributors (e.g., supermarkets) a loss leader promotion which they can advertise. While 4Ps makes very little from these special promotions, Alexander notes that this type of promotion keeps the company in "good standing with our distribution partners."

CUSTOMER SERVICE

4Ps offers two forms of service for its customers. For retailers and wholesalers, customer issues are primarily addressed by contacting the assigned salesperson or through phone calls with distribution support representatives. For consumers, the principal contact is through completion of a form on the company's website or by sending requests to a customer service email address. Currently, the 4Ps website does not offer an online chat option. Social media platforms, such as Twitter and Facebook, are also used to provide product/company updates and, to a lesser extent, offer promotional support, such as indicating when special promotions are occurring.

As Denise Alexander reviews 4Ps current marketing strategy, she wonders what if anything needs to change. While small adjustments that do not require much expense will not need upper-management approval, bigger changes involving larger investment will almost certainly require approval. Because of this, she decides to investigate both short-term changes and potential long-term changes.

Issues to Consider

1. What are the major problems facing 4Ps? What are short-term and long-term changes the company should make to remedy these problems? For the long-term changes, what are the primary arguments Denise Alexander needs to make to 4Ps upper-management?

2. What type of research did the consulting firm conduct? What do you think about the way the research was conducted?

3. Does the target market identified by 4Ps make sense? On what bases is their market currently segmented? How else do you think this market could be segmented?

4. What kind of pricing objective do you think this firm is following? What do you think of the idea to lower the price to compete against the retailer's own brand?

5. What are some of the reasons Alexander may have cited when discussing expanding the company's product mix? If expansion is approved, what options should they consider?

6. Research the pasta market. How does 4Ps compare with leading competitors? What can 4Ps learn from their competitors?

FOUR FALLS COFFEE COMPANY

Summary

Facing slower than expected sales growth, a small premium gourmet coffee company has set a goal of doubling sales within three years. To achieve this goal, the company's product manager believes a new marketing plan is needed. The product manager is open to making changes, though a limited budget will require a carefully planned and possibly creative use of funds.

Situation

John Maxwell is frustrated. Maxwell is product manager for the Four Falls Coffee Company, marketers of a relatively new line of premium gourmet coffees. His frustration stems from viewing the results of a survey request emailed to consumers, who had previously signed up to receive company information. The results show the vast majority of the 35 respondents who completed the survey really like the taste of Four Falls' products. However, consumers' feelings about the company's coffee products have yet to translate into significant sales as these products have barely penetrated the market. This also is the story he has heard from retailers distributing Four Falls' products, people seem to love the company's coffee, but sales have lagged below forecast.

At this point, Maxwell feels it is time to rethink Four Falls' marketing strategy. His boss, the company president, wants to see sales double within the next three years. Fortunately, with current yearly sales barely reaching $2 million, Maxwell feels growing sales to $4 million in three years seems somewhat reasonable. But Maxwell believes this will require a new plan to attract greater customer interest. Additionally, he has been told his budget will continue to be based on 15% of previous year's sales or $300,000 for the upcoming year (this does not include his salary and benefits, the salary and benefits of one full-time salesperson, and pay for one part-time assistant).

Before making any significant changes, Maxwell decides he must first reassess the existing marketing efforts. He begins by evaluating Four Falls' product decisions. Four Falls markets premium coffee produced from the finest beans obtained from Central and South America. The beans are shipped to and then roasted at Four Falls' facility in Virginia. The beans are then blended to create different coffee flavors. Currently, the company sells three different types of coffee blends - mild, medium, and dark roasted - each in 12-ounce packaging. Each type of coffee is available in ground and whole bean. There has been discussion of expanding options into flavored and decaffeinated products, though the company president is not inclined to invest in these products until Four Falls experiences an increase in sales for current products.

To distinguish its products from competitors on store shelves, Four Falls' coffees are packaged in a sealed paper bag that is then placed in a unique equilateral triangle-shaped metal container. Consumers can then pour the coffee from the bag into the container. The triangular package is designed to sit upright on store shelves, though some stores lay these flat to enable greater product stacking. The container is labeled on all sides so that the brand name does appear if laid flat. Consumers say the packaging is a nice additional option as it can be used to hold other items once the coffee is used. Compared to traditional paper and other flexible coffee packaging, which often costs less than 25-cents a package, the metal containers cost nearly $1 per package.

The company name, Four Falls, was developed by the company's founders, who started the business in an old textile building that sat next to a stream where water cascaded in four visible drop-offs (i.e., waterfalls). The company has since moved to a more modern building containing the administrative offices as well as the roasting, packaging, and shipping operations. The company founders are no longer involved in day-to-day business decisions but occasionally offer input, especially when attending company board meetings.

Four Falls targets above-average income consumers in the 35-55 age group located in the Southeastern region of the U.S. For the most part, these customers are light to moderate coffee consumers, who generally drink one or two cups of coffee per day. Consumer comments made on the survey indicate that almost all of this consumption takes place in their homes rather than outside the home (e.g., at work). Also, the company salesperson, who occasionally engages consumers in conversation while they shop in a store, indicates that those who buy Four Falls' products seem to genuinely enjoy it, though some view it as a "luxury" purchase given the price.

While Four Falls positions itself as a premium coffee producer, it does not attempt to compete against very high-end, expensive coffees that are mainly sold only online. Instead, Four Falls prices its products 10% to 15% higher than most direct competitors that may sit next to it on store shelves. From Four Falls' point of view, their direct competitors are other premium coffee brands sold in smaller food stores.

Four Falls' products are sold primarily in higher-end food stores, many of which are either single store operations or small chains (i.e., less than 5 outlets). The company ships product directly to retailers using a variety of services including UPS and USPS. The company does not operate its own delivery vehicles. Four Falls' products generally carry a six-month "best by" date and the company will accept unsold returns from retail customers, though the retailer must pay shipping expense or give the product to the salesperson on the next visit.

Currently Four Falls distributes in Virginia, North Carolina, South Carolina, and Georgia. Nearly all of the retailers distributing the company's products are located in metropolitan areas or vacation destinations. Additionally, there are also a small number of retailers in Maryland and West Virginia. These retailers were not solicited by the company's salesperson but instead reached out on their own to Four Falls asking to be distributors. The company does not fully understand how these retailers became aware of Four Falls' products, though an in-house customer service representative, who deals with these retailers, indicates they may have learned about Four Falls from online review postings, or they were exposed to the product when visiting a state where the coffee is distributed.

One idea that Maxwell has been considering is for the company to establish its own retail presence. While the idea of opening their own coffee stores might not be an option until Four Falls is larger, Maxwell believes there are other ways to expose customers to their coffee besides seeing it on food store shelves or through in-store product sampling.

Because Four Falls positions its coffees as high-quality products and also offers high profit margins to its retailers, the company sees no reason for offering sales incentives to their distributors. However, the company salesperson has stated that a growing competitive landscape, where retailers are inundated with coffee companies seeking to sell their products, is making it increasingly difficult for Four Falls to not offer some type of incentive to retailers. Four Falls does offer a 10% quantity discounts to retailers that purchase 150 or more coffee packages at one time, though the company salesperson reports that few retailers have the necessary storage space to stock this much inventory.

The highest percentage of Maxwell's marketing budget is spent on consumer-directed promotions with the most money allocated to in-store tastings, which is contracted to an outside firm. In the previous 12 months, Four Falls conducted 30 tastings, which generally occur on weekends. Four Falls also directs a small amount of promotional funds to online advertising, primarily on social media. The remainder of the company's marketing budget is used for occasional special events (e.g., providing coffee at charitable events).

Trade-directed promotional spending (e.g., promotion to retailers) is almost all associated with personal selling. For instance, expenses related to the company's lone salesperson would include such items as lunch with retail customers and travel expenses. Because the promotional budget is limited, Four Falls attempts to limit the salesperson's travel expenses to no more than $1,000 per month.

The Four Falls salesperson has two main goals:

1. Maintain good relations with current retail customers.

2. Expand distribution into new retail outlets.

Approximated 50% of the salesperson's time is spent on goal #1, 25% on goal # 2 and the remainder on internal work (e.g., company meetings, paperwork, etc.). Given the $1,000 per month travel expense limit, the salesperson generally spends less than 6 nights a month on the road.

The part-time office assistant is also engaged in promotional activity, though nearly all of this involves social media updates, and responding to customers' emails or website comments. The assistant has also recently started building a consumer email list by attracting consumers with the promise of offering *"great information and customer rewards."* Currently the list has only been used to invite consumers to complete the survey, though Maxwell believes that once the list has reached a sizable level more marketing programs can be communicated. Overall, these marketing efforts generally carry very low cost outside of this assistant's part-time pay.

Following the marketing strategy review, Maxwell wonders how to best meet the company's objective of doubling sales in three years. While he knows changes must be made, he also realizes Four Falls cannot afford to make changes that take time to show positive returns. He is also aware that trying to obtain an increase in the budget, at least in the first year, will not be easy unless he can make a strong case to the company president. He is scheduled to present a plan to the president in a few days, though he knows much work still needs to be done.

Issues to Consider

1. What issues do you believe are contributing to Four Falls' slower than expected growth? Make sure to provide support for each issue identified.

2. Evaluate Four Falls' current retail network. What advantages do these retailers offer to the company? What are the potential disadvantages to having this type of retail network?

3. What do you think of the way Four Falls sets its marketing budget? In what ways could this impact Four Falls' goal of doubling sales in three years? Also, what do you think of the president's reluctance to spend on new products until sales increase on existing products?

4. Maxwell has indicated that exposing more people to the company's products, besides on food store shelves or through in-store sampling, can help build sales. How else can the company expose customers to their coffee?

5. Evaluate the information Maxwell has received regarding customers' feelings about Four Falls' products. Are there any potential issues with the way this information was collected and interpreted?

6. Research the coffee market and identify companies that would "likely" be viewed as key competitors to Four Falls. Justify your reasons for selecting these companies.

7. Lay out a Marketing Plan intended to double sales within a three-year period. Note you should cover all key marketing decision areas.

PA DOCUMENT SYSTEMS

Summary

A manufacturer of affordably priced printing and document management equipment for large offices is introducing a new high-end product. However, some in the sales force have significant reservations about the new product and, in particular, the objectives management has set for selling it. Also, one of the top sales representatives wonders about the potential ramifications of management's decision to suddenly shift its marketing strategy in an attempt to reposition the company as a high-quality, premium cost provider.

Situation

Andrea Clements is not impressed with the presentation she is watching. For 90 minutes she has been sitting with her fellow sales representatives listening as their company's president discusses the firm's new product. Andrea works for PA Document Systems (PADS), a manufacturer of digital printing equipment headquartered in eastern Pennsylvania. The new product, branded as the PADS 1000, is a major advance for the company and is designed to replace the firm's principal product, the PADS 400. According to PADS' president, many experts in the printing industry feel the PADS 1000 is technologically superior to all competitive products that target organizations operating offices with 50 – 100 employees in a single location (e.g., within an office building). Because of this, PADS intends to position the new copier as the highest quality product in this market segment. Additionally, the pricing for the PADS 1000 is expected to exceed its closest competitors by a minimum of 20% and to be double the price of the PADS 400.

The marketing strategy for the PADS 1000 represents a significantly different approach for PADS, that in the past has positioned their products toward the more cost affordable end of the market. For example, the PADS 400 is regarded by many as meeting only average quality standards and, for a machine of its size, is believed to be the lowest priced product of its kind. In fact, PADS' competitors often tell prospects, who are considering the purchase of the PADS 400, *"You get what you pay for with PADS products."* With the new product, PADS is seeking to change the perceived image of the company. The president not only wants the sales force to sell the PADS 1000 into organizations not currently using the PADS 400, but the president is also instructing PADS' salespeople to go back to current customers of the PADS 400 and convince them to replace it with the PADS 1000. For customers, who purchased the PADS 400 within the last three years, the company will offer a trade-in incentive the amount of which is based on a formula comprised of the number of years the product has been in service and the number of copies that have been made. However, the trade-in value will not exceed more than 60% of the original purchase price. For customers, who are leasing the PADS 400, PADS will allow for termination of the lease without penalty if they lease or buy the PADS 1000.

Development of the PADS 1000 began twelve months ago when PADS negotiated a manufacturing and distribution deal with the D&D company, a small start-up focused on developing "*advanced printing solutions.*" Before partnering with PADS, D&D was displaying a prototype at industry trade shows that many regarded as a highly advanced printing machine. While the product design was considered to be cutting-edge, the company was less skilled with the manufacturing side of the business. D&D initially attempted to manufacture its product overseas, but delays and cost overruns forced the company to re-evaluate this decision. They gave strong consideration to bringing the manufacturing operation in-house, but they soon discovered that attempting to build their own manufacturing operation would create even greater delays and higher costs. With the company facing a precarious financial situation, the executives at D&D decided that if they wanted to see this product, and others in the development stage, marketed then they needed a business partner.

D&D and PADS negotiated an exclusive 10-year licensing deal in which PADS will manufacture, sell, and service D&D's products. The deal is limited to the U.S. and Canada only. However, the deal also allows D&D to use its own sales staff to sell their products in two markets, governments and educational institutions, and to brand products sold in these markets with their own name. Furthermore, the deal restricts PADS from directly targeting these markets with other printing machines, though PADS will still be permitted to sell supplies and to service their own printing machines that currently exist in these markets. PADS will also service D&D-branded machines in these two markets.

Compared to the PADS 400, the first product obtained from the licensing deal, the PADS 1000, is significantly more advanced. The key internal components are considered state of the art while the user input screen, where customers enter the work requirement (e.g., copy, scan, etc.), offers a unique graphical interface. Additionally, users can connect wirelessly from their desktop, can send data through mobile phones and tablets, and can also utilize cloud-based printing. Because the PADS 1000 is so advanced, user training is highly recommended and may last as much as a day in order for customers to understand the full functions of the product. Training is not part of the licensing deal so PADS and D&D will handle their own.

Unlike the PADS 400, which PADS could deliver to customers in just a few weeks, the PADS 1000 requires up to 90 days of lead time for delivery due to the highly complex nature of the manufacturing process. Additionally, there have been concerns raised by some in the industry regarding the durability of the PADS 1000 given the number of specialized internal components and its manufacturing complexity. However, PADS management has dismissed these concerns as being *"too nitpicky."* As the company's VP of Sales, Tom Lewis, explained to the sales staff, *"While the PADS 1000 may be a one-of-a-kind printer, it is a very solid product and we should promote it that way."*

As she listened to the presentation, Andrea grew more ambivalent toward the new product. In Andrea's mind, the PADS 1000 is far too advanced for the typical PADS customer. For Andrea, who has led the company for the last three years in sales of the PADS 400, the idea of suddenly changing from a low-priced, good value strategy to a high-priced, high-quality approach was puzzling. She understood the advantages the PADS 1000 offers over the PADS 400 (see Exhibit #1 below) but she believes the market for high-priced printing equipment is limited within the types of organizations PADS has typically targeted.

Exhibit #1

Key Advantages of PADS 1000 vs. PADS 400	
Size	20% smaller footprint
Speed	30% faster
Image Resolution	up to 40% sharper
Paper Capacity	holds 25% more paper
Reductions/Enlargements	up to 20% more effective
Routine Servicing	20% more copies before service
Energy Savings	uses 10% less electricity
Print Collation/Stapling	20% more in a single run
Connectivity	offers wireless, mobile and cloud printing
User Servicing	easier access to stuck paper path

What makes Andrea even more concerned is the firm's marketing plan for the introduction of the PADS 1000. In particular, the idea of having the sales force direct a good portion of their selling efforts towards getting current users of the PADS 400 to switch to the new product made her feel uneasy. To Andrea, these were customers she had cultivated for many years by convincing them to buy or lease her company's products on basis of being a good value. Now PADS is telling her to go back to these accounts and persuade them to replace the old product with a new one that costs twice as much. Andrea believes customers may not only be resistant to the PADS 1000 due to the significant financial investment they will need to make, but she feels customers may also question her credibility as her usual *"value is most important"* message to customers must now change to *"high quality is most important."* If so, she fears the relationships she has spent many years developing will be threatened.

Andrea is also bothered by the licensing deal which prevents PADS from selling printing machines to governments and educational institutions. Andrea and her fellow sales representatives have had much success in the past targeting these markets. In fact, for Andrea, these are some of her best accounts. Additionally, she believes quality is not an overwhelming issue when these customers make their purchase decisions. She feels when governments and educational institutions invest in printing equipment, they have only one thing in mind – getting a solid product at a low price. Andrea believes D&D will not only have difficulty selling their brand of the PADS 1000 into these markets but PADS may lose connection to these accounts altogether, especially if these customers can obtain printing supplies and service from other sources.

At the end of the meeting Andrea approaches Tom Lewis. Andrea has known Tom for 15 years dating back to when she started with the firm. *"So, Andrea this is really a great new product,"* Tom said excitedly. *"I bet you can't wait to hit the street with the 1000."* *"I guess so,"* Andrea said. *"But why do we have to replace the 400? Why can't we simply carry both?"* Tom looked at Andrea and smiling said, *"Because a new day has dawned at PADS. We can now call ourselves the best."* Andrea stared at Tom and wondered what he meant.

Issues to Consider

1. Evaluate Andrea's response to the PADS 1000? Is she right to be concerned about how existing customers will feel about PADS' objective of getting these customers to switch to the new product? Or should she accept what the company is laying out as its new marketing objectives? Also, should she really be concerned about losing credibility among existing customers because she is now selling a more expensive product?

2. What do you think of PADS shifting its marketing strategy to position the company as a manufacturer of high-end products? What risks and rewards does the company potentially face in taking this approach? What other marketing decisions will they need to adjust for this strategy to be successful?

3. What are the advantages and disadvantages if PADS had decided to sell both the PADS 1000 and the PADS 400 in the U.S. and Canada? Is there a way they could sell both products and still achieve the marketing objectives for the PADS 1000?

4. What impact could the 90-day lead time for acquiring the PADS 1000 have on customers' decision making? How should a salesperson address possible concerns raised by customers on this issue?

5. Assume you are a salesperson for PADS. Lay out a presentation, including listing the features, advantages and benefits of the PADS 1000, that is directed to existing purchasers of the PADS 400. What are the major objections salespeople are likely to hear from this targeted group and how should salespeople respond?

6. How do you feel about PADS's licensing deal with D&D? Does one company appear to have negotiated a better deal than the other company or are both companies getting equal benefit?

7. Research real licensing agreements that occur among companies. If possible, explain the features of these agreement and why each party likely agreed to the deal.

VISIONARY HEALTH PRODUCTS

Summary

William Park, marketing manager for a small company in the dietary supplements market, cannot understand why product sales are not expanding despite the launch of the company's first television advertising campaign. As he convenes a meeting with his marketing staff, William wonders if the ad was a mistake and whether it would have been wiser to spend the company's limited marketing funds on other promotional methods.

Situation

"I don't understand it. Why aren't these new ads working?" William Park is frustrated. He is looking at the previous week's sales report and is confused as to why sales are barely growing even though his company has recently launched a new television advertising campaign. Park is marketing manager for Visionary Health Products, an 8-year-old provider of digestive health aids. When the TV ad campaign started, the marketing staff saw this as a way to expand interest outside of the company's somewhat small but loyal customer base. However, in the first six weeks the advertisement has run, Visionary experienced very little change in sales. While William's marketing staff and others in the organization have suggested it is too soon to conclude that the campaign is not working, Park is not so sure. He is concerned the company has ventured into a promotional area that may not be the most effective for the type of product his company markets.

Visionary Health Products, which is a U.S. company based in Oregon, entered the market at a time when over-the-counter dietary supplements, and especially supplements targeting digestive health, were experiencing rapid growth. The company's main success within the dietary supplements market has been their probiotics product line. Probiotics contain live microorganisms that, when consumed over an extended period (e.g., taken daily for several months), are believed by some dietary supplements advocates to offer a number of benefits, particularly in terms of aiding certain gastrointestinal issues. Yet research on the level of effectiveness is generally not conclusive and the health advantages of using these supplements is controversial within the medical community.

Probiotics are found in many products including yogurt, specialized bottled water (i.e., water kefir), and snack bars. However, the primary method customers use to obtain probiotics is through pills, which often provide a higher concentration of microorganisms than are found in other delivery methods. Additionally, pill forms may offer several other benefits including: 1) being a better choice for those allergic to foods and drinks containing probiotics (e.g., allergy to yogurt); 2) often having a longer shelf life than food products; and 3) possibly delivering a more consistent amount of the probiotics per use. While pill forms include tablets and capsules, Visionary only sells probiotics in capsule form.

Visionary Health Products, like many of its direct competitors, markets its products as dietary supplements and, consequently, is prohibited by the U.S. Food and Drug Administration (FDA) from making specific health claims about its products. Despite this restriction, for the first few years Visionary enjoyed success thanks to extensive word-of-mouth support and through customers' public comments, particularly through postings on internet discussion forums and social media outlets. Visionary also participated in a large number of conventions, workshops, and other events that made it convenient for company representatives to interact with potential customers. While the company continues to engage in a limited number of in-person promotions, a significant percentage of their promotional effort is now directed at other types of non-personal promotions. As Park noted, *"Attending conventions and workshops is becoming too expensive and time consuming. We needed to find more efficient ways of getting our message out."*

In its third year on the market, customer awareness of the company received a big boost when a major television personality endorsed Visionary's probiotics during a syndicated daytime television program. At that time, Visionary's products were primarily sold through its online store, but the mention of their products on the TV program soon enabled the company to gain distribution into specialized health stores throughout the U.S and Canada. However, while retail distribution has been important for Visionary's success, the majority of sales continues to be derived from sales via their online store.

While Visionary has discussed expanding its product line in order to be less reliant on probiotics, it has yet to do so. Park believes company executives have been reluctant to diversify beyond Visionary's core product because, *"We just feel that doing one thing really well is better than trying to spread ourselves too thin by marketing many different products."* Visionary Health Products has also not explored gaining additional distribution through larger national and international retailers, and major online sellers. Park feels, that given their past track record, Visionary is better positioned to develop relationships with smaller chains and mom-and-pop health stores. Currently such retailers account for 20% of sales.

Production for Visionary's products is contracted to several U.S. manufacturers. While the company has investigated manufacturing outside the U.S., to date they have not chosen to do so even though they may be able realize 15%-to-20% lower production and packaging costs. Currently Visionary markets its probiotics in several configurations that differ in terms of pill size, number of pills in a package, and the number of active micro-organisms contained in a pill (commonly listed in terms of colony forming units or CFU).

As Visionary Health Products has grown and gained a level of credibility among targeted users, they have slowly increased the price of their products and, compared to competitors, are now viewed as being an above-average price seller. William reasons that charging a higher price offers a "psychological" effect that makes customers believe their products are of higher quality than competitors' products. However, recent discussion with a few small retailers that handle Visionary's probiotics revealed that many do not believe there is a significant difference between the brands they carry. Said one retailer, *"Our customers tell us they see very little difference between probiotics brands. If someone does ask me for a recommendation, I'll often suggest the brand that not only helps them but will also help us."*

The market for digestive supplements grew rapidly during the eight years in which the company has been in business. Yet while Visionary realized strong growth in its first four years, they have since seen sales grow at slower rates each of the last four years with last years' revenue reaching $15 million, a 6% increase over the previous year. The company's overall growth can be seen in their yearly sales figure shown in the table presented below.

Visionary Health Products Annual Sales	
Year	**Sales**
1	$450,000
2	$890,000
3	$2,100,000
4	$5,500,000
5	$9,600,000
6	$12,400,000
7	$14,300,000
8	$15,100,000

Park feels, that as the company enters year nine and as revenue is beginning to level off, they need to evaluate other promotional options. In the past, outside of trade shows and other in-person promotions, Visionary has relied primarily on emails (to existing customers) and online advertising for promoting its products. However, in the face of stiffer competition, Park believes they must consider other options. After much discussion within the marketing staff, William chose to venture into television advertising, which is Visionary's first foray into this medium. Their primary reasons for doing so include:

- TV advertising has potential to reach a wider audience.

- TV advertising can be repeated often and may have greater impact on the audience.

- Several competitors are also using this medium.

- TV advertising can encourage impulse purchasing by displaying easy ordering options.

While Park believes there is value in television ads, he is also aware a limited marketing budget places limitation on what they can do, thus requiring they carefully plan for the ad campaign. Consequently, William could not afford to spend large sums on advertising design. In fact, the company's television commercial is fairly simple as described below:

> At the beginning of the commercial an actress appears on screen with one of the company's probiotics in her hand. She begins to discuss the importance of living healthy and then suggests how Visionary can help. The viewer then sees pictures of the inside of the company's distribution warehouse while the actress discusses the company's products and its services. The camera returns to the actress who completes her talk by stating, *"Can you really afford to live without probiotics from Visionary Health Products?"* The ad ends with the actress encouraging viewers to learn more and to order either by calling the company's 800 telephone number or by visiting the company's website.

Visionary's relatively small budget also limits options for where the television advertisement can be placed. William decided to air the commercial on cable networks, where advertising rates are considerably less than major television networks. He selected two cable networks to run the commercial, one focused primarily on home improvement and another dealing with nature and the outdoors. Also, to conserve funds, Park decided to run the ad only on weekends between 6:00 AM and 10:00 AM and 11:00 PM and 3:00 AM.

William feels that unless they find new methods for attracting customer interest, sales will grow even slower in the upcoming year. He has called a marketing department meeting. As he looks across his desk at the two members of his staff, William wonders if the advertising campaign was a bad idea. He instructs those at the meeting to offer their thoughts on the campaign. He advises his staff that, *"Everything is on the table including pulling the TV ad if we feel it is not working. We need to make sure we are spending our money wisely so that we can grow sales."*

Issues to Consider

1. Is William right to be concerned about the new advertising campaign? Is six weeks a long enough period to judge the success of this campaign? What reasons can you cite for why the campaign may not be generating the expected bump in sales that William is expecting?

2. What is your opinion of Visionary's retail distribution strategy? William states Visionary can do better developing relationships with smaller chains and mom-and-pop health stores. What can Visionary learn from this and help them respond in a way that may benefit both its retailers and Visionary?

3. Assess the retailer's comment that product recommendations to customers depends not only on what helps the customer but also on what helps the retailer. How should Visionary respond to this?

4. William believes pricing Visionary's probiotics higher than some competitors has a "psychological" effect on customers' perception of product quality. Do you agree with this? Can price alone affect how customers view the quality of products? Can pricing products higher also affect retailers' perception of Visionary's products?

5. Are there other issues, marketing and otherwise, that also need to be addressed? If so, describe what these issues may be and how Visionary should address these.

6. What would you do to increase sales of the probiotics line if you were William? Lay out a promotional plan that assumes your marketing budget is somewhat restricted, though you do have some money to spend.

7. Research the dietary supplements industry. Discuss how this industry is viewed by the medical community. Also, identify companies and products that would "likely" be considered competitors to Visionary. Justify your reasons for selecting these.

Index

www.ingramcontent.com/pod-product-compliance
Lightning Source LLC
Chambersburg PA
CBHW082132210326
41599CB00031B/5954